Kaplan Publishing are constantly finding new ways to make a difference to y............... exciting online resources real............. different to students looking f.......

C000025695

This book comes with free MyKa............ .... **that you can study anytime, anywhere**

Having purchased this book, you have access to the following online study materials:

CONTENT	ACCA (including FFA,FAB,FMA)		FIA (excluding FFA,FAB,FMA)	
	Text	Kit	Text	Kit
iPaper version of the book	✓	✓	✓	✓
Interactive electronic version of the book	✓			
Progress tests with instant answers	✓			
Material updates	✓	✓	✓	✓
Latest official ACCA exam questions*		✓		
Extra question assistance using the signpost icon*		✓		
Timed questions with an online tutor debrief using the clock icon*		✓		
Interim assessment including questions and answers	✓		✓	
Technical articles	✓	✓	✓	✓

* Excludes F1, F2, F3, FFA, FAB, FMA

How to access your online resources

Kaplan Financial students will already have a MyKaplan account and these extra resources will be available to you online. You do not need to register again, as this process was completed when you enrolled. If you are having problems accessing online materials, please ask your course administrator.

If you are already a registered MyKaplan user go to www.MyKaplan.co.uk and log in. Select the 'add a book' feature and enter the ISBN number of this book and the unique pass key at the bottom of this card. Then click 'finished' or 'add another book'. You may add as many books as you have purchased from this screen.

If you purchased through Kaplan Flexible Learning or via the Kaplan Publishing website you will automatically receive an e-mail invitation to MyKaplan. Please register your details using this email to gain access to your content. If you do not receive the e-mail or book content, please contact Kaplan Flexible Learning.

If you are a new MyKaplan user register at www.MyKaplan.co.uk and click on the link contained in the email we sent you to activate your account. Then select the 'add a book' feature, enter the ISBN number of this book and the unique pass key at the bottom of this card. Then click 'finished' or 'add another book'.

Your Code and Information

This code can only be used once for the registration of one book online. This registration and your online content will expire when the final sittings for the examinations covered by this book have taken place. Please allow one hour from the time you submit your book details for us to process your request.

Please scratch the film to access your MyKaplan code.

Please be aware that this code is case-sensitive and you will need to include the dashes within the passcode, but not when entering the ISBN. For further technical support, please visit www.MyKaplan.co.uk

ACCA

Paper P5

Advanced Performance Management

Complete Text

British library cataloguing-in-publication data

A catalogue record for this book is available from the British Library.

Published by:
Kaplan Publishing UK
Unit 2 The Business Centre
Molly Millars Lane
Wokingham
Berkshire
RG41 2QZ

ISBN 978-1-78415-040-2

© Kaplan Financial Limited, 2014

Acknowledgements

We are grateful to the Association of Chartered Certified Accountants and the Chartered Institute of Management Accountants for permission to reproduce past examination questions. The answers have been prepared by Kaplan Publishing.

Contents

Paper Introduction

How to Use the Materials

These Kaplan Publishing learning materials have been carefully designed to make your learning experience as easy as possible and to give you the best chances of success in your examinations.

The product range contains a number of features to help you in the study process. They include:

(1) Detailed study guide and syllabus objectives

(2) Description of the examination

(3) Study skills and revision guidance

(4) Complete text or essential text

(5) Question practice

The sections on the study guide, the syllabus objectives, the examination and study skills should all be read before you commence your studies. They are designed to familiarise you with the nature and content of the examination and give you tips on how to best to approach your learning.

The **complete text or essential text** comprises the main learning materials and gives guidance as to the importance of topics and where other related resources can be found. Each chapter includes:

- The **learning objectives** contained in each chapter, which have been carefully mapped to the examining body's own syllabus learning objectives or outcomes. You should use these to check you have a clear understanding of all the topics on which you might be assessed in the examination.

- The **chapter diagram** provides a visual reference for the content in the chapter, giving an overview of the topics and how they link together.

- The **content** for each topic area commences with a brief explanation or definition to put the topic into context before covering the topic in detail. You should follow your studying of the content with a review of the illustration/s. These are worked examples which will help you to understand better how to apply the content for the topic.

- **Test your understanding** sections provide an opportunity to assess your understanding of the key topics by applying what you have learned to short questions. Answers can be found at the back of each chapter.

KAPLAN PUBLISHING

- **Summary diagrams** complete each chapter to show the important links between topics and the overall content of the paper. These diagrams should be used to check that you have covered and understood the core topics before moving on.

- **Question practice** is provided at the back of each text.

Quality and accuracy are of the upmost importance to us so if you spot an error in any of our products, please send an email to mykaplanreporting@kaplan.com with full details, or follow the link to the feedback form in MyKaplan.

Our Quality Co-ordinator will work with our technical team to verify the error and take action to ensure it is corrected in future editions.

Icon Explanations

 Definition – Key definitions that you will need to learn from the core content.

 Key Point – Identifies topics that are key to success and are often examined.

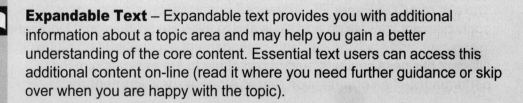 **Expandable Text** – Expandable text provides you with additional information about a topic area and may help you gain a better understanding of the core content. Essential text users can access this additional content on-line (read it where you need further guidance or skip over when you are happy with the topic).

 Illustration – Worked examples help you understand the core content better.

 Test Your Understanding – Exercises for you to complete to ensure that you have understood the topics just learned.

Some of the test your understandings in this material are shorter or more straightforward than questions in the P5 exam. They are contained in the material for learning purposes and will help you to build your knowledge and confidence so that you are ready to tackle past exam questions during the revision phase.

⚠ **Tricky topic** – When reviewing these areas care should be taken and all illustrations and test your understanding exercises should be completed to ensure that the topic is understood.

On-line subscribers

Our on-line resources are designed to increase the flexibility of your learning materials and provide you with immediate feedback on how your studies are progressing. If you are subscribed to our on-line resources you will find:

(1) On-line referenceware: reproduces your Complete or Essential Text on-line, giving you anytime, anywhere access.

(2) On-line testing: provides you with additional on-line objective testing so you can practice what you have learned further.

(3) On-line performance management: immediate access to your on-line testing results. Review your performance by key topics and chart your achievement through the course relative to your peer group.

Ask your local customer services staff if you are not already a subscriber and wish to join.

Syllabus

Paper background

The aim of ACCA Paper P5, Advanced performance management, is to apply relevant knowledge and skills and to exercise professional judgement in selecting and applying strategic management accounting techniques in different business contexts, and to contribute to the evaluation of the performance of an organisation and its strategic development.

Objectives of the syllabus

- Use strategic planning and control models to plan and monitor organisational performance.

- Assess and identify relevant macro-economic, fiscal and market factors and key external influences on organisational performance.

- Identify and evaluate the design features of effective performance management information and monitoring systems.

- Apply appropriate strategic performance measurement techniques in evaluating and improving organisational performance.

- Advise clients and senior management on strategic business performance evaluation and on recognising vulnerability to corporate failure.

- Identify and assess the impact of current developments in management accounting and performance management on measuring, evaluating and improving organisational performance.

Core areas of the syllabus

- Strategic planning and control.

- External influences on organisational performance.

- Performance measurement systems and design.

- Strategic performance measurement.

- Performance evaluation and corporate failure.

- Current developments and emerging issues in performance management.

Syllabus objectives

We have reproduced the ACCA's syllabus below, showing where the objectives are explored within this book. Within the chapters, we have broken down the extensive information found in the syllabus into easily digestible and relevant sections, called Content Objectives. These correspond to the objectives at the beginning of each chapter.

Syllabus learning objective	Chapter reference
A STRATEGIC PLANNING AND CONTROL	
1 Introduction to strategic management accounting	
(a) Explain the role of strategic performance management in strategic planning and control.[2]	1
(b) Discuss the role of corporate planning in clarifying corporate objectives, making strategic decisions and checking progress towards the objectives.[2]	1
(c) Compare planning and control between the strategic and operational levels within a business entity.[2]	1
(d) Assess the use of strategic management accounting in the context of multinational companies.[3]	1
(e) Discuss the scope for potential conflict between strategic business plans and short-term localised decisions.[2]	1
(f) Evaluate how SWOT analysis may assist in the performance management process.[2]	1
(g) Evaluate the methods of benchmarking performance.[3]	1

2 Performance management and control of the organisation

(a) Evaluate the strengths and weaknesses of alternative budgeting models and compare such techniques as fixed and flexible, rolling, activity based, zero based and incremental.[3] 3

(b) Assess how budgeting may differ in not-for-profit organisations from profit-seeking organisations.[3] 3

(c) Evaluate the impact to an organisation of a move to 'beyond budgeting'.[3] 3

3 Changes in business structure and management accounting

(a) Identify and discuss the particular information needs of organisations adopting a functional, divisional or network form and the implications for performance management.[2] 4

(b) Assess the influence of Business Process Re-engineering on systems development and improvements in organisational performance.[3] 4

(c) Discuss the concept of business integration and the linkage between people, operations, strategy and technology.[2] 4

(d) Analyse the role that performance management systems play in business integration using models such as the value chain and McKinsey's 7s's. [3] 4

(e) Identify and discuss the required changes in management accounting systems as a consequence of empowering staff to manage sectors of a business.[3] 4

4 Effect of information technology (IT) on strategic management accounting

(a) Assess the changing accounting needs of modern service orientated businesses compared with the needs of the traditional manufacturing industry.[3] 5

(b) Discuss how IT systems provide the opportunity for instant access to management accounting data throughout the organisation and their potential impact on business performance.[2] 5

(c) Assess how IT systems facilitate the remote input of management accounting data in an acceptable format by non-finance specialists.[2] 5

(d) Explain how information systems provide instant access to previously unavailable data that can be used for benchmarking and control purposes and help improve business performance (for example the use of enterprise resource planning systems and data warehouses).[2] 5

(e) Assess the need for businesses to continually refine and develop their management accounting and information systems if they are to maintain or improve their performance in an increasingly competitive and global market.[3] 5

5 Other environmental and ethical issues

(a) Discuss the ways in which stakeholder groups operate and how they effect an organisation and its strategy formulation and implementation (e.g. using Mendelow's matrix).[2] 2

(b) Discuss the ethical issues that may impact on strategy formulation and business performance.[3] 2

(c) Discuss the ways in which stakeholder groups may influence business performance.[2] 2

B EXTERNAL INFLUENCES ON ORGANISATIONAL PERFORMANCE

1 Changing business environment

(a) Assess the continuing effectiveness of traditional management accounting techniques within a rapidly changing business environment.[3] 2

(b) Assess the impact of different risk appetites of stakeholders on performance management.[3] 2

(c) Evaluate how risk and uncertainty play an important role in long term strategic planning and decision-making that relies upon forecast and exogenous variables. [3] 2

(d) Apply different risk analysis techniques in assessing business performance such as maximin, maximax, minimax regret and expected values. [3] 2

2 Impact of external factors on strategy and performance

(a) Discuss the need to consider the environment in which an organisation is operating when assessing its performance using models such as PEST and Porter's 5 forces, including areas:[2] 2

(i) political climate

(ii) market conditions

(iii) funding.

(b) Assess the impact of governmental regulations and policies on performance measurement techniques used and the performance levels achieved (for example, in the case of utility services and former state monopolies).[3]   2

C PERFORMANCE MEASUREMENT SYSTEMS AND DESIGN

1 Performance management information systems

(a) Discuss, with reference to performance management, ways in which the information requirements of a management structure are affected by the features of the structure.[2]   6

(b) Evaluate the compatibility of the objectives of management accounting and management accounting information.[3]   5

(c) Discuss the integration of management accounting information within an overall information system, for example the use of enterprise resource planning systems.[2]   5

(d) Evaluate whether the management information systems are lean and the value of the information that they provide.[3]   6

(e) Highlight the ways in which contingent (internal and external) factors influence management accounting and its design and use.[3]   6

(f) Evaluate how anticipated human behaviour will influence the design of a management accounting system.[3]   6

(g) Assess the impact of responsibility accounting on information requirements.[3]   6

2 Sources of management information

(a) Discuss the principal internal and external sources of management accounting information, their costs and limitations.[2]   6

(b) Demonstrate how the information might be used in planning and controlling activities, e.g. benchmarking against similar activities.[2]   5

(c) Discuss those factors that need to be considered when determining the capacity and development potential of a system.[2]   6

3 Recording and processing methods

(a) Demonstrate how the type of business entity will influence the recording and processing methods.[2]   6

(b) Discuss how IT developments, e.g. unified corporate databases, RFIDs and network technology, may influence management accounting systems.[2] 5

(c) Discuss the difficulties associated with recording and processing data of a qualitative nature.[2] 6

4 Management reports

(a) Evaluate the output reports of an information system in the light of [3] 6

(i) best practice in presentation

(ii) the objectives of the report/organisation

(iii) the needs of the readers of the report; and

(iv) avoiding the problem of information overload.

D STRATEGIC PERFORMANCE MEASUREMENT

1 Performance hierarchy

(a) Discuss how the purpose, structure and content of a mission statement impacts on business performance.[2] 1

(b) Discuss the ways in which high level corporate objectives are developed.[2] 1

(c) Identify strategic objectives and discuss how they may be incorporated into the business plan.[2] 1

(d) Discuss how strategic objectives are cascaded down the organisation via the formulation of subsidiary performance objectives.[2] 1

(e) Discuss social and ethical obligations that should be considered in the pursuit of corporate performance objectives.[2] 2

(f) Explain the performance 'planning gap' and evaluate alternative strategies to fill that gap.[3] 1

(g) Apply critical success factor analysis in developing performance metrics from business objectives.[3] 1

(h) Identify and discuss the characteristics of operational performance.[2] 1

(i) Discuss the relative significance of planning as against controlling activities at different levels in the performance hierarchy.[3] 1

2 Strategic performance measures in private sector

(a) Demonstrate why the primary objective of financial performance should be primarily concerned with the benefits to shareholders.[2] 8

4 Strategic performance measures in not-for-profit organisations

(a) Highlight and discuss the potential for diversity in objectives depending on organisation type.[3] 10

(b) Discuss the need to achieve objectives with limited funds that may not be controllable.[2] 10

(c) Identify and discuss ways in which performance may be judged in not-for-profit organisations.[2] 10

(d) Discuss the difficulties in measuring outputs when performance is not judged in terms of money or an easily quantifiable objective.[2] 10

(e) Discuss how the combination of politics and the desire to measure public sector performance may result in undesirable service outcomes.[3] 10

(f) Assess 'value for money' service provision as a measure of performance in not-for-profit organisations and the public sector.[3] 10

5 Non-financial performance indicators

(a) Discuss the interaction of non-financial performance indicators with financial performance indicators.[2] 11

(b) Discuss the implications of the growing emphasis on non-financial performance indicators.[3] 11

(c) Discuss the significance of non-financial performance indicators in relation to employees.[2] 11

(d) Identify and discuss the significance of non-financial performance indicators in relation to product/service quality e.g. customer satisfaction reports, repeat business ratings, customer loyalty, access and availability.[3] 11

(e) Discuss the issues in interpreting data on qualitative issues.[2] 11

(f) Discuss the significance of brand awareness and company profile and their potential impact on business performance .[3] 11

6 The role of quality in management information and performance measurement systems

(a) Discuss and evaluate the application of Japanese management practices and management accounting techniques, including: 12

   (i) Kaizen costing,

(ii) Target costing,

(iii) Just-in-time, and

(iv) Total Quality Management.[3]

(b) Discriminate between quality, quality assurance, quality control and quality management.[2] 12

(c) Assess the relationship of quality management to the performance management strategy of an organisation. [3] 12

(d) Advise on the structure and benefits of quality management systems and quality certification.[3] 12

(e) Justify the need and assess the characteristics of quality in management information systems.[3] 12

(f) Discuss and apply Six Sigma as a quality improvement method using tools such as DMAIC for implementation. [2] 12

7 Performance measurement and strategic Human Resource Management issues

(a) Explain how the effective recruitment, management and motivation of people is necessary for enabling strategic and operational success.[3] 7

(b) Discuss the judgemental and developmental roles of assessment and appraisal and their role in improving business performance.[3] 7

(c) Advise on the relationships of performance management to performance measurement (performance rating) and determine the implications of performance measurement to quality initiatives and process redesign.[3] 7

8 Performance measurement and the reward systems

(a) Explore the meaning and scope of reward systems.[2] 7

(b) Discuss and evaluate different methods of reward practice.[2] 7

(c) Explore the principles and difficulty of aligning reward practices with strategy.[2] 7

(d) Advise on the relationship of reward management to quality initiatives, process re-design and harnessing of e-business opportunities.[3] 7

(e) Assess the potential beneficial and adverse consequences of linking reward schemes to performance measurement, for example, how it can affect the risk appetite of employees.[3] 7

(c) Discuss how changing organisation's structure, culture and strategy will influence the adoption of new performance measurement methods and techniques.[3] 13

(d) Explore the role of the management accountant in providing key performance information for integrated reporting to stakeholders.[2] 2

The superscript numbers in square brackets indicate the intellectual depth at which the subject area could be assessed within the examination. Level 1 (knowledge and comprehension) broadly equates with the Knowledge module, Level 2 (application and analysis) with the Skills module and Level 3 (synthesis and evaluation) to the Professional level. However, lower level skills can continue to be assessed as you progress through each module and level.

The Examination

Examination format

- The examination will be a three hour paper plus 15 minutes of reading and planning time.

- The examination is in two sections:

	Number of marks
Section A	
One compulsory question	50
Section B	
A choice of two from three questions each worth 25 marks	50
Total	**100**

- There will be four professional marks available.

- The pass mark is 50%.

- Candidates will receive a present value table and an annuity table.

Paper-based examination tips

Spend the reading time reading the paper and planning your answers. You are allowed to annotate the question paper, so make use of this – e.g. highlighting key issues in the questions, planning calculations, brainstorming requirements – ensure that you understand the question. A key issue is to decide which questions you wish to attempt from section B – it is worth planning all three in outline before deciding.

Divide the time you spend on questions in proportion to the marks on offer. One suggestion **for this examination** is to allocate 1 and 4/5^{ths} minutes to each mark available, so a 10-mark requirement should be completed in approximately 18 minutes. A danger in P5 is that you spend too long on the calculation aspects and neglect the written elements, so allocate your time within questions as well as between them.

Stick to the question and **tailor your answer** to what you are asked. Pay particular attention to the verbs in the question.

Spend the last five minutes reading through your answers and making any additions or corrections.

If you **get completely stuck** with a question, leave space in your answer book and **return to it later**.

If you do not understand what a question is asking, state your assumptions. Even if you do not answer in precisely the way the examiner hoped, you should be given some credit, if your assumptions are reasonable.

You should do everything you can to make things easy for the marker. The marker will find it easier to identify the points you have made if your answers are legible.

Essay questions: Your essay should have a clear structure. It should contain a brief introduction, a main section and a conclusion. Be concise. It is better to write a little about a lot of different points than a great deal about one or two points.

Computations: It is essential to include all your workings in your answers. Many computational questions require the use of a standard format. Be sure you know these formats thoroughly before the exam and use the layouts that you see in the answers given in this book and in model answers.

Scenario-based questions: Most questions will contain a hypothetical scenario. To write a good case answer, first identify the area in which there is a problem, outline the main principles/theories you are going to use to answer the question, and then apply the principles/theories to the case. It is vital that you relate your answer to the specific circumstances given.

Reports, memos and other documents: some questions ask you to present your answer in the form of a report or a memo or other document. So use the correct format – there could be easy marks to gain here.

Study skills and revision guidance

This section aims to give guidance on how to study for your ACCA exams and to give ideas on how to improve your existing study techniques.

Preparing to study

Set your objectives

Before starting to study decide what you want to achieve - the type of pass you wish to obtain. This will decide the level of commitment and time you need to dedicate to your studies.

Devise a study plan

Determine which times of the week you will study.

Split these times into sessions of at least one hour for study of new material. Any shorter periods could be used for revision or practice.

Put the times you plan to study onto a study plan for the weeks from now until the exam and set yourself targets for each period of study - in your sessions make sure you cover the course, course assignments and revision.

If you are studying for more than one paper at a time, try to vary your subjects as this can help you to keep interested and see subjects as part of wider knowledge.

When working through your course, compare your progress with your plan and, if necessary, re-plan your work (perhaps including extra sessions) or, if you are ahead, do some extra revision/practice questions.

Effective studying

Active reading

You are not expected to learn the text by rote, rather, you must understand what you are reading and be able to use it to pass the exam and develop good practice. A good technique to use is SQ3Rs – Survey, Question, Read, Recall, Review:

(1) **Survey the chapter** – look at the headings and read the introduction, summary and objectives, so as to get an overview of what the chapter deals with.

(2) **Question** – whilst undertaking the survey, ask yourself the questions that you hope the chapter will answer for you.

(3) **Read** through the chapter thoroughly, answering the questions and making sure you can meet the objectives. Attempt the exercises and activities in the text, and work through all the examples.

(4) **Recall** – at the end of each section and at the end of the chapter, try to recall the main ideas of the section/chapter without referring to the text. This is best done after a short break of a couple of minutes after the reading stage.

(5) **Review** – check that your recall notes are correct.

You may also find it helpful to re-read the chapter to try to see the topic(s) it deals with as a whole.

Note-taking

Taking notes is a useful way of learning, but do not simply copy out the text. The notes must:

- be in your own words

- be concise

- cover the key points

- be well-organised

- be modified as you study further chapters in this text or in related ones.

Trying to summarise a chapter without referring to the text can be a useful way of determining which areas you know and which you don't.

Three ways of taking notes:

Summarise the key points of a chapter.

Make linear notes – a list of headings, divided up with subheadings listing the key points. If you use linear notes, you can use different colours to highlight key points and keep topic areas together. Use plenty of space to make your notes easy to use.

Try a diagrammatic form – the most common of which is a mind-map. To make a mind-map, put the main heading in the centre of the paper and put a circle around it. Then draw short lines radiating from this to the main sub-headings, which again have circles around them. Then continue the process from the sub-headings to sub-sub-headings, advantages, disadvantages, etc.

Highlighting and underlining

You may find it useful to underline or highlight key points in your study text – but do be selective. You may also wish to make notes in the margins.

Revision

The best approach to revision is to revise the course as you work through it. Also try to leave four to six weeks before the exam for final revision. Make sure you cover the whole syllabus and pay special attention to those areas where your knowledge is weak. Here are some recommendations:

Read through the text and your notes again and condense your notes into key phrases. It may help to put key revision points onto index cards to look at when you have a few minutes to spare.

Review any assignments you have completed and look at where you lost marks – put more work into those areas where you were weak.

Practise exam standard questions under timed conditions. If you are short of time, list the points that you would cover in your answer and then read the model answer, but do try to complete at least a few questions under exam conditions.

Also practise producing answer plans and comparing them to the model answer.

If you are stuck on a topic find somebody (a tutor) to explain it to you.

Read good newspapers and professional journals, especially ACCA's **Student Accountant** – this can give you an advantage in the exam.

Ensure you **know the structure of the exam** – how many questions and of what type you will be expected to answer. During your revision attempt all the different styles of questions you may be asked.

Further reading

You can find further reading and technical articles under the student section of ACCA's website.

Present value table

Present value of 1, i.e. $(1 + r)^{-n}$

Where   r = discount rate

         n = number of periods until payment

Periods (n)	Discount rate (r)									
	1%	2%	3%	4%	5%	6%	7%	8%	9%	10%
1	0.990	0.980	0.971	0.962	0.952	0.943	0.935	0.926	0.917	0.909
2	0.980	0.961	0.943	0.925	0.907	0.890	0.873	0.857	0.842	0.826
3	0.971	0.942	0.915	0.889	0.864	0.840	0.816	0.794	0.772	0.751
4	0.961	0.924	0.888	0.855	0.823	0.792	0.763	0.735	0.708	0.683
5	0.951	0.906	0.863	0.822	0.784	0.747	0.713	0.681	0.650	0.621
6	0.942	0.888	0.837	0.790	0.746	0.705	0.666	0.630	0.596	0.564
7	0.933	0.871	0.813	0.760	0.711	0.665	0.623	0.583	0.547	0.513
8	0.923	0.853	0.789	0.731	0.677	0.627	0.582	0.540	0.502	0.467
9	0.914	0.837	0.766	0.703	0.645	0.592	0.544	0.500	0.460	0.424
10	0.905	0.820	0.744	0.676	0.614	0.558	0.508	0.463	0.422	0.386
11	0.896	0.804	0.722	0.650	0.585	0.527	0.475	0.429	0.388	0.350
12	0.887	0.788	0.701	0.625	0.557	0.497	0.444	0.397	0.356	0.319
13	0.879	0.773	0.681	0.601	0.530	0.469	0.415	0.368	0.326	0.290
14	0.870	0.758	0.661	0.577	0.505	0.442	0.388	0.340	0.299	0.263
15	0.861	0.743	0.642	0.555	0.481	0.417	0.362	0.315	0.275	0.239

Periods (n)	Discount rate (r)									
	11%	12%	13%	14%	15%	16%	17%	18%	19%	20%
1	0.901	0.893	0.885	0.877	0.870	0.862	0.855	0.847	0.840	0.833
2	0.812	0.797	0.783	0.769	0.756	0.743	0.731	0.718	0.706	0.694
3	0.731	0.712	0.693	0.675	0.658	0.641	0.624	0.609	0.593	0.579
4	0.659	0.636	0.613	0.592	0.572	0.552	0.534	0.516	0.499	0.482
5	0.593	0.567	0.543	0.519	0.497	0.476	0.456	0.437	0.419	0.402
6	0.535	0.507	0.480	0.456	0.432	0.410	0.390	0.370	0.352	0.335
7	0.482	0.452	0.425	0.400	0.376	0.354	0.333	0.314	0.296	0.279
8	0.434	0.404	0.376	0.351	0.327	0.305	0.285	0.266	0.249	0.233
9	0.391	0.361	0.333	0.308	0.284	0.263	0.243	0.225	0.209	0.194
10	0.352	0.322	0.295	0.270	0.247	0.227	0.208	0.191	0.176	0.162
11	0.317	0.287	0.261	0.237	0.215	0.195	0.178	0.162	0.148	0.135
12	0.286	0.257	0.231	0.208	0.187	0.168	0.152	0.137	0.124	0.112
13	0.258	0.229	0.204	0.182	0.163	0.145	0.130	0.116	0.104	0.093
14	0.232	0.205	0.181	0.160	0.141	0.125	0.111	0.099	0.088	0.078
15	0.209	0.183	0.160	0.140	0.123	0.108	0.095	0.084	0.074	0.065

Annuity table

Present value of an annuity of 1, i.e. $\dfrac{1-(1+r)^{-n}}{r}$

Where r = discount rate

n = number of periods

Periods (n)	\multicolumn{10}{c}{Discount rate (r)}									
	1%	2%	3%	4%	5%	6%	7%	8%	9%	10%
1	0.990	0.980	0.971	0.962	0.952	0.943	0.935	0.926	0.917	0.909
2	1.970	1.942	1.913	1.886	1.859	1.833	1.808	1.783	1.759	1.736
3	2.941	2.884	2.829	2.775	2.723	2.673	2.624	2.577	2.531	2.487
4	3.902	3.808	3.717	3.630	3.546	3.465	3.387	3.312	3.240	3.170
5	4.853	4.713	4.580	4.452	4.329	4.212	4.100	3.993	3.890	3.791
6	5.795	5.601	5.417	5.242	5.076	4.917	4.767	4.623	4.486	4.355
7	6.728	6.472	6.230	6.002	5.786	5.582	5.389	5.206	5.033	4.868
8	7.652	7.325	7.020	6.733	6.463	6.210	5.971	5.747	5.535	5.335
9	8.566	8.162	7.786	7.435	7.108	6.802	6.515	6.247	5.995	5.759
10	9.471	8.983	8.530	8.111	7.722	7.360	7.024	6.710	6.418	6.145
11	10.368	9.787	9.253	8.760	8.306	7.887	7.499	7.139	6.805	8.495
12	11.255	10.575	9.954	9.385	8.863	8.384	7.943	7.536	7.161	6.814
13	12.134	11.348	10.635	9.986	9.394	8.853	8.358	7.904	7.487	7.103
14	13.004	12.106	11.296	10.563	9.899	9.295	8.745	8.244	7.786	7.367
15	13.865	12.849	11.938	11.118	10.380	9.712	9.108	8.559	8.061	7.606

Periods (n)	\multicolumn{10}{c}{Discount rate (r)}									
	11%	12%	13%	14%	15%	16%	17%	18%	19%	20%
1	0.901	0.893	0.885	0.877	0.870	0.862	0.855	0.847	0.840	0.833
2	1.713	1.690	1.668	1.647	1.626	1.605	1.585	1.566	1.547	1.528
3	2.444	2.402	2.361	2.322	2.283	2.246	2.210	2.174	2.140	2.106
4	3.102	3.037	2.974	2.914	2.855	2.798	2.743	2.690	2.639	2.589
5	3.696	3.605	3.517	3.433	3.352	3.274	3.199	3.127	3.058	2.991
6	4.231	4.111	3.998	3.889	3.784	3.685	3.589	3.498	3.410	3.326
7	4.712	4.564	4.423	4.288	4.160	4.039	3.922	3.812	3.706	3.605
8	5.146	4.968	4.799	4.639	4.487	4.344	4.207	4.078	3.954	3.837
9	5.537	5.328	5.132	4.946	4.772	4.607	4.451	4.303	4.163	4.031
10	5.889	5.650	5.426	5.216	5.019	4.833	4.659	4.494	4.339	4.192
11	6.207	5.938	5.687	5.453	5.234	5.029	4.836	4.656	4.486	4.327
12	6.492	6.194	5.918	5.660	5.421	5.197	4.968	4.793	4.611	4.439
13	6.750	6.424	6.122	5.842	5.583	5.342	5.118	4.910	4.715	4.533
14	6.982	6.628	6.302	6.002	5.724	5.468	5.229	5.008	4.802	4.611
15	7.191	6.811	6.462	6.142	5.847	5.575	5.324	5.092	4.876	4.675

Introduction to strategic management accounting

Chapter learning objectives

Upon completion of this chapter you will be able to:

- explain the role of strategic performance management in strategic planning and control

- discuss the role of corporate planning in clarifying corporate objectives, making strategic decisions and checking progress towards the objectives

- compare planning and control at the strategic and operational levels within a business entity

- assess the use of strategic management accounting in the context of multinational companies

- discuss the scope for potential conflict between strategic business plans and short-term localised decisions

- evaluate how SWOT analysis may assist in the performance management process

- evaluate the methods of benchmarking performance

- discuss how the purpose, structure and content of a mission statement impacts on business performance

- discuss the ways in which high-level corporate objectives are developed

- identify strategic objectives and discuss how they may be incorporated into the business plan

- discuss how strategic objectives are cascaded down the organisation via the formulation of subsidiary performance objectives

- explain the performance 'planning gap' and evaluate alternative strategies to fill the gap

- apply critical success factor analysis in developing performance metrics from business objectives

- identify and discuss the characteristics of operational performance

- discuss the relative significance of planning against controlling activities at different levels of the performance hierarchy.

1 Introduction to Paper P5

Paper P5 will require you to assess different approaches to performance management from a variety of perspectives. This will require you to know what the approaches are and, more importantly, you should be able to compare one with another.

Performance management systems are the systems within the organisation by which the performance of the organisation is measured, controlled and improved.

2 Assumed knowledge

Paper P5 builds on knowledge gained at other levels, specifically Paper F5 and, to a lesser extent, Paper P3.

Paper F5, Performance Management, tested your knowledge and application of core management accounting techniques. Paper P5 develops key aspects introduced at F5 level with a greater focus on linking the syllabus topics together and evaluation of the key topics and techniques. Therefore, you should not expect to be retested in a Paper F5 (or P3) style but need to be aware that all F5 knowledge (and some P3 knowledge) is assumed to be known.

Chapter 1 builds on the following knowledge from Paper P3:

- Strategy and strategic planning
- Critical success factors (CSFs) and key performance indicators (KPIs)
- Benchmarking
- SWOT
- Gap analysis
- Mission

3 Introduction to Chapter 1

This chapter sets the scene to Part A of the syllabus, '**strategic planning and control**'. It introduces the process of strategic planning and control and some of the tools used, i.e. benchmarking and SWOT analysis. In Paper P5 you should be able to use strategic planning and control models to plan and monitor an organisation's performance.

4 Introduction to planning and control

4.1 Definitions

Planning and control are fundamental aspects of performance management.

Strategic planning is concerned with:

- where an organisation wants to be (usually expressed in terms of its objectives) and
- how it will get there (strategies).

Control is concerned with monitoring the achievement of objectives and suggesting corrective action.

4.2 Planning and control at different levels within an organisation

Planning and control takes place at different levels within an organisation. The performance hierarchy operates in the following order:

(1) Mission

(2) Strategic (corporate) plans and objectives

(3) Tactical plans and objectives

(4) Operational plans and targets

4.3 Mission

A **mission statement** outlines the broad direction that an organisation will follow and summarises the reasons and values that underlie that organisation.

A mission should be:

- succinct

- memorable

- enduring, i.e. the statement should not change unless the entity's mission changes

- a guide for employees to work towards the accomplishment of the mission

- addressed to a number of stakeholder groups, for example shareholders, employees and customers.

Illustration 1 – Mission

Ben and Jerry's

'Our mission is to make, distribute and sell the finest quality ice cream and euphoric concoctions with a continued commitment to incorporating wholesome, natural elements and promoting business practices that respect the earth and the environment'.

Microsoft

'To enable people and business throughout the world to realise their full potential'.

The British Broadcasting Corporation (BBC)

'Inform, educate and entertain'.

Pepsi

'Beat Coke'.

The mission forms a key part of the planning process and should enhance organisational performance:

- It acts as a source of inspiration and ideas for the organisation's detailed plans and objectives.

- It can be used to assess the suitability of any proposed plans in terms of their fit with the organisation's mission.

- It can impact the day to day workings of an organisation, guiding the organisational culture and business practices used.

Drucker

Drucker concluded that a mission statement should address four fundamental questions.

Test your understanding 1

Required:

What are the potential benefits and drawbacks to an organisation of setting a mission statement?

The lifespan of a mission

There are no set rules on how long a mission statement will be appropriate for an organisation. It should be reviewed periodically to ensure it still reflects the organisation's environment.

If the market or key stakeholders have changed since the mission statement was written, then it may no longer be appropriate.

A change in the mission statement may result in **new performance measures** being established to monitor the achievement (or otherwise) of the new mission.

4.4 Strategic, tactical and operational plans

To enable an organisation to fulfil its mission, the mission must be translated into strategic, tactical and operational plans.

Each level should be consistent with the one above.

This process will involve moving from general broad aims to more specific objectives and ultimately to detailed targets.

In this chapter we will focus on strategic and operational plans.

Comparing planning and control between strategic and operational levels

Planning

Strategic
- Long-term
- Considers whole organisation as well as individual departments/divisions
- Considers internal and external environment and all stakeholders

Operational
- Short-term
- Considers the use of assets and resources
- Does not tend to consider the whole organisation

Illustration 2 – Strategic planning

Strategic planning is usually, but not always, concerned with the long-term. It raises the question of **which business shall we be in**? For example, a company specialising in production and sale of tobacco products may forecast a declining market for these products and may therefore decide to change its objectives to allow a progressive move into the leisure industry, which it considers to be expanding.

Strategic and operational planning

Planning

Strategic planning is characterised by the following:

- long-term

- considers the whole organisation as well as individual SBUs

- matches the activities of an organisation to its external environment

- matches the activities of an organisation to its resource capability and specifies future resource requirements

- will be affected by the expectations and values of all stakeholders, not just shareholders

- its complexity distinguishes strategic management from other aspects of management in an organisation. There are several reasons for this including:

  - it involves a high degree of uncertainty

  - it is likely to require an integrated approach to management

  - it may involve major change in the organisation.

Quite apart from strategic planning, the management of an organisation has to undertake a regular series of decisions on matters that are purely **operational** and short-term in character. Such decisions:

- are usually based on a given set of assets and resources

- do not usually involve the scope of an organisation's activities

- rarely involve major change in the organisation

- are unlikely to involve major elements of uncertainty and the techniques used to help make such decisions often seek to minimise the impact of any uncertainty.

- use standard management accounting techniques such as cost-volume-profit analysis, limiting factor analysis and linear programming.

Control

Strategic
Monitors the implementation of the organisation's strategy to ascertain how well the strategic objectives are being achieved

Operational
- Concerned with the management of existing assets and resources, given the existing strategic direction
- Will not lead to a change in strategy

Test your understanding 2

Required:

Is the activity of setting a profit-maximising selling price for a product a strategic or operational decision?

Give reasons for your answer.

The role of performance management in planning and control

Performance management is any activity that is designed to improve the organisation's performance and ensure that its goals are met.

- Planning will take place first to establish an appropriate mission and objectives.

- Performance management techniques will then be used to ensure that the most appropriate strategy is defined and executed in order to achieve the organisation's mission and objectives.

- Finally, performance management will aim to measure whether the mission and objectives are being achieved and to recommend any improvement strategies that are required.

Performance management aims to direct and support the performance of all employees and departments so that the organisation's goals are achieved. Therefore, any performance management system should be linked to performance measures at different levels of the hierarchy. One model of performance management that helps to link the different levels of the hierarchy is the performance pyramid.

The **performance pyramid** derives from the idea that an organisation operates at different levels, each of which has a different focus. However, it is vital that these levels support each other. It translates objectives from the top down and measures from the bottom up, the aim being that these are co-ordinated and support each other (this will be explored in more detail in Chapter 11).

5 Strategic (corporate) planning

We are now going to explore in more detail the role of strategic planning in performance management.

5.1 What is strategy?

The core of a company's strategy is about choosing:

- **where** to compete and
- **how** to compete.

It is a means to achieve **sustainable competitive advantage**.

In terms of performance management, the test of a good strategy is whether it enables an organisation to use its resources and competencies advantageously in the context of an ever changing environment.

 Strategic (or corporate) planning involves formulating, evaluating and selecting strategies to enable the preparation of a long-term plan of action and to attain objectives.

5.2 Strategic analysis, choice and implementation (rational model)

This three stage model of strategic planning is a useful framework for seeing the 'bigger picture' of performance management (and should be very familiar to you).

Strategic analysis
- External analysis to identify opportunities and threats
- Internal analysis to identify strengths and weaknesses
- Stakeholder analysis to identify key objectives and to assess power and interest of different groups
- Gap analysis to identify the difference between desired and expected performance.

↓

Strategic choice
- Strategies are required to 'close the gap'
- Competitive strategy – for each business unit
- Directions for growth – which markets/products should be invested in
- Whether expansion should be achieved by organic growth, acquisition or some form of joint arrangement.

↓

Strategic implementation
- Formulation of detailed plans and budgets
- Target setting for KPIs
- Monitoring and control.

Each of these areas will be explored in greater detail throughout the course. However, it is worth noting that although strategy is still included in this paper, the main thrust in P5 will be looking at where objectives come from, identifying critical success factors, choosing metrics and how to implement strategy. Theory will be secondary.

5.3 The role of strategic (corporate) planning in clarifying corporate objectives

Corporate objectives concern the business as a whole and focus on the desired performance and results that a business intends to achieve.

The first stage of the strategic planning process, strategic analysis, will generate a range of objectives, typically relating to:

- maximisation of shareholder wealth
- maximisation of sales
- growth
- survival
- research and development
- leadership
- quality of service
- contented workforce
- respect for the environment.

These need to be clarified in two respects:

- **conflicts need to be resolved**, e.g. profit versus environmental concerns
- to facilitate implementation and control, objectives need to be translated into **SMART** (specific, measurable, achievable, relevant and time bound) targets.

Illustration 3 – SMART objectives

A statement such as 'maximise profits' would be of little use in corporate planning terms. The following would be far more helpful:

- achieve a growth in EPS of 5% pa over the coming ten-year period
- obtain a turnover of $10 million within six years
- launch at least two new products per year.

5.4 Role of Strategic (corporate) planning in making strategic choices

The viability of a strategic choice should be assessed using three criteria:

Three criteria for evaluating potential strategies

Suitability
Does the strategy have a suitable strategic fit, i.e does it build on strengths, take advantage of opportunities and will new products fit with existing ones?

Acceptability
Is the strategy acceptable to the stakeholders of the organisation, both in terms of risk and return?

Feasibility
Can the necessary resources and competencies be obtained? Can the organisation manage the process of strategic change?

5.5 The role of strategic (corporate) planning in checking towards the objectives set

It is not enough merely to make plans and implement them.

- The results of the plans have to be compared against stated objectives to assess the firm's performance.

- Action can then be taken to remedy any shortfalls in performance.

Strategic (corporate) planning is not a once-in-every-ten-years activity, but an on going process which must react quickly to the changing circumstances of the firm and of the environment.

Diagram of strategic (corporate) planning activities

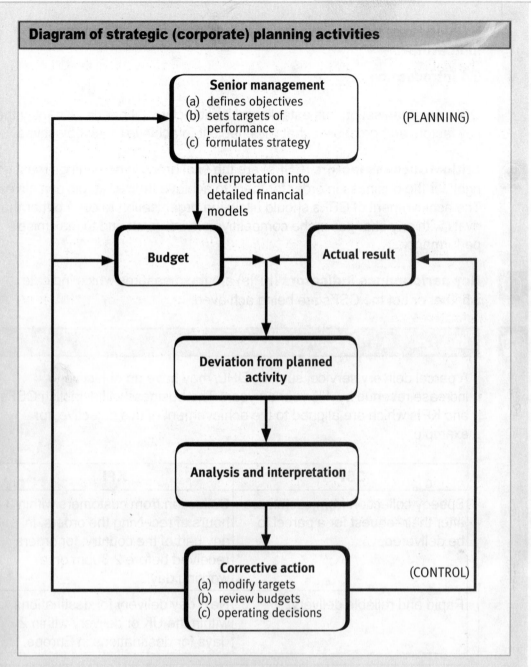

Senior management
(a) defines objectives
(b) sets targets of
    performance
(c) formulates strategy

(PLANNING)

Interpretation into
detailed financial
models

Budget

Actual result

**Deviation from planned
activity**

Analysis and interpretation

Corrective action
(a) modify targets
(b) review budgets
(c) operating decisions

(CONTROL)

Test your understanding 3

Required:

Why do you think managers need to understand strategic (corporate)
planning?

6 Objectives, critical success factors and key performance indicators

6.1 Introduction

Once an organisation has established its objectives, it needs to identify the key factors and processes that will enable it to achieve those objectives.

Critical success factors (CSFs) are the vital areas 'where things must go right' for the business in order for them to achieve their strategic objectives. The achievement of CSFs should allow the organisation to cope better than rivals with any changes in the competitive environment and to maximise performance.

Key performance indicators (KPIs) are the measures which indicate whether or not the CSFs are being achieved.

Illustration 4 – CSFs and KPIs

A parcel delivery service, such as DHL, may have an objective to increase revenue by 4% year on year. The business will establish CSFs and KPIs which are aligned to the achievement of this objective, for example:

CSF	KPI
Speedy collection from customers after their request for a parcel to be delivered.	Collection from customers within 3 hours of receiving the orders, in any part of the country, for orders received before 2.30pm on a working day.
Rapid and reliable delivery.	Next day delivery for destinations within the UK or delivery within 2 days for destinations in Europe.

6.2 CSFs

The organisation will need to have in place the **core competences** that are required to achieve the CSFs, i.e. something that they are able to do that is difficult for competitors to follow.

There are **five prime sources** of CSFs:

(1) **The structure of the industry** – CSFs will be determined by the characteristics of the industry itself, e.g. in the car industry 'efficient dealer network organisation' will be important where as in the food processing industry 'new product development' will be important.

(2) **Competitive strategy, industry position and geographic location**

- Competitive strategies such as differentiation or cost leadership will impact CSFs.

- Industry position, e.g. a small company's CSFs may be driven by a major competitor's strategy.

- Geographical location will impact factors such as distribution costs and hence CSFs.

(3) **Environmental factors** – factors such as increasing fuel costs can have an impact on the choice of CSFs.

(4) **Temporary factors** – temporary internal factors may drive CSFs, e.g. a supermarket may have been forced to recall certain products due to contamination fears and may therefore generate a short term CSF of ensuring that such contamination does not happen again in the future.

(5) **Functional managerial position** – the function will affect the CSFs, e.g. production managers will be concerned with product quality and cost control.

6.3 Classifying CSFs

Test your understanding 4

The directors of Dream Ice Cream (DI), a successful ice cream producer, with a reputation as a quality supplier, have decided to enter the frozen yogurt market in its country of operation. It has set up a separate operation under the name of Dream Yogurt (DY). The following information is available:

- DY has recruited a management team but production staff will need to be recruited. There is some concern that there will not be staff available with the required knowledge of food production.

- DY has agreed to supply yogurts to Jacksons, a chain of supermarkets based in the home country. They have stipulated that delivery must take place within 24 hours of an order being sent.

- DY hopes to become a major national producer of frozen yogurts.

- DY produces four varieties of frozen yogurt at present; Mango Tango, Very Berry, Orange Burst and French Vanilla.

Required:

Explain five CSFs on which the directors must focus if DY is to achieve success in the marketplace.

(10 marks)

Student accountant article: visit the ACCA website, www.accaglobal.com, to review the article on 'Defining managers' information requirements' from August 2006.

6.4 KPIs

KPIs are essential to the achievement of strategy since **what gets measured gets done**, i.e. things that are measured get done more often than things that are not measured.

Features of good performance measures

In addition, KPIs should be SMART (**s**pecific, **m**easurable, **a**ttainable, **r**elevant and **t**ime-bound).

Care must be taken when choosing what to measure and report. An unbalanced set of indicators may be valid for fulfilling the short-term needs of the organisation but will not necessarily result in long-term success. The balanced scorecard approach will seek to address this and is discussed in Chapter 11.

6.5 Past exam question

Some of the test your understandings in this material are shorter or more straightforward than questions in the P5 exam. They are contained in the material for learning purposes and will help you to build your knowledge and confidence so that you are ready to tackle past exam questions during the revision phase.

However, it is useful to look at some past exam/ exam standard questions right from the beginning of this course in order to understand how the areas covered may be tested in the real exam. You need to understand how to interpret the requirements, read and understand the scenario and plan and structure your answer. You may not be able to tackle the entire question at this point but you should read and learn from the answer.

Note: requirement (d) has been included for completeness but the areas tested have not been covered in the material as yet.

Test your understanding 5

Film Productions Co (FP) is a small international company producing films for cinema release and also for sale on DVD or to television companies. FP deals with all areas of the production from casting, directing and managing the artists to negotiating distribution deals with cinema chains and TV channels. The industry is driven by the tastes of its films' audience, which when accurately predicted can lead to high levels of profitability on a successful film.

The company's stated mission is to 'produce fantastic films that have mass appeal'. The company makes around $200 million of sales each year equally split between a share of cinema takings, DVD sales and TV rights. FP has released 32 films in the past five years. Each film costs an average of $18 million and takes 12 months to produce from initial commissioning through to the final version. Production control is important in order to hit certain key holiday periods for releasing films at the cinema or on DVD.

The company's films have been moderately successful in winning industry awards although FP has never won any major award. Its aims have been primarily commercial with artistic considerations secondary.

The company uses a top-down approach to strategy development with objectives leading to critical success factors (CSFs) which must then be measured using performance indicators. Currently, the company has identified a number of critical success factors. The two most important of these are viewed as:

(i)   improve audience satisfaction

(ii) strengthen profitability in operations

At the request of the board, the chief executive officer (CEO) has been reviewing this system in particular the role of CSFs. Generally, the CEO is worried that the ones chosen so far fail to capture all the factors affecting the business and wants to understand all possible sources for CSFs and what it means to categorise them into monitoring and building factors.

These CSFs will need to be measured and there must be systems in place to perform that role. The existing information system of the company is based on a fairly basic accounting package. However, the CEO has been considering greater investment in these systems and making more use of the company's website in both driving forward the business' links to its audience and in collecting data on them.

The CEO is planning a report to the board of Film Productions and has asked you to help by drafting certain sections of this report.

Required:

You are required to draft the sections of the CEO's report answering the following questions:

(a)   Explain the difference between the following two types of CSF: monitoring and building, using examples appropriate to FP.

(4 marks)

(b)   Identify information that FP could use to set its CSFs and explain how it could be used giving two examples that would be appropriate to FP.

(6 marks)

(c)   For each of the two critical success factors given in the question, identify two performance indicators (PIs) that could support measurement of their achievement and explain why each PI is relevant to the CSF.

(10 marks)

(d) Discuss the implications of your chosen PIs for the design and use of the company's website, its management information system and its executive information system.

(9 marks)

2 professional marks will be awarded for appropriateness of style and structure of the answer.

(Total: 31 marks)

7 Long-term and short-term conflicts

Strategic planning is a long-term, top-down process. The decisions made can conflict with the short-term localised decisions:

- Divisional managers tend to be rewarded on the short-term results they achieve. Therefore, it will be difficult to motivate managers to achieve long-term strategic objectives.

- Divisional managers need to be able to take advantage of short-term unforseen opportunities or avoid serious short-term crisis. Strict adherence to a strategy could limit their ability to do this.

Long-term and short-term conflicts

The whole concept of strategic planning explored earlier in this chapter implies a certain top-down approach. Even in the era of divisional autonomy and employee empowerment it is difficult to imagine that a rigorous strategic planning regime could be associated with a bottom-up management culture. There is a potential for conflict here.

- The idea of divisional autonomy is that individual managers operate their business units as if they were independent businesses – seeking and exploiting local opportunities as they arise.

- Managers are rewarded in a manner which reflects the results they achieve.

- The pressures on management are for short-term results and ostensibly strategy is concerned with the long-term. Often it is difficult to motivate managers by setting long-term expectations.

- Long-term plans have to be set out in detail long before the period to which they apply. The rigidity of the long-term plan, particularly in regard to the rationing and scheduling of resources, may place the company in a position where it is unable to react to short-term unforeseen opportunities, or serious short-term crisis.

- Strict adherence to a strategy can limit flair and creativity. Operational managers may need to respond to local situations, avert trouble or improve a situation by quick action outside the strategy. If they then have to defend their actions against criticisms of acting 'outside the plan', irrespective of the resultant benefits, they are likely to become apathetic and indifferent.

- The adoption of corporate strategy requires a tacit acceptance by everyone that the interests of departments, activities and individuals are subordinate to the corporate interests. Department managers are required to consider the contribution to corporate profits or the reduction in corporate costs of any decision. They should not allow their decisions to be limited by short-term departmental parameters.

- It is only natural that local managers should seek personal advancement. A problem of strategic planning is identifying those areas where there may be a clash of interests and loyalties, and in assessing where an individual has allowed vested interests to dominate decisions.

Test your understanding 6

Required:

How might an organisation take steps to avoid conflict between strategic business plans and short-term localised decisions?

8 The role of strategic management accounting

The role of the management accountant has changed from one of financial control to business support.

Strategic management accounting is a form of management accounting which aims to provide information that is relevant to the process of strategic planning and control. The focus is on both **external** and **internal** information and **non-financial** as well as **financial** factors.

```
        ┌─────────────────────┐
        │  Role of management │
        │     accountant      │
        └─────────────────────┘
         ·                   ·
        ·                     ·
```

Historically	Today
• Role limited to implementation stage, e.g. responsible for operational budgeting and control.	• Strategic role providing information on financial aspects of strategic planning e.g. competitors' costs.
• Focus is on internal factors and financial information.	• Uses internal and external information
• Focus is on the past	• Monitors performance in financial and non-financial terms.
	• Focus is on the future.

The strategic management accountant plays a **key role in performance management** helping to determine the financial implications of an organisation's activities and decisions and in ensuring that these activities are focused on shareholders' needs for profit.

Test your understanding 7

A company selling wooden garden furniture in northern Europe is facing a number of problems:

- demand is seasonal

- it is sometimes difficult to forecast demand as it varies with the weather – more is sold in hot summers than when it is cooler or wetter

- the market is becoming more fashion-conscious with shorter product life cycles

- there is a growth in the use of non-traditional materials such as plastics.

As a result the company finds itself with high inventory levels of some items of furniture which are not selling, and is unable to meet demand for others. A decision is needed on the future strategic direction and possible options which have been identified are to:

- use largely temporary staff to manufacture products on a seasonal basis in response to fluctuations in demand – however it has been identified that this could result in quality problems

- automate production to enable seasonal production with minimum labour-related problems

- concentrate on producing premium products which are smaller volume but high-priced and less dependent on fashion.

Required:

How could strategic management accounting help with the decision making?

9 Strategic management accounting in multinational companies

In the previous section we looked at the role of the strategic management accountant. Here we look at their role in multinational companies.

A **multinational company** has subsidiaries or operations in a number of countries, e.g. it may acquire raw materials in one country, manufacture the product in a second country, sell its products in the third country and have its head office in its home country.

Illustration 5 – The development of multinational companies

Typically, a multinational company takes the form of a central corporation with subsidiaries in each of the countries in which it operates. Well-known examples include Ford, Shell, Nestlé, General Motors, Toyota and Microsoft. By the early 1990s, 37,000 multinational companies with annual sales of $5.5 billion controlled about one-third of the world's private sector assets. The advent of these multinationals is associated with the apparent globalisation of the world economy. Various factors have contributed to this development, but one factor is critical. Increases in the scale of technology (in terms of cost, risk and complexity) have rendered even the largest national markets too small to be meaningful economic units on a stand-alone basis. Companies must expand internationally to support the technological development that is needed to remain competitive in many fields.

The modern trend in international business seems to be away from the old multinational corporations and towards networks and alliances. Strategic planning for the latter is another issue altogether.

The strategic process in a multinational company must take account of certain special features which have financial implications. These include:

- process specialisation
- product specialisation
- economic risk
- political sensitivities
- administrative issues.

Multinational strategic management accounting

Process specialisation. There may be a cost advantage in locating certain types of activity in certain countries. For example, a labour intensive operation may be best placed in a low wage area. Many companies (and not just traditional multinationals) have recently relocated customer service desks and telephone call centres to India.

Product specialisation. In spite of globalisation and the concept of 'world products', particular countries have characteristic tastes that the multinational must cater to.

Economic risk. The economics of a multinational operation may be highly sensitive to issues such as exchange rate fluctuations.

Political sensitivities. The multinational company operates across state boundaries and must be acutely aware of associated risk factors.

Administrative issues. A multinational company will find that even its own internal transactions are vulnerable to exchange rate movements, currency exchange controls and the existence (or absence) of international tax treaties. For example, if a multinational domiciled in country A tries to repatriate profits earned by its subsidiary in country B then it may find that those profits are taxed twice – once in A and again in B.

Impact of exchange rates

In the 1980s, many car manufacturers (Nissan, Toyota and Peugeot to name but three) built car assembly facilities in the UK to serve the whole of Europe – because the UK was perceived as a low-cost area. The UK's non-adoption of the Euro and the appreciation of the pound in the late 1990s suddenly made the UK a high-cost area. For a time, the viability of several high-profile plants was brought into question.

Test your understanding 8

Required:

A multinational company with subsidiaries in North America and Europe is considering launching its products in South America. As a management accountant supporting senior managers in making strategic decisions, what factors would you need to consider in your assessment of the options facing the company? How will these factors influence performance measurement/ management?

10 Tools used in strategic analysis

10.1 Benchmarking

Benchmarking is the process of identifying **best practice** in relation to the products (or services) and the processes by which those products (or services) are created and delivered. The objective of benchmarking is to understand and evaluate the current position of a business or organisation in relation to best practice and to identify areas and means of performance improvement.

Types of benchmarking

There are three basic types:

- **Internal**: this is where another function or department of the organisation is used as a benchmark. Can be straightforward but may lack innovative solutions due to there being no external focus.

- **Competitor**: uses a direct competitor in the same industry with the same or similar processes as the benchmark. The biggest problem will be obtaining information from the competitor.

- **Process or activity**: focuses on a similar process in another company which is not a direct competitor. Can prove easier to obtain information from a non-competitor and can still find innovative solutions.

KAPLAN PUBLISHING

Illustration 6 – Process benchmarking at Xerox

Among the pioneers in the benchmarking 'movement' were Xerox, Motorola, IBM and AT&T. The best known is the Xerox Corporation.

Some years ago, Xerox confronted its own unsatisfactory performance in **product warehousing and distribution**. It did so by identifying the organisation it considered to be the very best at warehousing and distribution, in the hope that 'best practices' could be adapted from this model. The business judged to provide a model of best practice in this area was L L Bean, a catalogue merchant (i.e. it existed in an unrelated sector). Xerox approached Bean with a request that the two engage in a co-operative benchmarking project. The request was granted and the project yielded major insights in inventory arrangement and order processing, resulting in major gains for Xerox when these insights were adapted to its own operations.

Strategic, functional and operational benchmarks

Benchmarks could include the following:

Strategic benchmarks

- market share
- return on assets
- gross profit margin on sales.

Functional benchmarks

- % deliveries on time
- order costs per order
- order turnaround time
- average stockholding per order.

Operational benchmarks

These are at a level below functional benchmarks. They yield the reasons for a functional performance gap. An organisation has to understand the benchmarks at the operational level in order to identify the corrective actions needed to close the performance gap.

The benchmarking process

Step 1: Set objectives and determine which areas or functions to benchmark.

Step 2: Identify key performance indicators and drivers that will be measured during benchmarking.

Step 3: Select organisations/partners for benchmarking comparison.

Step 4: Measure performance of all organisations/partners involved in benchmarking using measures identified in step 2.

Step 5: Measure own performance and compare it to the benchmark. Identify gaps in performance.

Step 6: Specify actions required to close the gap.

Step 7: Implement and monitor actions.

Benchmarking and the strategic planning process

Benchmarking can be used in all three areas of the strategic planning process:

- **Strategic analysis** – a company's mission may be to be 'the premium provider of its products' but without comparison through benchmarking how will they know if they are delivering premium products? In addition, a company's position can be summarised in a SWOT analysis. Each of these factors can be identified through benchmarking and any gaps identified.

- **Strategic choice** – benchmarking can help in assessing generic strategy. For example, an organisation may compare its costs to the leading competitor. If the organisation cannot better or equal those results then cost leadership is an inappropriate strategy to pursue.

- **Strategic implementation** – for example, budgetary targets should be benchmarked against other organisations to ensure that they are both challenging and attainable.

Benchmarking metrics

Once an organisation has decided which aspects of its performance should be benchmarked, it must then establish metrics for these, i.e. how can performance be measured? Some areas will be easy to measure (such as material used) where as others will be more difficult (such as customer service).

Illustration 7 – Benchmarking success at Kelloggs

Kelloggs' factories all use the same monitoring techniques, so it is possible to compare performance between sites, although there are always some things that are done differently.

They can interrogate this information to improve performance across every site. As things have improved, Kelloggs have also had to reassess their baseline figures and develop more sophisticated tools to monitor performance to ensure they continue to make progress.

They have seen a 20% increase in productivity in six years using this system.

Benchmarking evaluation

Benefits	Drawbacks
• Identifies gaps in performance and sets targets which are challenging but achievable. • Can help in assessing its current strategic position (more on SWOT analysis in section 10.2). • A method for learning and applying best practices. • Encourages continuous improvement. • A method of learning from the success of others. • Can help to assess generic strategy. • Minimises complacency and self-satisfaction with your own performance and can provide an early warning of competitive disadvantage.	• Best practice companies may be unwilling to share data. • Lack of commitment by management and staff. Staff need to be reassured that their status, remuneration and working conditions will not suffer. • Identifying best practice is difficult. • Costly in terms of time and money. • What is best today may not be so tomorrow. • Differences, for example in accounting treatment, may make comparisons meaningless. • Too much attention is paid to the aspects of performance that are measured as a result of the benchmarking exercise, to the detriment of the organisation's overall performance.

Performance comparison with the competition

Comparative analysis can be usefully applied to any value activity which underpins the competitive strategy of an organisation, an industry or a nation.

To find out the level of investment in fixed assets of competitors, the business can use physical observation, information from trade press or trade association announcements, supplier press releases as well as their externally published financial statements, to build a clear picture of the relative scale, capacity, age and cost for each competitor.

The method of operating these assets, in terms of hours and shift patterns, can be established by observation, discussions with suppliers and customers or by asking existing or ex-employees of the particular competitor. If the method of operating can be ascertained it should enable a combination of internal personnel management and industrial engineering managers to work out the likely relative differences in labour costs. The rates of pay and conditions can generally be found with reference to nationally negotiated agreements, local and national press advertising for employees, trade and employment associations and recruitment consultants. When this cost is used alongside an intelligent assessment of how many employees would be needed by the competitor in each area, given their equipment and other resources, a good idea of the labour costs can be obtained.

Another difference which should be noted is the nature of the competitors' costs as well as their relative levels. Where a competitor has a lower level of committed fixed costs, such as lower fixed labour costs due to a larger proportion of temporary workers, it may be able to respond more quickly to a downturn in demand by rapidly laying off the temporary staff. Equally, in a tight labour market and with rising sales, it may have to increase its pay levels to attract new workers.

In some industries, one part of the competitor analysis is surprisingly direct. Each new competitive product is purchased on a regular basis and then systematically taken apart, so that each component can be identified as well as the processes used to put the parts together. The respective areas of the business will then assess the costs associated with each element so that a complete product cost can be found for the competitive product.

A comparison of similar value activities between organisations is useful when the strategic context is taken into consideration. For example, a straight comparison of resource deployment between two competitive organisations may reveal quite different situations in the labour cost as a percentage of the total cost. The conclusions drawn from this, however, depend upon circumstances. If the firms are competing largely on the basis of price, then differentials in these costs could be crucial. In contrast, the additional use of labour by one organisation may be an essential support for the special services provided which differentiate that organisation from its competitors.

One danger of inter-firm analysis is that the company may overlook the fact that the whole industry is performing badly, and is losing out competitively to other countries with better resources or even other industries which can satisfy customers' needs in different ways. Therefore, if an industry comparison is performed it should make some assessment of how the resource utilisation compares with other countries and industries. This can be done by obtaining a measurement of stock turnover or yield from raw materials.

Benchmarking against competitors involves the gathering of a range of information about them. For quoted companies financial information will generally be reasonably easy to obtain, from published accounts and the financial press. Some product information may be obtained by acquiring their products and examining them in detail to ascertain the components used and their construction ('reverse engineering'). Literature will also be available, for example in the form of brochures and trade journals.

However, most non-financial information, concerning areas such as competitors' processes, customer and supplier relationships and customer satisfaction will not be so readily available. To overcome this problem, benchmarking exercises are generally carried out with organisations taken from within the same group of companies (intra-group benchmarking) or from similar but non-competing industries (inter-industry benchmarking).

Question practice

The following question is an exam standard and style question on benchmarking. Make sure that you take the time to attempt this question and to review the recommended answer.

Test your understanding 9

AV is a charitable organisation, the primary objective of which, is to meet the accommodation needs of persons within its locality.

In an attempt to improve its performance, AV's directors have started to carry out a benchmarking exercise. They have identified a company called BW which is a profit seeking private provider of rented accommodation.

BW has provided some operational and financial data which is summarised below along with the most recent results for AV for the year ended 31 May 2014.

Income and expenditure accounts for the year ended 31 May 2014 were as follows:

	AV ($)	BW ($)
Rents received	2,386,852	2,500,000
Less:		
Staff and management costs	450,000	620,000
Major repairs and planned maintenance	682,400	202,200
Day-to-day repairs	478,320	127,600
Sundry operating costs	305,500	235,000
Net interest payable and other similar charges	526,222	750,000
Total costs	2,442,442	1,934,800
Operating (deficit)/surplus	(55,590)	565,200

Operating information in respect of the year ended 31 May 2014 was as follows:

(1) Property and rental information:

AV – size of property	AV – number of properties	AV – rent payable per week ($)	BW – number of properties
1 bedroom	80	40	40
2 bedrooms	160	45	80
3 bedrooms	500	50	280
4 bedrooms	160	70	nil

AV had certain properties that were unoccupied during part of the year. The rents lost as a consequence of unoccupied properties amounted to $36,348. BW did not have any unoccupied properties at any point during the year.

(2) Staff salaries were payable as follows:

AV – number of staff	AV – salary per staff member per year ($)	BW – number of staff ($)	BW – salary per staff member per year ($)
2	35,000	3	50,000
2	25,000	2	35,000
3	20,000	20	20,000
18	15,000	–	–

(3) Planned maintenance and major repairs undertaken

Nature of work	AV – number of properties	AV – cost per property ($)	BW – number of properties	BW – cost per property ($)
Miscellaneous construction work	20	1,250	–	–
Fitted kitchen replacements (all are the same size)	90	2,610	10	5,220
Heating upgrades/ replacements	15	1,500	–	–
Replacement sets of windows and doors for 3 bedroomed properties	100	4,000	25	6,000

All expenditure on planned maintenance and major repairs may be regarded as revenue expenditure.

(4) Day-to-day repairs information:

Classification of repair	AV – number of repairs undertaken	AV – total cost ($)	BW – number of repairs undertaken
Emergency	960	134,400	320
Urgent	1,880	225,600	752
Non-urgent	1,020	118,320	204

Each repair undertaken by BW costs the same irrespective of classification of repair.

Required:

(a) Assess the progress of the benchmarking exercise to date, explaining the actions that have been undertaken and those that are still required.

(8 marks)

(b) Evaluate, as far as possible, AV's benchmarked position.

(9 marks)

(c) Discuss whether BW is a suitable benchmarking partner for AV to use.

(8 marks)

Student accountant article: visit the ACCA website, www.accaglobal.com to review the article on 'benchmarking'.

10.2 SWOT analysis

The purpose of **SWOT analysis** (corporate appraisal) is to provide a summarised analysis of the company's present situation in the market place. It can also be used to identify CSFs and KPIs.

Using a SWOT analysis

Once a SWOT analysis has been carried out strategies can be developed that:

- neutralise weaknesses or convert them into strengths.

- convert threats into opportunities.

- match strengths with opportunities – a strength is of little use without an opportunity.

Test your understanding 10

Required:

What types of strengths, weaknesses, opportunities and threats would a 'no frills' airline have?

SWOT analysis and performance management and measurement

SWOT analysis helps an organisation to understand its environment and its internal capacities and hence to evaluate the potential strategic options it could pursue in its quest to improve organisational performance and to close any performance gaps that exist.

It can also help an organisation to identify key aspects of performance (CSFs) that need measuring (through the establishment of KPIs).

Finally, it can help in determining the information needs of the business in relation to measuring and reporting on the KPIs set.

Test your understanding 11

Envie Co owns a chain of retail clothing stores specialising in ladies' designer fashion and accessories. Jane Smith, the original founder, has been pleasantly surprised by the continuing growth in the fashion industry during the last decade.

The company was established 12 years ago, originally with one store in the capital city. Jane's design skills and entrepreneurial skills have been the driving force behind the expansion. Due to unique designs and good quality control, the business now has ten stores in various cities.

Each store has a shop manger that is completely responsible for managing the staff and stock levels within each store. They produce monthly reports on sales. Some stores are continually late in supplying their monthly figures.

Envie runs several analysis programmes to enable management information to be collated. The information typically provides statistical data on sales trends between categories of items and stores. The analysis and preparation of these reports are conducted in the marketing department. In some cases the information is out of date in terms of trends and variations.

As the business has developed Jane has used the service of a local IT company to implement and develop their systems. She now wants to invest in website development with the view of reaching global markets.

Required:

(a) Construct a SWOT analysis with reference to the proposal of website development.

(b) Explain how the use of SWOT analysis may be of assistance to Envie Co's performance management and measurement process.

11 Gap analysis

Gap analysis is carried out as the final part of strategic analysis. It identifies the planning gap. This is the difference between the desired and the expected performance.

The planning gap is often measured in terms of demand but may also be reported in terms of earnings, return on capital employed etc.

The example below shows a gap for 'earnings'.

In the diagram showing the gap:

F_0 = initial forecast

F_1 = forecast adjusted for improvements in **internal efficiency**, e.g. internal cost savings through better use of resources or divestment of a loss-making business unit.

F_2 = forecast adjusted for **product-market expansion.** The expansion gap involves the development of a new product **or** market.

T = target. The gap between F_2 and the target represents the forecast adjusted for **product-market expansion**. The diversification gap involves the development of new products **and** markets.

Benchmarking and SWOT analysis can both be used to identify the gap and to help the organisation to identify strategies to address the gap.

Illustration 8 – SWOT analysis and gap identification

SWOT analysis would seek to identify:

- **Threats focusing on weaknesses** – This would have top priority and the company should seek to identify and consider possible solutions. This requires a defensive response of some kind and may well necessitate rapid change.

- **Threats focusing on strengths** – this requires a review of the supposed strength to ensure that it is still as strong as previously thought. Remember, what is good today, may not be so tomorrow.

- **Opportunity focusing on strengths** – this gives the organisation the chance to develop strategic competitive advantage in the marketplace. They should check the research and assess the strengths again.

- **Opportunity focusing on weakness** – this will require management to make a decision as to whether to change and pursue the opportunity or, alternatively, ignore the prospect and ensure resources are not wasted in this area in future. Usually substantial change will be required if the company is going to pursue the opportunity. The company should check that their internal competencies will allow them to exploit the opportunity.

12 Exam focus

Exam sitting	Area examined	Question number	Number of marks
June 2014	Mission	1 (v)	6
December 2013	KPIs, CSFs and gap analysis	1(i)(iii)(iv)(v)	35
June 2012	Benchmarking	4	17
June 2012	KPIs	2(a)	12
December 2011	KPIs	2(a)	7
December 2010	CSFs and KPIs	1 (a)-(c)	20
December 2010	KPIs	4(a)	4
December 2009	KPIs	2(b)(i)	12
December 2009	Mission, CSFs and KPIs	5	17
December 2008	Planning gap	3(a)	5
June 2008	Benchmarking	1(b)	7
December 2007	CSFs	3(b)	10
Pilot paper	Mission	2(a)(i)	5

Note:

- The current examiner has set the exam papers from the December 2010 sitting onwards.

- The format of the exam changed in June 2013. Section A now contains 1 × 50 mark question (previously 2 questions worth 60 marks in total) and Section B now contains a choice of 2 from 3 questions worth 25 marks each (previously a choice of 2 from 3 questions worth approximately 20 marks each).

Chapter summary

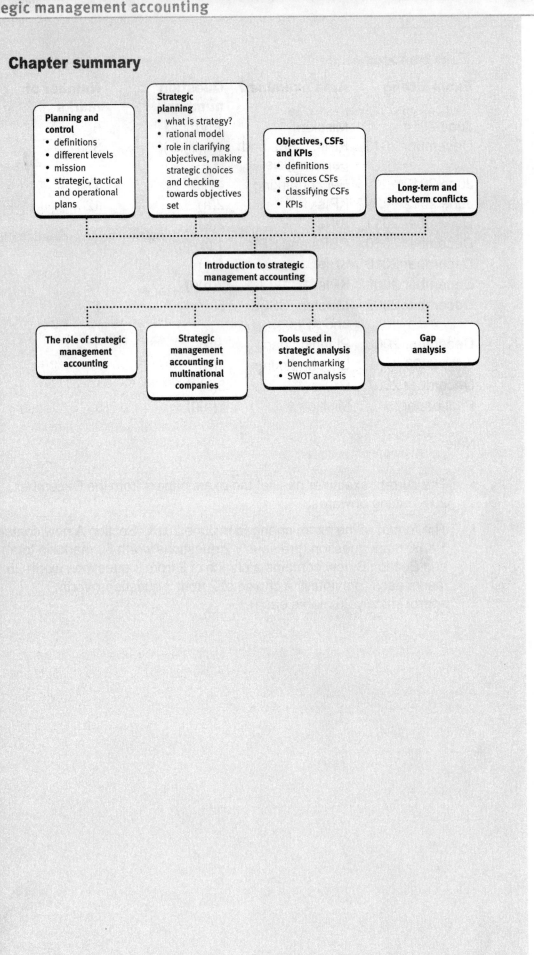

Planning and control
- definitions
- different levels
- mission
- strategic, tactical and operational plans

Strategic planning
- what is strategy?
- rational model
- role in clarifying objectives, making strategic choices and checking towards objectives set

Objectives, CSFs and KPIs
- definitions
- sources CSFs
- classifying CSFs
- KPIs

Long-term and short-term conflicts

Introduction to strategic management accounting

The role of strategic management accounting

Strategic management accounting in multinational companies

Tools used in strategic analysis
- benchmarking
- SWOT analysis

Gap analysis

Test your understanding answers

Test your understanding 1

Benefits	Drawbacks
• Provides strategic direction thereby assisting in the formation of acceptable strategies.	• They may be unclear or vague.
• Assists in resolving conflict between stakeholder groups.	• They may be unrealistic.
• Provides a framework within which managerial decisions can be made.	• There may be inconsistencies between the different elements of the mission statement.
• Assists in communicating key cultural values to employees and other stakeholders.	• They may be inconsistent with management action.
• Helps to prevent potential misinterpretations of the organisation's reason for being.	• They may lack sufficient external focus.
	• It may be difficult to measure the achievement of the mission statment or appropriate performance measures may not be established to begin with.

Test your understanding 2

This is an **operational** decision. Setting a profit-maximising selling price is an exercise based on forecast demand and marginal costs over a coming period such as a year. It does not involve asking whether a product should be sold at all, whether its design should be modified or how its selling price should be influenced by the position of the product in its life cycle or the product matrix of the business.

Test your understanding 3

- An understanding of corporate planning is essential for all management because lower-level objectives are inexorably linked to higher-level strategies. An appreciation of these strategies and how they are formulated can be an effective guide to action and improving performance.

- Moreover, whatever the level at which a manager operates within an organisation, he or she can have some influence over that organisation's strategic (corporate) strategy.

Test your understanding 4

Critical success factors (CSFs) are as follows:

Product quality – the fact that production staff may have no previous experience in a food production environment is likely to prove problematic. It is vital that a comprehensive training programme is put in place at the earliest opportunity. DY need to reach and maintain the highest level of quality as soon as possible.

Supply quality – the quality and timeliness of delivery into Jacksons supermarkets assumes critical significance. Hence supply chain management must be extremely robust as there is little scope for error.

Technical quality – compliance with existing regulators regarding food production including all relevant factory health and safety requirements is vital in order to establish and maintain the reputation of DY as a supplier of quality products. The ability to store products at the correct temperature is critical because yogurts are produced for human consumption and in extreme circumstances could cause fatalities.

External credibility – accreditation by relevant trade associations/regulators will be essential if nationwide acceptance of DY as a major producer of frozen yogurts is to be established.

New product development – while DY have produced a range of frozen yogurts it must be recognised that consumer tastes change and that in the face of competition there will always be a need for a continuous focus on new product development.

Margin – while DY need to recognise all other CSFs they should always be mindful that the need to obtain desired levels of gross and net margin remain of the utmost importance.

Note: only five CSFs were required. Alternative relevant discussion and examples would be appropriate.

Test your understanding 5

(a) Building and Monitoring critical success factors

Critical success factors (CSFs) are those areas of business performance where the company must succeed in order to achieve its overall strategic objectives. Monitoring CSFs are those that are used to keep abreast of ongoing operations, for example, comparison of actual results to budgets or industry averages. Building CSFs are those which look to the future of the organisation and its development, for example, the launch of niche products such as music concert films or the use of new distribution methods such as downloadable films.

(b) Information for establishing CSFs

The company can use information about the internal and external environment to set its CSFs. Relevant external information would include the structure of the industry and the strategy of FP's competitors. The geographical location of production and the main sales markets may also be relevant. Film is a hit driven industry where word of mouth can lead to success, therefore, recognition of the product and the brand ('Film Productions') by the public would lead to success. For example, the Walt Disney Company has achieved a high level of brand recognition that has enabled it to expand into other entertainment areas using characters from its films.

Relevant internal information would include measures of seasonality on sales which will dictate the timing of film releases and effectiveness of marketing campaigns. By forecasting the size of the market along with likely levels of competition, profit can be optimised. However, these forecasts will be subject to uncertainty and so the information systems will need to be flexible and allow probabilistic analysis. A CSF based on the quality of these forecasts would therefore be appropriate. Other internal sources could include measures of the cost per film and the time taken to produce a film.

Other possible information could include contingent factors (those that depend on specific threats or opportunities facing FP).

(c) **Performance indicators linked to the CSFs**

Audience satisfaction – performance indicators are:

- Sales per film – currently the company releases an average of 6.4 films per year and makes about $31.25 million on each one. These figures should be compared to industry averages. Trends on sales per film should be monitored for indications of changes in consumer taste.

- Brand recognition – consumers should be surveyed to identify if the FP name is known and used as an indicator of quality when selecting films. If FP regularly uses certain artists (directors or film stars) then positive consumer recognition of these names will indicate satisfaction.

- Repeat viewings – with TV showings, it will be possible to measure viewers for each showing of the film and monitor the decline in viewing over repetitions. The level of DVD purchases following a cinema release will also indicate customer satisfaction with customers actively wanting to own their own copy of a favourite film.

- Awards won – number of awards won will indicate success. However, the level of recognition of any award must be brought into account as major ones such as those voted on by the public or those whose ceremonies are widely reported have the greatest impact.

- Response of the media – scores by film critics often appear in the media and these give a measure of satisfaction although this category must be treated carefully as critics often look for artistic merit while FP is seeking commercial success and broad audience acceptance.

Profitability in operations – performance indicators are:

- Industry average margin – collect data on competitor companies to set an appropriate benchmark. This will require care to ensure that appropriate comparator companies are chosen, for example, those with a production budget similar to FP's of $18 million per film.

- Time in production – the cost of a film will depend on the length of time it takes to produce. If the film is intended to meet a current customer demand it may require to be produced quickly, in order to meet revenue targets. Therefore, the time in production will affect both sales and cost levels so altering the gross margin. Again, it would be helpful to identify if films meet their production schedule and if these schedules compare favourably to those of other film companies.

- Costs – the costs should be broken down into categories such as those for artists, production technicians and marketing. The cost structure for each film should be compared internally, to others that FP produces and also externally, to available figures for the industry.

(d) **Impact on FP's information systems**

The company website can collect audience survey results and comments posted on the site. Consumers can be drawn to the site with clips and trailers from current films and those in production. The site can log the frequency with which films are viewed and if audience members create accounts then further detail on the age, gender and location of the audience can be collected. This will allow a more detailed profile of the customer base for FP to be created and will be used to help in decisions about what films to commission in the future. The account members can be given the opportunity to score each film providing further information about satisfaction.

The company could also consider scanning the websites of its competitors to identify their performance – especially their published results which will provide benchmark information on gross margin levels.

A management information system (MIS) will collate the information from individual transactions recorded in the accounting system to allow middle level management to control the business. This system will allow customer purchases to be summarised into reports to identify both products that sell well and the customers (such as cinema chains and TV networks) who provide the main sources of revenue (indicators of satisfaction). The level of repeat business on a customer account will give an indication of the satisfaction with FP's output. The system will also produce management accounts from which gross margins will be drawn and it should be capable of breaking this down by film and by customer to aid decision-making by targeting FP's output to the most profitable areas. This will aid decision-making about the performance of the production team on a film and can be used to set rewards for each team.

An executive information system (EIS) is one that will supply information to the senior management of the organisation allowing them to drill down into the more detailed transaction reports where necessary. The EIS will provide summarised information, focused on the key performance indicators in order to allow the directors to quickly judge whether the company is meeting its CSFs. It will draw on internal sources such as the MIS and also external sources such as market data on revenues that different films are earning at the box office.

Test your understanding 6

Possible steps include:

- involving local managers in strategy formulation

- agreeing strategies with business units within certain boundaries

- ensuring performance management reflects a combination of short- and long-term issues

- permitting flexibility within the strategic planning process to allow for changes due to local circumstances

- a combination of strategic planning and freewheeling opportunism (no strategic plans). For example, strategic planning may be used for activities such as identifying the organisation's resource capability and its resources. Freewheeling opportunism may be used to exploit an organisation's competences, e.g. the skills of particular individuals or groups.

Test your understanding 7

Strategic management accounting may assist the decision making process as follows:

- analysis of the market for different types of product:
  - review of competitors' products
  - likely size and value of different market sectors
  - price comparison of different products

- forecasts of costs of manufacturing new products, comparing different levels of automation/ use of temporary staff

- forecasts of profitability of different products

- investigation of capital costs of different options and investment appraisal of possible options

- analysis of the cost of holding inventory under different options.

Test your understanding 8

Possible factors could include:

Process

In order to manage and improve performance, the company needs to determine where best to locate activities related to the new market, e.g. whether to manufacture products in South America as well as selling there. This will require a comparison of the total product costs with manufacture in different locations, including measurement of factors such as:

- labour costs

- materials – costs of purchasing in different areas, costs of sourcing elsewhere and transporting to manufacturing site

- distribution – costs under different scenarios including setting up own sales force, using existing distributors

- costs of after-sales support.

Product

In addition to changes in manufacturing costs due to the location of manufacture there may be additional costs if products need to be tailored for the South American market. These need to be estimated in order to manage performance and ensure that the goals are met.

Exchange rates

The company needs to assess the impact of exchange rate fluctuations on the value of income earned in South America. There is a need to consider how this risk will be managed, e.g. by hedging. An ongoing assessment should be made of exchange rates and risk management techniques.

Political risk

The company needs to be aware of the possibility of an unexpected politically motivated event in S.America affecting the outcome of the investment and hence the performance of the company, e.g. the government may decide to raise taxation. Again, an ongoing assessment should be made of any risk.

Administrative issues

The financial impact of a number of other factors needs to be incorporated into the evaluation of the options such as the impact on internal transactions of exchange rate movements, currency exchange controls and tax regimes. There will, e.g. be implications for any transfer pricing system. Exchange rate fluctuations also need to be taken into account in developing performance measures for business unit managers in overseas locations to ensure that they are not being penalised for changes in income which are out of their control.

Test your understanding 9

(a) The benchmarking process can be described using seven steps. These are outlined below, together with AV's current progress against these stages.

    (1) **Set objectives and decide areas to benchmark**

        It is not clear exactly what AV's objectives are here, as "improve performance" is too generic. AV must carefully identify what specific areas it is looking to improve upon – for example, reduced repair costs, improved staff productivity, better rental collections.

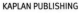

(2) Identify key performance drivers and indicators

To some extent these can be identified by looking at the expense headings in the Income statement. AV will improve performance by operating more efficiently across its major cost headings. It should be noted here that as a not for profit organisation performance will be measured in a different way from BW. For example, AV will not wish to increase rentals charged in order to report a surplus, so measures of efficiency become much more important so that it can provide good quality accommodation within the cost constraints imposed by the rents received.

(3) Select Organisations for benchmarking comparison

AV has selected a profit motivated company, BW, for benchmarking against, so this step has been carried out. However, it is not clear how this partner has been selected. Whilst there may be some examples of best practice to be learned from, it should again be noted that BW is profit motivated and so will have fundamentally different objectives from AV.

(4) Measure performance of all organisations involved

Some basic data has been gathered here.

(5) Compare performance

This is the stage that AV has now reached, as there is as yet no comparison of, or commentary on, the relative performance of the two organisations. Part (b) addresses this area.

(6) Specify areas for improvement

Once the comparisons above are made this should identify areas for improvement. Care should be taken that processes identified at BW can be transferred across to AV. Again, given their widely different objectives, this may not be possible. AV may also need to retrain some staff (or even recruit others) to ensure the requisite skills are in place.

(7) Implement and monitor improvements

Management must continuously monitor the impact of any changes implemented to make sure that the intended benefits are realised. Without this monitoring, any changes may be short lived because staff may soon revert back to their familiar way of doing things.

So, in conclusion, AV has identified a benchmarking partner (albeit one that may not be wholly suitable), and has collected some basic operational and financial data for comparison. It needs to more clearly define its objectives before it can proceed to specify actions for improvement.

(b) As discussed in part (c) below, it is not surprising that we see some major differences between the two organisations as they have very different objectives.

(1) Rental income

AV has average rental income per property of $52 per week compared to $120 per week for BW. This is not surprising, given that AV wants to make cheap housing available to as many people as possible, and BW seeks to charge higher rates for premium properties to tenants who can afford to pay. This should not be seen as an indicator that AV should increase its rents.

It should also be noted that the mix of properties is different. AV has a larger proportion of 3 and 4 bedroomed properties (presumably to cope with large families), whereas BW has no four bedroomed property. Taking this into account, the rentals on a "per room" basis are even higher for BW.

(2) Staff salaries

The average annual salary per employee in AV is $18000, whereas it is $24800 for BW. Again, this can largely be explained by the differing objectives that will encourage AV to keep costs to a minimum. It should be noted, however, that there may be a trade – off here between cost and productivity. If AV paid higher salaries would it be able to recruit better quality staff who are more productive? Staff numbers (25 in total)are the same for both companies, even though AV has 900 properties compared to only 400 for BW. This may lead to a reduced level of service for AV, which in turn could lead to a delay in dealing with problems such as repairs or collecting overdue rent.

(3) Planned maintenance and repairs

The major repair and maintenance cost for AV totalled $682,400, which is over three times as much as BW. There are two likely reasons for this. Firstly AV has more than twice as many properties (900 compared to 400), and secondly it may well be that their housing stock is in poorer condition and therefore needs more maintenance. It should also be noted that the repair costs are higher per property for BW (replacement kitchens cost twice as much as for BW for example), which will again reflect their different objectives and the needs of their clients. This should not be interpreted to mean that AV is "more efficient" as it is almost certainly not a like for like comparison. Hence, as noted in part (c) below, benchmarking against other not-for-profits may yield more meaningful comparisons.

One point that should be noted – there is always a possible trade off between cost and quality. If AV paid more per repair, would the quality be better and therefore the repairs last longer before further expenditure is needed?

(4) Day-to-day repairs

AV has undertaken a total of 3,860 repairs in the year at an average cost of $124 per repair. BW has carried out 1,276 repairs at a cost of $100 per repair. Whilst there is not a massive difference per repair, a saving of $24 per repair would result in overall cost savings of 3860 x $24 = $92,640.

AV should carry out further research as to how BW has obtained a fixed fee per repair, and see if it can obtain a similar contract as this could produce significant savings.

(5) Sundry operating costs

Whilst these are 30% higher for AV ($305,500 compared to $235,000), we have no breakdown of the figures and so cannot really comment further. It seems reasonable that, since AV has more than twice as many properties and tenants, it will incur a higher level of costs here.

(6) Net interest and other charges

Again no analysis is given, so no further comment is possible.

Conclusion

AV clearly operates at the "lower end" of the rental market compared with BW. It has more properties and charges lower rents per property. It is likely that the housing stock is in poorer condition, and so necessitates more ongoing repairs and maintenance. Attention should be given to getting the best possible deals from suppliers on repair work, perhaps negotiating a "fixed fee" in the same way as BW has done. It is surprising that staffing levels are the same for both companies as AW has more than twice as many properties.

Overall though, it should be noted that the two organisations have totally different objectives that may well go some way towards explaining these differences.

(c) As mentioned previously, the two organisations differ fundamentally because of their objectives. The objectives of not-for-profit organisations like AV can vary significantly. AV's primary objective is to "meet the accommodation needs of persons in its locality". So, it is likely to want to keep as many people as possible in accommodation regardless of cost. How can it measure whether or not it has met this non quantitative objective? Could it in fact have provided more properties if it had adopted different policies relating to staff or repairs?

BW has a primary objective of maximising profit. This is a clear and measureable objective that will probably lead BW to provide high quality accommodation in desirable areas that will generate high revenues and profits. This will support high rents (the average property rental for BW is $120 per week compared to $52 per week for AV) and will necessitate quality repairs and maintenance and customer service levels. Whilst efficiency will still be important for BW, to some extent it can pass on higher costs to its tenants by increasing rents.

AV on the other hand will seek to maintain low rents, and to provide as much housing as possible within its budgetary constraints. This will necessitate a very high level of efficiency as it will not seek to pass on high costs to its tenants. So, like any not-for-profit the critical measures of economy, efficiency and effectiveness must be considered.

Because of these fundamental differences AV would be better advised to consider benchmarking against other similar charities. This would give it much more meaningful comparisons as the objectives of the organisations would be more closely aligned. In addition, charitable organisations are generally more willing to share information to their mutual benefit, so such benchmarking partners may be readily found.

The use of a benchmarking partner that shares similar objectives would allow AV to obtain a much more objective comparison for its own performance.

Test your understanding 10

Strengths:	Weaknesses:
• Airports used are better than those used by competitors • Management skills • Lower costs than established airlines • Ease of booking flights • Recognised logo • IT facilities • Good employee relations.	• Airports used are worse than those used by the big carriers • Punctuality • Cash flows • No established safety record • Poorer than average customer service.
Opportunities:	**Threats:**
• Strong business demand for cheap air fares • Strong leisure demand for cheap air fares • Full exploitation of the Internet • Many secondary airports underused.	• Higher airport charges • Stringent security checks • Entry of subsidiaries of big carriers.

Test your understanding 11

(a)

Strengths:
Successful company
Steady increase in market share
Experience in the market
Founder's entrepreneurial skills
Good designs
Good quality control
Keen to exploit to technology
Strong IT

Weakness:
Management of information is often out of date
No in-house IT expertise
No web experience
Not sure if the new system will generate new sales
Lack of control over store managers
Out of date reporting from some stores
Over reliance on IT provider

Opportunities:
E-trading can provide a new sales channel and revenue stream
Identification and recording of customer details to enhance
customer relationships
Extension of customer base
Global market potential
Cut costs in many areas
Create a vision of a modern company
Develop product range further
Look at employing an IT specialist

Threats:
Customer resistance to on-line shopping
Loss of unique identity; may become just another website trader
Resistance within the company
Effects on existing personnel and working conditions
Costs of developing the website may outweigh the benefits
Security issues
Loss of competitive edge

Note: marks would be awarded for other relevant points.

(b) It is important to consider how these factors link to performance measurement in Envie Co:

- **Identifying weaknesses**: SWOT analysis has identified that Envie's lack of web experience is a weakness and therefore Envie needs to try to address this weakness and turn it into a strength by developing a website to reach global markets. It will be important for Envie Co to measure revenue and revenue growth for its website in order to assess how well it is performing. The use of SWOT analysis will focus management attention on current strengths and weaknesses of the organisation which will be of assistance in formulating the business strategy. It will also enable management to monitor trends and developments in the changing business environment. Each trend or development may be classified as an opportunity or a threat that will provide a stimulus for an appropriate management response. Management can make an assessment of the feasibility of required actions in order that the company may capitalise upon opportunities whilst considering how best to negate or minimise the effect of any threats.

- **Identifying CSFs**: SWOT analysis has identified unique designs and good quality control as key to the expansion of Envie Co. This therefore suggests that it will be important to have performance measures which look at the effectiveness of the design team and the quality of the products produced.

- **Setting targets**: one of the opportunities identified is 'the extension of the customer base'. This could be linked to financial objectives, such as revenue growth targets for new customers. Envie's managers will need to monitor the targets set to assess how well performance compares to them.

- **Information needs**: Envie Co will need to collect information in relation to measuring and reporting on the KPIs set.

2

Environmental influences

Chapter learning objectives

Upon completion of this chapter you will be able to:

- discuss the ways in which stakeholder groups operate and how they effect an organisation and its strategy formulation and implementation (e.g. using Mendelow's matrix)

- discuss the ethical issues that may impact on strategy formulation and business performance

- discuss the ways in which stakeholder groups may influence business performance

- assess the continuing effectiveness of traditional management accounting techniques within a rapidly changing business environment

- assess the impact of different risk appetites of stakeholders on performance management

- evaluate how risk and uncertainty play an important role in long term strategic planning and decision-making that relies upon forecasts and exogenous variables

- apply different risk analysis techniques in assessing business performance such as maximax, maximin, minimax regret and expected values

- discuss the need to consider the environment in which an organisation is operating when assessing its performance using models such as PEST and Porter's 5 forces, including areas:

  - political climate

  - market conditions

  - funding

- assess the impact of government regulations and policies on performance measurement techniques used and the performance levels achieved (for example, in the case of utility services and former state monopolies)

- discuss social and ethical obligations that should be considered in the pursuit of corporate performance objectives

- discuss the ways through which management accounting practitioners are made aware of new techniques and how they evaluate them

- assess the changing role of the management accountant in today's business environment as outlined by Burns and Scapens

- explore the role of the management accountant in providing key performance information for integrated reporting to stakeholders.

1 Assumed knowledge

Chapter 2 builds on the following knowledge from previous papers:

Paper F5
Risk and uncertainty including:

- expected values (EVs)

- maximax

- maximin

- minimax regret

Paper P3
Stakeholders
Porter's 5 forces and PEST

2 Introduction

This chapter focuses on Section B of the syllabus 'external influences on organisational performance'. All organisations will be impacted by the environment in which they operate and it is imperative that they consider the effect that factors such as risk, government regulations and social/ ethical issues will have on performance.

The changing business environment has also altered the work of the management accountant. These changes will be explored later on in this chapter.

3 External analysis

3.1 Introduction

As mentioned above, it is important that an organisation considers the impact of external factors on its performance. The organisation can use two different models when considering this impact. Each model focuses on a different level in the external environment.

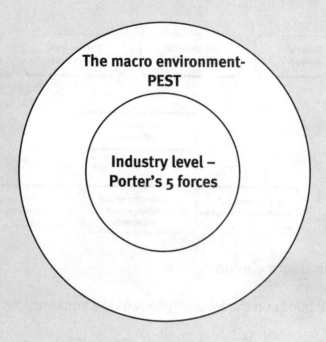

External analysis forms an important part of the 'strategic analysis' stage of the strategic planning process (as reviewed in Chapter 1).

3.2 PEST analysis

The PEST model looks at the macro-environment and its influence on organisational performance, using the following headings:

Heading	Examples
Political factors	• Taxation policy • Government stability • Foreign trade regulations • Taxation • Employment law • Monopoly legislation • Environmental protection legislation
Economic factors	• Interest rates • Inflation • Unemployment • Business cycles

Social factors	• Population demographics
	• Social mobility
	• Income distribution
	• Lifestyle changes
	• Attitudes to work and leisure
	• Levels of education and consumerism
	• How to produce goods with minimal environmental damage
Technological factors	• Speed of technological transfer
	• Rates of obsolescence

This model is sometimes referred to as PESTEL. The additional 'E' is for environmental factors (included as part of social factors in PEST) and the additional 'L' is for legal factors (included as part of political factors in PEST).

The key issue in P5 is to appreciate that, as well as being used for strategic analysis, **this model can be used to identify key performance management issues** (as discussed in the illustration below).

Illustration 1 – PEST and performance management

PEST can be used to identify key performance management issues:

Identifying CSFs and KPIs

Current trends have indicated that British consumers have moved towards 'one-stop' and 'bulk' shopping which is due to a variety of social changes. As a result, supermarkets such as Tesco have increased the amount of non-food items for sale. This may be seen as a CSF and necessary to meet the needs of the modern customer. Tesco may develop KPIs around this CSF, for example by measuring the number or proportion of non-food items for sale in each store.

Revising targets

Increasing public concern for the natural environment has resulted in many supermarkets setting targets for say, wastage, recycling and energy efficiency. These targets may need revising if the external environment changes. For example, in the UK in 2013 it was reported that more than two thirds of the bagged salad sold by Tesco ends up being thrown away. As a result of this investigation, Tesco (and a number of other retailers) have put more stringent wastage targets in place, recognising that performance would deteriorate if no action was taken.

PEST analysis

Environmental legislation may have been identified as being particularly important to a chemicals producer, in which case it should set up a series of targets to measure compliance. For example:

- level of fines

- number of environmental prosecutions

- number of environmental enforcement actions

- number of 'notifiable' incidents (local legislation will define what is 'notifiable' and what is not)

- percentage of employees working within an ISO 14001 compliant Environmental Management System

- the firm's rating in independent benchmarking such as the 'Business in the Environment' Index.

3.3 Porter's 5 forces model

The level of competition in the industry can also affect an organisation's performance. All businesses in a particular industry are likely to be subject to similar pressures that determine how attractive the sector is. Industry attractiveness depends on five factors or forces:

The **stronger each of the five forces is, the lower the profitability of the industry**.

KAPLAN PUBLISHING

Porter's 5 forces

- **Competitive rivalry**: There will be a tough environment if there are many competitors but a much easier one if there is a monopoly.

- **Buyer's bargaining power**: A few, large customers can exert powerful bargaining power. Many, small customers find it harder to apply pressure.

- **Supplier's bargaining power**: A monopoly supplier of a vital component can apply great pressure. Any one of many suppliers of an ordinary component cannot.

- **Threat from potential entrants**: The key issue here is to assess barriers to entry. For example, high capital costs, know-how and regulation of all present barriers to entry which will help to reduce competition.

- **Threat from substitutes**: The level of the threat is determined by relative price/performance.

Porter's 5 forces and performance management

Porter's 5 forces model can be used for strategic analysis and can also be used to identify key performance management issues. If they are able to, businesses should:

- avoid business sectors which are unattractive because of the five forces

- try to mitigate the effects of the five forces. For example, supplier power is lessened if a long-term contract is negotiated or competition is reduced by taking over a rival.

It is important that an organisation considers its performance in the context of its industry. For example, rising supplier prices may initially be blamed on an inefficient purchasing function. However, on further investigation it may be found that the industry is supplied by a relatively small number of large suppliers who have the power to increase prices.

Illustration 2 – Porter's 5 forces

A **Porter's** 5 forces analysis may have concluded that there is currently a low threat of new entrants due to the incumbent firm having economies of scale that create an effective barrier to entry. The firm concerned would be wise to monitor its cost per unit compared to those of potential new entrants to see if the threat increases.

PEST and Porter's 5 forces model

In the United Kingdom, railways are facing major challenges. Customers are complaining about poor services. The government is reluctant to spend vast amounts of public money on developing the decaying infrastructure. The inflated costs of commuting by car, such as fuel and congestion charges, are increasing the number of people wanting to use the railways.

Required:

Use PEST and Porter's 5 forces to identify the issues in the external environment and discuss the impact of these factors on the performance of the railways in the UK.

4 The impact of stakeholders

4.1 Introduction

A **stakeholder** of an organisation is anyone affected by the organisation.

The mission and objectives of an organisation need to be developed with the needs of the stakeholders in mind.

4.2 Stakeholders' influence on business performance

- The interest and power of different stakeholder groups can affect an organisation's performance. A stakeholder isn't simply any party that is affected by the organisation but **they can also have a huge influence on organisational performance**. This is explored in more detail in the discussion of 'stakeholder mapping' below.

- In addition, the **interests of different stakeholder groups might affect the areas of performance that are measured**.

Illustration 3 – Stakeholders influence

British Airways plc has regular labour relations problems with cabin attendants and check-in staff. The airline cannot operate without check-in staff, and particularly without legal minimum numbers of cabin attendants. So, these employees have great power and have shown over many years that they are happy to exercise that power.

Illustration 4 – Strategic planning and stakeholder needs

When planning, management has to take into account stakeholder requirements, power and ambition. For example, there is no point devising changes to production methodologies if:

- employees will not be prepared to adapt to them
- customers do not like the quality of what is offered
- suppliers cannot supply parts at the required frequency.

4.3 Stakeholder mapping

Mendelow's matrix looks at the level of power and interest of different stakeholder groups.

Managers can make use of Mendelow's matrix to help manage stakeholders' conflicting demands and to establish its priorities in terms of managing stakeholders' expectations.

Mendelow's matrix

- **Key players**: These stakeholders are the major drivers of change and could stop management plans and hinder success if not satisfied. Their participation in the planning process is vital.

- **Keep satisfied**: These stakeholders have high power and need to be reassured of the outcome of the strategy well in advance to stop them from gaining interest and negatively impacting business performance.

- **Keep informed**: These stakeholders are interested in the strategy but lack power. Managers must justify their plans to these stakeholders. Otherwise they will gain power by joining forces with other stakeholders.

- **Minimal effort**: These stakeholders lack interest and power and are more likely than others to accept what they are told and follow instructions.

Test your understanding 2

Chatman Theatre is a charitable trust with the objective of making multicultural films and stage productions available to a regional audience. The organisation is not for profit. The aim to bring diversity of films, plays and dance that would otherwise be inaccessible to a regional audience.

The theatre needs to have strict budget focus, since a charity can become bankrupt. In order to achieve the required income, relationships must be built with a range of stakeholders.

Required:

Identify a few key stakeholders and ideas that would assist in building relationships and hence improving performance.

4.4 Stakeholder conflict

Stakeholders' requirements and aspirations often conflict:

Shareholders want increased profit	⟷ Employees want increased wages
Shareholders want increased profit	⟷ Customers want lower prices and higher quality
Customers want 24/7 operations	⟷ Employees want 9 – 5, 5 days/week
Suppliers want long-term orders	⟷ Managers want to retain flexibility

Unless these conflicts are managed, performance will be affected.

Resolving conflicting objectives (Cyert and March)

Management can seek to manage conflicting objectives through the following.

- Prioritisation
- Negotiation and 'satisficing'
- Sequential attention
- Side payments
- Exercise of power

Resolving conflicting (Cyert and March)

Prioritisation – this could follow from Mendelow's matrix above.

Negotiation and 'satisficing' – finding the minimum acceptable outcome for each group to achieve a compromise.

Sequential attention – each period a different stakeholder group is focused upon, e.g. the workers' canteen could be updated this year with the implication that employees should not expect any improvements in working conditions for the next few years.

Side payments – this can often involve benefiting a group without giving them what they actually want, e.g. the local community may be concerned with cuts in jobs and increased pollution but the firm seeks to placate them by building new sports facilities and sponsoring a local fete.

Exercise of power – when a deadlock is resolved by a senior figure forcing through a decision simply based on the power they possess.

Test your understanding 3

The trustees of a museum are faced with the following conflicting objectives:

- to educate the public
- to preserve antiquities for study and research.

Required:

Give two examples of policies that would be affected by the prioritisation of these objectives.

5 The impact of ethical issues

5.1 Ethics

- Ethics is a set of moral principles that guide behaviour, based on what is 'felt' to be right.
- Comprises principles and standards that govern business behaviour.
- Actions can be judged to be right or wrong, ethical or unethical by individuals inside or outside the organisation.

For example, is it ethical to:

- experiment on animals?
- drill for oil?
- build roads through the countryside?
- allow smoking in public areas?
- pay senior executives large increases in salary?
- train students to pass exams?

Illustration 5 – Nestle and Ethics

Nestle was criticised in the past for taking advantage of the poor and uneducated populations in developing countries in order to increase their own profits.

The company gave gifts and incentives to local health officials, as encouragement in promoting their baby milk formula and therefore discouraging breast feeding. Nestle employees were heard telling midwives that 'all western women use formula to feed their babies, so that they grow up big and strong'.

Nestle didn't educate mothers about sterilising bottles and therefore mothers mixed the formula with dirty water at the cost of many babies' health. The free samples provided to mothers in hospitals and clinics soon dried up and mothers then had to pay almost western prices for the baby milk formula, a price that most families could not afford.

Ethics and performance management

Apart from any moral duty to be ethical, the prime purpose of a business is to maximise shareholder wealth and the chance of this happening is increased by the adoption of ethical behaviour.

Test your understanding 4

Required:

How can the adoption of ethical behaviour by an organisation help to assist to maximise shareholder wealth?

5.2 Corporate social responsibility

Corporate social responsibility (CSR) refers to the idea that a company should be sensitive to the needs of all stakeholders in its business operations and not just shareholders. As such, ethics is just one dimension of corporate social responsibility.

CSR and performance management

By aligning the company's core values with the values of society, the company can improve its reputation and ensure it has a long term future.

Benefits of a CSR strategy

- Differentiation – the firm's CSR strategy can act as a method of differentiation.

- High calibre staff will be attracted and retained due to the firm's CSR policies.

- Brand strengthening – due to the firm's honest approach.

- Lower costs – can be achieved in a number of ways, e.g. due to the use of less packaging or energy.

- The identification of new market opportunities and of changing social expectations.

- An overall increase in profitability as a result of the above – project NPVs will increase due to increased sales, lower costs, an extended project life and a lower level of risk.

Test your understanding 5

Required:

Many commentators believe that CSR is a morally correct pursuit, but there are powerful arguments against it. Identify and discuss these arguments.

CSR and metrics

- Remember, **things that get measured get done** more often than things that are not measured.

- Therefore, the company should measure the result of any CSR programme.

Test your understanding 6

RFG has set up manufacturing plants in many developing countries, some of which have much lower legislation standards regarding health and safety than RFG's target markets. To improve its global reputation, the firm wishes to improve its performance for health and safety.

Required:

Suggest some metrics for measuring health and safety.

6 The impact of government policy

6.1 Introduction

This area was introduced when we looked at PEST. However, it will now be explored in more detail.

Government policies will influence the performance levels achieved by an organisation and the performance measurement techniques chosen.

Test your understanding 7

Required:

Evaluate the circumstances in which a government can act as an aid to business performance.

Illustration 6 – The role of government policy

The capital engaged in some business operations is a direct function of relations with government. The following is an extreme example of this.

The UK Independent Television regional franchises were 'auctioned' in the early 1990s. The system is that a public body owns the transmitter network but franchises the right to broadcast programmes (and advertising) from regional centres every 10 years. Organisations interested in obtaining a franchise were required to submit sealed bids prior to certain dates. Those bids stated (among other things) the amount that the applicant was prepared to pay for the franchise.

Some of the franchises were keenly contested – particularly some of the more attractive ones in London and the south east. Several well-resourced consortia offered substantial nine-figure sums for the London franchises.

One organisation, Central Television, was preparing a bid for the Birmingham franchise. Through discreet enquiries it found that no other bids were going to be made for the franchise. So, it submitted a bid for £2,000 ($3,000) – which the government had to accept. A rich franchise, worth millions, was thereby acquired without any significant capital outlay.

The performance of Central Television on the basis of ROCE would have been phenomenal – but this had nothing to do with commercial success or efficiency. It was just an accident of the way that the industry is regulated.

Porter's view

The influence of government on an industry

Porter identifies seven ways in which a government can affect the structure of an industry.

- **Capacity expansion**. The government can take actions to encourage firms or an industry as a whole to increase or cut capacity. Examples include capital allowances to encourage investment in equipment; regional incentives to encourage firms to locate new capacity in a particular area, and incentives to attract investment from overseas firms. The government is also (directly or indirectly) a supplier of infrastructure such as roads and railways, and this may influence expansion in a particular area.

- **Demand**. The government is a major customer of business in all areas of life and can influence demand by buying more or less. It can also influence demand by legislative measures. The tax system for cars is a good example: a change in the tax relief available for different engine sizes has a direct effect on the car manufacturers' product and the relative numbers of each type produced. Regulations and controls in an industry will affect the growth and profits of the industry, for example minimum product quality standards.

- **Divestment and exit**. A firm may wish to sell off a business to a foreign competitor or close it down, but the government might prevent this action because it is not in the public interest (there could be examples in health, defence, transport, education, agriculture and so on).

KAPLAN PUBLISHING

- **Emerging industries may be controlled by the government**. For instance governments may control numbers of licences to create networks for next generation mobile phones.

- **Entry barriers**. Government policy may restrict investment or competition or make it harder by use of quotas and tariffs for overseas firms. This kind of protectionism is generally frowned upon by the World Trade Organisation, but there may be political and economic circumstances in which it becomes necessary.

- **Competition policy**. Governments might devise policies which are deliberately intended to keep an industry fragmented, preventing one or two producers from having too much market share.

- **New product adoption**. Governments regulate the adoption of new products (e.g. new drugs) in some industries. They may go so far as to ban the use of a new product if it is not considered safe (a new form of transport, say). Policies may influence the rate of adoption of new products, e.g. the UK government 'switch off' of the analogue television networks by 2012, effectively forcing users to buy digital cable or satellite services.

Legislation and regulation

Strategic planners cannot plan intelligently without a good working knowledge of the laws and regulations that affect their own companies and the businesses they operate in.

- There is an almost endless list of laws, or categories of legislation, that affect business enterprises in domestic, national or international dimensions. The main categories are listed below:
  - local by-laws (for example planning permission, construction of roads, licences)
  - labour legislation (such as safety at work, employee protection, redundancy payments)
  - trade union legislation
  - consumer protection legislation
  - company legislation
  - taxation legislation
  - anti-trust (monopolies) legislation and rulings
  - trade legislation (e.g. countries restricted for export)
  - business legislation (e.g. contract and agency law)
  - social legislation such as welfare benefits.

- At a more general level, laws are passed that enable government to levy taxes which will have an impact both on demand and the organisation's profits.

- There are special regulatory regimes for particular industries or sectors, such as nuclear energy, transport, broadcasting or food.

- Legislation is becoming more complex, particularly for those companies that trade internationally where the interface, indeed probable conflict, between domestic laws, the host country's laws, and probably also the laws of the trading block of nations the host country belongs to, provides an extremely complicated legal scenario.

Government and the public sector

In public sector organisations the government is the major stakeholder. This can have a number of particular impacts:

- the motivation to meet customer needs may be reduced

- the consequences of failure to provide an appropriate level of service for the organisation and the individual are reduced

- being dependent on government policy also means that objectives may change rapidly as policy changes and this political dimension reduces the scope of management options and increases the time for decisions to be taken

- when the public sector companies are privatised they may still remain subject to elaborate regulatory regimes. The performance of the operations involved is monitored and measured using various indicators, with the possibility of fines for poor performance or price restrictions imposed by regulators.

Planning for political change

The problem facing strategic planners is how to plan for changes in the political environment. It is necessary to consider what type of political change could affect the enterprise rather than trying to estimate all the political changes that might occur, by:

- examining changes in social behaviour and values, economic activity, and problems arising from the physical infrastructure or environment which can be related to the trend of political actions

- monitoring indicators of possible or intended future government actions and policy. These indicators are obtained from:
    - annual conferences of political parties
    - public utterances of party leaders and seniors
    - international events
    - directives from international trading groups
    - political commentators and analysts
    - international summit meetings
    - staged legislation
    - efforts of public pressure groups (particularly with regard to local government policy)
    - political manifestos.

Test your understanding 8

Required:

Give some examples of areas of government policy that are likely to affect a multinational electronics company and how the impact will be felt?

6.2 The impact of fiscal policy and monetary policy

Fiscal and monetary policies are the tools used by governments to control their economies.

Fiscal policy

- Looks at the balance between government income (taxation + borrowing) and expenditure.

Monetary policy

- Is the process by which the government and central bank controls the supply, availability and cost of money.

Fiscal policy	Monetary policy
Government adjusts: • taxation • public borrowing • public spending.	Government adjusts: • money supply • interest rates • exchange rates • availability of credit.

Fiscal and monetary policy – more detail

Fiscal policy

- To stimulate the economy, the government can spend more money. However, if the extra expenditure is met by raising taxes, the public will have less to spend and economic growth will be small. To really get things moving, the government needs to borrow and spend.

- The economy can also be stimulated by cutting tax and allowing individuals to spend more. If government expenditure is cut to match the tax cuts, there will be little stimulation, so government borrowing is needed to keep government spending high.

- Too much economic stimulation is likely to cause inflation as consumers compete for resources and services.

Monetary policy

Changes in monetary policy will influence the following factors.

- The availability and cost of finance. These in turn affect the level of investment and expenditure by firms.

- The level of consumer demand e.g. low interest rates will stimulate the economy as it is cheaper to borrow and savings do not earn a lot of interest. Similarly, the easy availability of credit also encourages borrowing and spending).

- The level of inflation.

- The level of exchange rates.

chapter 2

Impact of macroeconomics

In order for macroeconomic policy to work, its instruments must have an impact on economic activity. This means that it must affect the business sector. It does so in two broad forms.

Macroeconomic policy will influence the level of aggregate demand (AD) and thus activity in the economy as a whole.
 	
(AD is the total demand for goods and services in the economy.)
	• The level of AD is central to the determination of the level of unemployment and the rate of inflation.
	
	• If AD is too low, unemployment might result; if AD is too high, inflation induced by excess demand might result.
	
	• Changes in AD will affect all businesses to varying degrees. Thus effective business planning requires that businesses can:
	  – predict the likely thrust of macroeconomic policy in the short- to medium-term
	  – predict the consequences for sales growth of the overall stance of macroeconomic policy and any likely changes in it.
	
	• The more stable government policy is, the easier it is for businesses to plan, especially in terms of investment, employment and future output capacity.

Macroeconomic policy may influence the costs of the business sector.	• Macroeconomic policy may involve changes in **exchange rates**. This can have the effect of raising the domestic price of imported goods. Most businesses use some imported goods in the production process; hence this leads to a rise in production costs.

KAPLAN PUBLISHING

75

- **Fiscal policy** involves the use of **taxation:** changes in tax rates or the structure of taxation will affect businesses. For example, a change in the employer's national insurance contribution will have a direct effect on labour costs for all businesses. Changes in indirect taxes (for example, a rise in sales tax or excise duties) will either have to be absorbed or the business will have to attempt to pass on the tax to its customers.

- **Monetary policy** involves changes in **interest rates**; these changes will directly affect firms in two ways:

  - costs of servicing debts will change especially for highly geared firms

  - the viability of investment will be affected since all models of investment appraisal include the rate of interest as one, if not the main, variable.

Test your understanding 9

Required:

A carpet retailer imports carpets and sells them domestically. The domestic currency does not have a fixed exchange rate with any other currency. What are the likely effects on this business of a rise in domestic interest rates?

Test your understanding 10

Suppose the two main political parties in a hypothetical country have the following priorities:

	Party A (currently in government)	**Party B** (the opposition)
Priorities	• Low unemployment	• Low inflation
Policy choices	• Fiscal policy • Increase government spending to boost demand to create jobs • High government intervention in business	• Monetary policy • Increase interest rates to reduce inflation • Low taxes • Low levels of intervention

Recent polls suggest that Party B could win the next election.

Required:

Comment on the implications of this for a major construction company based in the country concerned.

7 The impact of government regulation

7.1 Introduction

Regulation is any form of government interference and is required to ensure that the needs of stakeholders can be met and that businesses act in the public interest.

7.2 Competition policy

Monopolies

Most governments consider the disadvantages of monopolies to outweigh the advantages.

Disadvantages to the economy as a whole	Possible **advantages**
• Supernormal profits • Economic inefficiency • Monopolies may be able to engage in price discrimination • Disincentive to innovate • Pricing practices	• Large firms may secure economies of scale reducing production costs • The special case of natural monopolies • Research and development (R&D) using profits

Disadvantages/advantages of monopolies

Disadvantages to the economy as a whole:

- **Supernormal profits:** the lack of competition allows monopolists to charge high prices at the expense of customers.

- **Economic inefficiency:** output is produced at a higher cost than necessary. For example, there may be no incentive to reduce costs by improving technology used.

- **Monopolies may be able to engage in price discrimination:** charging different prices to different customers for the same good or service, e.g. peak and off-peak pricing. This may act against the interests of customers.

- **Disincentive to innovate:** the absence of competition may reduce the incentive to develop new products or new production processes.

- **Pricing practices:** monopolies may adopt pricing practices to make it uneconomic for new firms to enter the industry, thus reducing competition in the long run.

Possible Advantages:

- **Large firms may secure economies of scale:** it is possible that there are significant economies of scale, reducing production costs, but that these require large firms and hence the number of firms in an industry is restricted.

- **The special case of natural monopolies:** this is the case where the economies of scale in the provision of some basic infrastructure are so great that only one producer is feasible. This may be the case in the public utilities of energy and water.

- **Research and development (R&D):** it may be that monopoly profits are both the reward for, and the source of finance for, technological and organisational innovation. Thus some static welfare losses have to be accepted in order to ensure a dynamic and innovative business sector.

Possible government responses to monopolies:

- The **control of monopolies**, e.g. the UK Competition Act prohibits anti-competitive agreements (such as illegal cartels) and prohibits the abuse of a dominant position.

- **Public regulation.** Many governments tried to increase the efficiency and performance of state-owned monopolies by privatisation, e.g. UK utilities were privatised in the 1980s. Privatisation needs to be controlled through the activities of an industry regulator.

- **Self regulation**, e.g. of the accounting and legal professions.

- **Public provision** through nationalisation, e.g. nationalisation of a number of large UK banks in 2008/09.

Privatisation

The regulator has to balance the following issues:

- protecting customer interests

- ensuring sufficient investment in infrastructure

- controlling quality (e.g. in the case of water utilities, water quality and the treatment of sewerage)

- ensuring shareholders and other investors achieve a reasonable return

- ensuring that the firm has, or can raise, the necessary funds for investment.

These are usually controlled by:

- setting a limit on price increases

- agreeing investment targets

- putting in place a detailed framework of KPIs that the firm must achieve to retain its licence and to avoid fines.

Test your understanding 11

Required:

Discuss whether and how a regulated water utilities company can improve its performance.

7.3 Supply-side policies

- Supply-side economists take the view that **the supply of suitable, cost-effective and adequate materials, services and labour is vital to an economy.**

- If these resources are made available, then they will be used to produce goods and services.

- The amounts paid to suppliers and employees will create the extra income necessary to buy the extra outputs.

- For example, improving education would increase the supply of educated workers in the workforce.

Supply side policies examples

Supply-side policies are therefore largely anti-regulation and anti-government interference. For example, supply-side economists would claim that:

- wage regulation prevents the labour market from achieving full employment

- government grants encourage weak businesses

- employment legislation limits risk taking and can lead to over-manning of industries

- high taxes act as a disincentive to work and enterprise and lead ultimately to lower output, employment and wealth.

7.4 Green policies/externalities

A **negative externality** is the cost of production experienced by society but not by producers or consumers themselves, for example:

- production, e.g. river pollution from manufacturing
- consumption, e.g. car emissions causing air pollution.

As a result, the government may impose green policies, e.g. an increase in tax on fuel.

8 The changing role of the management accountant

The role of the management accountant has changed as a result of environmental pressures. **Burns and Scapens** studied how the role has changed over the last 20 years.

8.1 Changes in the role of the management accountant

- The role has changed focus from financial control to **business support** making the management accountant more of a generalist. Management accountants may now spend much of their time as internal consultants and although they still produce standardised reports, more time is spent analysing and interpreting information rather than preparing reports.

- This new role has been called a **hybrid accountant** since the management accountant has a valuable combination of both accounting and operational/commercial knowledge.

- Traditionally, it was thought that accountants needed to be independent from operational managers in order to allow them to objectively judge and report their accounting information to senior managers. However, today accountants do **not necessarily work in a separate accounting department** but may be fully integrated into other departments, thus playing a key part in the operations and decision making process of the department.

Role of a management accountant

A scan of current job advertisements for management accountants would show that they are frequently being asked to:

- inform strategic decisions and formulate business strategies
- lead the organisation's business risk management
- ensure the efficient use of financial and other resources
- advise on ways of improving business performance
- liaise with other managers to put the finance view in context
- train functional and business managers in budget management
- identify the implications of product and service changes
- work in cross-functional teams involved in strategic planning or new product development.

8.2 Driving forces for change

Driving force	Explanation
Management structure	<ul><li>Head office has delegated much responsibility to the strategic business units thus reducing the involvement of management accountants in areas such as detailed budgeting.</li><li>The management accountant may now provide a link between the operational reports, the financial consequences and the strategic outcomes desired by the board.</li></ul>
Technology	<ul><li>Management Information Systems (MIS) allow access for users across the organisation to input data and run reports giving the type of analysis once only provided by the management accountant.</li></ul>
Competition	<ul><li>The competitive environment has driven organisations to take a more strategic focus.</li><li>Management accountants no longer focus their efforts on the final profit figure (this is seen as short-termism) but focus on a number of measures which try to capture long-term performance.</li></ul>

8.3 Benefits of the changes for performance management

- From an organisation's perspective, the accountant will be a guide to the strategic business unit manager to ensure that strategic goals are reflected in performance management.

- The management accountant will take a supporting role in assisting strategic business unit managers in getting the most from their management information system. This will entail the accountant understanding the needs of the particular manager and then working with them to extract valuable reports from the management information system.

- The management accountant can develop a range of performance measures to capture the different factors that will drive its success.

8.4 Sources of information

There are a number of sources of information for the management accountant who wants to learn about new techniques. For example:

- articles published in professional journals and the press

- studies published in specialised journals

- information provided by professional bodies

- networking and exchanging ideas

- seminars

- TV, radio, books and the Internet.

8.5 Role of the management accountant in providing information to stakeholders

Introduction

The demands placed on management accountants have grown in recognition of significant **sustainability** challenges.

These demands require a rich supply of information, capable of informing stakeholders of the financial and non-financial impact of the company's decisions.

Conventional management accounting systems often failed to provide this information.

The triple bottom line

Whilst all businesses are used to monitoring their profit figures, there are also environmental and social aspects to consider in the longer term.

The triple bottom line focuses on economic, environmental and social areas of concern.

Area of concern	Explanation
Economic performance	• The management accountant must monitor the financial performance of the organisation to ensure its continued prosperity and fulfilment of shareholders' needs.
Environmental performance	• Improved environmental practices may include taking steps to reduce waste, increase recycling and use energy efficient equipment. • The management accountant must monitor the costs and benefits of such actions to ensure that the needs of stakeholders are being met.
Social performance	• Many examples exist such as a contribution by a company to community projects. • Perhaps harder to measure than the economic and environmental aspects. • Many activities don't have to cost the organisation much (for example, giving staff time off every year to volunteer for charitable causes) but can have far reaching social benefits. • The management accountant must monitor the costs and benefits (as above).

The management accountant has an important role in preparing sustainability reports and capturing non-financial information.

There is a growing trend for companies to issue sustainability reports, sometimes as part of traditional financial reports. The problem with this type of 'add-on' to the annual financial report is that it is very selective and may communicate only the good news for readers, ignoring or obscuring the bad.

Integrated reporting

To tackle the problem discussed above, a new approach is being recommended called integrated reporting.

With integrated reporting, instead of having environmental and social issues reported in a separate section of the annual report, or a standalone 'sustainability' report, the idea is that one report should capture the strategic and operational actions of management in its holistic approach to business and stakeholder 'wellbeing'.

The management accountant must be able to collaborate with top management in the integration of financial wellbeing with community and stakeholder wellbeing.

Integrated reporting will bring statutory reporting closer to the management accountant and will make management accountants even more important in bridging the gap between stakeholders and the company's reports.

The management accountant will be expected to produce information that:

- is a balance between quantitative and qualitative information
- links past, present and future performance
- considers the regulatory impacts on performance
- provides an analysis of factors that could impact in the future.

There is clearly a need for the profession to accept the challenge for being the mechanism for a new type of transparency and accountability; one that incorporates social and environmental impacts as well as economic ones.

The role of the management accountant in sustainability is as yet not well established. However, it is anticipated that over time, integrated reporting will become the corporate reporting norm. This will offer a productive and rewarding future, not only for the management accountant but for society as a whole.

International Integrated Reporting Council (IIRC)

The IIRC was formed in August 2010 and aims to create a globally accepted framework for a process that results in communication by an organisation about value creation over time. The IIRC seeks to secure the adoption of and Integrated Reporting Framework (an alternative to the recommendations by the GRI) by report preparers. The Framework sets out several **guiding principles** and **content elements** that have to be considered when preparing an integrated report.

Illustration 7 – guiding principles

There are **seven** guiding principles, as follows:

Strategic focus and future orientation – the report should provide and insight into the organisation's strategy and how it relates to the organisation's ability to create value in the short, medium and long term.

Connectivity of information – the report should show a holistic picture of the combination, inter-relatedness and dependencies between the factors that affect the organisation's ability to create value over time.

Stakeholder relationships – the report should provide an insight into the nature and quality of the organisation's relationships with its stakeholders.

Materiality – the report should disclose information about matters that substantively affect the organisation's ability to create value.

Conciseness – the report should be concise and include relevant information only.

Reliability and completeness – the report should include all material matters, both positive and negative, in a balanced way and without material error.

Consistency and comparability – the report should be consistent and comparable over time.

Illustration 8 – content elements

There are **eight** content elements:

Organisational overview and external environment – what does the organisation do and what are the circumstances under which it operates?

Governance – how does the organisation's governance structure support its ability to create value in the short, medium and long term?

Business model – what is the organisation's business model?

Risks and opportunities – what are the risks and opportunities that affect the organisation's ability to create value over the short, medium and long term and how is the organisation dealing with them?

Strategy and resource allocation – where does the organisation want to go and how does it intend to get there?

Performance – to what extent has the organisation achieved its strategic objectives for the period?

Outlook – what challenges and uncertainties is the organisation likely to encounter in pursuing its strategy and what are the implications for future performance?

Basis of preparation and presentation – how does the organisation determine what matters to include in the integrated report and are such matters quantified or evaluated?

The Global Reporting Initiative (GRI)

The most accepted framework for reporting sustainability is the GRI's Sustainability Reporting Guidelines, the latest of which 'G4' – the fourth of the guidelines – was issued in May 2013. The G4 Guidelines consist of principles and disclosure items.

- The principles help to define report content, quality of the report and give guidance on how to set the report boundary.

- The disclosure items include disclosures on management of issues as well as performance indicators themselves.

Reporting principles and disclosures

Reporting principles

Reporting principles are essentially the required characteristics of the Report Content and the Report Quality. The Principles for Defining Report Content are given as:

- Stakeholder Inclusiveness

- Sustainability Context

- Materiality

- Completeness

The Principles for Defining Report Quality are given as:

- Balance

- Comparability

- Accuracy

- Timeliness
- Clarity
- Reliability

Standard Disclosures

Two types of disclosure are required:

General standard disclosures:

- Strategy and Analysis
- Organisational Profile
- Identified Material Aspects and Boundaries
- Stakeholder Engagement
- Report profile
- Governance
- Ethics and Integrity

Specific Standard Disclosures

- Disclosures on Management's Approach
- Indicators

The G4 guidelines encourage disclosure of various 'aspects' in the three categories: Economic, Environmental and Social.

Illustration 9 – Categories and aspects in the G4 guidelines

The aspects grouped by category are:

Economic

- Economic Performance
- Market Presence
- Indirect Economic Impacts
- Procurement Practices

Environmental

- Materials
- Energy

- Water
- Biodiversity
- Emissions
- Effluents and Waste
- Products and Services
- Compliance
- Transport
- Overall
- Supplier Environmental Assessment
- Environmental Grievance Mechanisms

Social – this category is split into four sub-categories, each with several aspects associated with it as follows:

Labour Practices and Decent Work

- Employment
- Labour/Management Relations
- Occupational Health and Safety
- Training and Education
- Diversity and Equal Opportunity
- Equal Remuneration for Men and Women
- Supplier Assessment for Labour Practices
- Labour Practices Grievance Mechanisms

Human rights

- Investment
- Non-discrimination
- Freedom of Association and Collective Bargaining
- Child Labour
- Forced or Compulsory Labour
- Security Practices
- Indigenous Rights
- Assessment
- Supplier Human Rights Assessment
- Human Rights Grievance Mechanisms

> **Society**
>
> - Local Communities
> - Anti-corruption
> - Public Policy
> - Anti-competitive Behaviour
> - Compliance
> - Supplier Assessment for Impacts on Society
> - Grievance Mechanisms for Impacts on Society
>
> **Product Responsibility**
>
> - Customer Health and Safety
> - Product and Service Labelling
> - Market Communications
> - Customer Privacy
> - Compliance

9 Risk and uncertainty

9.1 Introduction

Strategic planning deals with future events but these future events cannot always be accurately predicted. Planning must therefore take risk and uncertainty into account.

 Risk is the variability of possible returns. There are a number of possible outcomes and the probability of each outcome is known.

 Uncertainty also means that there are a number of possible outcomes. However, the probability of each outcome is not known.

 Exogenous variables are variables that do not originate from within the organisation itself and are not controllable by management, e.g. government policy, weather conditions, state of the economy, competitors' actions etc. Their existence means that strategic planning will always be subject to some risk and uncertainty.

All business face risk/uncertainty. Risk management is the process of understanding and managing the risks that an organisation is inevitably subject to.

The impact of exogenous variables

A hospital has developed a new surgical technique as a more expensive alternative to existing treatments. It is considering whether to begin to provide the treatment to all its patients, which would mean building a new facility. In order to inform the decision, the hospital is considering the likely effect of a number of variables.

- The likelihood that another alternative cheaper treatment, either a surgical technique or a drug regime, will be discovered.

- The likelihood that other hospitals will begin to offer similar services which will limit demand.

- Government policy – changes in the way that treatment is funded and therefore whether the costs of the treatment will be paid for.

9.2 Dealing with risk/uncertainty

A number of tools can be used to incorporate the impact of risk/uncertainty.

Tool	Explanation
Scenario planning	Looks at a number of different but plausible future situations. For example, Shell was the only major oil company to have prepared for the shock of the 1970s oil crisis through scenario planning and was able to respond faster than its competitors.
Computer simulations	A modelling technique which shows the effect of more than one variable changing at a time and gives management a view of the likely range and level of outcomes so that a more informed decision can be taken.
Sensitivity analysis	Takes each uncertain factor in turn, and calculates the change that would be necessary in that factor before the original decision is reversed.
Expected values (EVs)	Shows the weighted average of all possible outcomes.
Maximax, maximin and minimax regret	Three different tools for incorporating risk/uncertainty. The attitude of management towards risk will determine which of the three tools is used.

EVs and maximin, maximax and minimax regret will be explored in more detail below.

9.3 Expected values (EVs)

The expected value is the average return that will be made if a decision is repeated again and again.

Each of the possible outcomes is weighted with their relative probability of occurring. It is the weighted arithmetic mean of the outcomes.

The formula for expected values is: **EV = $\sum$px**

where: x = the value of the possible outcome

p = the probability of the possible outcome.

Illustration 10 – Simple EV calculation

Returns from a new restaurant depend on whether a company decides to open in the same area. The following estimates are made:

Competitor opens up	Probability (p)	Project NPV (x)	px
Yes	0.30	($10,000)	($3,000)
No	0.70	$20,000	$14,000
			$11,000

The EV = $\sum$px = $11,000. Since the expected value shows the long run average outcome of a decision which is repeated time and time again, it is a useful decision rule for a **risk neutral decision maker**. This is because a risk neutral decision maker neither seeks or avoids risk; he is happy to accept the average outcome.

Pay-off (profit) tables

A pay-off (profit) table is useful for calculating EVs when there is a range of possible outcomes and a variety of possible responses.

Illustration 11 – Simple pay-off (profit) table

Geoffrey Ramsbottom runs a kitchen that provides food for various canteens throughout a large organisation. A particular salad generates a profit of $2 based on a selling price of $10 and a cost of $8. Daily demand is as follows:

Demand	Probability
40 salads	0.10
50 salads	0.20
60 salads	0.40
70 salads	0.30
	1.00

Required:

The kitchen must prepare the salad in batches of 10. Its staff have asked you to help them decide how many salads it should supply per day.

Answer:

There are a range of possible outcomes (levels of demand) and a variety of possible responses (number of salads to supply) and therefore it is useful to construct a payoff table:

Daily demand	Prob (p)	Daily supply profit/(loss) outcome (x)			
		40 salads	50 salads	60 salads	70 salads
40 salads	0.10	$80 (W1)	$0	($80)	($160)
50 salads	0.20	$80	$100	$20	($60)
60 salads	0.40	$80	$100	$120	$40
70 salads	0.30	$80	$100	$120	$140
	EV =	$80	$90	$80	$30 (W2)

Workings:

(W1) Profit is calculated as follows = 40 salads × $2 = **$80**

(W2) EV is calculated as follows = (0.10 × –$160) + (0.20 × –$60) + (0.40 × $40) + (0.30 × $140) = **$30**

Conclusion:

Therefore, based on EVs, daily supply should be **50 salads** since this yields the highest expected value of $90.

In the illustration above, there was only one variable outcome, i.e. the level of demand. However, in some situations there may be more than one variable outcome, e.g. demand and inflation. In this case, a **two way data table** should be prepared before the EV is calculated.

Test your understanding 12

Confused Company is seeking to establish the likely profit to be generated for the forthcoming year. This is very much dependent upon the anticipated demand, and the impact of inflation upon the fixed costs of the business.

Probabilities have been estimated for both demand and inflation as shown below.

Demand	Probability	Inflation	Probability
Strong	0.20	None	0.30
Normal	0.50	2%	0.50
Weak	0.30	4%	0.20

A **two way data table** has been prepared which estimates the changes in net profit (in $) for a range of changes in demand and inflation:

		Inflation				
		None	1%	2%	3%	4%
Demand	Strong	95,000	85,000	75,000	65,000	55,000
	Normal	60,000	50,000	40,000	30,000	20,000
	Weak	25,000	15,000	5,000	(5,000)	(15,000)

Required:

Prepare a summary that shows:

- the range of possible net profit and loss outcomes
- the combined probability of each outcome
- the expected value of the profit for the year.

Management will be awarded a bonus if profit exceeds $50,000. What are the chances of this occurring?

Usefulness of EVs

Since the expected value shows the long-run average outcome of a decision which is repeated again and again, it is a useful decision tool for a risk neutral decision maker. This is because a risk neutral person neither seeks risk nor avoids it; they are happy to accept an average outcome. This technique would not be useful for decisions which occur only once.

9.4 Maximax, maximin and minimax regret

The **maximax rule** looks at the best possible outcome for each course of action and selects the alternative that maximises the maximum pay-off achievable.

The **maximin rule** looks at the worst possible outcome for each course of action and selects the alternative that maximises the minimum pay-off achievable.

The **minimax regret** looks at the maximum regret (opportunity cost) for each course of action and aims to choose the strategy that minimises the maximum regret.

Illustration 12 – Geoffrey Ramsbottom

Required:

Using the information from illustration 7 decide how many salads should be supplied per day using:

(a) the maximax rule

(b) the maximin rule

(c) the minimax regret rule.

Answer:

(a) Maximax

Daily demand	Prob (p)	Daily supply profit/(loss) outcome (x)			
		40 salads	50 salads	60 salads	70 salads
40 salads	0.10	$80	$0	($80)	($160)
50 salads	0.20	$80	$100	$20	($60)
60 salads	0.40	$80	$100	$120	$40
70 salads	0.30	$80	$100	$120	$140
		———	———	———	———
	Maximum profit =	$80	$100	$120	**$140**
		———	———	———	———

The maximax rule involves selecting the alternative that maximises the maximum pay-off achievable. Looking at the table above, the maximum profit achievable is $140. This will be achieved if **70 salads** are supplied.

(b) Maximin

Daily demand	Prob (p)	Daily supply profit/(loss) outcome (x)			
		40 salads	50 salads	60 salads	70 salads
40 salads	0.10	$80	$0	($80)	($160)
50 salads	0.20	$80	$100	$20	($60)
60 salads	0.40	$80	$100	$120	$40
70 salads	0.30	$80	$100	$120	$140
		———	———	———	———
	Minimum profit =	**$80**	$0	($80)	($160)
		———	———	———	———

The maximin rule involves selecting the alternative that maximises the minimum pay-off achievable. Looking at the table above, the maximum of the minimum profits is $80. This will be achieved if **40 salads** are supplied.

(c) Minimax regret

The minimax regret strategy is the one that minimises the maximum regret (opportunity cost). A regret table should be used:

Daily demand	Daily supply regret (opportunity cost)			
	40 salads	50 salads	60 salads	70 salads
40 salads	Right decision	$80 (w1)	$160 (w1)	$240 (w1)
50 salads	$20	Right decision	$80	$160
60 salads	$40	$20	Right decision	$80
70 salads	$60	$40	$20	Right decision
	——	——	——	——
Maximum regret =	**$60**	$80	$160	$240
	——	——	——	——

Therefore, to minimise the maximum regret, **40 salads** should be supplied.

W1: If daily demand is 40 salads, it would be the right decision for the business to supply 40 salads since the profit of supplying 40 salads is the highest, i.e. $80.

- If the business decided instead to supply 50 salads, the regret (opportunity cost) would be the $80 it could have made supplying 40 salads minus the $0 it did make supplying the 50 salads = $80.

- If the business decided instead to supply 60 salads, the regret (opportunity cost) would be the $80 it could have made supplying 40 salads minus the $80 loss it did make supplying the 60 salads = $160.

- If the business decided instead to supply 70 salads, the regret (opportunity cost) would be the $80 it could have made supplying 40 salads minus the $160 loss it did make supplying the 70 salads = $240.

Usefulness of maximin, maximax and minimax regret

With **maximin** the decision maker chooses the outcome which is guaranteed to minimise his losses. In the process, he loses out on the opportunity to make big profits. It is often seen as a pessimistic approach to decision making (assuming the worst outcome will occur) and is used by decision makers who are **risk averse**.

With **maximax** the decision maker chooses the outcome which is guaranteed to maximise his profit. In this process he risks making a lower profit. It is often seen as an optimistic approach to decision making (assuming the best outcome will occur) and is used by decision makers who are **risk seeking**.

With **minimax regret** the decision maker chooses the outcome which minimises the maximum regret. In the process, he risks making a lower profit. It is often seen as a technique for a '**sore loser**' who does not want to make the wrong decision.

Each of the above techniques can be used for one-off or repeated decisions.

Question practice

It is useful to take the time to look at scenario-based questions that are in a similar style as the exam questions. Make sure that you attempt the question below and that you also carry out a detailed review of the recommended answer.

Test your understanding 13

Cement Co is a listed company specialising in the manufacture of cement, a product used in the building industry. The company has been a major player in the construction sector of European country, Q, since its formation in 1987. It is passionate about customer care and proud of its active approach to safety and sustainability (recognising the need to minimise any adverse environmental impact of its operations).

The company operates in a very traditional industry but profits can be volatile. Q's economy has been in recession for the last three years and this has had a direct impact on Cement Co's profitability. Shareholders are concerned about this fall in profit and have expressed their desire for a secure return. Competitors, keen to find ways of increasing profit and market share, in these difficult economic circumstances, have started to increase the level of investment in research and development, ensuring their products anticipate and meet the needs of its customers.

When Q entered recession, many workers left the country in search of more lucrative and secure work. This has had a significant impact on Cement Co which is now facing labour shortages and increased labour costs. At the same time, suppliers have also increased their prices putting further pressure on Cement Co's margins.

The company has found that when weather conditions are good, the demand for cement increases since more building work is able to take place. Last year, the weather was so good, and the demand for cement was so great, that Cement Co was unable to meet demand. Cement Co is now trying to work out the level of cement production for the coming year in order to maximise profits. The company doesn't want to miss out on the opportunity to earn large profits by running out of cement again. However, it doesn't want to be left with large quantities of the product unsold at the end of the year, since it deteriorates quickly and then has to be disposed of. The company has received the following estimates about the probable weather conditions and corresponding demand levels for the coming year:

Weather	Probability	Demand
Good	25%	350,000 bags
Average	45%	280,000 bags
Poor	30%	200,000 bags

Each bag of cement sells for $9 and costs $4 to make. If cement is unsold at the end of the year, it has to be disposed of at a cost of $0.50 per bag.

Cement Co has decided to produce at one of the three levels of production to match forecast demand. It now has to decide which level of cement production to select.

As an incentive to increase profitability a new bonus scheme has just been introduced for a select group of Cement Co's directors. A bonus will be received by each of these directors if annual profit exceeds a challenging target.

Required:

(a) Identify the risks facing Cement Co and assess the impact of different risk appetites of managers and shareholders on their response to these risks.

(10 marks)

(b) Evaluate the proposed levels of cement production using methods for decision making under risk and uncertainty and assess the suitability of the different methods used.

(15 marks)
(Total: 25 marks)

9.5 Impact of risk appetite of stakeholders on performance management

As mentioned earlier in the chapter, a business must consider the needs of its stakeholders when making decisions. Different stakeholders will have different risk perspectives or different risk appetites. For example:

- **Shareholders** – may be prepared to take a risk (**risk seeking**) in order to maximise the possible return, especially since shareholders are able to spread their risk by holding a portfolio of investments. However, shareholders are not always classed as risk seeking. For example, the shareholders of a company that is in financial distress may prefer the business to take a more risk neutral or risk averse approach in order to secure the future of the business.

- **Employees and managers** – they should act in the best interests of the shareholders but this does not always happen since they may be:
  - **risk averse**: employees and managers may be reluctant to take risks, e.g. to invest in a new project, if an unsuccessful outcome would impact their performance evaluation or the survival of the company (and hence their job). Therefore, even though risk taking may be in the best interests of the company and its shareholders they tend to exercise caution and are unwilling to take risks.

  - **risk seeking**: employees and managers may be encouraged to take risks by the promise of huge rewards or bonuses.

- **Financiers** – these include:
  - **Venture capitalists** (VCs) – VCs are likely to be rational investors seeking the maximum return for minimum risk. However, they will invest in a number of companies and so are prepared for some of their investments to fail, provided that some of their investments perform well. Steps will be taken to reduce risks, for example performance will be monitored on a regular basis to ensure that any agreed exit strategy can be achieved. In addition, the VCs will also place employees on the management team so that they can influence decisions.

- **Banks** – traditionally, banks would have been considered to have a reasonably conservative approach to risk with a desire to secure their funds and guarantee returns. However, the financial crisis which commenced in 2007 was triggered by US banks giving high risk loans (sub-prime mortgages) to people with poor credit histories. A sharp rise in US interest rates resulted in a huge number of American home owners defaulting on their mortgages. The impact of these defaults were felt across the financial system as many of the mortgages had been sold to big banks who turned them into supposedly low risk securities. However, this assumption proved wrong. In fact, huge uncalculated risks had been taken with the bankers being spurred on by the potential to earn huge bonuses.

Therefore, in order to effectively manage business performance, it will be necessary for the business to align its decisions with the stakeholder's risk appetite.

Illustration 13 – Risk appetite of employees

The collapse of Lehman brothers, a sprawling global bank, in September 2005, almost brought down the world's financial system. The then governor of the bank of England, Mervyn King, criticised City banks who rewarded staff with huge sums for taking risks and concluded that the credit crisis was caused, in part, by bankers betting on high-risk complex financial products. A culture of risk taking had developed due to the huge potential bonuses and rewards offered to bankers.

Student accountant articles: visit the ACCA website, accaglobal.com, to review two articles on 'the risks of uncertainty' from 2009.

10 Exam focus

Exam sitting	Area examined	Question number	Number of marks
June 2014	Risk	3(a)(b)	17
December 2013	PEST	1(ii)	11
June 2013	Porter's 5 forces and risk	3(a)(c)	21
December 2012	Changing role of management accountant	5(a)	12
December 2011	Risk	1	35
June 2011	Stakeholders	2(c)	6
December 2010	PEST	4(a)	4
June 2010	Expected values	2(b)(i)(ii)	12
December 2009	Economic, financial and social considerations	4(b)	14
June 2009	Maximax, maximin and minimax regret	2(d)	7
December 2008	Ethical issues/CSR, how government can aid business performance	3(c)(d)	10
June 2008	Strategic and economic factors	3(a)	14
December 2007	Porter's 5 forces	5(a)	10
Pilot paper	Ethics	1(d)	3
Pilot paper	Risk	3(b)	10

Note:

- The current examiner has set the exam papers from the December 2010 sitting onwards.

- The format of the exam changed in June 2013. Section A now contains 1 × 50 mark question (previously 2 questions worth 60 marks in total) and Section B now contains a choice of 2 from 3 questions worth 25 marks each (previously a choice of 2 from 3 questions worth approximately 20 marks each).

Chapter summary

The impact of stakeholders
- definitions
- stakeholders' influence
- stakeholder mapping
- conflict

External analysis
- PEST
- Porter's 5 forces

The impact of ethical issues
- ethics
- CSR

The impact of government policy
- policy areas
- fiscal and monetary policy

Environmental influences

The impact of government regulation
- competition policy
- supply-side policy
- green policies/ externalities

Changing role of management accountant
- changes
- driving forces
- benefits
- sources of information
- providing information to stakeholders

Risk and uncertainty
- definitions
- dealing with risk
- EVs
- maximax, maximin and minimax regret
- risk appetite of stakeholders

Test your understanding answers

Test your understanding 1

PEST analysis for UK railways

Political

The balance of public – private involvement in the running costs and capital investment for rail development is a major issue. Any changes in government policy could have dramatic consequences for companies operating in the rail industry.

Economic

The growth of commuter travel on the rail system means it is working at close to full capacity. This trend is likely to continue with the rising costs of fuel, making car travel expensive. This, however, can be seen as a positive for rail companies who can cease the opportunity to increase profits and improve performance.

However, there is a need for investment in infrastructure in areas such as longer platforms and new signal systems. Financing this investment may be difficult but the performance of railway companies will deteriorate in the long-term if the investment is not made.

Social

Increasing concerns about reliability, particularly in rural areas, could detract from profitability as passengers switch to more reliable forms of transport.

Concerns about the effect that railway construction and travel has on the environment could again detract from profitability since customers may be lost.

Safety issues on trains and at railway stations – train travel is comparatively very safe but it is still necessary for the railway companies to monitor safety and address any issues identified.

Technological

The development of new train technologies such as high speed railways could result in a long term boost in profit but will require significant investment.

Also following the trends set by air travel by introducing ways to improve the customer experience. For example, offering Internet access and on-train entertainment. Fulfilment of customers' needs could, once again, result in improved performance.

Porter's 5 forces model – UK railways

Competitive rivalry

In certain areas rail operators may be directly competing over the same routes. If the force is medium or high then performance will be negatively impacted.

Threats from substitutes

There are other forms of transport available such as travel by road (e.g. cars and buses) and travel by air. However, the rising cost of petrol and diesel and the inappropriateness of air travel for shorter journeys may make this force low and the performance of the railway companies should not suffer as a result.

Buyers' bargaining power

Severe competition over price with low-cost airlines on longer city routes (but again this would not be a suitable alternative for shorter routes).

Online price comparisons make it easy for customers to select lowest cost option but transparency of ticket prices and types in the UK is still poor.

Overall, this force may be classed as medium and the impact on performance will be limited.

Threat from potential entrants

New companies may enter the market when rail franchises become available for re-tender. For example, Virgin entered the UK market some years ago. Any threat should be investigated and acted on since the entry of any new players could seriously reduce market share and profitability.

Suppliers' bargaining power

With an increasing number of discrete rail and train operators, the allocation of capacity becomes an issue. This is similar to landing slots at airports. Close working relations with suppliers could help to understand this issue and to negotiate the level of service required. If these steps are taken, performance may not suffer.

Test your understanding 2

Loyal customers

Chatman Theatre, which is a charity, can make use of a database to profile their interests and wants. A tailored communication can then be sent.

Given the need to contain costs, this might be by getting customers to sign up to an e-list to get up-to-date news and information on future performances.

They could set up a website with booking facilities and send confirmation by email rather than post.

Develop a friend of the theatre group, giving discounts to regular loyal customers.

First time customers

The website could be linked to other relevant websites, such as local attractions and tourist boards, to attract new customers.

The theatre could produce an information pack to attract new mailing list subscribers. These could be made available in local churches and shops.

Local arts groups

A partnership agreement could be established with arts groups, to co-sponsor events of special interest to given groups of customers.

Local organisations

Try to obtain commercial sponsorship from local companies. Acknowledgement could be given in the monthly programme mailings and preferential facilities offered for corporate hospitality.

Media

Personal invitations could be issued to opening nights, to interview the performers and give an overview of the show.

Note: The above is just a selection of potential relationships with stakeholders.

Test your understanding 3

- **Whether or not the museum should charge an entry fee** – this would discourage some people from going to the museum (compromising the first objective) but would provide extra cash for funding research.

- **Which artefacts should be displayed** – education would require a wide range of exhibits with the most prestigious on display. An emphasis on preservation would prevent the most significant items from being displayed for fear of damage.

Test your understanding 4

- Ethical behaviour is likely to be favoured by:
    - customers: resulting in higher sales volumes and/or prices.

    - employees: resulting in the attraction/retention of the best employees and increased employee productivity.

    - business collaborators: resulting in increased opportunities for profitable projects.

- Ethical behaviour reduces risk and gives access to cheaper funds which in turn increase project NPVs.

- Unethical behaviour will, at some point be discovered resulting in a damage to reputation and potential legal charges.

Test your understanding 5

- The purpose of a business is to make profits. Profit is a good thing in its own right as it supports stable employment, innovation, allows higher taxes to be paid and makes economies richer. Companies have no need to feel guilty about making profits and buying off some of that guilt by embarking on good works.

- The prime stakeholders are the shareholders and directors should always attempt to maximise shareholder wealth. If directors embark on a CSR programme, have shareholders given permission? It is, after all, shareholders' money that is being used.

- CSR allows directors to feel generous and righteous – but with someone else's money. Better, perhaps, that directors and shareholders make private donations out of their remuneration and dividends.

- What is the democratic basis which companies use to choose between CSR projects? Simply choosing a project because the chief executive likes it does not mean the money is being well spent – the project could be already well-funded.

Test your understanding 6

Suitable metrics could include:

- number of fatalities

- number of permanently disabling injuries

- number of enforcement actions

- accident frequency rate (AFR) e.g. the number of reportable accidents per 100,000 hours worked

- lost time incident frequency rate (LTIFR)

- sickness absence rate

- health and safety training rate (days/employee)

- percentage of employees working within an ISO 18001 compliant Health and Safety Management System.

Test your understanding 7

Governments can act as an aid to business performance in the following ways:

- A government can increase aggregate demand for goods and services by increased government spending and/or by reducing taxation so that firms (and individuals) have more income available to spend.

- Government policy may encourage firms to locate in particular areas. This is particularly the case where there is high unemployment in such areas.

- Government policy via the use of quotas and import tariffs might make it more difficult for overseas firms to compete in domestic markets.

- A government can regulate monopolies in particular with regard to the prices they charge and the quality of their goods and services.

- Government policy can regulate the activities of those firms which do not act in the best interests of the environment.

Test your understanding 8

Areas could include:

Interest rates

Changes in the interest rates for consumer debt may affect demand for luxury goods which may include high-value electronic products.

The company's cost of debt may change, affecting the cost of developing new facilities.

Exchange rates

Changes in interest rates may change the value of profits earned in different countries or the price to consumers of imported goods.

Taxation levels

The level of personal taxation will affect the demand for products. Changes in the company tax regime will affect the returns to shareholders.

Incentive schemes

The availability of incentive schemes may make expanding into certain countries more attractive.

Worker protection

Legislation in this area may have an impact on the requirements for facilities and their costs.

Restrictive practices

These may affect the company's ability to export to certain countries.

Environment protection

The company may need to develop new products which are more economical to run or which use materials which are less harmful to the environment when thrown away.

Test your understanding 9

(1) Customers' mortgages and loans will become more expensive, giving less net disposable income for major purchases, such as new carpets.

(2) Customers will be less motivated to borrow to finance carpet purchase.

(3) The cost of capital will rise so the retailer will be less prepared to undertake major projects.

(4) The domestic currency will strengthen, reducing the cost of imports.

Test your understanding 10

- Higher interest rates will increase the cost of borrowing and the gearing risk of the firm, making it less likely that long-term earnings targets will be met.

- A fall in government spending could see a downturn in orders, particularly if the firm currently is engaged in government contracts (e.g. building roads, hospitals). Future plans may have to be revised to reflect this and alternative strategies sought. Analysis of sales mix between public and private sector contracts will become more important.

- Potentially lower levels of taxation could increase profitability.

- Lower inflation will reduce business uncertainty, making planning easier. Plans may have to be revised to reflect lower inflation.

- Higher unemployment in the economy could allow the firm to reduce planned pay increases.

Test your understanding 11

Depending on the degree of regulation in the country concerned the firm could find it difficult to improve performance due to the following:

- It may be difficult to win new customers as the firm already has a regional monopoly.

- Price rises will probably be capped by the regulator.

- Minimum spending plans will be agreed with the regulator. These could be delayed to boost short-term ROCE.

- Quality targets make it difficult to cut corners to reduce operating costs.

These emphasise the importance of negotiating a 'good deal' with the regulator when spending plans are agreed.

The company should also look to developing non-core activities (though these may also be regulated).

- Water sports facilities, such as sailing.

- Whether land could be developed, e.g. building apartments.

Test your understanding 12

Possible demand	Possible inflation	Net profit $ = x	Combined prob = p	px ($)	Bonus prob (profit > $50,000)
Strong (prob = 0.20)	None (prob 0.30)	95,000	0.20 × 0.30 = 0.06	5,700	0.06
	2% (prob = 0.50)	75,000	0.20 × 0.50 = 0.10	7,500	0.10
	4% (prob = 0.20)	55,000	0.20 × 0.20 = 0.04	2,200	0.04
Normal (prob = 0.50)	None (prob 0.30)	60,000	0.50 × 0.30 = 0.15	9,000	0.15
	2% (prob = 0.50)	40,000	0.50 × 0.050 = 0.25	10,000	–
	4% (prob = 0.20)	20,000	0.50 × 0.20 = 0.10	2,000	–
Weak (prob = 0.30)	None (prob 0.30)	25,000	0.30 × 0.30 = 0.09	2,250	–
	2% (prob = 0.50)	5,000	0.30 × 0.50 = 0.15	750	–
	4% (prob = 0.20)	(15,000)	0.30 × 0.20 = 0.06	(900)	–
				———	———
			EV = $\sum$px	**38,500**	**0.35**
				———	———

Test your understanding 13

(a) The primary objective of Cement Co, a listed company, will be to maximise shareholder wealth. The directors should, in theory, be acting in the best interests of the shareholders. The shareholders appear to be reasonably risk averse at the moment since they have expressed concern over the fall in profit.

Cement Co is open to a lot of risk and uncertainty:

- Firstly, Q's economy is in recession which will have a direct impact on Cement Co as house building falls and government contracts are cut.

- At the same time, the company's costs are increasing due to increases in wages and in suppliers' prices.

- Cement Co is risking falling behind its competitors who have increased investment in research and development. There is a risk that Cement Co will not be able to meet the needs of its customers as well as its competitors.

- Cement Co does pride itself on its approach to sustainability and safety. However, the industry is characterised by its negative impact on the environment and poor safety record and therefore it is imperative that Cement Co does not lose focus on achieving their sustainability and safety targets.

- Finally, volatile weather conditions can have a huge impact on the building industry and on Cement Co's profitability. The weather is clearly something that cannot be controlled but the risk should be appropriately managed.

Directors can take one of three approaches to managing risk:

- Risk averse directors – will assume the worst outcome and will seek to minimise its effect. Some of Cement Co's directors will be keen to take this approach in the hope of securing a satisfactory return for shareholders and securing their positions.

- Risk seeking directors – will assume the best outcome and will seek to maximise its effect. Some of the directors will be risk seeking, hoping to secure an outcome that will maximise profitability and their annual bonus.

- Risk neutral directors – these directors will be interested in the most probable outcome. This would be a sensible approach in situations where the risks remain unaltered and decisions are repeated many times.

(b) Level of cement production

Before any of the techniques for decision making under risk and uncertainty are applied, it will be necessary to construct a pay off table:

DEMAND	Weather	Probability	SUPPLY		
			350,000	280,000	200,000
			Profit $000	Profit $000	Profit $000
350,000	Good	0.25	1,750 (W1)	1,400	1,000
280,000	Average	0.45	1,085 (W2)	1,400	1,000
200,000	Poor	0.30	325	640	1,000

Workings

Profit per bag sold in coming year = $9 − $4 = $5

Loss per bag disposed of = $4 + $0.50 = $4.50

(W1) 350,000 × $5 = $1,750,000

(W2) [280,000 × $5] − [70,000 × $(4.50)] = $1,085,000 etc

We can now evaluate the proposed levels of cement production using four different methods:

Method 1: Expected Values

Use the probabilities provided in order to calculate the expected value of each of the supply levels.

Good: (0.25 × $1,750,000) + (0.45 × $1,085,000) + (0.30 × $325,000) = $1,023,250

Average: (0.7 × $1,400,000) + (0.3 × $640,000) = $1,172,000

Poor: 1 × $1,000,000 = $1,000,000

The expected value of producing 280,000 bags when conditions are average is the highest at $1,172,000, therefore this supply level should be chosen.

Method 2: Maximin

Identify the worst outcome for each level of supply and choose the highest of these worst outcomes.

	SUPPLY		
	350,000 Profit $000	280,000 Profit $000	200,000 Profit $000
Worst	325	640	1,000

The highest of these is $1,000,000 therefore choose to supply only 200,000 bags to meet poor conditions.

Method 3: Maximax

Identify the best outcome for each level of supply and choose the highest of these best outcomes.

	SUPPLY		
	350,000 Profit $000	280,000 Profit $000	200,000 Profit $000
Best	1,750	1,400	1,000

The highest of these is $1,750,000 therefore choose to supply 350,000 bags to meet good conditions.

Method 4: Minimax Regret

For each level of demand, identify the right decision (the supply level which results in the highest profit) and the regret for the other supply levels. Choose the maximum level of regret at each possible supply level and then choose the level of supply that minimises this maximum regret.

	SUPPLY		
DEMAND	350,000 Regret $000	280,000 Regret $000	200,000 Regret $000
350,000	Right decision	350 (W3)	750
280,000	315 (W4)	Right decision	400
200,000	675	360	Right decision
Maximum regret	675	360	750

(W3) Regret (opportunity cost) = $1,750,000 – $1,400,000 = $350,000

(W4) Regret (opportunity cost) = $1,400,000 – $1,085,000 = $315,000

Suitability of the different methods

The **maximin** decision rule looks at the worst possible outcome at each supply level and then selects the highest one of these. It is used when the outcome cannot be assessed with any level of certainty. The decision maker therefore chooses the outcome which is guaranteed to minimise his losses. In the process, he loses out on the opportunity of making big profits. It is often seen as the pessimistic approach to decision-making (assuming that the worst outcome will occur) and is used by decision makers who are risk averse. It can be used for one-off or repeated decisions.

The **expected value** rule calculates the average return that will be made if a decision is repeated again and again. It does this by weighting each of the possible outcomes with their relative probability of occurring. It is the weighted arithmetic mean of the possible outcomes. Since the expected value shows the long run average outcome of a decision which is repeated time and time again, it is a useful decision rule for a risk neutral decision maker. This is because a risk neutral person neither seeks risk or avoids it; they are happy to accept an average outcome. The problem often is, however, that this rule is often used for decisions that only occur once. In this situation, the actual outcome is unlikely to be close to the long run average. For example, with Cement Co, the closest actual outcome to the expected value of $1,172,000 is the outcome of $1,085,000. This is not too far away from the expected value but many of the others are significantly different.

The **maximax** decision rule looks at the best possible outcome at each supply level and then selects the highest one of these. It is used when the outcome cannot be assessed with any level of certainty. The decision maker therefore chooses the outcome which is guaranteed to maximise his gain. In the process, he risks making a lower profit. It is often seen as an optimistic approach to decision making (assuming the best outcome will occur) and is used by decision makers who are risk seeking. It can be used for one-off or repeated decisions.

The **minimax regret** decision rule looks at the maximum regret (opportunity cost) at each level of supply and aims to choose the level of supply which minimises the maximum regret. In the process, he risks making a lower profit. It is often seen as a technique for a 'sore loser' who doesn't want to make the wrong decision.

Approaches to budgets

Chapter learning objectives

Upon completion of this chapter you will be able to:

- evaluate the strengths and weaknesses of alternative budgeting models and compare such techniques as fixed and flexible, rolling, activity based, zero based and incremental

- assess how budgeting may differ in not-for-profit organisations from profit-seeking organisations

- evaluate the impact to an organisation of a move to 'beyond budgeting'

- discuss and evaluate the application of activity-based management.

1 Assumed knowledge

Chapter 3 builds on the following knowledge from Paper F5:

- Absorption costing and activity-based costing
- Budgeting
- Standard costing and variances
- Forecasting

2 Introduction

In chapter 1 we said that 'performance management is any activity that is designed to improve an organisation's performance and ensure that its goals are being met'. Budgeting will assist with performance management since it is an important tool for **planning** and **control** within an organisation and contributes to performance management by providing benchmarks against which to compare actual results (through variance analysis) and develop corrective measures.

It is important that the organisation understands the relative merits of the different budgeting approaches and chooses the approach that is most suitable for them.

'Traditional' budgeting is not without its problems, however, and later on in this chapter we introduce 'beyond budgeting' which will aim to address some of these issues.

3 Purposes of budgeting

A **budget** is a quantitative plan prepared for a specific time period. It is normally expressed in financial terms and prepared for one year.

Budgeting serves a number of purposes:

- Planning
- Control
- Communication
- Co-ordination
- Evaluation
- Motivation
- Authorisation
- Delegation

Purposes of budgeting

Budgeting serves a number of purposes:

Planning

A budgeting process forces the business to look into the future. This is essential for survival since it stops management from relying on ad hoc or poorly co-ordinated planning.

Control

Actual results are compared against the budget and action is taken as appropriate.

Communication

The budget is a formal communication channel that allows junior and senior staff to converse.

Co-ordination

The budget allows co-ordination of all parts of the business towards a common corporate goal.

Evaluation

Responsibility accounting divides the organisation into budget centres, each of which has a manager who is responsible for its performance. The budget may be used to evaluate the actions of a manager within the business in terms of costs and revenues over which they have control.

Motivation

The budget may be used as a target for managers to aim for. Rewards should be given for operating within or under budgeted levels of expenditure. This acts as a motivator for managers.

Authorisation

The budget acts as a formal method of authorisation for a manager for expenditure, hiring staff and the pursuit of plans contained within the budget.

Delegation

Managers may be involved in setting the budget. Extra responsibility may motivate managers. Management involvement may also result in more realistic targets.

4 Participation in budget setting

 A **top-down** (or non-participative) budget is one that is imposed on the budget holder by senior management.

 A **bottom-up** (or participative) budget involves the divisional managers of an organisation having the opportunity to participate in the setting of the budgets.

It is important that you can discuss the relative merits of these two approaches and recommend the most appropriate method for a given organisation.

KAPLAN PUBLISHING

Advantages of bottom-up budgeting	Advantages of top-down budgeting
• Improved motivation due to a sense of ownership and empowerment. • It increases divisional managers' understanding (which has an additional benefit if personal targets are set from the budget). • Frees up senior management resource. • Improves the quality of decision making since divisional managers are close to their product markets.	• Avoids budgetary slack (i.e. divisional managers may be tempted to set targets that are too easy to achieve). • Avoids dysfunctional behaviour (i.e. divisional managers lack a strategic perspective, focusing on the needs of the division and, as a result, budgets may not be in line with corporate objectives). • Senior managers retain control. • Budget setting process can be quicker. • Avoids the problem of bad decisions from inexperience managers.

An organisation may use a mix of the two approaches and each approach may be used to a greater or lesser extent in different divisions. It will be up to senior management to decide on the level of central control to exercise, based on the skills and needs of the divisional managers.

5 Methods of budgeting

Different approaches to budgeting were studied in Paper F5. In this exam it is important that you not only understand each of the techniques but that you can compare the techniques and evaluate their relative strengths and weaknesses.

5.1 Fixed and flexible budgeting

A fixed budget is a budget prepared at a single level of activity.

A flexible budget is a budget prepared with the cost behaviour of all cost elements known and classified as either fixed or variable. The budget may be prepared at a number of activity levels and can be 'flexed' or changed to the actual level of activity for budgetary control purposes.

Test your understanding 1

A company has the following budgeted and actual information for a department.

	Budget	Actual
Level of activity (units of output)	1,000	1,200
Cost ($)	20,000	23,000

Required:

(a) Assuming all costs are variable, has the company done better or worse than expected?

(b) If $10,000 of the budgeted costs are fixed costs, the remainder being variable, has the company performed better or worse than expected?

Advantages and disadvantages of flexible budgeting

Advantages	Disadvantages
Should enable better performance evaluation as comparing like with like.	• May be perceived by some as 'moving the goal posts' resulting in demotivation – especially if bonuses are lost despite beating the original budget. • Difficulties splitting costs into fixed and variable elements. • In the long run it could be argued that all costs are variable.

Test your understanding 2

Redfern hospital is a government funded hospital in the country of Newland. Relevant cost data for the year ended 31 December 20X0 is as follows:

(1) Salary costs per staff member were payable as follows:

	Budget ($)	Actual ($)
Doctors	100,000	105,000
Nurses	37,000	34,500

Budgeted and actual staff were 60 doctors and 150 nurses.

(2) Budgeted costs for the year based on 20,000 patients per annum were as follows:

	$	Variable cost (%)	Fixed cost (%)
Other staff costs	1,440,000	100	–
Catering	200,000	70	30
Cleaning	80,000	35	65
Other operating costs	1,200,000	30	70
Depreciation	80,000	–	100

Variable costs vary according to the number of patients.

(3) The actual number of patients for the year was 23,750. Actual costs (excluding the cost of doctors and nurses) incurred during the year were as follows:

	$
Other staff costs	1,500,000
Catering	187,500
Cleaning	142,000
Other operating costs	1,050,000
Depreciation	80,000

Required:

Prepare a statement which shows the actual and budgeted costs for Redfern hospital in respect of the year ended 31 December 20X0 on a comparable basis.

5.2 Incremental budgets

An **incremental budget** starts with the previous period's budget or actual results, and adds (or subtracts) an incremental amount to cover inflation and other known changes.

Suitability

- It is suitable for stable businesses, where costs are not expected to change significantly.

- There should be good cost control.

- There should be limited discretionary costs.

Advantages	Disadvantages
• Quickest and easiest method. • Assuming that the historic figures are acceptable, only the increment needs to be justified. • Avoids 'reinventing the wheel'.	• Builds in previous problems and inefficiencies. • Uneconomic activities may be continued. • Managers may spend up to their budget to ensure that they get an increment from the highest possible base figure in the following year.

Incremental approach to budgets

AW produces two products, A and C. In the last year (20X4) it produced 640 units of A and 350 units of C incurring costs of $672,000. Analysis of the costs has shown that 75% of the total costs are variable. 60% of these variable costs vary in line with the number of A produced and the remainder with the number of C.

The budget for the year 20X5 is now being prepared using an incremental budgeting approach. The following additional information is available for 20X5:

- All costs will be 4% higher than the average paid in 20X4.

- Efficiency levels will remain unchanged.

- Expected output of A is 750 units and of C is 340 units.

Required:

What is the budgeted total variable cost of product C (to the nearest $100) for the full year 20X5?

Solution:

20X4 costs:

Total variable costs	= 75% × $672,000	= $504,000
Proportion relating to product C	= 40% × $504,000	= $201,600
Cost per unit of product C	= $201,600/350	= $576

20X5 budget costs:

Inflated cost per unit of C	= 1.04 × $576	= $599.04
Total variable cost for product C	= 340 × $599.04	= $203,674

i.e. $203,700 to nearest $100.

Question practice

The NW Entertainments Company (NWEC) is a privately owned organisation which operates an amusement park in a rural area within the North West region of a country which has a good climate all year round. The amusement park comprises a large fairground with high-quality rides and numerous attractions designed to appeal to people of all ages.

The park is open for 365 days in the year.

Each day spent by a guest at the park is classed as a 'Visitor Day'. During the year ended 30 November 20X3 a total of 2,090,400 visitor days were paid for and were made up as follows:

Visitor category	% of total visitor days
Adults	40
14–18 years of age and Senior Citizens	20
Under 14 years of age	40

Two types of admission pass are available for purchase, these are:

The 'One-day Visitor's pass' and the 'Two-day Visitor's pass', which entitles the holder of the pass to admission to the amusement park on any two days within the year commencing 1 December.

The pricing structure was as follows:

(i) The cost of a One-day pass for an adult was $40. Visitors aged 14–18 years and Senior Citizens receive a 25% discount against the cost of adult passes. Visitors aged below 14 years receive a 50% discount against the cost of adult passes.

(ii) The purchase of a Two-day Visitor's pass gave the purchaser a 25% saving against the cost of two One-day Visitor's passes.

(iii) 25% of the total visitor days were paid for by the purchase of One-day passes. The remainder were paid for by the purchase of Two-day passes.

Total operating costs of the park during the year amounted to $37,600,000.

NWEC receives income from traders who provide catering and other facilities to visitors to the amusement park. There are 30 such traders from whom payments are received. The amount of the payment made by each trader is dependent upon the size of the premises that they occupy in the amusement park as shown in the following summary:

Size of premises	No. of Annual Traders	Payment per Trader
		$
Large	8	54,000
Medium	12	36,000
Small	10	18,000

The income from each trader is received under 3 year contracts which became effective on 1 December 20X3. The income is fixed for the duration of each contract.

All operating costs of the park incurred during the year ending 30 November 20X4 are expected to increase by 4%. This has led to a decision by management to increase the selling price of all categories of admission passes by 4% with effect from 1 December 20X3. Management expect the number of visitor days, visitor mix and the mix of admission passes purchased to be the same as in the previous year.

NWEC also own a 400 bedroom hotel with leisure facilities, which is located 20 kilometres from the amusement park.

During the year ended 30 November 20X3, the charge per room on an all-inclusive basis was $100 per room, per night. The total operating costs of the hotel amounted to $7,950,000. Average occupancy during the year was 240 rooms per night. The hotel is open for 365 days in the year.

It is anticipated that the operating costs of the hotel will increase by 4% in the year ending 30 November 20X4. Management have decided to increase the charge per room, per night by 4% with effect from 1 December 20X3 and expect average occupancy will remain at the same level during the year ending 30 November 20X4.

The revenue of the hotel is independent of the number of visitors to the amusement park.

Required:

Prepare a statement showing the budgeted net profit or loss for the year to 30 November 20X4.

Answer

NWEC Budgeted Profit and Loss Statement for year to 30 November 20X4

	$	$
Amusement Park – admission receipts:		
One-day pass:		
Adults:	8,696,064	
14–18 years, senior citizens	3,261,024	
Under 14 years	4,348,032	
Two-day pass:		
Adults:	19,566,144	
14–18 years, senior citizens	7,337,304	
Under 14 years	9,783,072	
		52,991,640
Other revenue Income from traders		1,044,000
Total revenue – park		54,035,640
Operating costs		39,104,000
Budgeted profit of park		14,931,640
Hotel income	9,110,400	
Hotel operating costs	8,268,000	
Budgeted profit of hotel		842,400
		15,774,040

Workings:

No. of Visitor days for year to 30 November 20X4 = 2,090,400
One-day passes = 2,090,400 × 25% = 522,600
Two-day passes (2,090,400 × 75%)/2 = 783,900

Admission fees applicable from 1 December 20X3. (increased by 4% per annum).

	One-day pass ($)	Two-day pass ($)
Adults	41.60 (40*1.04)	62.40 (41.60*2 less 25%)
14–18 years; senior citizens	31.20 (30*1.04)	46.80 (31.20*2 less 25%)
Under 14's	20.80 (20*1.04)	31.20 (20.80*2 less 25%)

Split	One-day pass revenue			Two-day pass revenue		
40%	209,040	$41.60	$8,696,064	313,560	$62.40	$19,566,144
20%	104,520	$31.20	$3,261,024	156,780	$46.80	$ 7,337,304
40%	209,040	$20.80	$4,348,032	313,560	$31.20	$ 9,783,072
	———			———		
	522,600			783,900		

5.3 Zero based budgets

Zero based budgeting (ZBB) is a method of budgeting that requires each cost element to be specifically justified, as though the activities to which the budget relates were being undertaken for the first time. Without approval, the budget allowance is zero.

Suitability

- Fast moving businesses/industries
- Discretionary costs such as research and development (R&D).
- Public sector organisations such as local authorities.

ZBB process

There are four distinct stages in the implementation of ZBB:

(1) Managers should specify for their responsibility centres those activities that can be individually evaluated.

(2) Each of the individual activities is then described in a decision package. The decision package should state the costs and revenues expected from the given activity. It should be drawn up in such a way that the package can be evaluated and ranked against other packages.

(3) Each decision package is evaluated and ranked usually using cost/benefit analysis.

(4) The resources are then allocated to the various packages.

ZBB

A decision package was defined by Peter Pyhrr (who first formulated the ZBB approach at Texas Instruments) as:

'A document that identifies and describes a specific activity in such a manner that senior management can:

A evaluate it and rank it against other activities competing for limited resources and

B decide whether to approve or disapprove it.'

A decision package is a document that does the following:

- Analyses the cost of the activity. (Costs may be built up from a zero base, but costing information can be obtained from historical records or last year's budget.)

- States the purpose of the activity.

- Identifies alternative methods of achieving the same purpose.

- Assesses the consequence of not doing the activity at all, or performing the activity at a different level.

- Establishes measures of performance for the activity.

Pyhrr identifies two types of package:

I   Mutually-exclusive packages. These contain different methods of obtaining the same objective.

II   Incremental packages. These divide the activity into a number of different levels of activity. The base package describes the minimum effort and cost that is needed to carry out the activity. The other packages describe the incremental costs and benefits when added to the base.

ZBB exercise

A company is conducting a ZBB exercise, and a decision package is being prepared for its materials-handling operations.

- The manager responsible has identified a base package for the minimum resources needed to perform the materials-handling function. This is to have a team of five workers and a supervisor, operating without any labour-saving machinery. The estimated annual cost of wages and salaries, with overtime, would be $375,000.

- In addition to the base package, the manager has identified an incremental package. The company could lease two forklift trucks at a cost of $20,000 each year. This would provide a better system because materials could be stacked higher and moved more quickly. Health and safety risks for the workers would be reduced, and there would be savings of $5,000 each year in overtime payments.

- Another incremental package has been prepared, in which the company introduces new computer software to plan materials-handling schedules. The cost of buying and implementing the system would be $60,000, but the benefits are expected to be improvements in efficiency that reduce production downtime and result in savings of $10,000 each year in overtime payments.

The base package would be considered essential, and so given a high priority. The two incremental packages should be evaluated and ranked. Here, the forklift trucks option might be ranked more highly than the computer software.

In the budget that is eventually decided by senior management, the forklift truck package might be approved, but the computer software package rejected on the grounds that there are other demands for resources with a higher priority.

Test your understanding 3

For a number of years, the research division of Z has produced its annual budget (for new and continuing projects) using incremental budgeting techniques. The company is now under new management and the annual budget for 20X4 is to be prepared using ZBB techniques.

Required:

Explain how Z could operate a ZBB system for its research projects.

Advantages	Disadvantages
• Inefficient or obsolete operations can be identified and discontinued. • ZBB leads to increased staff involvement at all levels. This should lead to better communication and motivation. • It responds to changes in the business environment. • Knowledge and understanding of the cost-behaviour patterns of the organisation will be enhanced. • Resources should be allocated efficiently and economically.	• The time involved and the cost of preparing the budget are much greater than for less elaborate budgeting methods. • It may emphasise short-term benefits to the detriment of long-term benefits. • The budgeting process may become too rigid and the company may not be able to react to unforeseen opportunities or threats. • There is a need for management skills that may not be present in the organisation. • Managers may feel demotivated due to the large amount of time spent on the budgeting process. • It is difficult to compare and rank completely different types of activity. • The rankings of packages may be subjective where the benefits are of a qualitative nature.

5.4 Rolling budgets

A **rolling budget** is one that is kept continuously up to date by adding another accounting period (e.g. month or quarter) when the earliest accounting period has expired.

Suitability

- Accurate forecasts cannot be made, e.g. in a dynamic business environment or in a new business.

- For any area of business that needs tight control.

Advantages	Disadvantages
• The budgeting process should be more accurate.	• More costly and time consuming.
• Much better information upon which to appraise the performance of management.	• An increase in budgeting work may lead to less control of the actual results.
• The budget will be much more 'relevant' by the end of the traditional budgeting period.	• There is a danger that the budget may become the last budget 'plus or minus a bit'.
• It forces management to take the budgeting process more seriously.	• The budget may be demotivating because the targets are changing regularly.

Test your understanding 4

A company uses rolling budgeting and has a sales budget as follows:

	Quarter 1 $	Quarter 2 $	Quarter 3 $	Quarter 4 $	Total $
Sales	125,750	132,038	138,640	145,572	542,000

Actual sales for Quarter 1 were $123,450. The adverse variance is fully explained by competition being more intense than expected and growth being lower than anticipated. The budget committee has proposed that the revised assumption for sales growth should be 3% per quarter for Quarters 2, 3 and 4.

Required:

Update the budget figures for Quarters 2–4 as appropriate.

Question practice

The question below is taken from the December 2012 exam and is an excellent example of how the examiner may expect you to compare the different budgeting techniques. Make sure that you attempt this question and review the recommended answer.

Test your understanding 5

The Drinks Group (DG) has been created over the last three years by merging three medium-sized family businesses. These businesses are all involved in making fruit drinks. Fizzy (F) makes and bottles healthy, fruit-based sparkling drinks. Still (S) makes and bottles fruit-flavoured non-sparkling drinks and Healthy (H) buys fruit and squeezes it to make basic fruit juices. The three companies have been divisionalised within the group structure. A fourth division called Marketing (M) exists to market the products of the other divisions to various large retail chains. Marketing has only recently been set up in order to help the business expand. All of the operations and sales of DG occur in Nordland, which is an economically well-developed country with a strong market for healthy non-alcoholic drinks.

The group has recruited a new finance director (FD), who was asked by the board to perform a review of the efficiency and effectiveness of the finance department as her first task on taking office. The finance director has just presented her report to the board regarding some problems at DG.

Extract from the finance director's Report to the Board

'The main area for improvement, which was discussed at the last board meeting, is the need to improve profit margins throughout the business. There is no strong evidence that new products or markets are required but that the most promising area for improvement lies in better internal control practices.

Control

As DG was formed from an integration of the original businesses (F, S, H), there was little immediate effort put into optimising the control systems of these businesses. They have each evolved over time in their own way. Currently, the main method of central control that can be used to drive profit margin improvement is the budget system in each business. The budgeting method used is to take the previous year's figures and simply increment them by estimates of growth in the market that will occur over the next year. These growth estimates are obtained through a discussion between the financial managers at group level and the relevant divisional managers. The management at each division are then given these budgets by head office and their personal targets are set around achieving the relevant budget numbers.

Divisions

H and S divisions are in stable markets where the levels of demand and competition mean that sales growth is unlikely, unless by acquisition of another brand. The main engine for prospective profit growth in these divisions is through margin improvements. The managers at these divisions have been successful in previous years and generally keep to the agreed budgets. As a result, they are usually not comfortable with changing existing practices.

F is faster growing and seen as the star of the Group. However, the Group has been receiving complaints from customers about late deliveries and poor quality control of the F products. The F managers have explained that they are working hard within the budget and capital constraints imposed by the board and have expressed a desire to be less controlled.

The marketing division has only recently been set up and the intention is to run each marketing campaign as an individual project which would be charged to the division whose products are benefiting from the campaign. The managers of the manufacturing divisions are very doubtful of the value of M, as each believes that they have an existing strong reputation with their customers that does not require much additional spending on marketing. However, the board decided at the last meeting that there was scope to create and use a marketing budget effectively at DG, if its costs were carefully controlled. Similar to the other divisions, the marketing division budgets are set by taking the previous year's actual spend and adding a percentage increase. For M, the increase corresponds to the previous year's growth in group turnover.'

End of extract

At present, the finance director is harassed by the introduction of a new information system within the finance department which is straining the resources of the department. However, she needs to respond to the issues raised above at the board meeting and so is considering using different budgeting methods at DG. She has asked you, the management accountant at the Group, to do some preliminary work to help her decide whether and how to change the budget methods. The first task that she believes would be useful is to consider the use of rolling budgets. She thinks that fast-growing F may prove the easiest division in which to introduce new ideas.

F's incremental budget for the current year is given below. You can assume that cost of sales and distribution costs are variable and administrative costs are fixed.

	Q1 $000	Q2 $000	Q3 $000	Q4 $000	Total $000
Revenue	17,520	17,958	18,407	18,867	72,752
Cost of sales	9,636	9,877	10,124	10,377	40,014
Gross profit	7,884	8,081	8,283	8,490	32,738
Distribution costs	1,577	1,616	1,657	1,698	6,548
Administration costs	4,214	4,214	4,214	4,214	16,856
Operating profit	2,093	2,251	2,412	2,578	9,334

The actual figures for quarter 1 (which has just completed) are:

	$000
Revenue	17,932
Cost of sales	9,863
Gross profit	8,069
Distribution costs	1,614
Administration costs	4,214
Operating profit	2,241

On the basis of the Q1 results, sales volume growth of 3% per quarter is now expected.

The finance director has also heard you talking about bottom-up budgeting and wants you to evaluate its use at DG.

Required:

(a) Evaluate the suitability of incremental budgeting at each division.

(8 marks)

(b) Recalculate the budget for Fizzy division (F) using rolling budgeting and assess the use of rolling budgeting at F.

(8 marks)

(c) Recommend any appropriate changes to the budgeting method at the Marketing division (M), providing justifications for your choice.

(4 marks)

(d) Analyse and recommend the appropriate level of participation in budgeting at Drinks Group (DG).

(6 marks)

(Total: 26 marks)

5.5 Activity-based budgeting (ABB)

Before we look at activity-based budgeting, it is useful to review the activity based models in general.

5.5.1 Activity-based costing (ABC)

Aim: the aim of ABC is to calculate the full production cost per unit. It is an alternative to absorption costing in a modern business environment.

Reasons for the development of ABC

- Absorption costing is based on the principle that production overheads are driven by the level of production. This was true in the past when businesses tended to produce only one product or a few simple and similar products. However, a higher level of competition has resulted in the **diversity** and **complexity** of the products increasing. As a result, there are a number of different factors that drive overheads, not simply the level of production.

- Production overheads are a **larger proportion** of total costs in modern manufacturing since manufacturing has become more machine intensive and less labour intensive. Therefore, it is important that an accurate estimate is made of the production overhead per unit.

Steps in ABC

Step 1: Group production overheads into activities (cost pools), according to how they are driven.

Step 2: Identify cost drivers for each activity, i.e. what causes the activity costs to be incurred.

Step 3: Calculate an overhead absorption rate (OAR) for each activity.

Step 4: Absorb the activity costs into the product.

Step 5: Calculate the full production cost and/or the profit or loss.

The question below recaps the calculation of the full production cost per unit using traditional absorption costing and using ABC. Make sure that you understand the calculation and that you can comment on the reasons for the differences between the full production cost per unit under the two costing methods.

Test your understanding 6

Trimake makes three main products, using broadly the same production methods and equipment for each. A conventional absorption costing system is used at present, although an activity based costing (ABC) system is being considered. Details of the three products for a typical period are:

| Product | Hours per unit | | Materials per unit | Volumes |
	Labour	Machinery	$	Units
X	½	1½	20	750
Y	1½	1	12	1,250
Z	1	3	25	7,000

Direct labour costs $6 per hour and production overheads are absorbed on a machine hour basis. The rate for the period is $28 per machine hour (i.e. the OAR) and a total of 23,375 machine hours were worked.

Traditional **absorption costing** would give a full production cost per unit as follows:

	X ($)	Y ($)	Z ($)
Materials	20	12	25
Labour	3	9	6
Total direct cost	23	21	31
Production overhead @ $28 per hour	42	28	84
Total	64	49	115

Further analysis shows the total production overhead of $654,500 is not entirely driven by machine hours and can be divided as follows:

	%
Costs relating to set-ups	35
Costs relating to machinery	20
Costs relating to materials handling	15
Costs relating to inspection	30
Total production overhead	100

The following total activity volumes are associated with the product line for the period as a whole:

	Number of set-ups	Number of movements of materials	Number of inspections
Product X	75	12	150
Product Y	115	21	180
Product Z	480	87	670
Total	670	120	1,000

Required:

Calculate the cost per unit for each product using ABC principles.

Advantages and disadvantages of ABC

Advantages	Disadvantages
• Provides a more accurate cost per unit leading to better pricing, decision making and performance management.	• Limited benefit if overheads are primarily volume related or a small proportion of total costs.
• It provides a better insight into what drives overhead costs resulting in better control of costs.	• It is impossible to allocate all overheads to specific activities.
• It recognises that overhead costs are not all related to production and sales volumes.	• The choice of activities and cost drivers might be inappropriate.
• It can be applied to all overhead costs, not just production overheads.	• The benefits might not justify the costs since a large amount of data must be collected.
• It can be used just as easily in service costing as product costing.	

5.5.2 Activity based management (ABM)

Activity based management (ABM) is the use of ABC information for management purposes to improve operational and strategic decisions. Performance should improve as a result.

- By identifying the underlying drivers of activities, ABM provides an understanding of the resource implications of various courses of action and therefore **ensures that unfeasible courses of action are not taken**.
- It can assist in **re-pricing or eliminating unprofitable products**.
- It may **eliminate the need to carry out certain activities** which do not add value to the customer.
- It may identify ways to **produce a product more efficiently** by understanding what drives the costs.
- It may identify **design improvements**.
- It can assist in **improving relationships with customers and suppliers**.
- Can be used to decide which **products to develop and which strategies to pursue**.

In summary, ABM can help middle managers to make decisions that benefit the whole organisation, not just their activities' bottom line and ensure that the needs of the customer are being met.

Two types of ABM

Two types of ABM

Operational ABM
- Uses ABC information to improve efficiency
- Activities which add value to a product are indentified and improved
- Activities that don't add value to the product can be reduced to cut costs without reducing product value

Strategic ABM
- Uses ABC information to to decide which products to develop and which activities to use
- Uses ABC information to identify which customers are the most profitable and focuses more on them

Test your understanding 7

Required:

Briefly discuss the potential risks associated with ABM.

Illustration 1 – The application of ABM at DHL

In the 1990s, DHL saw its margins decreasing and used ABM to reverse this trend.

- Falling margins were mainly due to changes in product, destination and customer mixes.

- DHL concluded that they did not have sufficient visibility of margins to enable better pricing policies (and had different policies in different countries) so implemented ABC.

- A greater understanding of margins allowed DHL to design and implement a new pricing structure that was adopted worldwide.

Question practice

The question below is from the June 2013 exam and is an excellent question showing the step-up from Paper F5 to P5. Calculations may be tested but they will be used to form the basis of your decisions and will generally only be worth a small number of marks. Make sure that you attempt this question and learn from the answer. You may find it difficult to attempt a past exam question in full at this stage of your studies but it is important that you understand the level that you are expected to reach by the time you come to sit the exam.

Test your understanding 8

Navier Aerials Co (Navier) manufactures satellite dishes for receiving satellite television signals. Navier supplies the major satellite TV companies who install standard satellite dishes for their customers. The company also manufactures and installs a small number of specialised satellite dishes to individuals or businesses with specific needs resulting from poor reception in their locations.

The chief executive officer (CEO) wants to initiate a programme of cost reduction at Navier. His plan is to use activity-based management (ABM) to allocate costs more accurately and to identify non-value adding activities. The first department to be analysed is the customer care department, as it has been believed for some time that the current method of cost allocation is giving unrealistic results for the two product types.

At present, the finance director (FD) absorbs the cost of customer care into the product cost on a per unit basis using the data in table 1. He then tries to correct the problem of unrealistic costing, by making rough estimates of the costs to be allocated to each product based on the operations director's impression of the amount of work of the department. In fact, he simply adds $100 above the standard absorbed cost to the cost of a specialised dish to cover the assumed extra work involved at customer care.

The cost accountant has gathered information for the customer care department in table 2 from interviews with the finance and customer care staff. She has used this information to correctly calculate the total costs of each activity using activity-based costing in table 3. The CEO wants you, as a senior management accountant, to complete the work required for a comparison of the results of the current standard absorption costing to activity-based costing for the standard and specialised dishes.

Once this is done, the CEO wants you to consider the implications for management of the customer care process of the costs of each activity in that department. The CEO is especially interested in how this information may impact on the identification of non-valued added activities and quality management at Navier.

Navier Dishes (information for the year ending 31 March 2013)

Customer care (CC) department

Table 1: Existing costing data

	$000
Salaries	400
Computer time	165
Telephone	79
Stationery and sundries	27
Depreciation of equipment	36
	707

Note:

(1) CC cost is currently allocated to each dish based on 16,000 orders a year, where each order contains an average of 5.5 dishes.

Table 2: Activity-costing data

Activities of CC dept	Staff time	Comments
Handling enquiries and preparing quotes for potential orders	40%	relates to 35,000 enquiries/quotes per year
Receiving actual orders	10%	relates to 16,000 orders in the year
Customer credit checks	10%	done once an order is received
Supervision of orders through manufacture to delivery	15%	
Complaints handling	25%	relates to 3,200 complaints per year

Notes:

(1) Total department cost is allocated using staff time as this drives all of the other costs in the department.

(2) 90% of both enquiries and orders are for standard dishes. The remainder are for specialised dishes.

(3) Handling enquiries and preparing quotes for specialised dishes takes 20% of staff time allocated to this activity.

(4) The process for receiving an order, checking customer credit and supervision of the order is the same for both a specialised dish order and a standard dish order.

(5) 50% of the complaints received are for specialised dish orders.

(6) Each standard dish order contains an average of six dishes.

(7) Each specialised dish order contains an average of one dish.

Table 2: Activity-based costs

	Total	Standard	Specialised
	$	$	$
Handling enquiries and preparing quotes	282,800	226,240	56,560
Receiving actual orders	70,700	63,630	7,070
Customer credit checks	70,700	63,630	7,070
Supervision of order through manufacture to delivery	106,050	95,445	10,605
Complaints handling	176,750	88,375	88,375
Total	707,000	537,320	169,680

Required:

(a) Evaluate the impact of using activity-based costing, compared to the existing costing system for customer care, on the cost of both types of product.

(13 marks)

(b) Assess how the information on each activity can be used and improved upon at Navier in assisting cost reduction and quality management in the customer care department.

Note: There is no need to make comments on the different product types here.

(12 marks)

(Total: 25 marks)

Student accountant article: visit the ACCA website, www.accaglobal.com, to review the article on 'activity-based management'.

5.5.3 Activity-based budgeting (ABB)

Now that we understand the concepts of ABC and ABM, we can review the final approach to budgeting, ABB.

Activity-based budgeting (ABB) uses the principles of ABC to estimate the firm's future demand for resources and hence can help the firm to acquire these resources more efficiently.

Illustration 2 – Steps in ABB

The operating divisions of Z have in the past always used a traditional (absorption costing) approach to analysing costs into their fixed and variable components. A single measure of activity was used which, for simplicity, was the number of units produced. The new management does not accept that such a simplistic approach is appropriate for budgeting in the modern environment and has requested that the managers adopt an activity-based approach to their budgets in the future.

Required

Explain how ABB would be implemented by the operating divisions of Z.

Solution

Step 1: Estimate the production and sales volumes of individual products or customers.

Step 2: Estimate the demand for organisational activities.

Step 3: Determine the resources that are required to perform organisational activities.

Step 4: Estimate for each resource the quantity that must be supplied to meet the demand.

Step 5: Take action to adjust the capacity of resources to match the projected supply.

Advantages	Disadvantages
• ABB draws attention to the costs of 'overhead activities' which can be a large proportion of total operating costs.	• A considerable amount of time and effort might be needed to establish an ABB system. (identifying the key activities and their cost drivers).
• It recognises that it is activities that drive costs. If we can control the causes (drivers) of costs, then costs should be better managed and understood.	• ABB might not be appropriate for the organisation and its activities and cost structures.
• It provides information for the control of activity costs, by assuming that they are variable, at least in the longer-term.	• It may be difficult to identify clear individual responsibilities for activities.
• ABB can provide useful information for a total quality management (TQM) environment, by relating the cost of an activity to the level of service provided.	• It could be argued that in the short-term many overhead costs are not controllable and do not vary directly with changes in the volume of activity for the cost driver. The only cost variances to report would be fixed overhead expenditure variances for each activity.

ABB

A company has prepared an activity-based budget for its stores department. The budgeted costs are:

	Cost driver	Budgeted cost
Receiving goods	Number of deliveries	$80 per delivery
Issuing goods from store	Number of stores' requisitions	$40 per requisition
Ordering	Number of orders	$25 per order
Counting stock	Number of stock counts	$1,000 per count
Keeping records	–	$24,000 each year
Supervision	–	$30,000 each year

Activity		Actual cost
		$
Receiving goods	45 orders delivered	3,450
Issuing goods	100 requisitions	4,400
Ordering	36 orders	960
Counting	2 stock counts	1,750
Record keeping		1,900
Supervision		2,700
		_____
		15,160
		_____

Required:

Prepare a variance report for the month.

Solution:

Activity		Expected cost	Actual cost	Variance
		$	$	$
Receiving goods	45 orders delivered	3,600	3,450	150 F
Issuing goods	100 requisitions	4,000	4,400	400 A
Ordering	36 orders	900	960	60 A
Counting	2 stock counts	2,000	1,750	250 F
Record keeping		2,000	1,900	100 F
Supervision		2,500	2,700	200 A
		_____	_____	_____
		15,000	15,160	160 A
		_____	_____	_____

6 Beyond budgeting

6.1 Introduction

As mentioned previously, the aim of traditional budgeting is to provide benchmarks against which to compare actual results and develop corrective measures. However, many critics would argue that in an ever-changing business environment the use of traditional budgetary control is costly, reinforces poor working methods and discourages innovation and reactive behaviour. As a result of these criticisms, the concept of beyond budgeting has been embraced and developed by many.

6.2 Criticisms of traditional budgeting

Traditional budgets based on fixed annual periods and centrally set budgets with variances:

- encourage rigid planning and a lack of flexibility. This may not be appropriate in a fast moving business environment

- are time consuming

- encourage managers and employees to meet only the lowest target rather than attempting to beat the target set (this is inconsistent with a total quality management approach)

- encourage managers and employees to achieve the budget even if this results in undesirable action

- encourage managers and employees to spend what is in the budget, even if it is not necessary, to guard against next year's budget

- reinforce the barriers between departments rather than encourage knowledge sharing

- are seen as a mechanism for top-down control by senior management but organisations should be empowering individuals on the front-line

- ignore key drivers of shareholder value by focusing on short term financial performance

- produced inadequate variance reports leaving the 'how' and 'what' unanswered.

6.3 What is beyond budgeting?

- The beyond budgeting model rejects the traditional approach in favour of **continuous rolling plans** and a flexible system of targets designed to support the overall strategic aims of the company.

- The power to decide on these targets, and to revise forecasts to assist in cash flow planning, is **devolved downwards**, the aim being to motivate and inspire staff rather than restrict behaviour.

- Performance is measured against suitable indicators designed to **show progress towards achievement of the targets**, rather than historical variance analysis.

Traditional versus beyond budgeting

Below is a summary of the main differences between the traditional and the new beyond budgeting model as outlined by Jeremy Hope:

	Traditional Budgeting Management Model	Beyond Budgeting Management Model
Targets & rewards	Incremental targets Fixed incentives	Stretch goals Relative targets & rewards
Planning & controls	Fixed annual plans Variance controls	Continuous planning KPIs & rolling forecasts
Resource & coordination	Pre-allocated resources Central co-ordination	Resources on demand Dynamic coordination
Organisational culture	Central control Focus on managing numbers	Local control of goals/plans Focus on value creation

6.4 Advantages of beyond budgeting

- Employees will be responsible for setting appropriate targets which are linked to the strategy of the organisation and their pay will be linked to their success in achieving these. Remember, 'what gets measured gets done' but 'what gets measured and fed back gets done well' and 'what gets rewarded gets repeated'.

- Targets may be linked to external benchmarks and not past performance.

- Beyond budgeting should help to empower employees and engage them in helping the organisation to achieve its overall goals rather than simply explaining past performance.

- The beyond budgeting approach should encourage innovative solutions since flexible budgets which encourage coordination and new ideas are used as opposed to formal, restrictive budgets.

- Flexibility to respond quickly to new developments.

6.5 Suitability of beyond budgeting

- Industries where there is rapid change in the business environment and/or where the product range is innovative. Flexible targets will be responsive to change.

- Organisations using management methods such as TQM. Continuous improvement will be key.

- Organisations with skilled staff who want to be empowered.

- Organisations undergoing radical change, e.g. using business process re-engineering. Budgets may be hard to achieve in such circumstances.

Beyond budgeting in the public and private sector

Beyond budgeting in the private sector

This entails devolved managerial responsibility where power and responsibility go hand in hand.

- The focus moves from beating other managers to beating the competition.

- It motivates people giving them challenges, responsibilities and clear guidelines.

- Rewards are team based.

- Performance responsibilities are given to operational management who are closer to the action.

- It empowers managers to remove resource constraints

- Creation of open information systems throughout the organisation.

Beyond budgeting in the public sector

The greater flexibility that lies at the heart of beyond budgeting may prevent successful application of the model in the public sector.

Beyond budgeting would require a mindset which not only moves away from control but also requires a reduction in internal politics which has been at the heart of the public sector for many years.

The managers within the public sector may have the desire for flexibility but are likely to remain constrained by the inability of their organisation to change.

Student accountant article: visit the ACCA website, www.accaglobal.com, to review the article on 'beyond budgeting'.

7 Budgeting in not-for-profit organisations

7.1 Introduction

Not-for-profit organisations, NFPOs, include organisations of many different forms, for example schools and universities, social clubs, sports clubs, sports governing bodies, hospitals, museum/library/arts organisations, government organisations/local authorities and charities.

7.2 Things to consider when preparing a budget in a NFPO

- **No profit motive** – but these organisations still need to control costs.

- **Non-quantifiable benefits** – many of the benefits arising from expenditure by these bodies are non-quantifiable (certainly not in monetary terms, e.g. social welfare). So how can measurable budgets be prepared which meet the organisation's objectives?

- **No revenue generated** – often revenue is not generated and there is a fixed budget for spending within which they have to keep. 'Value for money' is often quoted as an objective here but it does not get round the problem of measuring 'value'.

- **Multiple stakeholders** – give rise to multiple objectives so there is a need to prioritise/compromise (e.g. hospital – patients, staff, government, taxpayers, local community, society at large, contractors, management, donors/contributors, etc.).

- **Objectives** – may be difficult to define, may change as a result of the political process and may be achievable in different ways.

Objectives

A further consideration is that the distinction between objectives and ways of achieving these is often misunderstood. For example, one public objective is 'to contain crime within reasonable limits'. One means of achieving that objective is to have police officers patrolling the streets on foot. In fact, police foot patrols are a very inefficient method of containing crime. The use of video surveillance cameras and police response units using fast cars is much more cost effective.

7.3 Public sector budgets

- Budgets tend to concentrate on planning for one year ahead.

- Incremental budgeting is traditionally used.

- Other budgeting approaches such as ZBB and planned programme budgeting systems (PPBS) have been used.

Planned programme budgeting system (PPBS)

- PPBS breaks work down into programmes designed towards achieving various objectives.

- Several departments may contribute towards a single programme.

- Budget targets may spread over more than one year.

- The means used to achieve programmes should be efficient and cost-effective.

Efficiency

Efficiency revolves around making the maximum possible use of a given set of resources. That is, it involves a straight comparison of output and input.

Many UK local authorities in the 1970s were judged to be making an inefficient use of the resources available to them. They undertook most of their activities (e.g. council house maintenance, road repairs, maintenance of parks and gardens, etc.) using large numbers of direct council employees. It was often found that the use of obsolete equipment and inefficient working practices (strict job demarcation was widespread) resulted in the operation involving excessive costs.

Financial management initiatives in the 1980s required local authorities to put many of their activities 'out to tender'. Private contractors may submit bids in order to undertake programmes of work for the local authorities. If the councils retain a direct works department, then that department has to bid in competition with private contractors for most available work.

The advent of executive agencies in national government is another example of this approach. Government has devolved some of its functions to agencies (e.g. the DVLA at Swansea) which are run on semi-commercial lines. The performance of these agencies is monitored using target performance indicators (e.g. the average time it takes to issue a new driving licence or the average time it takes to respond to a police enquiry concerning a vehicle).

8 Forecasting

8.1 Introduction

A number of forecasting methods were reviewed in paper F5 including:

- the hi-low method
- regression analysis
- time series analysis
- the learning curve model.

The learning curve model will be recapped below.

8.2 The learning curve effect

As workers become more familiar with the production of a new product, the average labour time (and average labour cost) per unit will decline.

Wright's Law states that as output doubles, the average time per unit falls to a fixed percentage (referred to as the learning rate) of the previous average time.

The learning curve effect can be calculated using the following formula:

$y = ax^b$

where:

y = the average time (or average cost) per unit/batch

a = time (or cost) for the first unit/batch

x = output in units/batches

b = log r/log 2 (r = rate of learning, expressed as a decimal).

The formula can be used to forecast the cost of labour but would normally be examined as part of a bigger forecasting question such as the one below.

The learning curve and the steady state

The learning effect will only apply for a certain range of production. Once the steady state is reached the direct labour hours will not reduce any further.

Test your understanding 9

BFG is investigating the financial viability of a new product, the S-pro. The S-pro is a short-life product for which a market has been identified at an agreed design specification. The product will only have a life of 12 months.

The following estimated information is available in respect of the S-pro.:

(1) Sales should be 120,000 in the year in batches of 100 units. An average selling price of $1,050 per batch of 100 units is expected.

(2) An 80% learning curve will apply for the first 700 batches after which a steady state production time will apply, with the labour time per batch after the first 700 batches being equal to the time of the 700th batch. The labour cost of the first batch was measured at $2,500. This was for 500 hours at $5 per hour.

(3) Variable overhead is estimated at $2 per labour hour.

(4) Direct material will be $500 per batch for the S-pro for the first 200 batches produced. The second 200 batches will cost 90% of the cost per batch of the first 200 batches. All batches from then on will cost 90% of the batch cost for each of the second 200 batches.

(5) S-pro will require additional space to be rented. These directly attributable fixed costs will be $15,000 per month.

A target net cash flow of $130,000 is required in order for the project to be acceptable.

Note: At the learning curve rate of 80% the learning factor (b) is equal to -0.3219.

Required:

Prepare detailed calculations to show whether S-pro will provide the target net cash flow.

Exam focus

The examiner is more likely to give you a completed or part completed forecast and ask you about flaws or assumptions.

Limitations of the learning curve model

The learning curve model on applies if:

- **there are no breaks in production**: a break in production may result in the learning effect being lost.

- **the product is new**: the introduction of a new product makes it more probable that there will be a learning effect.

- **the product is complex**: the more complex the product, the more probable that the learning effect will be significant and the longer it will take for the learning effect to reach the steady state.

- **the process is repetitive**: if the process is not repetitive, a learning effect will not be enjoyed.

- **the process is labour intensive**: the learning effect will not apply if machines limit the speed of labour.

9 Exam focus

Exam sitting	Area examined	Question number	Number of marks
June 2014	Variances, budgeting evaluation, beyond budgeting	4	25
June 2013	ABC and ABM	2	25
December 2012	Budgeting	2	25
December 2010	ABC, beyond budgeting	2	25
June 2010	ABC and ABM	4	20
June 2010	Calculation of budgeted net profit/(loss)	2(a)	7
December 2009	Preparation of budgeted and actual income statement	1(i)	10
December 2009	Beyond budgeting	2(a)	14
December 2008	ABC and ABM	5	20
June 2008	Problems with budgeting	2	24
December 2007	Forecasting	3(a)	5
December 2007	ABC	4(b)(c)	15
Pilot paper	Actual vs budget comparison	1(a)	14
Pilot paper	Uses of budgeting, ABB, beyond budgeting	5	20

Note:

- The current examiner has set the exam papers from the December 2010 sitting onwards.

- The format of the exam changed in June 2013. Section A now contains 1 × 50 mark question (previously 2 questions worth 60 marks in total) and Section B now contains a choice of 2 from 3 questions worth 25 marks each (previously a choice of 2 from 3 questions worth approximately 20 marks each).

Chapter summary

Test your understanding answers

Test your understanding 1

(a) At first sight, the costs are higher meaning the company has done worse, from a cost control angle, but then the activity level is 20% higher than planned. If all costs are variable, we would expect costs to rise in line with activity, making expected costs 20,000 x 1.2 = $24,000. In this case the company has done better than expected.

(b) The fixed costs of $10,000 will NOT rise in line with activity levels where as the variable costs of $10,000 will increase in line with activity levels. Therefore, the expected cost of the actual level of activity will be ($10,000 x 1.2) + $10,000 = $22,000. The actual cost is $23,000 so the company has spent more than expected.

Test your understanding 2

(W1) Actual patient numbers were 18.75% above budget, i.e. ((23,750 – 20,000) ÷ 20,000) × 100 = 18.75%. Therefore, budgeted variable costs should be increased by 18.75%.

Cost statements for the year ended 31 December 20X0

	Budget ($)	Actual ($)
Doctors	60 × $100,000 = 6,000,000	60 × $105,000 = 6,300,000
Nurses	150 × $37,000 = 5,550,000	150 × $34,500 = 5,175,000
Other staff costs	1.1875 (W1) × 1,440,000 = 1,710,000	1,500,000
Catering	(1.1875 (W1) × $200,000 × 70%) + ($200,000 × 30%) = 226,250	187,500
Cleaning	(1.1875 (W1) × $80,000 × 35%) + ($80,000 × 65%) = 85,250	142,000
Other operating costs	(1.1875 (W1) × $1,200,000 × 30%) + ($1,200,000 × 70%) = 1,267,500	1,050,000
Depreciation	80,000	80,000
Total costs	**14,919,000**	**14,434,500**

Test your understanding 3

The managers/researchers responsible for each project should decide which projects they wish to undertake in the forthcoming period. These projects will be a mixture of continued projects and new projects.

For the projects which have already been started and which the managers want to continue in the next period, we should ignore any cash flows already incurred (they are sunk costs), and we should look only at future costs and benefits. Similarly, for the new projects we should only look at the future costs and benefits.

Different ways of achieving the same research goals should also be investigated and the projects should go ahead only if the benefit exceeds the cost.

Once all the potential projects have been evaluated, if there are insufficient funds to undertake all the worthwhile projects, then the funds should be allocated to the best projects on the basis of a cost-benefit analysis.

ZBB is usually of a highly-subjective nature. (The costs are often reasonably certain, but usually a lot of uncertainty is attached to the estimated benefits.) This will be even more true of a research division where the researchers may have their own pet projects which they are unable to view in an objective light.

Test your understanding 4

The revised budget should incorporate 3% growth starting from the actual sales figure of Q1.

	Quarter 2 $	Quarter 3 $	Quarter 4 $
Sales	127,154	130,969	134,898

Workings

- Q2: Budget = $123,450 × 103%

- Q3: Budget = $127,154 × 103%

- Q4: Budget = $130,969 × 103%

Test your understanding 5

(a) The current method of budgeting at all divisions is incremental budgeting. The advantages of incremental budgeting are that it is simple and easy; therefore, it does not take up much time and resources in the finance department, which is constrained by the new information system implementation. It is suitable in organisations where the business is stable and so historic figures represent a solid base from which to consider small changes. The problems associated with incremental budgeting are that it consolidates existing practices into the targets and so tends to stifle innovation. As a result, inefficient and uneconomic activities will not be challenged and opportunity for cost savings may be missed. Also, managers may deliberately spend up to their budget limits in order to ensure that they get an increment from the highest possible base figure in the next budget.

At the different divisions

As S and H are stable businesses, it makes sense to continue to use incremental budgeting at these divisions. Change at these divisions may not seem necessary as it would create resistance from the divisional managers. However, incremental budgeting is not consistent with continuous improvement which may be required to reduce costs and improve profit margins in these divisions.

At F, the incremental budgets will be rapidly out of date in such a growing business. The current problems of management dissatisfaction and poor quality control may be resulting from divisional management trying to meet their targets with a budget that is not suitable for the growth occurring. They may be cutting corners to meet budget and so buying poorer materials or failing to increase capacity and so not making deliveries.

At M, incremental budgeting is intensifying complaints from the other divisions, who already see M as an unnecessary expense. Incremental budgeting is insufficiently critical of the existing spending and it can lead to unjustified increases.

(b) A rolling budget is one where the budget is kept up to date by adding another accounting period when the most recent one expires. The budget is then rerun using the new actual data as a basis. At Drinks Group, with its quarterly forecasting, this would work by adding another quarter to the budget and then rebudgeting for the next four quarters.

Rolling budgets are suitable when the business environment is changing rapidly or when the business unit needs to be tightly controlled.

KAPLAN PUBLISHING

The new budget at F would be:

	Current year Q1	Q2	Q3	Q4	Total	Next year Q1
	$000	$000	$000	$000	$000	$000
Revenue	17,932	18,470	19,024	19,595	75,021	20,183
Cost of sales	9,863	10,159	10,464	10,778	41,264	11,101
Gross profit	8,069	8,311	8,560	8,817	33,757	9,082
Distribution costs	1,614	1,662	1,712	1,764	6,752	1,817
Administration costs	4,214	4,214	4,214	4,214	16,856	4,214
Operating profit	2,241	2,435	2,634	2,839	10,149	3,051

Based on the assumptions that cost of sales and distribution costs increase in line with sales and that administration costs are fixed as in the original budget.

The budget now reflects the rapid growth of the division. Using rolling budgets like this will avoid the problem of managers trying to control costs using too small a budget and as a result, choking off the growth of the business. The rolling budgets will require additional resources as they now have to be done each quarter rather than annually but the benefits of giving management a clearer picture and more realistic targets more than outweigh this.

However, it may also be worth considering going beyond budgeting altogether in order to avoid this constraint problem.

(c) At M, as noted in part (a), incremental budgeting may not be a suitable choice of budget method. A more appropriate budgeting system for such a project-based function is zero-based budgeting (ZBB). Marketing operates around campaigns that often run for fixed periods of time and do not fit neatly into accounting periods which further undermines the use of incremental budgeting. It can be seen as a series of projects. This type of operation is best controlled by having individual budgets for each campaign that the divisional managers must justify to senior management at the start. ZBB requires each cost element to be justified, otherwise no resources are allocated. This approach would please the manufacturing divisional managers, as they will see tight control. It will not hobble M as there are few fixed overheads in marketing as it mainly involves human capital. ZBB is often used where spending is discretionary in areas such as marketing and research and development.

(d) The management style currently used at DG is top-down, budget-based with some degree of participation by divisional managers. Given the irritation being expressed by the divisional managers, the senior management could consider making the control process more participatory. This would involve shifting to more bottom-up setting of control targets. This could involve the divisions preparing budgets or else dropping budgeting altogether.

Bottom-up control involves the divisional managers at DG having an opportunity to participate in the setting of their budgets/targets. It is also known as participative control for that reason. It has the advantages of improving motivation of the divisional managers by creating a greater sense of ownership in the budget/targets. It increases the manager's understanding, which has additional benefits if personal targets are then set from the budget. Bottom-up processing frees up senior management resource as the divisional managers do more of the work. It can also improve the quality of decision making and budgeting as divisional managers are closer to their product markets.

Bottom-up control can be contrasted with top-down budgeting. A top-down budget is one that is imposed on the budget holder by the senior management. It is controlled by senior management and avoids budgets that are not in line with overall corporate objectives or that are too easily achieved.

At DG, the current approach does have involvement from the budget holders and so is participatory. This is important as the managers are set targets based on budgets, although the finance department involvement should help to avoid the issues of lack of strategic focus and slack that are noted above. The introduction of rolling budgets could be delegated to the F managers as they will be happy to take on the solution to their constraint problems. It would be wise to keep some involvement by senior finance staff in reviewing the budget – particularly, the key growth assumptions. The introduction of ZBB at M will require the involvement of budget holders as they will prepare the original proposal. These suggestions will have the advantage of encouraging innovation although it will loosen central control. Senior management will need to assess whether the managers of the stable divisions (H and S) can be relied on to drive down costs without the close oversight of the head office that is provided by a top-down approach.

Thus, some level of bottom-up budgeting fits well with both the current and future plans for financial control at Drinks Group. Although, the senior management will have to decide on the different level of central control to exercise, based on the skills of the divisional management and the degree of latitude that they require in order to improve their operations.

Test your understanding 6

(W1) Overheads

Type of overhead	%	Total overhead
		$
Set-ups	35 X 654500	229,075
Machining	30	130,900
Material's handling	15	98,175
Inspection	30	196,350
	100	654,500

Step 1: Group production overhead into activities	Step 2: Identify cost drivers for each activity
Set-ups	Number of set-ups
Machining	Number of machine hours
Material's handling	Number of movements of materials
Inspection	Number of inspections

Step 3: Calculate an OAR for each activity

Activity cost (W1)	Cost driver	OAR = activity cost ÷ cost driver
35% x 654500		
Set-ups = $229,075	670 set ups	$341.90 per set up
Machining = $130,900	23,375 machine hours	$5.60 per machine hour
Materials handling = $98,175	120 material movements	$818.13 per movement of material
Inspection = $196,350	1,000 inspections	$196.35 per inspection

1·5 x 750
1125 x 5.6

Step 4: Absorb activity costs into products

	Product X ($)	Product Y ($)	Product Z ($)	Total ($)
Set-ups	25,642.50	39,318.50	164,112.00	229,073
Machining	6,300	7,000	117,600	130,900
Materials handling	9,817.56	17,180.73	71,177.31	98,175.60
Inspection	29,452.50	35,343.00	131,554.50	196,350
Total production overhead	71,212.56	98,842.23	484,443.81	654,498.60
Production overhead per unit	**94.95**	**79.07**	**69.21**	

Step 5: Calculate the full production cost per unit

	Product X ($)	Product Y ($)	Product Z ($)
Direct costs (from question)	23.00	21.00	31.00
Production overhead (step 4)	94.95	79.07	69.21
Full production cost under ABC	**117.95**	**100.07**	**100.21**
Full production cost under absorption costing	64	49	115

ABC has resulted in a significant change in the full production cost per unit. The cost of products X and Y have approximately doubled where as the cost of product Z has decreased by approximately 13%.

Test your understanding 7

Some activities will have an implicit value which is not necessarily reflected in the financial value of the product. For example:

- A pleasant workplace can help attract/retain the best staff. A risk of operational ABM is that this activity is eliminated.

- A low value customer may open up new leads in the market. A risk of strategic ABM is that this customer is eliminated.

Test your understanding 8

(a) **Current absorption costing**

(Workings to support quantitative results are given below.)

The CC department represents an overhead to the operations at Navier. Its costs are currently allocated in a simple fashion by dividing the total departmental cost by the number of dishes to obtain a cost of customer care for each dish as $8.03. This cost will then be added to other costs (such as materials and labour used in production) to obtain a total cost per dish. This cost can then be compared to the selling price per dish in order to obtain a figure for the profit per dish.

In addition, the FD adds a further $100 per specialised dish in order to compensate for the extra work involved. However, this leads to an over-absorption of total cost since the $8.03 will absorb fully the CC costs and an additional $160,000 (1,600 specialised dishes at $100) of costs may be incorrectly absorbed.

ABC costing

The problem at Navier is that it sells two different types of dish and these products use different amounts of the company's resources. The activity-based analysis shows that the cost of customer care per standard dish is in fact lower than the current cost allocated at $6.22 per dish. This means that these dishes are making a higher profit per unit than would be given using the existing costing system. The specialised dishes are costing $106.05 each in customer care so it is vital that their price reflects this much higher cost base. The major activities that contribute to this higher cost are dealing with initial sales enquiries and handling complaints. This is not surprising, as the specialised dishes represent a bespoke service which will not be easily reduced to a standard set of steps.

Given the size of the difference between the ABC cost ($106.05) and the current initial estimate of absorbed cost ($8.03), it is not surprising that there have been efforts to correct for this difference. The finance director's estimate of $108.03 to cover the costs of customer care for the specialised dishes is fairly accurate but, of course, the addition of this extra amount should have required the cost for the standard dishes to be reduced from $8.03 in order to compensate for the allocation of more cost to the specialised dishes. It is not clear if this is being done.

The advantage of the ABC analysis is that it shows the activities that are driving the higher costs and, therefore, this analysis opens the opportunity to consider if the customers of the specialised dishes value the additional work. If not, then ABM would require the non-value adding processes be removed/reduced. A survey of customer attitudes and a comparison with competitors' service standards would shed light on the perceived value of these activities.

A question that should arise in relation to the ABC exercise undertaken here is whether it has been worth the effort, given that the finance director does appear capable of reasonably accurately estimating the costs without undertaking the time-consuming ABC analysis. Of course, the problem of over-allocation of total costs would have to be corrected in any case.

(b) The information in the workings below shows that the main cost activities of the CC department are pre-sale preparation (handling enquiries and quotes) and post-sale complaints handling. Together, these activities consume 65% of the resources of the customer care department.

The pre-sale work is essential for the organisation and the department converts 46% (16,000/35,000) of enquiries to orders. It would be beneficial to try to benchmark this ratio to competitor performance although obtaining comparable data will be difficult, due to its commercially sensitive nature.

However, the complaints handling aspect is one which would be identified as non-value adding in an activity-based management analysis. Non-value adding activities are those that do not increase the worth of the product to the customer, common examples are inspection time and idle time in manufacturing. It is usually not possible to eliminate these activities but it is often possible to minimise them. Complaints handling is not value adding as it results from failure to meet the service standards expected (and so is already included in the price paid).

Complaints handling links directly to issues of quality management at Navier as improved quality of products should reduce these costs. These costs are significant at Navier as complaint numbers are 20% (3,200/16,000) of orders. Complaints may arise in many ways and these causes need to be identified. As far as the operation of the CC department is concerned, it may cause complaints through poor work at the quotation stage where the job is improperly understood or incorrectly specified to the manufacturing or installation teams. This leads to non-conformance costs as products do not meet expected standards and, in this case, complaints imply that these are external failure costs as they have been identified by customers.

Quality of the end product could also be affected by the supervision activity and in order to ensure that this is functioning well, the CC department will need to have the authority to intervene with the work of other departments in order to correct errors – this could be a key area for prevention of faults and so might become a core quality activity (an inspection and prevention cost).

The other activities in the department are administrative and the measures of their quality will be in the financial information systems. Order processing quality would be checked by invoice disputes and credit note issuance. Credit check effectiveness would be measured by bad debt levels.

Workings:

Customer care (CC) department

Standard absorption cost per dish

	$000
Salaries	400
Computer time	165
Telephone	79
Stationery and sundries	27
Depreciation of equipment	36
	707

Total CC cost	$707,000
Number of dishes (5.5 × 16,000)	88,000
Standard absorption cost per dish	$8.03
Finance director's adjusted cost per specialised dish	$108.03

Activity-based costs

	Total $	Standard $	Specialised $
Handling enquiries and preparing quotes	282,800	226,240	56,560
Receiving actual orders	70,700	63,630	7,070
Customer credit checks	70,700	63,630	7,070
Supervision of order through manufacture to delivery	106,050	95,445	10,605
Complaints handling	176,750	88,375	88,375
Total	707,000	537,320	169,680

	Standard	Specialised
Average dishes per order	6	1
No of orders	14,400	1,600
Total number of dishes	86,400	1,600
ABC absorption cost per dish	$6.22	$106.06

Test your understanding 9

BFG net cash flow calculation

Sales units	120,000
	$
Sales revenue	1,260,000
Costs:	
Direct material (W1)	514,000
Direct labour (W2)	315,423
Variable overhead (W3)	126,169
Rent	180,000
	———————
Net cash flow	124,408
Target cash flow	130,000

The target cash flow will not be achieved.

Workings:

(W1) **Direct material**

	$
Batches	
First 200 @ $500	100,000
Second 200 @ $450	90,000
Remaining 800 @ $405	324,000
	———————
Total	514,000

(W2) **Direct labour**

$v = ax^b$

where; a = 2,500 and b = −0.3219

Total cost for first 700 batches (x = 700);

$700 \times 2.500 \times 700^{-0.3219}$	$212,423
Total cost for first 699 batches (x = 699);	
$699 \times 2.500 \times 699^{-0.3219}$	$212,217
Cost of 700th batch ($212,423 − $212,217)	$206
Total cost of final 500 batches;	
$206 × 500	$103,000
Total labour cost ($212,423 + $103,000)	$315,423

(W3) **Variable overhead**

Variable overhead is $2 per labour hour, or 40% of the direct labour cost.

Changes in business structure and management accounting

Chapter learning objectives

Upon completion of this chapter you will be able to:

- identify and discuss the particular information needs of organisations adopting a functional, divisional or network form and the implications for performance management

- assess the influence of business process re-engineering (BPR) on systems development and improvements in organisational performance

- discuss the concept of business integration and the linkages between people, operations, strategy and technology

- analyse the role that performance management systems play in business integration using models such as the value chain and McKinsey's 7S's

- identify and discuss the required changes in management accounting systems as a consequence of empowering staff to manage sectors of a business.

1 Assumed knowledge

Chapter 4 builds on your knowledge of organisational structure and the value chain from Paper P3.

2 Organisational forms

2.1 Introduction

In this paper you could be asked to:

- discuss the information needs of organisations adopting a particular structure

- discuss the implications of a particular structure for performance management.

KAPLAN PUBLISHING

2.2 Functional structure

What is a functional structure?

```
                        ┌──────────────┐
                        │   Board of   │
                        │  Directors   │
                        └──────────────┘
```

| Production | Research and development | Marketing | Personnel | Accounting and finance |

- The organisation is divided into activities or functions.

- A manager is placed in charge of each function.

- A narrow band of senior management co-ordinates the functions and retains the authority to make most of the decisions, i.e. decision making tends to be centralised.

Information needs of a functional structure

The centralised structure results in:

- Data being passed from the functional level to the upper level.

- Data is then aggregated and analysed at the upper level for planning and control purposes.

- Feedback is then given at functional level.

Test your understanding 1

Required:

Discuss ONE potential advantage and ONE disadvantage of a functional structure for performance management.

2.3 Divisional structure

What is a divisional structure?

- A divisional organisation is divided along product or geographical lines.
- Divisional structures tend to be decentralised, i.e. the divisional managers have the authority to make most of the decisions.

Information needs of a divisional structure

The decentralised structure results in:

- Information being required lower down the hierarchy.
- For example, information will be required by the divisions for budgeting purposes.

Test your understanding 2

Required:

Discuss the potential advantages and disadvantages of a divisional structure for performance management.

Note: Divisional performance appraisal will be reviewed in detail in chapter 9.

Test your understanding 3

Company A is a diversified business with strategic business units (SBUs) in very different business areas. It is organised with each SBU being a separate division.

Company B is a multinational with different parts of the supply chain in different countries. It is also divisionalised.

Required:

Comment on the differences in performance management issues for each company.

2.4 Network (virtual) structures

A **network (virtual) organisation** uses computer and telecommunications technologies to extend its capabilities by working routinely with employees or contractors located throughout the country or world. Using email, faxes, instant messages and videoconferencing, it implies a high degree of working away from the office as well as using remote facilities.

Illustration 1 – Network structures

Amazon.com

Many internet companies are examples of networks – Amazon being perhaps one of the best known on-line retailers.

- Amazon operates its website but relies on external book publishers, book warehouses, couriers and credit card companies to deliver the rest of the customer experience.

- These partners are also expected to provide Amazon with information on, for example, stock availability, delivery times, promotional material, etc.

- The customer feels that they are dealing with one organisation, not many.

Information needs of a network structure

With network structures, targeted information is needed to make decisions:

- Each party needs to have feedback as to how it is performing in relation to others.

- Those responsible for regulating the performance of the organisation will also need information for decision making to enable them to take resource allocation decisions.

- Control is normally exercised via shared goals and, in the case of inter-organisational collaborations, contractual agreements.

Test your understanding 4

The idea of the network organisation emphasises:

- the decentralisation of control
- the creation of more flexible patterns of working
- a greater empowerment of the workforce
- the displacement of hierarchy by team working
- the development of a greater sense of collective responsibility
- the creation of more collaborative relationships among co-workers.

Required:

Comment on the importance of information to such an organisation.

3 Business integration

3.1 What is business integration?

Business integration means that all aspects of the business must be aligned to secure the most efficient use of the organisation's resources so that it can achieve its objectives effectively.

Hammer and Davenport

Modern writers such as **Hammer** and **Davenport** argue that many organisations have departments and functions that try to maximise their own performance and efficiency at the expense of the whole.

Their proposed solution is twofold:

(1) Processes need to be viewed as complete entities that stretch from initial order to final delivery of a product.

(2) IT needs to be used to integrate these activities.

Four aspects in particular need to be linked.

- people
- operations
- strategy
- technology.

Test your understanding 5

Required:

XYZ has a conventional functional structure. Assess how many different people in the organisation may have to deal with customers, and the problems this creates.

There are two frameworks for understanding integrated processes and the linkages within them:

- Porter's value chain model.
- McKinsey's 7S model

3.2 Porter's value chain

The value chain is the linked set of value-creating activities from the acquisition of raw materials to the delivery of the final product to the customer.

- Margin, i.e. profit will be achieved if the customer is willing to pay more for the product/service than the sum of the costs of all the activities in the value chain.
- Value chain analysis aims to maximise margin by understanding how the value chain activities are performed and how they interact with each other.
- There are five primary activities and four support activities.

Illustration 2 – Value chain activities

Primary activity	Description	Example
Inbound logistics	Receiving, storing and handling raw material inputs	A just-in-time stock system could give a cost advantage (see chapter 12)
Operations	Transformation of raw materials into finished goods and services	Using skilled craftsmen could give a quality advantage
Outbound logistics	Storing, distributing and delivering finished goods to customers	Outsourcing activities could give a cost advantage
Marketing and sales	Market research and the marketing mix (product, price, place, promotion)	Sponsorship of a sports celebrity could enhance the image of a product
After sales service	All activities that occur after the point of sale, such as installation, training and repair	A flexible approach to customer returns could enhance a quality image
Firm infrastructure	How the firm is organised	Centralised buying could result in cost savings due to bulk discounts
Technology development	How the firm uses technology	Modern computer-controlled machinery gives greater flexibility to tailor products to meet customer specifications
Human resource management	How people contribute to competitive advantage	Employing expert buyers could enable a supermarket to purchase better wine than their competitors
Procurement	Purchasing, but not just limited to materials	Buying a building out of town could give a cost advantage over High Street competitors

Illustration 3 – Value chain

Value chain analysis helps managers to decide how individual activities might be changed to reduce costs of operation or to improve the value of the organisation's offerings. Such changes will increase margin.

For example, a clothes manufacturer may spend large amounts on:

- buying good quality raw materials (inbound logistics)
- hand-finishing garments (operations)
- building a successful brand image (marketing)
- running its own fleet of delivery trucks in order to deliver finished clothes quickly to customers (outbound logistics).

All of these should add value to the product, allowing the company to charge a premium for its clothes.

Another clothes manufacturer may:

- reduce the cost of its raw materials by buying in cheaper supplies from abroad (inbound logistics)
- making all its clothes using machinery that runs 24 hours a day (operations)
- delaying distribution until delivery trucks can be filled with garments for a particular location (outbound logistics).

All of these should enable the company to gain economies of scale and to sell clothes at a cheaper price than its rivals.

Evaluation of the value chain

Advantages of the value chain model

- Particularly useful for focusing on how each activity in the process adds to the firm's overall competitive advantage.
- Emphasises critical success factors (CSFs) within each activity and overall.
- Examines both primary activities (e.g. production) and support activities, such as HRM, which may otherwise be dismissed as overheads.
- Highlights linkages between activities.

Disadvantages of the value chain model

- It is more suited to a manufacturing environment and can be hard to apply to a service provider.

- It is intended as a quantitative analysis tool but this can be time consuming since it often requires recalibrating the system to allocate costs to individual activities.

Test your understanding 6

Many European clothing manufacturers, even those aiming at the top end of the market, outsource production to countries with lower wage costs such as Sri Lanka and China.

Required:

Comment on whether you feel this is an example of poor integration (or poor linkage in Porter's terminology).

Uses in performance management

- As well as being part of strategic analysis to identify strengths or weaknesses, the value chain can be used for ongoing performance management as targets can be set and monitored for the different activities.

- This enables the performance of the overall process to be assessed and managed.

Value system

More recently, organisations have started to consider supply chain partnerships. The value system looks at linking the value chains of suppliers and customers to that of the organisation. A firm's performance depends not only on its own value chain, but on its ability to manage the value system of which it is part.

Illustration 4

In Chapter 2 we looked at an illustration on the UK supermarket giant, Tesco and its high wastage levels of products such as bagged salads. Tesco's 'farm to fork' methodology has engaged with producers, suppliers and customers to collect data on the levels and causes of food waste and to give an overall waste 'footprint' for a selection of products. This has shown where waste 'hotspots' have occurred and has enabled Tesco to develop a waste reduction action plan and targets for each product. For example, 'display until' dates have been removed from fruit and vegetables.

3.3 McKinsey's 7s model

The **McKinsey 7S model** describes an organisation as consisting of seven interrelated internal elements.

A change in one element will have repercussions on the others. All seven elements must be aligned to ensure organisational success, e.g.:

- to determine how best to implement a strategy
- to improve organisational performance
- to examine the effects of future changes within a company
- to align departments or processes during a merger or acquisition.

McKinsey's 7S model

There are three **hard** elements of business behaviour

- Strategy – what will the company do?
- Structure – how should it be organised?
- Systems – what procedures need to be in place (few or many)?

Hard elements are easier to define or identify and management can directly influence them.

There are four **soft** elements

- Staff – what staff will we require?
- Style – what management style will work best?
- Shared values – what culture (attitudes) will be most suitable?
- Skills – what skills will our staff/company need?

Soft elements are more difficult to describe, less tangible and are more influenced by culture.

4 Business Process Re-engineering (BPR)

4.1 What is BPR?

BPR is the **fundamental rethinking and radical redesign of business processes** to achieve dramatic improvements in critical, contemporary measures of performance, such as cost, quality, service and speed. Improved customer satisfaction is often the primary aim.

Illustration 5 – IBM and BPR

Prior to re-engineering, it took IBM Credit between one and two weeks to issue credit, often losing customers during this period.

- On investigation it was found that performing the actual work only took 90 minutes. The rest of the time (more than seven days!) was spent passing the form from one department to the next.

- The solution was to replace specialists (e.g. credit checkers) with generalists – one person (a deal 'structurer') processes the entire application from beginning to end.

- Post re-engineering, the process took only minutes or hours.

Test your understanding 7

A business process is a series of activities that are linked together in order to achieve given objectives. For example, materials handling might be classed as a business process in which the separate activities are scheduling production, storing materials, processing purchase orders, inspecting materials and paying suppliers.

Required:

Suggest ways in which materials handling might be re-engineered.

Features of a re-engineered process

The following are common features of re-engineered processes:

- several jobs are combined into one
- workers make real decisions
- work is performed where it makes most sense
- checks and controls are reduced
- reconciliation processes are reduced
- a case manager provides a point of contact.

4.2 The influence of BPR on organisational performance

- Despite some success stories, e.g. at IBM and Ford, BPR became unpopular in the late 1990s due to some widely discussed failures.

- Numerous organisations have attempted to redesign their business processes but have failed to enjoy the enormous improvements in organisational performance that were promised.

- The key to realising these improvements in performance seems to be continuous learning. As problems emerge, they must be identified, analysed and communicated in order to improve the future success rate of BPR.

Advantages and disadvantages of BPR

Advantages of BPR

- BPR revolves around customer needs and helps to give an appropriate focus to the business.

- BPR provides cost advantages that assist the organisation's competitive position.

- BPR encourages a long-term strategic view of operational processes by asking radical questions about how things are done and how processes could be improved.

- BPR helps overcome the short-sighted approaches that sometimes emerge from excessive concentration on functional boundaries. By focusing on entire processes the exercise can streamline activities throughout the organisation.

- BPR can help to reduce organisational complexity by eliminating unnecessary activities.

Criticisms of BPR

- BPR was sometimes seen (incorrectly) as a means of making small improvements in existing practices. In reality, it should be a more radical approach that questions whether existing practices make any sense in their present form.

- BPR was often perceived (incorrectly) as a single, once-for-all cost-cutting exercise. In reality, it is not primarily concerned with cost cutting (though cost reductions often result), and should be regarded as on-going rather than once-for-all. This misconception often creates hostility in the minds of staff who see the exercise as a threat to their security.

- BPR requires a far-reaching and long-term commitment by management and staff. Securing this is not an easy task, and many organisations have rejected the whole idea as not worth the effort.

- In many cases business processes were not redesigned but merely automated.

- In some cases the efficiency of one department was improved at the expense of the overall process. To make BPR work requires a focus on integrated processes (as discussed above) that often involves obliterating existing processes and creating new ones.

- Some companies became so focused on improving internal processes that they failed to keep up with competitors' activities in the market.

Most companies are now more likely to talk about 'business process redesign' instead.

4.3 The influence of BPR on systems development

BPR results in more automation and greater use of IT/IS to integrate processes.

Some of the key technologies that allow fundamental shifts in business operations to occur are:

- shared database access from any location
- expert systems (a database system providing expert knowledge and advice) to devolve expertise
- powerful communication networks for remote offices
- wireless communication for on-the-spot decision making
- tracking technology for warehouses and delivery systems
- Internet services to re-engineer channels of distribution.

Another example was seen in the previous chapter with bottom-up budgeting.

5 Staff empowerment

5.1 Introduction

Empowerment is the delegation of certain aspects of business decisions to those lower down in the hierarchy.

For example, customer service staff may have the discretion to issue on-the-spot refunds or discounts.

5.2 Information needs of an empowered organisation

Characteristics of the information needs of an empowered organisation:

- There may have to be a budget for each empowered team of members of staff.

- Transparency and immediacy.

- Common definitions to allow comparison across the organisation.

- Mixture of financial and non-financial information.

- Relevant to each empowered team of members of staff.

5.3 Changes to management accounting systems as a result of staff empowerment

If staff are empowered to manage sectors of a business then typically there will need to be a number of changes in the management accounting system.

- these individuals or teams will need targeted information to make decisions

- individuals and teams will need feedback on their performance

- information must be captured and aggregated to give users further up the hierarchy a broad picture of performance.

In Chapter 2 we looked at 'the changing role of the management accountant' and said that one of the driving forces for change was technology; management information systems (MIS) have empowered employees allowing users access across the organisation to input data and run reports giving the type of analysis once only provided by the management accountant.

5.4 Staff empowerment and quality

In Chapter 12 we will look at the role of quality in performance management and the importance of quality in reducing costs, improving products and fulfilling customers' needs.

There is a strong link between quality practices and staff empowerment. Techniques such as Kaizen costing, total quality management and just-in-time rely on highly skilled and well trained staff seeking out, identifying and correcting quality problems. These techniques will be explored in more detail in Chapter 12.

6 Exam focus

Exam sitting	Area examined	Question number	Number of marks
June 2014	BPR	2(a)(b)	17
June 2013	Change in divisional structure	4(c)	9
June 2012	Performance management and measurement in complex business structures	5	17

Note:

- The current examiner has set the exam papers from the December 2010 sitting onwards.

- The format of the exam changed in June 2013. Section A now contains 1 × 50 mark question (previously 2 questions worth 60 marks in total) and Section B now contains a choice of 2 from 3 questions worth 25 marks each (previously a choice of 2 from 3 questions worth approximately 20 marks each).

Chapter summary

Test your understanding answers

Test your understanding 1

One **advantage** of a functional structure for performance management is that it is easier to control the performance of various functions due to the centralised approach taken.

One **disadvantage** of a functional structure for performance management is that it is difficult to assess the performance of individual products or markets and it is therefore unsuitable for diversified organisations.

Test your understanding 2

Advantages	Disadvantages
• Easier to assess the performance of individual products or markets. • There is clear responsibility for the performance of each division. • Performance management systems can be tailored to meet divisional needs.	• Potential loss of goal congruence. • Difficult to allocate head office costs. • Difficult to set a transfer price to fairly reflect the performance of the divisions.

Test your understanding 3

Company A

- Given that business units are in unrelated markets, there is likely to be more devolved management, with the use of divisional performance measures and reliance on the measurement systems, particularly financial reporting, for control.

Company B

- There is a need for a high level of interaction between business units, so senior management control is more important, whether in terms of standardisation or detailed operational targets.

- The performance measurement system may aid communication between managers and provide a common language.

Test your understanding 4

Information is key to a successful network organisation:

- this is mainly through the systems that facilitate co-ordination and communication, decision making and the sharing of knowledge, skills and resources

- information systems can reduce the number of levels in an organisation by providing managers with information to manage and control larger numbers of workers spread over greater distances and by giving lower-level employees more decision-making authority

- it is no longer necessary for these employees to work standard hours every day, nor work in an office or even the same country as their manager

- with the emergence of global networks, team members can collaborate closely even from distant locations

- information technology permits tight co-ordination of geographically dispersed workers across time zones and cultures

- different companies can join together to provide goods and services.

Test your understanding 5

(1) Sales staff to make the original sale.

(2) Delivery staff to arrange delivery.

(3) Accounts staff chasing up payment if invoices are overdue.

(4) Customer service staff if there is a problem with the product.

Possible problems include:

- delivery staff may be unaware of any special delivery requirements agreed by the sales staff

- accounts staff may be unaware of any special discounts offered

- aggressive credit controllers could damage sales negotiations for potential new sales

- credit controllers might not be aware of special terms offered to the client to win their business

- customers may resent having to re-explain their circumstances to each point of contact

- customer service may be unaware of the key factors in why the client bought the product and hence not prioritise buying.

Customer service could be improved by having one customer-facing point of contact.

Test your understanding 6

Firms following a cost leadership strategy have found that outsourcing to China, say, has cut costs considerably, even after taking into account distribution costs.

Differentiators have, on the whole, found that they have saved costs without compromising quality. Thus the apparent conflict between low cost production and high quality branding has not been a problem. Furthermore the perceived quality of Chinese garments is rising with some manufacturers claiming that quality is higher than in older European factories.

Note: Commercial awareness – given that many firms do it, be wary of criticising the approach too heavily! They must have their reasons.

Test your understanding 7

In the case of materials handling, the activity of processing purchase orders might be re-engineered by:

- integrating the production planning system with that of the supplier (an exercise in supply chain management (or SCM)) and thus sending purchase orders direct to the supplier without any intermediate administrative activity

- joint quality control procedures might be agreed thus avoiding the need to check incoming materials. In this manner, the cost of material procurement, receiving, holding and handling is reduced.

The impact of information technology

Chapter learning objectives

Upon completion of this chapter you will be able to:

- assess the changing accounting needs of modern service orientated businesses compared with the needs of traditional manufacturing industry

- discuss how IT systems provide the opportunity for instant access to management accounting data throughout the organisation and their potential impact on business performance

- assess how IT systems facilitate the remote input of management accounting data in an acceptable format by non-finance specialists

- explain how information systems provide instant access to previously unavailable data that can be used for benchmarking and control purposes and help improve performance (for example, through the use of enterprise resource planning systems and data warehouses)

- assess the need for businesses to continually refine and develop their management accounting and information systems if they are to maintain or improve their performance in an increasingly competitive and global market

- evaluate the compatibility of the objectives of management accounting and management accounting information

- discuss the integration of management accounting information within an overall information system, for example the use of enterprise resource planning systems

- demonstrate how the information might be used in planning and controlling activities, e.g. benchmarking against similar activities

- discuss how IT developments, e.g. unified corporate databases, RFIDs and network technology may influence management accounting systems.

1 Introduction

This chapter discusses the influence of information technology (IT) on strategic management accounting.

2 IT developments

There has been a wealth of recent IT developments. These include:

Data warehouses

A data warehouse is a:

- database: data is combined from multiple and varied sources (internal and external) into one comprehensive, secure and easily manipulated data store. A unified corporate database allows all users to access the same information.

- data extraction tool: data can be extracted from the database to meet the individual user's needs.

- a decision support system: data mining is used to analyse the data and unearth unknown patterns or correlations in data.

Illustration 1 – Influence of IT on Sainsbury plc

Sainsbury plc, the UK supermarket giant, has a data warehouse with information about purchases made by the company's eight million customers.

Transactional details are tied to specific customers through the company's Nectar loyalty programme, producing valuable information about buying habits.

Initial analysis of the information quickly showed Sainsbury's how ineffective its traditional mass-mailing approaches were – where large numbers of coupons were widely distributed in an attempt to get customers through its doors. Rather than buying more, many customers would cherry-pick the specials and go to its competitors for other items. This meant many advertising campaigns were running at a loss.

Since those initial findings, a concerted focus on timely data analysis and relevant marketing has helped Sainsbury to design far more effective direct marketing campaigns based on customers' actual purchasing habits.

In one campaign designed to increase the value of customers' shopping baskets, Sainsbury's analysed purchases and identified the product category from which each customer purchased most frequently. A coupon for that category would then be sent, along with five other coupons for areas in which it was hoping to boost sales – to encourage customers to buy other types of products. The response rate was 26%, a tremendous amount in retail.

Data mining

This is the analysis of data contained within a data warehouse to unearth relationships between them.

Illustration 2 – Data mining relationships

Data mining results may include:

- **Associations** – when one event can be correlated to another, e.g. beer purchasers buy peanuts a certain percentage of the time.

- **Sequences** – one event leading to another event, e.g. a rug purchase followed by a purchase of matching curtains.

- **Classifications** – profiles of customers who make purchases can be set up.

Networks

Most organisations connect their computers together in local area networks (LANs), enabling them to share data (e.g. via email) and to share devices such as printers. Wide area networks (WANs) are used to connect LANs together, so that computer users in one location can communicate with computer users in another location. Improvements in broadband speed and security have eased communication across sites and from home.

Intranet

This is a private network contained within an organisation. It allows company information and computing resources to be shared among employees.

Extranet

This is a private, secure extension of an Intranet. It allows the organisation to share information with suppliers, customers and other business partners.

Internet

A global system of interconnected networks carrying a vast array of information and resources.

Illustration 3 – The internet and management information

An Internet site that allows customers to place orders on-line can provide the following useful management accounting information:

Data	Use
Customer details	For delivery purposes; also to build up a record of customer interests and purchases.
Product details accessed and products bought	For delivery purposes; also to build up patterns such as products that are often bought together.
Value of products bought	Sales accounting and customer profiling.
Product details accessed but product not bought	Other items that the customer might be interested in. Why were they not bought? Has a rival got better prices?
Date of purchase	Seasonal variations; tie in with special offers and advertising campaigns.

Time of purchase	Some web-sites might be particularly busy at certain times of the day. Why that pattern? Avoid busy times when carrying out web-site maintenance.
Delivery method chosen	Most Internet sellers give a choice of delivery costs and times. Analysis of this information could help the company to increase its profits.

Enterprise resource planning system (ERPS)

- It is important that management accounting data does not exist in isolation but is part of the wider information system of the organisation.

- An ERPS is a way of integrating the data from all operations within the organisation, e.g. operations, sales and marketing, human resources and purchasing, into one single system.

- It is an accounting orientated system that helps to identify and plan the resources needed to fulfil customers' orders.

- It ensures that everyone is working off the same system aiding the data flow of information within the organisation as well as managing connections outside the organisation, e.g. with suppliers.

- It includes decision support features to assist management with decision making.

- Software companies like SAP and Oracle have specialised in the provision of ERPS across many different industries.

Test your understanding 1

Required:

Explain how the introduction of an ERPS could impact on the role of management accountants.

Radio frequency identification (RFID)

Organisations can use small radio receivers to tag items and hence to keep track of their assets. It can be used for a variety of purposes, for example:

- to track inventory to retail stores

- to tag livestock after the BSE crisis in the UK in 2002

- to track the location of doctors in a hospital.

Illustration 4 – RFID

Many clothing retailers began the phased rollout of item-level radio frequency identification (RFID) tags in 2007 following extensive testing of the technology. Stock accuracy has improved and stores and customers have commented on the more consistent availability of sizes in the pilot departments.

The tags allow staff to carry out stocktaking 20 times faster than bar code scanners by passing an RFID reader over goods. At the end of each day, stock on the shop floor will be scanned and the data collected will be compared with information in a central database containing each store's stock profile, to determine what products need to be replaced. This has led to improved sales through greater product availability.

Test your understanding 2

Required:

Discuss the impact of recent IT developments on management accounting and on business performance.

3 Compatibility of management accounting and management accounting information

Management accounting information may be used to:

- **assess the performance** of the business as a whole or of individual divisions or products

- **value inventories**

- **make future plans** – the provision of management accounting information may assist in making future business plans

- **control the business** – for example, through variance reporting

- **make decisions** – for example, through the provision of summary information (which can be used to make strategic decisions) or through the provision of more detailed information (which can be used to make tactical and operational decisions).

Management accounting involves the provision and analysis of detailed information to help managers to run the business today and in the future, i.e. they provide the management accounting information which is used in the ways detailed above. However, for this information to be useful the management accountant must ensure that it is:

- **relevant** – to the needs of the user

- **accurate and complete** – to inspire confidence in the user

- **timely** – in the right place at the right time

- **appropriately communicated** – using a suitable format and communication medium

- **cost < benefit**.

It is important that the management accountant is **available** to answer any questions that arise as a result of the provision of the management accounting information. They also need to be **flexible** in order to respond to the changing needs of the organisation.

In summary, the objectives of management accounting should be compatible with management accounting information.

4 Instant access to data

4.1 Introduction

- The information systems discussed in section 2 provide instant access to previously unavailable data. The impact on a business is as follows:
    - real time transaction processing
    - real time billing
    - real time performance monitoring.

    This information can be used by managers for benchmarking and control purposes (see below) and will allow targets and strategies to be updated on a regular basis.

- The new systems also facilitate the remote input of management accounting data in an acceptable format by non-finance specialists.

4.2 IT systems and benchmarking

Benchmarking was reviewed in Chapter 1. Instant access to data allows managers continuous access to:

- internal data so that they can see patterns, trends and changes quickly

- external data so that they can revise benchmarks quickly.

Together these ensure that decision makers have the most up-to-date information about relative performance and can act accordingly:

(1) Organisational performance compared with the performance of 'best in class' organisations.

(2) Gaps in performance identified.

(3) Methods of improving performance identified.

(4) New methods implemented.

(5) Benefits monitored and necessary control action taken.

IT systems and benchmarking: Pricechallenger.com

This site claims the following:

'Pricechallenger.com is a web-enabled solution that allows companies to benchmark, control and then substantially reduce costs.'

The data at the heart of the system is drawn from the results of thousands of real negotiations and genuine purchases – not published price lists from supplier catalogues.

Reports provide each member with straight forward benchmarks which allow them to:

- assess their own suppliers

- measure the effectiveness of their buying team

- discover where and how to find better prices – the result being savings often between 10% and 20%.

The system searches out individual savings across hundreds of product and service lines, and presents them to the buyer who gains great efficiencies by focusing on the categories with the greatest savings potential. What is more, the savings are on-going and sustainable. Through live market benchmarking there is no need to repeatedly issue tenders. Now members access benchmarking tools to sustain their buying position within the market.

4.3 IT systems and budgetary control

A **budgetary control system** compares actual financial performance to budgeted financial performance.

The elements of the control system are:

- **standard**: the budget
- **sensor**: the method of recording the actual output
- **feedback**: the actual results for the period, collected by the sensor
- **comparator**: the comparison between actual and budget (e.g. variance analysis)
- **effector**: the manager of the department, in consultation with others, takes action to minimise future adverse variances and to exploit opportunities resulting from favourable variances.

Improvements in IT systems have resulted in a more robust system of budgetary control:

Problems caused by traditional accounting systems	How a modern accounting system can address the problem
Problem 1: Delays	
For example, sales have to be recorded manually by accounting staff, analysed, posted, compared to budget, variances calculated and action effected. Typically, there could be weeks of delay before knowing whether actual results were in line with those planned.	Sales are recorded and processed in real time by non-accounting staff. Results and comparisons are continually available, certainly by the end of each day. Amended orders to suppliers can be placed quickly. There is a much closer alignment between customers' requirements and goods available.
Problem 2: Environmental impact	
From time to time, budgets need to be adjusted to stay in line with environmental developments. This can be slow and time consuming using traditional accounting.	Budgets and financial models set up on spreadsheets can be changed very quickly.
Problem 3: Incomplete measurement	
For example, traditional accounting methods rarely used activity based costing (ABC), preferring to use a simple, single overhead absorption rate – even if this did not properly reflect the cost of production.	ABC procedures can be built into modern accounting systems so that more complete and accurate measurements can be achieved.

5 Remote input of data

New data capture techniques allow **non-finance specialists** to **remotely** input **management accounting data** into an organisation's system. For example:

- Mobile sales staff can record orders using laptops or hand held computers.

- Shop floor sales staff use multi-purpose barcode scanners to collect information about what products are being bought, at what time and by which customers.

Test your understanding 3

Required:

How would equipping a mobile sales force with laptops capable of communicating accounting information to and from head office help to improve a company's profitability?

6 The need for continual systems development

Information and accounting systems need to be developed continually otherwise they will become out of date either because of advances in technology or because of environmental changes.

Test your understanding 4

Blueberry is a quoted hotel resort chain based in Europe. It is considering the use of an activity-based management approach and has identified five activity areas (cost pools) and cost drivers.

The company has recently invested in a 'state of the art' IT system which has the capability to collate all of the data necessary for budgeting in each of the activity areas.

Required:

Explain the problems that Blueberry might experience in the successful implementation of an activity-based costing system using its recently acquired 'state of the art' IT system.

Illustration 5 – The need for continual systems development

New technology, such as radio frequency identification (RFID) technology allows individual items of inventory (like individual tins of beans) to be uniquely identified and tagged.

Marks and Spencer became an early adopter of RFID in autumn 2002, using tags embedded into standard trays which transported fresh food from suppliers to depots. Their aim was to achieve high stock accuracy throughout the supply chain in a very efficient and cost-effective manner.

There are now 4.5 million trays in the Marks and Spencer's supply chain, used by 100 food suppliers. This makes 90% of its food supply RFID-compliant. The data collected is used to confirm deliveries and automate procurement four times more quickly than previous barcode scanning methods, with 100% accuracy.

Test your understanding 5

Lead times are becoming increasingly important within the clothing industry. An interesting example of a company going against the conventional wisdom is Zara International, part of the Inditex group (Spain).

- Zara produces half of its garments in-house, where as most retailers outsource all production. Although manufacturing in Spain and Portugal has a cost premium of 10 to 15%, local production means the company can react to market changes faster than the competition.

- Instead of predicting months before a season starts what women will want to wear, Zara observes what is selling and what is not and continuously adjusts what it produces on that basis. This is known as a 'design-on-demand' operating model.

- Rather than focusing on economies of scale, Zara manufactures and distributes products in small batches.

- Instead of using outside partners, Zara manages all design, warehousing, distribution, and logistics functions itself.

- The result is that Zara can design, produce, and deliver a new garment to its 600-plus stores worldwide in a mere 15 days.

KAPLAN PUBLISHING

By comparison a typical shirt manufacturer may take 30 days just to source fabric and then a further ten days to make the shirt. For some firms overall lead time could be between three and eight months from conception to shelf.

Required:

Comment on the importance of IT systems to Zara's competitive strategy.

The use of Intranets to enhance performance

HI is a large importer of cleaning products; HI has its head office situated in the centre of the capital city. This head office supports its area branches; a branch consists of an area office and a warehouse. The branches are spread geographically throughout the country; a total of seven area branches are supported.

Currently each HI area office and warehouse supports and supplies its own dealers with the required products. When stocks become low they place a Required Stock Form (RSF) with head office. On receipt of the RSF, head office despatch the goods from their central warehouse to the appropriate area office. When the central warehouse becomes low on any particular item(s) HI will raise purchase orders and send them to one of their many international suppliers.

Typically, each area office has its own stock recording system, running on locally networked personal computer systems (PCs). RSFs are e-mailed to head office.

Required:

How would the introduction of an Intranet enhance performance within HI?

Solution:

An Intranet could provide an excellent opportunity for HI to link all the areas in a number of ways: i.e. allowing access to a central database would be a substantial improvement on the current system, where updates are faxed or e-mailed to head office. This may possibly lead to the development of an integrated database system.

An automatic stock replenishment system could be introduced for the branches, replacing RSFs. If some branches were short of specific items and other branches had ample stocks, then movement between branches may be possible. Currently head office may order goods from suppliers when the organisation has sufficient stocks internally.

Dissemination of best practice throughout the organisation can be encouraged and savings in terms of printing and distributing paper based manuals, catalogues and handbooks. All the current internal documentation can easily be maintained and distributed.

The Intranet would enable the establishment of versatile and standard methods of communication throughout the company.

The Intranet could encourage group or shared development, currently several area offices have their own IT systems working independently on very similar projects.

An Intranet could also enable automatic transfer of information and data i.e. the quarterly figures could be circulated. Monthly returns of business volumes could be calculated on an as required basis.

Information can be provided to all in a user-friendly format.

7 The needs of modern service industries

7.1 Introduction

Traditional manufacturing companies have been replaced by modern service industries, e.g. insurance, management consultancy and professional services.

The differences between the products of manufacturing companies and those of service businesses:

- can create **problems in measuring and controlling performance** and
- this, in turn, **affects the information needs of service organisations**.

7.2 Characteristics of services

Five Key Characteristics

Intangibility
• The output is not a tangible product
• There is not a single measurable output e.g intangible factors such as professionalism may be difficult to value

Heterogeneity
The output differs due to:
• The high level of human intervention
• Demand for customised services

Simultaneity
The service is produced and consumed at the same time making it difficult to apply all relevant tests and checks before its use

Perishability
Refers to an inability to carry stocks of a service to cover unexpectedly high demand

No transfer of ownership
Customers can use the service for a limited period only

7.3 Measuring service quality

Service providers do not have a physical product so base competitive advantage on less tangible customer benefits such as:

- soundness of advice given

- attitude of staff

- ambience of premises

- speed of service

- flexibility/responsiveness

- consistent quality.

Test your understanding 6

Required:

State the performance measures that may be used in order to assess the surgical quality provided by a hospital indicating how each measure may be addressed.

8 Exam focus

Exam sitting	Area examined	Question number	Number of marks
December 2013	RFID	3(a)	12
June 2013	Differences between services and manufacturing organisations	1(i)	5
December 2011	Control and development of IS	3	20
June 2010	IT systems and ABC	4(a)(ii)	4
June 2010	Characteristics of services	3(iii)	8
December 2009	Measurement of service quality	5(c)	3
December 2008	Service quality	2(c)(d)	10
Pilot paper	Service quality	1(e)	6

Note:

- The current examiner has set the exam papers from the December 2010 sitting onwards.

- The format of the exam changed in June 2013. Section A now contains 1 × 50 mark question (previously 2 questions worth 60 marks in total) and Section B now contains a choice of 2 from 3 questions worth 25 marks each (previously a choice of 2 from 3 questions worth approximately 20 marks each).

Chapter summary

IT developments

Compatibility of management accounting and management accounting information

Instant access to data
- IT systems and benchmarking
- IT systems and budgetary control

The impact of information technology

Remote input of data

The need for continual systems development

The needs of modern service industries
- characteristics
- measuring service quality

Test your understanding answers

Test your understanding 1

The introduction of ERPS has the potential to have a significant impact on the work of management accountants.

- The use of ERPS causes a substantial reduction in the gathering and processing of routine information by management accountants.

- Instead of relying on management accountants to provide them with information, managers are able to access the system to obtain the information they require directly via a suitable electronic access medium.

- ERPS perform routine tasks that not so long ago were seen as an essential part of the daily routines of management accountants, for example perpetual inventory valuation. Therefore, if management accountants are not to be diminished then it is of necessity that management accountants should seek to expand their roles within their organisations.

- Management accountants may be involved in interpreting the information generated from the ERPS and to provide business support for all levels of management within an organisation.

Test your understanding 2

- IT developments, such as networks and databases, provide the opportunity for instant access to management accounting information.

- It is possible to directly access and manipulate information from both internal and external sources.

- Information is relatively cheap to collect, store and manipulate.

- Many of the modern forms of management accounting have been developed in conjunction with IT systems, e.g. it may be difficult to run a meaningful ABC system without IT support.

- Data mining techniques can be used to uncover previously unknown patterns and correlations and hence improve performance.

Test your understanding 3

The principal accounting information that will be provided by the sales force to head office will be about new sales orders. This information can be used for instant initiation of despatch/manufacture and ordering components.

The information can also be used to produce sales analyses and comparisons to budgets. If sales of certain components are lower than expected, quick decisions can be made about lowering their prices.

The principal accounting information to be provided to the sales force from head office is likely to be the latest selling prices, stock availability and customer related information, such as current balances.

Test your understanding 4

- A large amount of data will need to be collected initially on each activity. Therefore, the cost of buying, implementing and maintaining a system of activity-based costing will be high.

- Incorrect identification of cost pools and cost drivers would result in inaccurate information being produced by the ABC system and hence incorrect decisions by managers.

Test your understanding 5

IT systems are critical to Zara's short lead times.

Zara needs comprehensive information in the following areas:

- which garments are selling, at what price points and in what quantities – key information will relate to both Zara stores and those of competitors

- detailed product specifications for these garments to enable design of new products

- compatibility between reporting and design software systems

- supply chain management

- order and delivery systems.

Test your understanding 6

- The percentage of satisfied patients which could be measured by using the number of customer complaints or via a patient survey.

- The time spent waiting for non-emergency operations which could be measured by reference to the time elapsed from the date when an operation was deemed necessary until it was actually performed.

- The number of successful operations as a percentage of total operations performed which could be measured by the number of remedial operations undertaken.

- The percentage of total operations performed in accordance with agreed schedules which could be measured by reference to agreed operation schedules.

- The standards of cleanliness and hygiene maintained which could be measured by observation or by the number of cases of hospital bugs such as MRSA.

- The staff to patient ratio which could be measured by reference to personnel and patient records.

- The responsiveness of staff to requests of patients which could be measured via a patient survey.

KAPLAN PUBLISHING

6

Performance measurement systems and design

Chapter learning objectives

Upon completion of this chapter you will be able to:

- discuss, with reference to performance management, ways in which the information requirements of a management structure are affected by the features of the structure

- evaluate whether the management information systems are lean and the value of the information that they provide

- highlight the ways in which contingent (internal and external) factors influence management accounting and its design and use

- evaluate how anticipated human behaviour will influence the design of a management accounting system

- assess the impact of responsibility accounting on information requirements

- discuss the principal internal and external sources of management accounting information, their costs and limitations

- discuss those factors that need to be considered when determining the capacity and development potential of a system

- demonstrate how the type of business entity will influence the recording and processing methods

- discuss the difficulties associated with recording and processing data of a qualitative nature

- evaluate the output reports of an information system in the light of:

    (i)   best practice in presentation

    (ii) the objectives of the report/organisation

    (iii) the needs of the readers of the reports

    (iv) avoiding the problem of information overload

- discuss the problems encountered in planning, controlling and measuring performance levels, e.g. productivity, profitability, quality and service levels, in complex business structures

- discuss the impact on performance management of the use of business models involving strategic alliances, joint ventures and complex supply chain structures.

1 Assumed knowledge

This chapter builds on your knowledge of performance management information systems from Paper F5.

2 Introduction

This chapter focuses on a number of important topics with regards to performance measurement systems. These include:

- the points to consider when designing a system
- the different types of system
- the sources of information
- the control and quality of management report information.

3 Performance management information systems

3.1 Information systems at different business levels

Good decision making is at the heart of good management. A hierarchy of decision-based systems may be used:

Executive information system
(EIS): gives senior executives access to internal and external information. Information is provided in a summarised form with the option to 'drill down' to a greater level of activity

Decision support system
DSS: an aid to making decisions. The system predicts the consequences of a number of possible scenarios and the manager then uses their judgement to make the final decision

Transaction processing system
TPS: a system for processing routine business transactions, often in large volumes, e.g sales and purchase information

- **Expert systems:** hold specialist knowledge, e.g. on law and taxation, and allow non-experts to interrogate them for information, advice and recommended decisions. Can be used at **all levels** of management.

- **Management information systems (MIS):** EIS, DSS and expert systems are all types of MIS. They convert data from internal and external sources and provide information to all levels of management to enable them to make timely and effective decisions for **planning and controlling** the activities for which they are responsible.

Management information systems (MIS)

- A MIS will collate information from individual transactions recorded in the accounting system to allow middle managers to control the business.

- Customer purchases are summarised into reports to provide information about the customers and products providing the most revenue.

- The level of repeat business can be viewed giving an indication of customer satisfaction.

- Management accounts can be produced by the system showing margins for individual products and customers. This will assist in setting individual/ team rewards.

Test your understanding 1

CB publishing is considering the impact of a new system based on an integrated, single database which would support a management information system (MIS) and an executive information system (EIS). A network update would allow real time input of data.

Required:

Evaluate the potential impact of the introduction of the new system on performance management.

3.2 Lean management information systems

Introduction

A lean management information system is a specific type of MIS. The system is based on the Toyota production system whose overall goal is to get the right things in the right place at the right time. Additional aims are to minimise waste and be open to change.

Before we can fully understand the concept of lean management information systems we need to introduce the philosophy of lean production.

Lean production is a philosophy of management based on **cutting out waste** and unnecessary activities including:

- **inventory**, e.g. holding unnecessary raw material

- **waiting**, e.g. idle time

- **defective units** which need to be scrapped/ reworked

- unnecessary **effort** of people or equipment

- delays in **transportation**

- **over-processing**, i.e. unneccesary steps which do not add value

- **over-production**, i.e. ahead of demand.

Organisations can become 'lean and mean' if they get rid of their unnecessary fat. Two elements in lean manufacturing are:

- just-in-time production and purchasing (JIT)

- total quality management (TQM).

These will be reviewed in detail in chapter 12.

Application of lean to management information systems

A lean approach would aim to identify and eliminate waste in the MIS and improve the efficiency of the flow of information to users. The system should be simplified but also improved as a result.

Management should be provided with statements that are:

- instantly accessible through an IT system, and
- simple to read.

Illustration 1 – JIT and management accounting control systems

Management accounting systems within a JIT environment must be capable of producing performance and control information consistent with a JIT philosophy. Information must therefore be produced that directs management attention to the following issues:

- elimination of waste
- reduction in set-up time
- continuous improvement.

The five Ss concept

The five Ss concept is often associated with lean principles and has the aim of creating a workplace which is in order. The five Ss are:

- **Structurise** – introduce order where possible, e.g. think about optimal locations for storage.
- **Systemise** – arrange and identify items for ease of use and approach tasks systematically.
- **Sanitise** – be tidy, avoid clutter.
- **Standardise** – be consistent in the approach taken.
- **Self-discipline** – sustain by motivation. Do the above daily.

4 The influence of structure on information requirements

4.1 Introduction

In Chapter 4 we looked at the information requirements of a functional, divisional and network structure. In this section we look at the information system requirements of different business structures and the particular performance management and performance measurement problems surrounding complex business structures.

Characteristics of organisation structure	Information system
Large, complex structure.	A sophisticated system will be beneficial and cost effective.
High level of interaction between business units.	System should aid communication between managers.
Responsibility centres in place, i.e. the business is split into parts which are the responsibility of a single manager. The area of responsibility may be a cost centre, profit centre or investment centre (see chapter 9).	Management accounting systems should be designed to reflect the responsibility structure in place and ensure that costs and revenues can be traced to those responsible. Managers of responsibility centres will require: • the correct information • in the correct form • at the correct intervals.

Responsibility centres

Responsibility accounting is a system of accounting based upon the identification of individual parts of a business which are the responsibility of a single manager.

Budgetary control and responsibility accounting are inseparable.

• An organisation chart must be drawn up in order to implement a budgetary control system satisfactorily. It may even be necessary to revise the existing organisation structure before designing the system.

• The aim is to ensure that each manager has a well-defined area of responsibility and the authority to make decisions within that area, and that no parts of the organisation remain as 'grey' areas where it is uncertain who is responsible for them.

- This area of responsibility may be simply a cost centre, or it may be a profit centre (implying that the manager has control over sales revenues as well as costs) or an investment centre (implying that the manager is empowered to take decisions about capital investment for his department). Appropriate performance measures for such structures are discussed in later chapters .

- Once senior management have set up such a structure, with the degree of delegation implied, some form of responsibility accounting system is needed.

- Each centre will have its own budget, and the manager will receive control information relevant to that budget centre.

- Costs (and possibly revenue, assets and liabilities) must be traced to the person primarily responsible for taking the related decisions, and identified with the appropriate department.

- Some accountants would go as far as to advocate charging departments with costs that arise strictly as a result of decisions made by the management of those departments.

Management accounting systems should be designed to reflect the responsibility structure in place and ensure that costs and revenues can be traced to those responsible.

Controllability

The principal of controllability is very important in responsibility accounting. Whilst controllability refers mainly to costs, it is important to remember that its principles can also apply to revenues and investments.

- Controllability can depend on the time scale being considered.
  - Over a long enough time-span, most costs are controllable by someone in the organisation.
  - In the short-term some costs, such as rent, are uncontrollable even by senior managers, and certainly uncontrollable by managers lower down the organisational hierarchy.

- There may be no clear-cut distinction between controllable and non-controllable costs for a given manager, who may also be exercising control jointly with another manager.

- The aim under a responsibility accounting system will be to assign and report on the cost to the person having primary responsibility. The most effective control is thereby achieved, since immediate action can be taken.

- Some authorities would favour the alternative idea that reports should include all costs caused by a department, whether controllable or uncontrollable by the departmental manager. The idea here is that, even if he has no direct control, he might influence the manager who does have control.

Test your understanding 2

Required:

Explain why, as businesses become larger and more diverse, strict financial controls are more likely to be used by top management.

Test your understanding 3

A production manager will have control over the usage of raw materials but not over price, as buying is done by a separate department.

Responsibility accounting would suggest that the price and usage variances are separated and, under the first approach, the production manager would be told only about the usage variance, a separate report being made to the purchasing manager about the price variance.

Required:

Give an alternative argument as to why the production manager should also be told about the price variance.

4.2 Complex business structures

Complex business structures include:

- joint ventures
- strategic alliances

- multinationals
- virtual organisations
- supply chains
- divisional structures

The high level of interaction and inter-dependence between partners makes performance management and measurement difficult.

Problems associated with complex business structures

Business Structure	Problems in planning, controlling and measuring performance
Joint venture – a separate business entity whose shares are owned by two or more business entities. Useful for sharing costs, risks and expertise	• Reporting of joint profits/losses difficult if partners are unwilling to share information or do not have an integrated system • Quality, cost control and risk management difficult if partners have different opinions • Security of confidential information a concern
Strategic alliance – similar to a joint venture but a separate business entity is not formed	• Independence is retained making it difficult to put common performance measures in place and to collect and analyse management information • Security of confidential information a concern
Multinationals – have subsidiaries or operations in a number of countries	• Open to greater levels of uncertainty, e.g. due to exchange rate movements, changes in government policy, recession

Question practice with additional assistance

The question below is taken from the June 2012 exam. It is an excellent test of your ability to add depth to your answer and to use the scenario since there is only one requirement worth 17 marks.

Additional guidance has been included within both the question and the answer. Take the time to read this guidance and use the advice given when attempting future questions.

This is an excellent question to learn from. Ensure that you attempt it and take time to review the answer before sitting the exam.

Test your understanding 4

Callisto Retail (Callisto) is an on-line reseller of local craft products related to the historic culture of the country of Callistan. The business started ten years ago as a hobby of two brothers, Jeff and George. The brothers produced humorous, short video clips about Callistan which were posted on their website and became highly popular. They decided to use the website to try to sell Callistan merchandise and good initial sales made them believe that they had a viable business idea.

Callisto has gone from strength to strength and now boasts sales of $120m per annum, selling anything related to Callistan. Callisto is still very much the brothers' family business. They have gathered around themselves a number of strategic partners into what Jeff describes as a virtual company. Callisto has the core functions of video clip production, finance and supplier relationship management. The rest of the functions of the organisation (warehousing, delivery and website development) are outsourced to strategic partners.

The brothers work from their family home in the rural North of Callistan while other Callisto employees work from their homes in the surrounding villages and towns. These employees are involved in video editing, system maintenance, handling customer complaints and communication with suppliers and outsourcers regarding inventory. The employees log in to Callisto's systems via the national internet infrastructure. The outsourced functions are handled by multinational companies of good reputation who are based around the world. The brothers have always been fascinated by information technology and so they depend on email and electronic data interchange to communicate with their product suppliers and outsourcing partners.

Recently, there have been emails from regular customers of the Callisto website complaining about slow or non-delivery of orders that they have placed. George has commented that this represents a major threat to Callisto as the company operates on small profit margins, relying on volume to drive the business. He believes that sales growth will drive the profitability of the business due to its cost structure.

Jeff handles the management of outsourcing and has been reviewing the contracts that exist between Callisto and its strategic partner for warehousing and delivery, RLR Logistics. The current contract for warehousing and delivery is due for renewal in two months and currently, has the following service level agreements (SLAs):

(1) RLR agree to receive and hold inventory from Callisto's product suppliers.

(2) RLR agree to hold 14 days inventory of Callisto's products.

(3) RLR agree to despatch from their warehouse any order passed from Callisto within three working days, inventory allowing.

(4) RLR agree to deliver to customers anywhere in Callistan within two days of despatch.

Breaches in these SLAs incur financial penalties on a sliding scale depending on the number and severity of the problems. Each party to the contract collects their own data on performance and this has led to disagreements in the past over whether service levels have been achieved although no penalties have been triggered to date. The most common disagreement arises over inventory levels held by RLR with RLR claiming that it cannot be expected to deliver products that are late in arriving to inventory due to the product suppliers' production and delivery issues.

Required:

Assess the difficulties of performance measurement and performance management in complex business structures such as Callisto, especially in respect of the performance of their employees and strategic partners.

(Total: 17 marks)

Question assistance

Step 1 – Review the requirements

Assessment = is an alternative to 'evaluate' where both pros and cons are needed and final judgement on their balance is required.

Performance measurement AND performance management – so need to go further than just the measures and think about how to improve performance.

'Complex business structures such as Callisto' – what constitutes a complex business structure and how does Callisto meet this definition?

Ensure employees and strategic partners are specifically addressed.

Step 2 – Review scenario for relevant information relating to requirements

Examples here include:

- 'on-line reseller'
- 'They have gathered around themselves a number of strategic partners into what Jeff describes as a virtual company'
- 'The rest of the functions of the organisation (warehousing, delivery and website development) are outsourced to strategic partners'
- 'The employees log in to Callisto's systems via the national internet infrastructure'
- 'outsourced functions are handled by multinational companies of good reputation'
- 'so they depend on email and electronic data interchange to communicate with their product suppliers and outsourcing partners'
- 'complaining about slow or non-delivery of orders'
- 'the company operates on small profit margins'
- 'The current contract for warehousing and delivery is due for renewal in two months'
- 'Each party to the contract collects their own data on performance and this has led to disagreements in the past'.

Step 3 – Plan the answer

You need to plan your answer identifying sufficient points for each part of the requirement. Use headings to structure your plan – this will help you keep focused when you write your answer

Difficulties for Performance Measurement

- Employees
- Strategic partners

Difficulties for Performance Management

- Employees
- Strategic partners

For each heading you need to be identifying the difficulties for a virtual organisation (the 'textbook' answer) and combine this with relevant examples and information regarding Callisto. Both of these elements are essential for your answer otherwise you are either just describing the scenario or merely repeating textbook content.

Step 4 – Check requirements

Quick recap of requirements – have you covered everything?

Step 5 – Write your answer

Use space, headings and short paragraphs to clearly signpost to the marker that you have covered all the necessary parts. If you have planned properly this will be the easiest part of the whole question!

5 Sources of management information

5.1 Introduction

Managers need information for planning and decision making and in order to manage and control their organisations effectively. In addition, as mentioned earlier on in the chapter, information requirements will vary according to the type of decision being made. As a result, managers will need a range of **internal and external information**.

5.2 Internal sources

Internal sources of information may be taken from a variety of areas such as the sales ledger (e.g. volume of sales), payroll system (e.g. number of employees) or the fixed asset system (e.g. depreciation method and rate).

Examples of internal sources of information	

Examples of internal data:

Source	Information
Sales ledger system	Number and value of invoices Volume of sales Value of sales, analysed by customer Value of sales, analysed by product
Purchase ledger system	Number and value of invoices Value of purchases, analysed by supplier
Payroll system	Number of employees Hours worked Output achieved Wages earned Tax deducted

Fixed asset system	Date of purchase Initial cost Location Depreciation method and rate Service history Production capacity
Production	Machine breakdown times Number of rejected units
Sales and marketing	Types of customer Market research results

5.3 External sources

In addition to internal information sources, there is much information to be obtained from external sources such as suppliers (e.g. product prices), customers (e.g. price sensitivity) and the government (e.g. inflation rate).

Examples of external sources of information

External source	Information
Suppliers	Product prices Product specifications
Newspapers, journals	Share price Information on competitors Technological developments National and market surveys
Government	Industry statistics Taxation policy Inflation rates Demographic statistics Forecasts for economic growth
Customers	Product requirements Price sensitivity
Employees	Wage demands Working conditions
Banks	Information on potential customers Information on national markets
Business enquiry agents	Information on competitors Information on customers
Internet	Almost everything via databases (public and private), discussion groups and mailing lists

Test your understanding 5

Required:

What are the limitations of using externally generated information?

5.4 Use of internal and external information in performance management

The internal and external information may be used in **planning** and **controlling** activities. For example:

*   Newspapers, the Internet and business enquiry agents (such as Dun and Bradstreet) may be used to obtain external competitor information for benchmarking purposes.

*   Internal sales volumes may be obtained for variance analysis purposes.

Test your understanding 6

Required:

Briefly explain the use of customer data for control purposes.

5.5 The costs of internal and external information

The benefit of management information must exceed the cost (**benefit > cost**) of obtaining the information.

Benefits and costs of information

The design of management information systems should involve a cost/benefit analysis. A very refined system offers many benefits, but at a cost. The advent of modern IT systems has reduced that cost significantly. However, skilled staff have to be involved in the operation of information systems, and they can be very expensive to hire.

Let us illustrate this with a simple example. Production costs in a factory can be reported with varying levels of frequency ranging from daily (365 times per year) to annually (once per year). Costs or benefits of reporting tend to move as follows in response to increasing frequency of reporting.

- Information has to be gathered, collated and reported in proportion to frequency and costs will move in line with this. Experience suggests that some element of diseconomy of scale may set in at high levels of frequency.

- Initially, benefits increase sharply, but this increase starts to tail off. A point may come where 'information overload' sets in and benefits actually start to decline and even become negative. If managers are overwhelmed with information, then this actually starts to get in the way of the job.

The position may be represented graphically as follows:

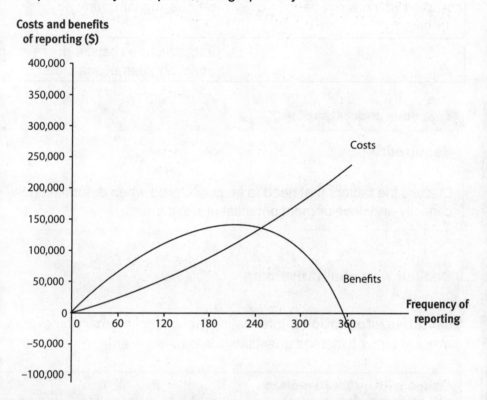

An information system is just like any part of a business operation. It incurs costs and it offers benefits. In designing an information system, the accountant has to find some means of comparing the two for different options and determining which option is optimal. In this sense, system design follows the same practices for investment appraisal and decision making which are explored later in this text.

In the above case it can be seen that net benefits (benefits less costs) are maximised at around 120 reports per year – suggesting an optimal information cycle of about 3 days. The system should be designed to gather, collate and report information at three-day intervals. This is an over-simplified example but it serves to illustrate a general logic which can be applied to all aspects of information system design.

The costs of information can be classified as follows:

Costs of internal information	Costs of external information
Direct data capture costs, e.g. the cost of barcode scanners in a supermarket.	Direct costs, e.g. newspaper subscriptions.
Processing costs, e.g. salaries paid to payroll processing staff.	Indirect costs, e.g. wasted time finding useful information.
Indirect costs, e.g. information collected which is not needed or is duplicated.	Management costs, e.g. the cost of processing information.
	Infrastructure costs, e.g. of systems enabling Internet searches.

Test your understanding 7

Required:

Discuss the factors that need to be considered when determining the capacity and development potential of a system.

6 Dealing with qualitative data

Qualitative information is information that cannot normally be expressed in numerical terms (whereas quantitative information can).

Issues with qualitative data

In both decision making and control, managers should be aware that an information system may provide a limited or distorted picture of what is actually happening. In many situations, sensitivity has to be used in interpreting the output of an information system.

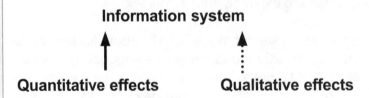

Information system

Quantitative effects   **Qualitative effects**

It is worth noting that as many economies move from being manufacturing based to service based there may be fewer opportunities to use quantitative measures and that qualitative measures become more important.

Qualitative information is often in the form of opinions, for example:

- **employees** – who will be affected by certain decisions which may threaten their continued employment, or cause them to need re-training

- **customers** – who will be interested to know about new products, but will want to be assured that service arrangements, etc. will continue for existing products

- **suppliers** – who will want to be aware of the entity's plans, e.g a move to a just-in-time (JIT) environment.

It is difficult to record and process data of a qualitative nature but qualitative factors still need to be considered when making a decision. These include:

- **The effects on the environment**: certain decisions may affect emissions and pollution of the environment. The green issue and the entity's responsibility towards the environment may seriously affect its public image.

- **Legal effects**: there may be legal implications of a course of action, or a change in law may have been the cause of the decision requirement.

- **Political effects**: government policies, in both taxation and other matters, may impinge on the decision.

- **Timing of decision**: the timing of a new product launch may be crucial to its success.

These factors must be considered before making a final decision. Each of these factors is likely to be measured by opinion. Such opinions must be collected and co-ordinated into meaningful information.

> ### Illustration 2 – Dealing with qualitative data
>
> Here are some examples of qualitative effects.
>
> - The impact of a decreased output requirement on staff morale is something that may be critical but it is not something that an information system would automatically report.
>
> - The impact of a reduction in product range may have a subtle impact on the image that a business enjoys in the market – again something that an information system may not report.

Test your understanding 8

Information and Investment

Moffat commenced trading on 01/12/X2, it supplies and fits tyres and exhaust pipes and services motor vehicles at thirty locations. The directors and middle management are based at the Head Office of Moffat.

Each location has a manager who is responsible for day-to-day operations and is supported by an administrative assistant. All other staff at each location are involved in the fitting and servicing operations.

The directors of Moffat are currently preparing a financial evaluation of an investment of $2 million in a new IT system for submission to its bank. They are concerned that sub-optimal decisions are being made because the current system does not provide appropriate information throughout the organisation. They are also aware that not all of the benefits from the proposed investment will be quantitative in nature.

Required:

(a) Explain the characteristics of **three** types of information required to assist in decision-making at different levels of management and on differing timescales within Moffat, providing two examples of information that would be appropriate to each level.

(b) Identify and explain **three** approaches that the directors of Moffat might apply in assessing the **qualitative** benefits of the proposed investment in a new IT system.

(c) Identify **two qualitative** benefits that might arise as a consequence of the investment in a new IT system and explain how you would attempt to assess them.

7 Output reports

The output reports (performance reports) produced for management should contain good information.

Qualities of output reports

The output reports from an information system should allow the organisation to run the business effectively both today and in the future. Output reports should have the following characteristics:

Characteristic	Explanation
Accurate	For example, figures should add up and there should be no typos.
Complete	The reports should include all the information that is needed by the readers of the report and should be aligned to the overall objectives of the report or of the organisation.
Cost < benefit	The benefit of having the information must be greater than the cost of providing it.
Understandable	The readers of the report must be able to understand the contents and use the contents to fulfil their needs. Presentation should be clear and in line with best practice.

Relevant	Information that is not needed by the reader(s) of the report should be omitted. Information overload can be a huge problem and can detract from the usefulness of the report. The problem of information overload may be overcome using, for example, drill-down reports (provide users with the capability to look at increasingly detailed information about a particular item) and exception reports (which are only triggered when a situation is unusual or requires management action).
Adaptable	The output reports should have the capability of being adapted to meet the needs of the user or the organisation.
Timely	The information should be provided when needed and should not be provided too frequently (this can result in information overload and the cost of providing the information exceeding the benefit).
Easy to use	Information should be presented in a form recommended by the industry or organisation's best practice. It should not be too long (to prevent information overload) and it should be sent using the most appropriate communication channel to ensure user needs are met.

Test your understanding 9

Required:

Discuss the weaknesses in an information system that could result in poor output reports.

Question practice

The question below is an extract from the June 2012 exam. Take the time to complete and review this question. It will help to give you a broader understanding of some of the areas covered above.

Test your understanding 10

Metis is a restaurant business in the city of Urbanton. Metis was started three years ago by three friends who met at university while doing courses in business and catering management. Initially, their aim was simply to 'make money' although they had talked about building a chain of restaurants if the first site was successful.

The three friends pooled their own capital and took out a loan from the Grand Bank in order to fit out a rented site in the city. They designed the restaurant to be light and open with a menu that reflected the most popular dishes in Urbanton regardless of any particular culinary style. The dishes were designed to be priced in the middle of the range that was common for restaurants in the city. The choice of food and drinks to offer to customers is still a group decision amongst the owners.

Other elements of the business were allocated according to each owner's qualifications and preferences. Bert Fish takes charge of all aspects of the kitchen operations while another, Sheila Plate, manages the activities in the public area such as taking reservations, serving tables and maintaining the appearance of the restaurant. The third founder, John Sum, deals with the overall business issues such as procurement, accounting and legal matters.

Competition in the restaurant business is fierce as it is easy to open a restaurant in Urbanton and there are many competitors in the city both small, single-site operations and large national chains. The current national economic environment is one of steady but unspectacular growth.

The restaurant has been running for three years and the founders have reached the point where the business seems to be profitable and self-sustaining. The restaurant is now in need of refurbishment in order to maintain its atmosphere and this has prompted the founders to consider the future of their business. John Sum has come to you as their accountant looking for advice on aspects of performance management in the business. He has supplied you with figures outlining the recent performance of the business and the forecasts for the next year (see the performance report below). This table represents the quantitative data that is available to the founders when they meet each quarter to plan any short-term projects or initiatives and also, to consider the longer-term future. Bert and Sheila have often indicated to John that they find the information daunting and difficult to understand fully.

Metis Performance Report

	Year to 31 March					
	Actual 2010 ($)	Actual 2011 ($)	Actual 2012 ($)	Forecast 2013 ($)	Latest quarter to 31 March 2012 (Q4 2012) ($)	Previous quarter (Q3 2012) ($)
Revenue						
Food	617,198	878,220	974,610	1,062,180	185,176	321,621
Wine	127,358	181,220	201,110	219,180	38,211	66,366
Spirits	83,273	118,490	131,495	143,310	24,984	43,394
Beer	117,562	167,280	185,640	202,320	35,272	61,261
Other beverages	24,292	34,850	38,675	42,150	7,348	12,763
Outside catering	9,797	13,940	15,470	16,860	2,939	5,105
Total	979,680	1,394,000	1,547,000	1,686,000	293,930	510,510
Cost of sales						
Food	200,589	284,422	316,748	345,209	60,182	104,527
Wine	58,585	83,361	92,511	100,821	17,577	30,528
Spirits	21,651	30,807	34,189	37,261	6,496	11,283
Beer	44,673	63,566	70,543	76,882	13,403	23,279
Other beverages	3,674	5,228	5,801	6,323	1,102	1,914
Outside catering	3,135	4,461	4,950	5,395	941	1,634
Total	332,307	472,845	524,742	571,891	99,701	173,165
Gross profit	647,373	921,155	1,022,258	1,114,109	194,229	337,345
Staff costs	220,428	313,650	348,075	379,350	66,134	114,865
Other operating costs						
Marketing	25,000	10,000	12,000	20,000	3,000	3,000
Rent/ mortgage	150,800	175,800	175,800	193,400	43,950	43,950
Local property tax	37,500	37,500	37,500	37,500	9,375	9,375
Insurance	5,345	5,585	5,837	6,100	1,459	1,459
Utilities	12,600	12,978	13,043	13,173	3,261	3,261

Waste removal	6,000	6,180	6,365	6,556	1,591	1,591
Equipment repairs	3,500	3,658	3,822	3,994	956	956
Depreciation	120,000	120,000	120,000	120,000	30,000	30,000
Building upgrades				150,000		
Total	360,745	371,701	374,367	550,723	93,592	93,592
Manager salary	35,000	36,225	37,494	38,806	9,373	9,373
Net profit/ loss before interest and corporate taxes	31,200	199,579	262,322	145,230	25,130	119,515
Net margin	3.2%	14.3%	17.0%	8.6%	8.5%	23.4%

Required:

Critically assess the existing performance report and suggest improvements to its content and presentation.

(12 marks)

8 Exam focus

Exam sitting	Area examined	Question number	Number of marks
June 2014	Evaluation of performance report	1(i)	15
June 2014	Complex business structures	3(c)	8
December 2013	Lean management and accountability	3(b)(c)	13
June 2013	Evaluation of strategic performance report	1(ii)	8
June 2012	Assessment of performance report	1(i)	12
June 2012	Complex business structures	5	17
December 2011	Suitability of branch information given	4(a)	8
June 2011	EIS	1(c)	5
December 2010	Impact of KPIs on system design	1(d)	9

Note:

- The current examiner has set the exam papers from the December 2010 sitting onwards.

- The format of the exam changed in June 2013. Section A now contains 1 × 50 mark question (previously 2 questions worth 60 marks in total) and Section B now contains a choice of 2 from 3 questions worth 25 marks each (previously a choice of 2 from 3 questions worth approximately 20 marks each).

KAPLAN PUBLISHING

Chapter summary

```
                    ┌─────────────────────┐
                    │ The influence of    │
                    │ structure on        │
                    │ information         │   ┌─────────────────────┐
   ┌──────────────┐ │ requirements        │   │ Sources of          │
   │ Performance  │ │ • different         │   │ management          │
   │ management   │ │   information       │   │ information         │
   │ information  │ │   requirements      │   │ • internal sources  │
   │ systems      │ │ • complex business  │   │ • external sources  │
   │ • IS at      │ │   structures        │   │ • use in performance│
   │   different  │ └─────────────────────┘   │   management        │
   │   business   │                           │ • cost              │
   │   levels     │                           └─────────────────────┘
   │ • lean MIS   │
   └──────────────┘
```

Performance management information systems
- IS at different business levels
- lean MIS

The influence of structure on information requirements
- different information requirements
- complex business structures

Sources of management information
- internal sources
- external sources
- use in performance management
- cost

Performance measurement systems and design

Dealing with qualitative data

Output reports

Test your understanding answers

Test your understanding 1

Advantages	Disadvantages
• Benefit of real time data input and access. • Improved decision making, e.g. the EIS should allow drill-down access of data to operational level but presentation of data should be based on the KPIs of the company. • The EIS will link to external data sources thus reducing the risk of ignoring issues from the wider environment. • The database will reduce/eliminate the problem of data redundancy since data is only held in one place. • Improved data integrity. Data is only held in one place and therefore time and effort will be taken to ensure it is 'ACCURATE'.	• Cost of real time data input. • Cost of linking the EIS to new, external data sources. • Cost of implementation and training. • Risk that the system does not work properly or that training is inadequate. • Increased security threat since the data is only held in one place. • Potential information overload, especially for senior managers.

Test your understanding 2

As businesses become larger and more diverse, it becomes more difficult for top management to control them in any way other than by strict financial controls. The diversity of information and complexity is simply too great. Targets on profitability, return on investment and residual income are easy to set and monitor without knowing much about the details of business activities.

If there is high diversity, then sub-units are largely independent of one another so that each can be judged fairly in isolation, i.e. poor performance in one division should have no effect on another.

Test your understanding 3

With additional information the production manager may attempt to persuade the purchasing manager to try alternative sources of supply.

Test your understanding 4

Tutor tip: Splitting your answer into the measurement and management sections is a good start. You can break it down further by separating employees, strategic partners and other issues.

Performance measurement problems at Callisto

In a virtual organisation such as Callisto, performance measurement can be difficult due to the fact that key players in the business processes and in the supply chain are not 'on site'. Callisto has the problem of collecting and monitoring data about its employees working from home and the outsourcing partners.

Tutor tip: This identifies the key issue relating to the 'virtual' nature of a company like Callisto.

At Callisto, there is a reliance placed on information technology for handling these remote contacts. Collecting and monitoring performance should therefore be done automatically as far as possible. A large database would be required that can be automatically updated from the activities of the remote staff and suppliers. This will require the staff and supplier systems to be compatible.

Tutor tip: Another specific issue relating to virtual organisations that has been linked to information regarding Callisto. This paragraph goes further than just identifying the issue and explains the implications.

Employees

The employees can be required to use software supplied by Callisto and in fact, at Callisto, they use the internet to log in remotely to Callisto's common systems. Although this solution requires expenditure on hardware and software, it is within the control of Callisto's management.

Tutor tip: Part of 'assessing' the difficulty may involve explaining why it is not too much of an issue – so here identifying the fact that Callisto still have control over their employees.

Even with reviews of system logs to identify the hours that staff spend logged in to the systems, there are still the difficulty of measuring staff outputs in order to ensure their productivity. These outputs must be clearly defined by Callisto's managers, otherwise there will be disputes between staff and management.

> **Tutor tip:** *Again, the implication of the problem has been described.*

One further outstanding issue is the need to ensure that such communication is over properly secured communication channels, especially if it contains customer or financial data. There are likely to be significant penalties if data protection regulations are breached, not to mention the reputational impact.

Strategic partners

The strategic partners, such as RLR, will have their own systems. A problem for Callisto is that there is disagreement over the measurement of the key SLAs. In order to resolve such disputes, lengthy reconciliations between Callisto's and RLR's systems will have to be undertaken otherwise there are no grounds for enforcement of the SLAs and the SLAs represent Callisto's key control over the relationship.

> **Tutor tip:** *The implication has been explained with specific reference to information in the scenario. This ensures your answer is not just a generic 'textbook' answer.*

The solution would be for the partners to agree a standard reporting format for all data that relates to the SLAs which would remove the need for such reconciliations

> **Tutor tip:** *Part of 'assessing' a difficulty may involve thinking about how it can be resolved.*

Finally, there is the problem that Callisto and the partner organisation may have differing objectives – the obvious conflict over price between supplier and customer being one. However, at Callisto, this is being addressed by the use of detailed SLAs which both organisations can use to develop performance measures such as inventory levels and delivery times.

Performance management problems at Callisto

> **Tutor tip:** *Performance management goes a step further than merely measuring output and considers how improvements can be made.*

Employees

The performance management of employees is complicated due to the inability of management to 'look over their shoulder' since they are not present in the same building. However, employees will enjoy the advantages of home-working, such as lower commuting times, more contact with family and greater flexibility in working hours. The disadvantages are the difficulties in measuring outputs mentioned above and ensuring motivation and commitment.

Tutor tip: This nicely combines an identification of the problem, the implications of the problem along with an upside to the situation.

This nicely combines an identification of the problem, the implications of the problem along with an upside to the situation.

Tutor tip: Further assessment of the problem considers the possible solutions.

Strategic partners

When managing the performance of the strategic partners it is crucial that there is a balance between consideration of security and control issues and encouraging a positive and collaborative relationship.

Tutor tip: This introduces the difficulty faced regarding performance management of strategic partners.

One difficulty which may arise concerns confidentiality as the partners will have access to commercially sensitive information about customers' locations and suppliers' names and lead times. Callisto must control access to this information without affecting the relationship. Leakage of such data will have a detrimental effect on the company's reputation. However interface between the organisations can create wasteful activity if there is not an atmosphere of trust. At Callisto, this is illustrated by the problem of reconciliation of performance data.

Tutor tip: The problem is further explained and the possible implications considered.

It is also important to consider reliability where the partner is supplying a business critical role (as for RLR with Callisto) such that it would take considerable time to replace such a relationship and affect customer service while this happened.

Finally Callisto must carefully consider profit sharing. The collaborative nature of the relationship and the difficulty of breaking it combine to imply that it will be in the interest of both parties to negotiate a contract that is motivating and profitable for both sides. For Callisto, the business aim is to increase volume and this will require customer loyalty so the quality of service is important.

Tutor tip: The 'difficulty' identified here is how to determine the appropriate split of profit between Callisto and its partners.

Test your understanding 5

- External information may not be accurate.

- External information may be out of date.

- The company publishing the data may not be reputable.

- External information may not meet the exact needs of the business.

- It may be difficult to gather external information, e.g. from customers or competitors.

Test your understanding 6

Historical customer data will give information about:

- product purchases and preferences

- price sensitivity

- where customers shop

- who customers are (customer profiling).

For a business that prioritises customer satisfaction this will give important control information. Actual customer data can be compared with plans and control action can be taken as necessary, e.g. prices may be changed or the product mix may be changed.

Test your understanding 7

An information system can be developed to varying levels of refinement. Specifically:

- **Reporting frequency** – information can be collected and reported with varying levels of frequency, e.g. for example, the management accounting system of a manufacturer can report actual production costs on a daily, weekly, monthly or even annual basis

- **Reporting quantity and level of detail** – information can be collected and reported at varying levels of detail e.g. in absorbing overheads into product costs one can use a single factory overhead absorption rate (OAR) or one can operate a complex ABC system. The information requirements of the latter are far more elaborate than those of the former

- **Reporting accuracy and back-up** – subtle qualitative factors can be incorporated into information systems at varying levels, e.g. information can be rigorously checked for accuracy or a more relaxed approach can be adopted.

Broadly, **the more refined the system** is, then **the more expensive it is** to establish and operate. The organisation has to decide if the increased benefits outweigh the increased costs.

Test your understanding 8

Information and Investment – Moffat

(a) The management of an organisation need to exercise control at different levels within an organisation. These levels are often categorised as being strategic, tactical and operational. The information required by management at these levels varies in nature and content.

Strategic information

Strategic information is required by the management of an organisation in order to enable management to take a longer term view of the business and assess how the business may perform during the period. The length of this long term view will vary from one organisation to another, being very much dependent upon the nature of the business and the ability of those responsible for strategic decisions to be able to scan the planning horizon.

Strategic information tends to be holistic and summary in nature and would be used by management, when for example, undertaking SWOT analysis.

In Moffat strategic information might relate to the development of new services such as the provision of a home-based vehicle recovery service or the provision of 24hr servicing. Other examples would relate to the threats posed by Moffat's competitors or assessing the potential acquisition of a tyre manufacturer in order to enhance customer value via improved efficiency and lower costs.

Tactical information

Tactical Information is required in order to facilitate management planning and control for shorter time periods than strategic information. Such information relates to the tactics that management adopt in order to achieve a specific course of action. In Moffat this might involve the consideration of whether to open an additional outlet in another part of the country or whether to employ additional supervisors at each outlet in order to improve the quality of service provision to its customers.

Operational information

Operational information relates to a very short time scale and is often used to determine immediate actions by those responsible for day-to-day management.

In Moffat the manager at each location within Moffat would require information relating to the level of customer sales, the number of vehicles serviced and the number of complaints received during a week. Operational information might be used within Moffat in order to determine whether staff are required to work overtime due to an unanticipated increase in demand, or whether operatives require further training due to excessive time being spent on servicing certain types of vehicle.

(b) One approach that the directors of Moffat could adopt would be to **ignore the qualitative benefits** that may arise on the basis that there is too much subjectivity involved in their assessment.

The problem that this causes is that the investment will probably look unattractive since all the costs will be included in the valuation where as significant benefits and savings will have been ignored. This approach lacks substance and would not be recommended.

An alternative approach would involve **attempting to attribute values to each of the identified benefits that are qualitative in nature**. Such an approach will necessitate the use of management estimates in order to derive the cash flows to be incorporated in a cost benefit analysis. The problems inherent in this approach include gaining consensus amongst interested parties regarding the footing of the assumptions from which estimated cash flows have been derived. Furthermore, if the proposed investment does take place then it may well prove impossible to prove that the claimed benefits of the new system have actually been realised.

Perhaps the preferred approach is to **acknowledge the existence of qualitative benefits and attempt to assess them in a reasonable manner acceptable to all parties including the company's bank**. The financial evaluation would then not only incorporate 'hard' facts relating to costs and benefits that are qualitative in nature, but also would include details of qualitative benefits which management consider exist but have not attempted to assess in financial terms. Such benefits might include, for example, the average time saved by location managers in analysing information during each operating period.

Alternatively, the management of Moffat could attempt to express qualitative benefits in specific terms linked to a hierarchy of organisational requirements.

For example, qualitative benefits could be catergorised as being:

(1) Essential to the business

(2) Very useful attributes

(3) Desirable, but not essential

(4) Possible, if funding is available

(5) Doubtful and difficult to justify

(c) One of the main qualitative benefits that may arise from an investment in a new IT system by Moffat is the **improved level of service to its customers in the form of reduced waiting times** which may arise as a consequence of better scheduling of appointments and inventory management. This could be assessed via the introduction of a questionnaire requiring customers to rate the service that they have received from their recent visit to a location within Moffat according to specific criteria such as adherence to appointed times, time taken to service a vehicle, cleanliness of the vehicle and attitude of staff.

Alternatively a follow-up telephone call from a centralised customer services department may be made by Moffat personnel in order to gather such information.

Another qualitative benefit may arise in the form of competitive advantage. **Improvement in customer specific information and service levels may give Moffat a competitive advantage**.

Likewise **improved inventory management may enable costs to be reduced** thereby enabling a 'win-win' relationship to be enjoyed with customers.

Test your understanding 9

- **Unreliable information**: Information must be sufficiently reliable (e.g. accurate and complete) so that managers trust it to make judgements and decisions.

- **Presentation**: The information system may not be capable of presenting the information in a user-friendly format.

- **Appropriate information**: The information produced by the system should assist in meeting the organisation's objectives and should meet the needs of the users.

- **Timeliness**: Information must be available in time for managers to use it to make decisions.

- **Responsibility and controllability**: Information systems might fail to identify controllable costs, or indicate management responsibility properly. Information should be directed to the person who has the authority and the ability to act on it.

- **Information overload:** In some cases, managers might be provided with too much information, and the key information might be lost in the middle of large amounts of relatively unimportant figures.

- **Cost and value**: The cost of providing the information should not exceed the benefits obtained.

Test your understanding 10

Current performance report

The existing performance report has some good elements and many weaknesses. The current report shows clearly the calculation of profit and the profit margin from the business and shows how this has changed over the past three years along with a forecast of the next year. There is also a breakdown of the performance in the last two quarters which gives a snapshot of more immediate performance. The report breaks revenue and costs into product categories and so might allow a review of selling and procurement activities.

However, there are a number of weaknesses with the existing report. Firstly, the report only clearly answers the question 'what was the profit?' The owners have indicated that their aim is to 'make money' and it is possible that making money and profit may not be entirely compatible in the short term. For example, there are no cash measures of performance on the report. These are likely to assume greater importance given the planned improvements and any long-term expansion of the business. The owners might wish to consider refining their long-term goal in order to make it a more precise statement.

The current report does not present its information clearly. There is too much unnecessary information (e.g. the detail on operating costs). The style of presentation could easily be confusing to a non-accountant as it shows a large table of numbers with few clear highlights. The use of more percentage figures rather than absolute numbers may help (e.g. gross margins, change on comparative period percentages). Also, the numbers are given to the last $ where it would probably be sufficient to work in thousands of dollars.

The current report does not break down conveniently according to the functional areas over which each owner-manager has control. It summarises the overall build up of profit but, for example, it cannot be easily used to identify performance of the service staff except indirectly through growth in total revenue. In order to improve this aspect of the report, the critical success factors associated with each functional area will need to be identified and then suitable performance measures chosen. For example, Sheila's area is customer-facing and so a measure of customer satisfaction based on number of complaints received or changes over time in average scores in customer surveys would be helpful. Bert's area is kitchen management and so staff efficiency (measured by number of meals produced per staff hour) and wastage control (measured by gross margin) may be critical factors. In your own financial and legal areas, costs are mostly fixed and so absolute measures such as the cost of capital may be helpful. In the area of procurement, purchasing the appropriate quality of food and drink for the lowest price is critical and so a gross margin for each product category would aid management.

The timescales reported in the current format are possibly not helpful for quarterly meetings. The existing report shows evidence of seasonality in the large change between Q3 and Q4 performance (42% fall in revenue). The figures for two years ago may not be particularly relevant to current market conditions and will not reflect recent management initiatives. It may be useful to consider reporting the last quarter's monthly performance giving comparative figures from the previous year and drop the use of the detailed 2010 and 2011 figures in favour of just supplying net profit figures for those years in order to give an overview of long-term performance.

The current report does not give much benchmark data to allow comparisons in order to better understand the results. It would be helpful to have budget figures for internal comparison and competitor figures for an external comparison of performance. Such external data is often difficult to obtain although membership of the local trade association may give access to a suitably anonymised database provided Metis is willing to share its data on the same basis.

Finally, the current document only reports financial performance. I have already indicated that this may not be sufficient to capture the critical factors that drive the business. A restaurant will be judged on the service and quality of its products as well as its pricing. It would be an improvement to include this style of reporting although gathering reliable data on these non-financial areas is more demanding.

Human resource aspects of performance management

Chapter learning objectives

Upon completion of this chapter you will be able to:

- explain how the effective recruitment, management and motivation of people is necessary for enabling strategic and operational success

- discuss the judgemental and developmental role of assessment and appraisal and their role in improving business performance

- advise on the relationship of performance management to performance measurement (performance rating) and determine the implications of performance measurement to the quality initiatives and process redesign

- explore the meaning and scope of reward systems

- discuss and evaluate different methods of reward practices

- explore the principles and difficulty of aligning reward practices with strategy

- advice on the relationship of reward management to quality initiatives, process re-design and harnessing e-business opportunities

- assess the potential beneficial and adverse consequences of linking reward schemes to performance measurement, for example, how it can affect the risk appetite of employees

- discuss the accountability issues that might arise from performance measurement systems

- evaluate the ways in which performance measurement systems may send the wrong signals and result in undesirable business consequences

- demonstrate how management style needs to be considered when designing an effective performance measurement system

Student accountant articles: visit the ACCA website, www.accaglobal.com to review the following articles on the topics in this chapter:

- Human resource management and the appraisal system from July 2013.
- Reward schemes for employees and managers from January 2013.

1 Assumed knowledge

Chapter 7 builds on your knowledge of Hopwood's management styles from Paper F5.

2 Introduction

This chapter looks at the link between human resource management and performance management and considers the impact of the employee appraisal system and the reward system on the behaviour of employees and on the performance of the organisation as a whole. It also looks at the undesirable business consequences that may arise from a chosen performance measurement system and discusses how management style needs to be considered when designing an effective performance measurement system.

3 Introduction to human resource management (HRM)

3.1 Definition of HRM

HRM is the strategic and coherent approach to the management of an organisation's most valued assets: the people working there who individually and collectively contribute to the achievement of its objectives for sustainable competitive advantage (Armstrong).

HRM includes the recruitment of employees, the development of policies relating to human resources (e.g. reward systems) and the management and development of employees (e.g. through training and development and through the appraisal system).

3.2 Importance of human resources

Human resource management has grown in importance from the traditional view of the personnel department, whose role was primarily seen as that of hiring and firing employees. Today, employees are seen less as an expensive necessity but as a strategic resource that may provide the organisation with competitive advantage.

> ### Illustration 1 – Importance of human resources
>
> In service industries, such as restaurants, employees have direct contact with customers. Having employees that are friendly and helpful has a large impact on how customers will view the business. Teams must be passionate about delivering an amazing guest experience to each and every customer and they should be provided with the right tools and training to deliver this brilliant experience.

An organisation uses HRM to ensure that it has the correct people in place to fulfil its strategic and operational objectives.

People are fundamental to an organisation

Strategic significance - the creation and fulfilment of the strategy relies on the skills, knowledge and creativity of the people

Operational significance - successful completion of a task relies on having employees with appropriate skills and abilities to carry out their work

Illustration 2 – HRM and competitive advantage

Some examples of the link between HRM and strategy are as follows:

If competitive advantage is sought through differentiation then HRM needs to ensure that high quality, skilled staff are recruited, that these staff are given the freedom to be creative and innovate, that a culture of service and quality is prevalent, and that rewards are geared towards long-term success and beyond short-term financial measures.

On the other hand, if a strategy of cost leadership was pursued, then HRM needs to focus on recruiting low skilled workers, providing repetitive, simple tasks, minimising staff numbers, providing strict controls, and focusing appraisals and rewards on short-term cost measures.

Test your understanding 1

Required:

If an organisation planned to grow through acquisition, how might HRM contribute to the achievement of this strategy?

The problem with human resources is that they require more management than other resources since humans are complex, emotional creatures.

3.3 Recruitment and selection

Recruitment involves attracting a field of suitable candidates for the job where as **selection** is aimed at choosing the best person for the job from the field of candidates sourced at recruitment.

The recruitment and selection process is important for a number of reasons:

- Individuals with the right skills and the right attitudes to contribute to the strategic goals of the organisation are required.

- Employees should have a personality which fits with the culture of the organisation.

- The process provides potential employees with the opportunity to see if the organisation matches their expectations. This should minimise disappointment and staff turnover later on.

3.4 Competency frameworks

In many organisations, competency frameworks may be developed prior to the recruitment stage. A competency framework shows a set of behaviour patterns and skills that the candidate needs in order to perform a job with competence.

4 Using appraisal to improve business performance

4.1 Introduction

Performance appraisal is the process of evaluating employee performance against predetermined objectives and providing feedback to the employee so that any necessary adjustments to performance can be made.

4.2 Reasons for the appraisal process

```
              Two main reasons
               for appraisal
```

Control purpose
- appraisal has a **judgemental** role
- the strategic objectives of the organisation are linked to the goals of employees
- measurable targets are set for employees based on these goals
- performance against these targets will be assessed during the appraisal
- organisational performance should improve as a result of this

Identifying development needs
- the appraisal identifies any training and development needs that the individual may have
- a personal development plan is made to develop the individual in any area(s) of weakness

Illustration 3 – Conflicts in the appraisal process

The appraisal may lead to an assessment that the employee has failed to achieve goals or targets that had been agreed upon in advance. This judgement might result in the employee not receiving a pay rise or promotion or a bonus. The employee will therefore feel that he/she has been criticised during this part of the assessment and build up resistance to the appraiser and the appraisal process.

But at the same time the appraiser will want to make a developmental appraisal. They will want to determine why the employee has failed and offer support in avoiding these failures in the future by developing the employee's skills (e.g. via training).

It is therefore important that the employee understands that the appraisal is as much for their benefit as for the employers. This is why feedback and open communication is important.

4.3 Difficulties in appraisal

Lockett suggests that appraisal barriers can be identified as follows:

Barrier	Example
Appraisal is confrontation	Differing views regarding performance since appraisal is subjective
	Feedback is subject to bias in favour of some and against others
	Feedback is badly delivered - employees may react negatively to criticism, blame others for their short comings and lose motivation
Appraisal is judgement	Appraisal is one-sided
	Appraisal is imposed
Appraisal is chat	An unproductive conversation
Appraisal is bureaucracy	Form filling and depersonalised
	No real purpose or worth
Appraisal is an event	A traditional ceremony
	No real purpose or worth
Appraisal is unfinished business	No belief that issues will be followed up

Test your understanding 2

Required:

Critically evaluate the statement that appraisal will lead to improvements in business performance.

4.4 Improving the appraisal process

In order for appraisals to work:

- The targets set should be discussed between and agreed by the manager and employee.

- These targets should reflect areas that the employee can control.

- Feedback should be balanced to include a mix of positive and negative aspects.

- The appraisal conversation should be two-way between the manager and employee.

- More emphasis should be placed on continuous, informal feedback as opposed to a more formal annual or bi-annual process.

- Issues should be followed up and addressed.

4.5 The importance of target selection

Appraisal (performance management) will only be beneficial and achieve its aims if appropriate targets (performance measures) are set. Targets should be:

- **Relevant** to the organisation's overall objective, e.g. if the organisation has an objective of 100% quality then an individual production worker may be set a target to produce products with zero defects. (It is worth noting that quality initiatives are often undermined by targets that focus on short-term profits).

- **Achievable** – employees may be unmotivated if they consider targets are very difficult or impossible to achieve, e.g. zero defects may be seen as impossible. However, it is worth noting that the same may be true if targets are too easy to achieve.

- **Controllable** – the individual will be unmotivated if they feel they can't control the target set, e.g. a production worker may not be responsible for defects if poor quality materials are purchased.

- **Prioritised** – employees will be overwhelmed and hence unmotivated if they are set a large number of targets.

4.6 Measurement of performance

Each of these will be explored in turn.

Measurement of inputs

This aims to identify whether the staff member has the competencies (or traits) for a job, for example, leadership, commitment or the ability to work within a team. Reference to the competency framework may be necessary.

Psychometric tests may be used to measure the abilities and personal skills of an individual and to avoid the subjectivity of this exercise being carried out by the employee's manager.

Behaviour in performance

Quantitative and qualitative information is collected on a regular basis relating to the behaviour of the employee during work.

Measurement of results and outcomes

Individuals are assessed on quantifiable outcomes, e.g. the level of sales achieved by a salesman. Performance will be judged against targets set.

4.7 Linking appraisal to the reward system

The appraisal process may be linked to a reward scheme whereby employees and managers earn some incentive, such as promotion or financial incentives, if targets are met. Reward schemes are discussed in more detail below.

4.8 The relationship between the achievement of targets and motivation

Motivated staff are more likely to achieve targets and organisational goals.

Vroom believed that people will be motivated to do things to reach a goal if they believe in the worth of that goal and if they can see that what they do will help them in achieving it. Vroom's expectancy model is stated as:

Force = valence × expectancy

where:

Force = the strength of a person's motivation

Valence = the strength of an individual's desire for an outcome

Expectancy = the probability that they will achieve that outcome

5 Reward schemes for employees and managers

5.1 Introduction

A reward system refers to all the monetary, non-monetary and psychological payments that an organisation provides for its employees in exchange for the work they perform.

5.2 The purpose of reward systems

- To further the organisation's objectives through the achievement of the employee's objectives.

Illustration 4 – Alignment of goals

The reward scheme should support the organisation's goals and must be consistent with its strategy. For example, the UK supermarket Waitrose has a strategy of differentiation. Staff receive generous pay and benefits which are linked to the achievement of certain skills and pre-agreed targets. The supermarket, Lidl, on the other hand has a strategy of cost leadership. It has a simple reward scheme offering fairly low wages as staff are less skilled and new staff are easy to recruit and need little training.

- To ensure the recruitment and retention of appropriately skilled staff.
- To provide a fair and consistent basis for rewarding employees.
- To motivate staff and maximise performance (see discussion on Vroom above).

Reward schemes and employee motivation

A well known theory of motivation is Maslow's hierarchy of needs.

Maslow stated that people's wants and needs follow a hierarchy. As employees become progressively more highly paid, monetary rewards become less important as other needs such as recognition and an ability to achieve one's potential become more important.

- To reward performance through promotion or progression.

- To control salary costs.

- To comply with legal requirements and ethical obligations.

Illustration 5 – Reward systems and ethics

Awarding huge salaries and large bonuses to the senior executives of big companies may be seen as unethical when the economy is in recession and there is a climate of job cuts and pay freezes. However, others would argue that in order for a company to survive and thrive, the best senior executives must be attracted and retained. Therefore, executives must be offered a competitive and attractive reward package.

- To ensure the employees' attitude to risk is aligned with that of the organisation.

As mentioned above, one of the problems associated with linking reward schemes to performance is that employees will prioritise the achievement of their reward which may impact their risk appetite.

UK banking executive's pay has received widespread political and media coverage since the 2008 financial crisis. It is argued that performance related bonuses have incentivised excessive risk taking and short-termism and there are widespread concerns that remuneration policies may have been a contributory factor to the financial crisis.

5.3 Methods of reward

Employee rewards fall into four categories:

- **Basic pay** – this is the minimum amount that an employee receives for working in an organisation and is determined in a number of ways such as market rates or job evaluation. Hourly rates or fixed annual salaries may be paid. Basic pay may be supplemented by other types of remuneration.

- **Performance-related pay** – pay is based on the level of performance. Rewards may be based on individual, group or organisational performance, all of which aim to motivate employees to work harder.

- **Benefits** – a wide range of rewards other than wages or pensions, such as company cars or health insurance. These can provide additional incentives at a lower cost and can be designed in a flexible way to suit the individual employee.

- **Share options** – these give employees the right to purchase shares at a specified exercise price at a specified time in the future. Share options will generally be exercisable on a specific date. They are often given to senior managers and should motivate them to increase share price. However, there is an argument that many of the factors that influence share price will be outside of the manager's control or that (previously risk averse) managers could be tempted to take risks in the hope of increasing the share price.

> ### Test your understanding 3
>
> **Required:**
>
> Evaluate the four different reward methods.

5.4 Types of performance-related pay

There are a number of different types of performance-related pay:

- **Piecework schemes** – a price is paid for each unit of output. Often viewed as a fair system but quality control will be required.

- **Individual performance-related pay** – a pay rise or bonus is given to an employee on achievement of pre-agreed objectives or based on the assessment by a manager. Advantages include the ability to align individual objectives with organisational goals and the controllability of rewards by the employee. However, such schemes may result in a lack of teamwork and in tunnel vision (sole concentration on areas which are measured and rewarded).

- **Group performance-related pay** – rewards are based on the achievement of group targets. Encourages teamwork but may not be seen as fair by employees.

- **Knowledge contingent pay** – for example, an accountant may receive a bonus or pay rise on passing their ACCA exams.

- **Commission** – normally used for sales staff and is based on a percentage of their sales. Can motivate staff but may lead to short termism and manipulation of results.

- **Profit-related pay** – part of the employee's remuneration is linked to organisational profit. Can motivate employees to increase company profit and increase loyalty but may lead to short termism and lack of motivation if employees feel they have no control over organisational profit.

5.5 Benefits and problems of linking reward schemes to performance

Benefits of linking reward schemes and performance	Potential problems of linking reward schemes and performance
• It gives individuals an incentive to achieve a good performance level since they know that this will be rewarded. • Schemes based on shares can motivate employees/managers to act in the long-term interests of the organisation. • Effective schemes also attract and keep the employees valuable to an organisation. • By tying an organisation's key performance indicators to a scheme, it is clear to all employees that performance creates organisational success. • By rewarding performance, an effective scheme creates an organisation focused on continuous improvement.	• Employees will prioritise the achievement of their reward which may impact their risk appetite. Employees may become too cautious and risk averse or conversely they may take bigger risks. • Employees may be unmotivated if they feel that they were penalised financially for circumstances outside of their control, e.g. an employee may have hit their quality target but did not receive a reward because the company's annual performance was poor. • Employees may become highly stressed if a significant proportion of their income is performance related. • Employees will have an extra incentive towards the dysfunctional behaviour, i.e. making decisions that are not in the best interests of the business. • Should targets be based on individual, team, division or group performance?

5.6 Reward management in the modern business environment

We have already discussed the need for individual staff targets and hence rewards to be aligned with strategic goals. There have been some common changes to strategic goals in the modern business environment:

• **Quality** – as mentioned previously, strategic quality objectives should be translated into individual quality objectives. Pay or rewards should then be linked to the achievement of these targets.

- **Process re-design** – a change to a process and hence job roles will result in changes to organisational and individual goals. Rewards should be based on the achievement of these new goals. Managers should be aware that employees may be resistant to changes in their job role and must therefore ensure that the reward scheme provides sufficient incentives for change.

- **E-business** – an organisation embarking on a strategy of e-business (i.e. using the Internet to connect with customers, partners and suppliers) will have to ensure that an individual's objectives and rewards reflect the new process and technological objectives of the organisation.

Question practice

The question below is an extract from question 1 of the December 2012 exam. Make sure that you take the time to attempt the question and review the answer.

Test your understanding 4

Lincoln & Lincoln Advertising (LLA) is an advertising agency based in Veeland, which is a large well-developed country considered to be one of the wealthiest in the world. LLA operates out of three regional offices (North, East and West) with its head office functions based in the East offices. The business offers a wide range of advertising services:

Strategic: Advising on an overall advertising campaign (mix of advertising channels and overall themes);

Buying: Advising and buying advertising space (on television, radio, websites and in newspapers and magazines); and

Creative: Designing and producing specific adverts for the customers' use.

The company is one of the three largest agencies in Veeland with many years of experience and many awards won. Competition in advertising is fierce, as advertising spending by businesses has suffered recently during a general economic downturn. Most new business is won in tender competitions between different advertising agencies.

Remuneration policy and regional offices

There are broadly five grades of staff at each regional office. The following is an outline of their remuneration packages. (The head office staff are treated separately and are not part of this exercise.)

Senior management

All staff at this level are paid a basic fixed salary, which reflects industry norms over the last few years, plus a bonus dependent on the net income of their office.

Creative staff

The 'creatives' are on individual packages which reflect the market rates in order to recruit them at the time that they were recruited. Some are fixed salary and some have a fixed element plus a bonus based on their office's revenues.

Buying staff

The buyers are paid a fixed salary plus a bonus based on the prices for advertising space that they negotiate compared to the budgeted cost of space. The budget is set by the finance team at head office based on previous years' experience and their forecast for supply and demand in the year in question.

Account management staff

Account management handles relationships with clients and also develops new clients. They are paid a fixed market-based salary.

Administration staff

These staff are paid the market rate for their jobs as a fixed salary based on hours worked.

Required:

Using the information provided, evaluate LLA's remuneration policy suggesting changes as appropriate.

(10 marks)

6 Problems of performance measurement

There are many ways in which poorly designed performance measurement can result in wrong signals and dysfunctional behaviour. Berry, Broadbent and Otley identified the following problem areas:

- **Misrepresentation** – 'creative' reporting to suggest that a result is acceptable. For example, an organisation may report that 98% of customers were 'satisfied' or 'more than satisfied' with the level of service they were provided with. However, on further investigation it may be found that feedback was only sought from a small selection of customers.

- **Gaming** – is dysfunctional behaviour where an individual manager is trying to meet their individual targets while ignoring the good of the whole organisation. For example, a manager may decide to cut divisional investment to boost divisional return on investment but this may result in a long-term fall in profits.

- **Misinterpretation** – failure to recognise the complexity of the environment in which the organisation operates. For example, looking at the financial aspects of performance an organisation may be assessed as performing well. However, on further investigation it may be discovered that non-financial factors such as customer satisfaction are less favourable and therefore performance has been misinterpreted.

- **Short-termism** – leading to the neglect of longer-term objectives. Financial measures such as return on capital employed (ROCE) may lead to short-termism. The use of a mix of financial and non-financial measures may lead to an improved focus on long term success.

- **Measure fixation** – measures and behaviour in order to achieve specific performance indicators which may not be effective. For example, an excessive focus on cost cutting to the detriment of quality and long term performance.

- **Tunnel vision** – undue focus on stated performance measures to the detriment of other areas. For example, an undue focus on ROCE to the detriment of employee satisfaction due to their needs, for say training or competitive remuneration, not being met.

- **Sub-optimisation** – focus on some objectives so that others are not achieved. For example, a focus on winning new customers may result in a reduced focus on the satisfaction of existing customers.

- **Ossification** – an unwillingness to change the performance measurement scheme once it has been set up, especially when it shows that good or adequate results are being achieved. The example of customer surveys being sent to only a select group of customers is also relevant here.

A number of actions might be taken in order to minimise the impact of imperfections that may exist within the performance measurement system. These methods will be explored in later chapters.

7 Management styles

Hopwood identified three distinct management styles of performance appraisal. The style needs to be considered when designing an effective performance measurement system.

Hopwood styles

Budget constrained style

The manager's performance is primarily evaluated upon the basis of his ability to continually meet the budget on a short-term basis. The manager will receive unfavourable feedback from his superior if, for instance, his actual costs exceed the budgeted costs, regardless of other considerations.

Profit-conscious style

The manager's performance is evaluated on the basis of his ability to increase the general effectiveness of his unit's operations in relation to the long-term purposes of the organisation.

Non-accounting style

The budgetary information plays a relatively unimportant part in the superior's evaluation of the manager's performance.

	Budget constrained	Profit-conscious	Non-accounting
Characteristics	Pressure to hit short-term financial targets.	Focus on longer-term performance.	• Little emphasis on financial performance. • Look at non-financial aspects instead.
Performance measurement systems	Short-term financial performance is measured using, say, ROCE or annual gross profit.	Measures of long-term profitability may be used. For example, the net present value (NPV) of a project over its entire life may be used when making decisions.	Non-financial measures such as customer satisfaction, employee morale or innovation may be used.
Advantages	Should ensure short-term targets are met.	Give flexibility to go 'off plan' if justifiable.	• Focus on causes rather than effects. • Targets may be more meaningful to staff.
Disadvantages	• Short-termism (e.g. cost cutting). • Results may be 'distorted'. • Stress for employees and difficult working relationships. • Lack of flexibility. • Stifles ingenuity.	Loss of short-term control.	Financial implications of behaviour may be neglected.

Accountability and performance measurement

In the case of **performance measurement:**

- the principal is the employer
- the agent is the employee.

The problem is how the agent can be motivated and monitored so that they do what the principal wants. In reality this may be achieved by aligning the principal's goals with the agent's goals and the reward system (as previously discussed).

8 Exam focus

Exam sitting	Area examined	Question number	Number of marks
June 2014	Appraisals	2(c)	8
December 2013	Wrong signals and dysfunctional behaviour	2(b)	10
December 2012	Reward schemes	1(iii)	10
December 2011	Performance appraisal system, Hopwood	4(b) and (c)	12
December 2009	Acceptance of a performance measurement system	1(iii)	6
June 2009	Agency and expectancy theory	3(a)	12

Note:

- The current examiner has set the exam papers from the December 2010 sitting onwards.

- The format of the exam changed in June 2013. Section A now contains 1 × 50 mark question (previously 2 questions worth 60 marks in total) and Section B now contains a choice of 2 from 3 questions worth 25 marks each (previously a choice of 2 from 3 questions worth approximately 20 marks each).

Chapter summary

Introduction to HRM
- definition
- importance
- recruitment and selection
- competency frameworks

Using appraisal to improve business performance
- definition
- reasons for process
- difficulties
- improving the process
- target selection
- measurement of performance
- linking appraisal to the reward system

Reward schemes for employees and managers
- definition
- purpose of reward systems
- methods
- performance-related pay
- linking performance and rewards
- modern environment

Human resource aspects of performance management

Problems of performance measurement

Management styles

Test your understanding answers

Test your understanding 1

HRM may have to:

- plan potential redundancies when staff are measured
- facilitate and manage the changes in culture and performance that are necessary
- ensure that corporate goals and missions are understood and communicated
- unify reward systems
- redesign jobs
- plan training.

This is just one further example of the link between HRM and strategy, but it should illustrate how HRM plays a role in contributing to the achievement of an organisation's objectives.

Test your understanding 2

Appraisal may lead to business improvements because:

- employees will be more motivated (and hence more productive) since they feel that they are rewarded for achieving their objectives
- employees will be more motivated since they feel that their developmental needs are being addressed
- individual employee objectives should be aligned with business objectives. Therefore, if an employee achieves their objectives the performance of the business should also improve.

However, the judgemental purpose of appraisal has the ability to demotivate (and hence to reduce productivity) because:

- employees may feel that they are being criticised
- employees may not consider the assessment to be fair
- employees may not think that the appraisal has any purpose or worth.

Test your understanding 3

	Advantages	Disadvantages
Basic pay	• Easy to administer • Basic employee needs taken care of	• Does not motivate employees to achieve strategy • Does not motivate employees to improve performance
Performance-related pay	• Motivates employees to achieve strategy • Motivates employees to improve performance	• Can be subjective and inconsistent • Can be viewed as unfair if based on team/ company performance • Stressful for employee if they rely on this to pay for basic needs
Benefits	• Can be tailored to the individual employee	• Employees may not want • Does not motivate employees to achieve strategy • Big additional cost
Share options	• Should motivate employees to increase share price	• Factors that influence share price may be outside of employee's control • May tempt managers to take excessive risks

Test your understanding 4

Remuneration packages

Generally, using industry norms as a basic benchmark will help to ensure that staff are kept broadly happy, although it will not motivate them to outperform their peers.

Taking each of the staff levels in turn:

Senior management

Their basic salary reflects historic norms and the bonus should motivate performance. It is notable that no account is taken of the different economic conditions that each office may find itself in and so there may be resentment from those in offices where the general economy is doing poorly to those who are in a region with good performance and so profits are growing easily. It may be worthwhile trying to benchmark the performance of each office against its regional competitors, although it can be hard to obtain such detailed information.

Creative staff

The creatives' packages are set when recruited. This could lead to a loss of motivation, especially for those who get only a fixed salary. If a bonus is paid, then it is currently based on revenue and not profits and so there is no mechanism to control costs on projects with these employees. There will be tension between the need for imaginative ideas and cost efficient ones. Overall, it is likely that each staff member should have a personalised package with a performance element that would be based on the assessment of a superior manager. In order to maintain some sense of objectivity, the criteria that the manager might use to judge performance should be agreed across the firm and could include, primarily, winning new business in tender competitions and, secondarily, winning industry awards.

Buying staff

The packages for the buying staff appear to be based on appropriate performance, although the setting of such targets depends heavily on the expertise of the finance team and, as they are based in the East office, they may lack the local knowledge to set the budget accurately. It may be wise to maintain the bulk of the buyers' remuneration as a fixed salary element as a result.

Account management staff

It is surprising that this group of client-facing staff are not paid on performance. It would seem that their performance could be directly measured by client retention and new business won, so it would be common for such staff to have a high percentage of their remuneration based on performance and not be wholly fixed. Measures such as numbers of clients and total client revenues would be appropriate for these posts.

Administration staff

This is a common method of remuneration for these types of jobs and in line with the general market. A small bonus based on the overall performance of the firm may help to create a culture of loyalty throughout the business. It is unlikely to be efficient to set individual targets for such employees, given that there will probably be a large number of them.

Financial performance measures in the private sector

Chapter learning objectives

Upon completion of this chapter you will be able to:

- demonstrate why the primary objective of financial performance should be primarily concerned with the benefits to shareholders

- justify, for a profit-seeking organisation, the crucial objectives of survival and business growth

- discuss the appropriateness of, and apply the following as measures of performance:

  - return on capital employed (ROCE)

  - earnings per share (EPS)

  - earnings before interest, tax and depreciation adjustment (EBITDA)

  - net present value (NPV)

  - internal rate of return and modified internal rate of return (IRR, MIRR)

- discuss why indicators of liquidity and gearing need to considered in conjunction with profitability

- compare and contrast short and long run financial performance and the resulting management issues

- explore the traditional relationship between profits and share value with the long-term profit expectations of the stock market and recent financial performance of new technology/communications companies

- assess the relative financial performance of the organisation compared to appropriate benchmarks.

1 Assumed knowledge

Chapter 8 builds on your knowledge of financial performance measures from Paper F5.

2 Introduction

In the exam, you may be required to look at performance measures in a variety of contexts. In this chapter we focus on the principal measures used by the private sector. The emphasis will be on financial measures (non-financial measures will be reviewed in Chapter 11).

3 The objectives of profit-seeking organisations

3.1 Maximising shareholder wealth

- The primary objective of a profit seeking organisation is to maximise shareholder wealth.

- This is based on the argument that shareholders are the legal owners of a company and so their interests should be prioritised.

- Shareholders are generally concerned with the following:
    - current earnings
    - future earnings
    - dividend policy
    - relative risk of their investment.

All of these are driven by financial performance.

Test your understanding 1

Required:

What will be the primary objective of a commercial bank? What might be some of its subsidiary or secondary objectives?

Objectives according to Drucker

Peter Drucker has suggested that profit-seeking organisations typically have objectives relating to the following:

- market standing
- innovation
- productivity
- physical and financial resources
- profitability
- manager performance and development
- worker performance and attitude
- public responsibility.

3.2 Survival and growth

A profit-seeking organisation will also have the crucial objectives of survival and growth:

- to continue in existence (**survival**) – survival is the ultimate measure of success of a business. Without survival then obviously there will be no fulfilment of other objectives. In order to survive in the long-term a business must be financially successful

- to maintain **growth** and development – growth is generally seen as a sign of success, provided it results in improvements in financial performance.

Achieving the objectives of survival and growth will depend upon making profits.

Measuring growth

Growth can be identified in a number of ways both financial and non-financial.

Financial:

- profitability
- revenue
- return on investment (ROI)
- cash flow.

Non-financial:

- market share
- number of employees
- number of products.

Illustration 1 – Prioritising survival and growth over profit

Survival

In 2013 the UK roadside restaurant chain, Little Chef, was saved from closure after being bought by a Kuwaiti company for £15 million. The offer price was much lower than the value first discussed when the chain was put up for sale. However, it was recognised that in order to survive, the business had to take urgent action.

Growth

Blogging has become an extremely popular way to try to make a full-time living. Revenue may be received from a variety of sources including:

- fees charged for advertising on the blogging site – a high number of hits will be required on the blogging site if an organisation is to even consider paying for advertising on the site.

- fees paid by an organisation when a blogger recommends the organisation's products/services within the blog – again, a high number of hits on the blogging site will be required to secure such fees.

- sale of e-books written by the blogger – the higher the number of hits on the blog, the higher the sales of e-books that would be expected.

Therefore, most bloggers realise that they still need to concentrate on growth first and foremost. Without this growth, a regular revenue stream and profitability will not be achieved.

3.3 The relationship between profits and shareholder value

Rather than focusing on achieving higher profit levels, companies are under increasing pressure to look at the long-term value of the business. This is due to the following factors.

- research has suggested a poor correlation between shareholder return and profits

- investors are increasingly looking at long-term value

- reported profits may not be comparable between companies.

The correlation between shareholder return and profits

Total shareholder return (TSR) is the return shareholders receive both in dividends and capital growth.

Studies have found that there is little correlation between TSR and earnings per share (EPS) growth, and virtually no relationship at all with return on equity, yet many companies are still using profit as their only measure of performance.

Even where companies state that their objective is to maximise shareholder value, often directors' bonuses are still based on short-term profitability or EPS targets.

However strong evidence has been found between shareholder value and future cash flows.

While these issues have been known for some time, they have come into sharp focus due to the performance of new technology/communications companies.

Illustration 2 – Profits and shareholder value

Timescales

In calculating shareholder value it is customary to make a distinction between the 'planning' period (usually less than 5 years), and the 'continuing period' beyond. Results for different industries show the following:

Industry	% of value in the planning period	% of value in the continuing period
Tobacco	40	60
Sporting goods	20	80
Skin care	5	95
High tech	−20	120

High tech companies, such as Apple, need to make decisions based on the long-term value of the business since these companies tend to make initial losses due to the high level of research and development required.

3.4 How to measure the long-term value of a business

A **value based management** (VBM) approach aligns the strategic, operational and management processes to focus management decision making on what activities create wealth for shareholders (VBM will be explored in more detail in Chapter 9).

4 Financial performance measures

4.1 Introduction

This chapter is concerned with measuring:

- the financial performance of the organisation as a whole

- the performance of the key projects.

Chapter 9 will cover divisional performance and Chapter 11 will cover non-financial performance.

Although most of these indicators will be familiar to you from Paper F5, there will be a different emphasis in P5 questions. A common problem of P5 candidates is that they throw every indicator that they can remember at a problem in an uncritical fashion. P5 is all about the critical approach. It is about selecting from the range of indicators that you know from F5 and using those which are most appropriate to the scenario. In addition, the examiner will not only expect you to calculate the numbers but to also give performance management advice based on what you have calculated.

Each of these measures will be reviewed in turn.

Performance measurement systems

A good performance measurement system should have the following characteristics:

- Support corporate strategy, its communication and implementation.

- Measure performance from a financial, non-financial, quantitative and qualitative perspective.

- Attuned to the needs of decision makers and their activities.

- Reporting is produced at sufficient regularity to properly support decision-making.

- Attention to the accuracy of data and calculation of measures is important for trust in the information.

Any performance measurement system requires the identification of indicators which can identify past, current or potential future outcomes.

The aim:

- Report past outcomes, both good and bad;
- Identify where improvements should be made and what resources are required;
- Determine the quality and robustness of business processes; and
- Allow stakeholders to independently judge an organisation's performance.

By embodying the key measures that are important for the organisation's strategy they can indicate to the organisation what is important. (Often incorporated in strategic frameworks such as scorecards).

NB: As a general rule these measures are only meaningful when compared with:

- other time periods
- other measures of performance
- other companies
- other industries
- budget.

4.2 Return of capital employed (ROCE)

ROCE is a key measure of **profitability**. It shows the operating profit that is generated from every $1 of assets employed.

$$ROCE = \frac{\text{Profit from operations}}{\text{Capital employed}} \times 100$$

Note:

- ROCE is sometimes calculated using PBIT instead of profit from operations. Use whichever figure is given in the exam.
- Capital employed = total assets less current liabilities or total equity plus long-term debt.
- Capital employed may be based on net book value (NBV), gross book value or replacement cost. Use whichever figure is given in the exam.

A high ROCE is desirable. An increase in ROCE could be achieved by:

- Increasing profit, for example through an increase in sales price or better control of costs.

- Reducing capital employed, for example through the repayment of its debt.

Advantages	Disadvantages
• Easy to calculate. • Figures are readily available. • Measures how well a business is utilising the funds invested in it. • Often used by external analysts/investors.	• Research shows a poor correlation between ROCE and shareholder value. • Care must be taken to ensure that like is compared with like, when comparing with different companies – e.g. inclusion of intangibles in capital employed. • Can be distorted by accounting policies. • ROCE can be improved by cutting back investment – this may not be in the company's long-term best interest.

4.3 Other profitability measures

ROCE is usually calculated as part of a range of profitability measures. These include:

Measure	Calculation
Gross profit margin	(Gross profit ÷ Sales) × 100%
Net profit margin	(Net profit ÷ Sales) × 100%
Asset turnover	Sales ÷ Capital employed
Dividend cover	PAT ÷ Dividends paid during the year
Dividend yield	(Dividend per share ÷ Current share price) × 100%
P/E ratio	Share price ÷ EPS
Earnings yield	(EPS ÷ Share price) × 100%
EPS	Covered below
EBITDA	Covered below
Return on equity	Net profit after tax ÷ average shareholder's equity

One additional measure of performance is economic value added (EVA). This will be discussed in Chapter 9.

EPS and EBITDA will be reviewed in more detail below.

Test your understanding 2

	Company A	Company B
	$	$
Profit from operations	20,000	1,000,000
Sales	200,000	2,000,000
Capital employed	100,000	10,000,000

Required:

For companies A and B, which of the following statements are true?

(1) Company A has a higher ROCE than company B.

(2) Company B has a higher ROCE than company A.

(3) Company A is more profitable than company B.

(4) Company A is better utilising the funds invested in it than company B.

Choose:

A   (1), (3) and (4)

B   (2) only

C   (1) and (4)

D   None of these

4.4 EPS

EPS is a measure of the profit attributable to each ordinary share.

$$EPS = \frac{\text{Profit after tax less preference dividends}}{\text{Weighted average number of ordinary shares in issue}}$$

For EPS to be truly meaningful, it must be set in context.

- Is EPS growing or declining over time?
- Is there likely to be significant dilution of EPS?
- Is it calculated consistently?

Advantages	Disadvantages
• Easily understood by shareholders. • Calculation is precisely defined accounting standards. • Figures are readily available. • Often used as a performance measure between companies, sectors, periods within the same organisation.	• Research shows a poor correlation between EPS growth and shareholder value. • Accounting treatment may cause ratios to be distorted.

Test your understanding 3

A company's share capital is as follows:

Ordinary shares ($1 each)	$6,000,000
9% Preference shares	$1,000,000

The company made profits before tax of $5,500,000. Corporation tax on this is calculated as $2,100,000

Required:

Calculate the company's EPS.

4.5 EBITDA

EBITDA is earnings before interest, tax and depreciation adjustment.

Advantages	Disadvantages
• It is a proxy for cash flow from operations and is therefore a measure of underlying performance.	• It ignores changes in working capital and their impact on cash flow.
• Tax and interest are externally generated and therefore not relevant to the underlying success of the business.	• It fails to consider the amount of fixed asset replacement needed by the business.
• Depreciation and amortisation represent a write off of expenditure over a number of years and might therefore be excluded when examining the performance of a particular year.	• It can easily be manipulated by aggressive accounting policies related to income recognition and capitalisation of expenses.
• Easy to calculate.	
• Easy to understand.	

4.6 Net present value (NPV)

The **NPV** is the present value (PV) of all cash inflows less the PV of all cash outflows of a project.

- NPV represents the increase or decrease in the value of an organisation today as a result of accepting the project being reviewed.

- **Decision rule**: any project that generates a positive NPV is viable.

Advantages	Disadvantages
• Strong correlation with shareholder value. • It considers the time value of money. • Risk can be allowed for by adjusting the cost of capital. • Cash flows are less subject to manipulation and subjective decisions than accounting profits. • Considers all cash flows of a project. • Superior measure to IRR for mutually exclusive projects.	• Difficult to calculate/understand. • It does not easily allow two projects of very different scales to be compared. • It is based on assumptions about cash flows, the timing of those cash flows and the appropriate cost of capital. • Many firms use NPV for investment appraisal and then switch to profit-based measures to motivate managers.

Test your understanding 4

Oracle invests in a new machine at the beginning of Year 1 which costs $15,000. It is hoped that the net cash flows over the next five years will correspond to those given in the table below.

Year	1	2	3	4	5
Net cash flow ($)	1,500	2,750	4,000	5,700	7,500

Required:

(i) Calculate the NPV assuming a 15% cost of capital.

(ii) Calculate the NPV assuming a 10% cost of capital.

(iii) Draw a conclusion based on your findings.

Sensitivity analysis

Sensitivity analysis calculates the percentage change in a variable, e.g. sales volume, that would have to occur before the original investment decision is reversed, i.e. the project NPV changes to $0.

$$\text{Sensitivity} = \frac{\text{NPV}}{\text{PV of flows under consideration}} \times 100$$

Benchmarking

Benchmarking has already been covered in chapter 1. In the exam, you may be required to assess the relative financial performance of an organisation compared to appropriate benchmarks.

Test you understanding 5

JDL manufactures a range of solar panel heating. They have recently developed the new EF solar panel. The directors of JDL recently spent $20,000 on market research, the findings of which led them to believe that a market exists for the EF panels

The finance director of JDL has gathered relevant information and prepared the following evaluation relating to the proposed manufacture and sale of the EF solar panels:

(1) Sales are expected to be 2,700 units per annum at a selling price of $3,000 per unit.

(2) Variable material, labour, and overhead costs are estimated at $1,580 per unit.

(3) In addition, a royalty of $250 per unit would be payable to EF (Environmental Friends), for the use of their brand name.

(4) Fixed overheads are estimated at $900,000 per annum. These overheads cannot be avoided until the end of the year in which the EF solar panels is withdrawn from the market.

(5) An initial investment of $7 million would be required. A government grant equal to 50% of the initial investment would be received on the date the investment is made. No tax allowances would be available on this initial investment. The estimated life cycle of the EF solar panels is six years.

(6) Corporation tax at the rate of 30% per annum is payable in the year in which profit occurs.

(7) The cost of capital is 12%.

Required:

(a) Calculate the net present value (NPV) of the EF solar panels proposal and recommend whether it should be undertaken by the directors of JDL.

(b) Using sensitivity analysis, estimate by what percentage each of the under-mentioned items, taken separately, would need to change before the recommendation in (a) above is varied:
   (i)   Initial outlay of $7,500
   (ii) Annual contribution.

(c) Comment on THREE factors other than NPV that the directors of JDL should consider when deciding whether to manufacture the EF solar panels.

(d) Explain the term 'benchmarking' and briefly discuss the potential benefits that JDL can obtain as a result of undertaking a successful programme of benchmarking.

4.7 Internal rate of return (IRR)

The **IRR** is the discount rate when the NPV = 0.

$$IRR = L + \frac{NPVL}{NPVL - NPVH} \times (H - L)$$

where:

L = lower cost of capital

H = higher cost of capital

NPVL= the NPV at the lower cost of capital

NPVH= the NPV at the higher cost of capital

- When presented with uncertainty about the cost of capital, some managers prefer to assess projects by reference to the IRR.

- **Decision rule**: the project should be accepted if the IRR is greater than the firm's cost of capital.

Test you understanding 6

A project's predicted cash flows give:

- a NPV of $50,000 at a cost of capital of 10%
- a NPV of ($10,000) at a cost of capital of 15%.

Required:

Calculate the IRR.

4.8 Modified internal rate of return (MIRR)

- One drawback of IRR is that it is possible to get multiple rates of return.
- MIRR eliminates this possibility.

The **MIRR** represents the actual return generated by a project.

The MIRR assumes that funds will be reinvested at the investor's required return (cost of capital). It is calculated as follows:

Method:

Step 1: The cash inflows after the initial investment are converted to a single cash inflow at the end of the last year of the project by assuming that the cash inflows are reinvested at the investor's required rate of return (cost of capital).

Step 2: The present value of the cash outflows is then calculated.

Step 3: The MIRR is calculated as the return which equates to the present value of the outflows to this single inflow, using present value tables

Illustration 3 – MIRR

The following information is available for a project:

Year	0	1	2	3	4
Cash flow ($)	(5,000)	2,000	(1,000)	3,500	3,800

The cost of capital is 10%.

Required:

Calculate the MIRR of the project.

Solution:

Step 1: Find the value of the cash inflows at the end of the project.

Year	Cash inflows ($)	Value at the end of year 4 ($)
1	2,000	$2.000 \times (1.10)^3 = 2.662$
3	3,500	$3,500 \times 1.10 = 3,850$
4	3,800	$= 3,800$
		Total = 10,312

Step 2: Find the present value of the cash outflows

Year	Cash outflows ($)	Value in year 0 ($)
0	5,000	5,000
2	1,000	$1000 \div (1.10)^2 = 826$
		Total = 5,826

Step 3: Calculate the MIRR

$10,312 \times$ Discount factor $_{\text{yr 4 @ MIRR}} = 5,826$

Discount factor $_{\text{yr 4 @ MIRR}} = 5,826 \div 10,312$

$$= 0.565$$

From tables, MIRR is approximately **15%**

Alternatively, a formula can be used to calculate the MIRR:

(Present value of inflows ÷ present value of outflows)$^{1/n} \times$ (1 + cost of capital) − 1

where n = the life of the project in years

Illustration 4 – MIRR alternative solution

Required:

Using the information from the previous illustration, calculate the MIRR using the formula.

Solution:

Start by calculating the present value of the cash inflows:

Year	Cash inflows ($)	DF 10%	Present value ($)
1	2,000	0.909	1,818
3	3,500	0.751	2,629
4	3,800	0.683	2,595
			Total = 7,042

Next, calculate the present value of the cash outflows:

Year	Cash outflows ($)	DF 10%	Present value ($)
0	5,000	1	5,000
2	1,000	0.826	826
			Total = 5,826

Finally, use the formula to calculate the MIRR:

$$\text{MIRR} = (7{,}042 \div 5{,}826)^{1/4} \times 1.1 - 1$$

MIRR = **15.3%** (as per illustration 3)

Decision rule: the project should be accepted if the MIRR is greater than the firm's cost of capital.

KAPLAN PUBLISHING

4.9 Liquidity and gearing indicators

Liquidity ratios

These ratios measure the ability of the company to meet its short-term obligations:

Measure	Calculation
Current ratio	Current assets ÷ Current liabilities
Acid test or quick ratio	(Current assets – inventories) ÷ Current liabilities
Raw material period	(Ave. value of raw materials ÷ Purchases) ×365
WIP period	(Ave. value of WIP ÷ Cost of sales) × 365
Finished goods period	(Ave. value of finished goods ÷ Cost of sales) × 365
Receivables period	(Ave. receivables ÷ Sales) ×365
Payables period	(Ave. payables ÷ Purchases) ×365

There is often a trade-off between liquidity and profitability. Companies can be highly profitable but get into trouble when they run out of cash (overtrading).

Therefore liquidity needs to be considered alongside profitability when appraising a company's financial situation.

Risk ratios

These ratios measure the ability of the company to meet its long-term liabilities:

- Financial gearing = (Long-term debt/Shareholder funds) × 100% **or**

  Financial gearing = (Long-term debt/(Long-term debt + Shareholders funds)) × 100%

- Operating gearing = (Fixed costs/Variable costs)
- Interest cover = (PBIT/Interest charges)

4.10 Assessing performance and giving performance management advice

The examiner will expect you to be able to assess and comment on the financial performance of an organisation using a range of appropriate measures. In Paper P5 it is more important that you can give performance management advice rather than just being able to calculate a long list of ratios. Bear this in mind when attempting the questions below.

Test your understanding 7

AK is a privately owned manufacturing company and has been experiencing difficulties.

Required:

You have been asked to assess the current position of AK using appropriate performance measures:

	20X6	20X5
	$000	$000
Receivables	5,200	3,120
Inventory	2,150	2,580
Cash	350	1,350
Total current assets	7,700	7,050
Non Current assets	14,500	14,500
Total payables	4,500	3,150
Sales	17,500	16,625
Operating costs	14,000	12,950
Operating profit	3,500	3,675
Earnings	2,625	2,756

There are 2.5 million share in issue.

Assessing financial performance

BPG is a Telecommunications company that commenced trading in 20X1 in the country of Brean. In 20X6 it established a similar division in the country of Porlet.

Required:

Assess the financial performance of BPG and its operations in Brean and Portlet during the years ended 20X8 and 20X9. Using the data provided below.

Note: you should highlight any information that would be required to make a more comprehensive assessment of financial performance.

Summary Income Statements

	20X9			20X8		
	Brean	**Portlet**	**Company**	**Brean**	**Portlet**	**Company**
	$000	$000	$000	$000	$000	$000
Revenue	14,400	2,900	17,300	14,040	1,980	16,020
Salaries	4,450	1,340	5,790	4,125	1,185	5,310
Consumables	2,095	502	2,597	1,950	380	2,330
Other operating costs	2,921	695	3,616	2,754	620	3,374
	9,466	2,537	12,003	8,829	2,185	11,014
Marketing	2,456	600	3,056	2,092	480	2,572
Interest			850			900
Depreciation and amortisation	400	160	560	400	100	500
	2,856	760	4,466	2,492	580	3,972
Total costs	12,322	3,297	16,469	11,321	2,765	14,986
Profit/(loss)	2,078	(397)	831	2,719	(785)	1,034

Statement of financial position

	20X9			20X8		
	Brean	Portlet	Company	Brean	Portlet	Company
	$000	$000	$000	$000	$000	$000
Assets						
Non current assets	9,000	1,600	10,600	8,000	1,000	9,000
Current assets	4,550	1,000	5,550	5,000	800	5,800
Total assets	13,550	2,600	16,150	13,000	1,800	14,800
Equity and liabilities			9,150			7,800
Share capital						
Non-current liabilities						
Long term borrowings			4,000			4,500
Current liabilities	2,400	600	3,000	2,000	500	2,500
			16,150			14,800

Solution:

Company		20X9	20X8
ROCE =	PBIT/D+E	12.8%	15.7%
EBITDA =	EBITDA	2,241	2,434
Gearing =	D/E	43.7%	57.7%
or gearing =	D/D+E	30.4%	36.6%

Each operation		20X9	20X9	20X8	20X8
		Brean	Portlet	Brean	Portlet
Sales Margin =	Profit/ Revenue (%)	14.4	(13.7)	19.4	(39.6)
Non Current asset turnover =	Revenue / non curr assets	1.6	1.8	1.76	1.98

	Brean	Portlet	Company
% Revenue growth	2.6	46.5	8
% Profit growth	(23.6)	49.4	
% Increase in costs:			
Salaries	7.9	13.1	
Marketing	7.4	32.1	
Operating costs	6.1	12.1	

The turnover in Brean has increased by 2.6% whilst in Portlet turnover has increased by 46.5% which is excellent since the business only commenced trading in 20X6. The overall growth amounted to 8% which is an acceptable level.

The profits in Brean are down by nearly 24% whilst in Portlet the loss has fallen by 49%. Portlet will need to make further growth in sales and monitor costs in order to become more profitable.

The costs within Brean have risen by 8% for salaries, 7% for marketing and 6% for operating costs yet sales have only increased by 2.6%.

The costs within Portlet have risen substantially more than in Brean. Marketing for example has risen by 32%. This may be due to the fact that this is a necessary cost to develop the growth in revenue within the newly established operation.

Salaries and operating costs have risen by between 12 and 13%, yet sales have increased by 46%. These costs should be monitored as the business grows further.

The EBITDA has fallen by 8% from $2,434,000 to $2,241,000 and ROCE has also fallen from 13.1% to 10.4%. This is not a very good sign for the company.

The non current asset utilisation ratios of Brean shows a decrease from 20X8 to 20X9. Portlet also shows a decrease from 2 to 1.8, this is less surprising given that the operation has only recently been established. Portlet is clearly in a rapid growth phase hence the need for investment in non-current assets.

It would be useful to have previous years data for Brean to observe longer term trends for revenue and costs. Data for Portlet from its first year of operation in 20X6 would enable a complete picture to be taken.

Competitor information would allow us to establish the market share and establish how well the operations are performing in comparison to competitors.

It is clear that long term borrowings have decreased from 20X8 to 20X9 and that BPG has sufficient cash flow to repay some of the debt finance. However it would be useful to have a breakdown of working capital for each operation.

It would also be useful to have future market and financial projections for Brean and Porlet, which should reflect the actual results in 20X8 and 20X9.

Budgeted data would be useful to see if they have managed to meet the targets set.

Note: You may be tempted to review the cash flows. This is not required in the question and the examiner is unlikely to expect this from you in this type of question.

Test your understanding 8

Water Supply Services (WSS) and Enterprise Activities (EA) are two wholly-owned subsidiaries of Aqua Holdings. You have recently qualified as an accountant and have joined the finance team of Aqua Holdings at headquarters. Your finance director is not satisfied with the performance of these two subsidiaries and has asked you to prepare a report covering the following issues:

(1) The profitability of the two subsidiaries.

(2) The competence of the EA manager to make financial decisions.

(3) The consequences of having a common management information system serving both companies.

The finance director has also provided you with the following background information on the two companies.

WSS

The company holds a licence issued by the government to be the sole supplier of drinking water to a large town. The business necessitates a considerable investment in infrastructure assets and is therefore highly capital intensive. To comply with the licence the company has to demonstrate that it is maintaining guaranteed service standards to its customers. WSS is extensively regulated requiring very detailed annual returns concerning costs, prices, profits and service delivery standards. The government enforces a price-capping regime and therefore the company has limited freedom in tariff determination – the government will normally only sanction a price increase following a demonstrable rise in costs.

EA

In contrast to WSS, EA operates in a very competitive market offering a plumbing service to domestic properties. The business has the following characteristics:

- rapidly changing market conditions
- a high rate of new entrants and business failures
- occasional shortages of skilled plumbers
- fluctuating profits.

In addition to this background information you also have summarised income statements and statements of financial position for the last two years for both companies.

Water Supply Services
Summary income statement

	Year	
	20X9	**20X8**
	$m	$m
Turnover	31	30
Less: Staff costs	3	2
General expenses	2	2
Depreciation	12	9
Interest	5	5
Profit	9	12

Summary statement of financial position

	Year	
	20X9	**20X8**
	$m	$m
Non-current assets	165	134
Current assets	5	6
Total assets	170	140
Current liabilities	(3)	(6)
Debentures	(47)	(47)
Net assets	120	87
Shareholders equity	120	87

Enterprise activities – summary income statement

	Year	
	20X9	**20X8**
	$m	$m
Turnover	20	35
Less: Staff costs	5	6
General expenses	10	10
Materials	3	6
Depreciation	1	1
Profit	1	12

Summary statement of financial position

	Year	
	20X9	**20X8**
	$m	$m
Non-current assets	22	22
Current assets	13	12
Total assets	35	34
Current liabilities	(4)	(4)
Net assets	31	30
Shareholders equity	31	30

Required:

Prepare a report on the comparative financial performance of Water Supply Services and Enterprise Activities from the above financial statements. Your report should incorporate an assessment of the potential limitations of undertaking such a comparison.

5 Short and long-term financial performance

5.1 Introduction

Short-term financial performance measures are used for:

- control purposes, e.g. variance analysis is carried out comparing actual and budgeted results and investigating any differences.

- determining executive rewards – rewards may be linked to the achievement of short-term targets.

- assessing the quality of past decisions and assessing the impact of decisions yet to be made.

5.2 Problems of using short-term targets to appraise performance

A focus on short-term performance (and the measurement of manager's performance on short-term results) can threaten a company's ability to create long-term value for its shareholders. Managers may feel the pressure to achieve short-term targets (such as a target ROCE or gross profit margin) and, as a result, long-term performance may be compromised. For example:

- Investment in new assets is cut. This may lead to a short-term boost in profits but long-term profitability may suffer as a result of old, and potentially inefficient, assets being used.

- The development and training budget may be cut to boost short-term profitability. However, employees are now a key resource for many organisations and a lack of investment in this area could lead to a loss of competitive advantage and a resultant fall in long-term profits.

5.3 Steps to reduce short termism

- **Use financial and non-financial measures**: these should focus manager's attention on long-term financial performance. Methods such as the balanced scorecard can be used (these methods will be discussed in detail in chapter 11).

- **Switch from a budget-constrained style**: a switch should be made to a profit-conscious or non-accounting style (Hopwood). Both of these approaches have a more long-term focus.

- **Share options**: if these are given to management they should focus their attention on improving share price and hence long-term performance.

- **Bonuses**: these should be linked to profits over timescales greater than one year.

- **NPV and IRR**: should be used to appraise investments. Discounted cash flow techniques recognise the future economic benefits of current investments.

- **Reduce decentralisation**: this should increase central control and reduce the problem of dysfunctional behaviour.

- **Value-based techniques**: focus on the key drivers of shareholder wealth. These techniques can be incorporated and will be discussed in more detail in chapter 9.

5.4 Should a short-term approach ever be taken?

It is generally accepted that a focus on long-term performance is superior. However, there are some situations when it is important to measure the achievement of short-term targets and to link rewards to these targets.

The best example of this would be an organisation which is fighting to survive. It is only by overcoming short-term hurdles and building short-term profits that long-term survival (and profitability) can be achieved. Cashflow measures may be more important than profit measures at this stage.

6 Exam focus

Exam sitting	Area examined	Question number	Number of marks
June 2014	Fixed and variable costs	1(ii)	6
June 2013	Evaluation of strategic performance report and metrics	1(ii)	8
December 2012	ROCE	3(b)	7
December 2012	Financial performance evaluation and choice of measures	1(i)(ii)	20
June 2012	Evaluation of performance measures	1(ii)(iii)	24
December 2009	Evaluation of financial performance	4(a)	6
June 2009	NPV calculation	2(a)	6
December 2008	Assessment of financial performance	2(a)	14
June 2008	NPV and sensitivity analysis	4(i)(ii)	8
Pilot paper	Assessment of financial performance and EBITDA	4	20

Note:

- The current examiner has set the exam papers from the December 2010 sitting onwards.

- The format of the exam changed in June 2013. Section A now contains 1 × 50 mark question (previously 2 questions worth 60 marks in total) and Section B now contains a choice of 2 from 3 questions worth 25 marks each (previously a choice of 2 from 3 questions worth approximately 20 marks each).

Chapter summary

```
┌─────────────────────────────────┐
│   Financial performance         │
│   measures in the private sector│
└─────────────────────────────────┘
```

The objectives of profit-seeking organisations

- maximising shareholder wealth
- survival and growth
- relationship between profits and shareholder value
- measuring the long-term value of a business

Financial performance measures

- ROCE
- other profitability measures
- EPS
- EBITDA
- NPV
- IRR
- MIRR
- liquidity and gearing ratios
- assessing performance and giving performance management advice

Short and long-term financial performance

- problems of using short-term targets
- steps to reduce short termism
- should a short-term approach ever be taken?

Test your understanding answers

Test your understanding 1

A bank's primary objective will be **profit maximisation** for the benefit of the shareholders.

Secondary objectives may include:

- market share
- customer satisfaction
- revenue growth
- employee satisfaction.

Test your understanding 2

Answer is C.

Company A has a ROCE of 20% ($20k ÷ $100k) compared with only 10% for Company B ($1m ÷ $10m). A higher ROCE means that the company is better at utilising the funds invested in it.

Test your understanding 3

Profits before tax	$5,500,000
Less tax	$2,100,000
Less preference dividends (9% × 1,000,000)	$90,000
	_____
Earnings	$3,310,000
	_____
Number of ordinary shares	6,000,000

EPS = (Profit after tax, − preference dividends)/Weighted average number of ordinary shares in issue

= $3.31m/6m

= 55.2 cents

Test your understanding 4

Year	Cash flow	DF	PV	DF	PV
	$	15%	$	10%	$
0	(15,000)	1.00	(15,000)	1.00	(15,000)
1	1,500	0.870	1,305	0.909	1,364
2	2,750	0.756	2,079	0.826	2,272
3	4,000	0.658	2,632	0.751	3,004
4	5,700	0.572	3,260	0.683	3,893
5	7,500	0.497	3,727	0.621	4,657
NPV			**(1,997)**		**190**

(i) NPV @ 15% = ($1,997)

(ii) NPV @ 10% = $190

(iii) If the company's cost of capital is 10% the project would be accepted, if it were 15% it wouldn't.

Test you understanding 5

(a)

All figures in $000	0	1	2	3	4	5	6
Sales revenue		8,100	8,100	8,100	8,100	8,100	8,100
Variable costs		(4,266)	(4,266)	(4,266)	(4,266)	(4,266)	(4,266)
Royalties		(675)	(675)	(675)	(675)	(675)	(675)
Fixed costs		(900)	(900)	(900)	(900)	(900)	(900)
Cash inflow from operations		2,259	2,259	2,259	2,259	2,259	2,259
Tax payable (30%)		(678)	(678)	(678)	(678)	(678)	(678)
Initial investment	(7,000)						
Government grant received	3,500						
	(3,500)	1,581	1,581	1,581	1,581	1,581	1,581
Discount factor @ 12%	1	0.893	0.797	0.712	0.636	0.567	0.507
	(3,500)	1,412	1,260	1,126	1,006	897	802
NPV	**3,002**						

Alternatively, an annuity approach can be taken:

Time	Narrative	CF	DF	PV
0	Investment	(7,000)	1	(7,000)
0	Grant	3,500	1	3,500
1 – 6	Net inflow (see above)	2,259	4.111	9,287
1 – 6	Tax 30%	(678)	4.111	(2,787)
NPV				**3,000**

(b) (i)

$$\text{Sensitivity} = \frac{\text{NPV}}{\text{PV of initial outlay}} \times 100$$

$$= \frac{3,002}{7,000} \times 100$$

= 42.9% i.e. the initial outlay would have to increase by 42.9% before decision is reversed

(ii)

Figures in $000	1	2	3	4	5	6
Sales revenue	8,100	8,100	8,100	8,100	8,100	8,100
Variable costs	(4,266)	(4,266)	(4,266)	(4,266)	(4,266)	(4,266)
Royalties	(675)	(675)	(675)	(675)	(675)	(675)
Contribution before tax	3,159	3,159	3,159	3,159	3,159	3,159
Tax payable (30%)	(948)	(948)	(948)	(948)	(948)	(948)
Contribution after tax	2,211	2,211	2,211	2,211	2,211	2,211
Discount factor @ 12%	0.893	0.797	0.712	0.636	0.567	0.507
	1,975	1,762	1,574	1,406	1,254	1,121

NPV contribution = **9,089**

Or using annuities:

Time	Narrative	CF	DF	PV
1 – 6	Contribution	3,159	4.111	12,987
1 – 6	Tax @ 30%	(948)	4.111	3,897
PV contribution				9,089

Sensitivity = NPV/PV of contribution = 3002/9089 = 33%
i.e the annual contribution would have to decrease by 33% before the project was rejected.

(c) Factors that should be considered by the directors of JDL include:

- How the cash flows are estimated. How accurate they are requires detailed consideration.

- The cost of capital used by the finance director might be inappropriate. For example if the EF solar panels proposal is less risky than other projects undertaken by JDL then a lower cost of capital should be used.

- How strong is the EF brand name? The directors are proposing to pay royalties equivalent to 8% of sales revenue during the six years of the anticipated life of the project. Should they market the EF solar panels themselves?

- Would competitors enter the market and what would be the likely effect on sales volumes and selling prices?

N.B: Only three factors were required.

(d) Benchmarking is the use of a yardstick to compare performance. The yardstick for benchmarking is based on best in class.

A major problem facing the management of JDL lies in the accessing of information regarding the activities of a competitor firm that may be acknowledged to display best practice. Internal benchmarking i.e. using another function within the same firm as the standard can help in the avoidance of the problems of information access, but that clearly limits the scope of what can be achieved. The most common approach is process benchmarking, where the standard of comparison is a firm which is not a direct competitor but is best in practice for a particular process or activity.

The objective is to improve performance. This is best achieved by means of the sharing of information which should prove of mutual benefit to both parties to the benchmarking programme. As a result of receiving new information each party will be able to review their policies and procedures. The very process of comparing respective past successes and failures can serve as a stimulus for greater innovation within each organisation.

To evaluate the performance JDL they need to establish a basis for targets which reflects the performance of an organisation which displays 'Best Practice'. As a direct consequence of a comparison of existing standards with the 'Best Practice' organisation, managers can focus upon areas where improvements can be achieved and evaluate measures to help attain those improvements.

A principal benefit that will be derived by JDL as a result of undertaking a successful programme of benchmarking will be the identification of areas where cost savings are possible. Hence the levels of cost of sales and operating expenses can be reduced leading to increased profitability.

Test you understanding 6

$$IRR = 10\% + \frac{50{,}000}{50{,}000 - 10{,}000} \times (15\% - 10\%)$$

$$= 14.17\%$$

16.83%

Test your understanding 7

	20X6	20X7
Current ratio	7,700 ÷ 4,500 = 1.7	7,050 ÷ 3,150 = 2.2
Acid test ratio	5,550 ÷ 4,500 = 1.2	4,470 ÷ 3,150 = 1.4
Receivable days	(5,200 ÷ 17,500) × 365 = 108 days	(3,120 ÷ 16,625) × 365 = 68 days
Inventory days	(2,150 ÷ 14,000) × 365 = 56 days	(2,580 ÷ 12,950) × 365 = 73 days
Asset turnover	17,500 ÷ 17,700 = 1.0 times	16,625 ÷ 18,400 = 0.9 times
ROCE	(3,500 ÷ 17,700) × 100 = 19.8%	(3,675 ÷ 18,400) × 100 = 20.0%
EPS	2,625 ÷ 2,500 = 1.05	2,756 ÷ 2,500 = 1.10

The company has high receivables, low inventories, a low cash balance and high trade payables.

The philosophy is to chase sales by offering lax trade credit to customers, while attempting to maintain adequate liquidity by taking extensive credit from suppliers.

This is a risky policy since it involves the risk of:

- long-standing receivables balances going bad

- discouraging potential customers since low inventory means an increased risk of goods being out of stock.

The low cash balance means that unexpected expenditures cannot be paid for out of cash. Specific funds would have to be organised.

The high trade payables will upset the suppliers; they may even stop supply until the balance outstanding is paid.

Test your understanding 8

Report on the comparative financial performance of WSS and EA.

(i) **Summary of financial ratios**

	WSS		EA	
	20X9	**20X8**	**20X9**	**20X8**
Profitability (W1)				
ROCE	8.4%	12.7%	3.2%	40.0%
Profit margin	45.2%	56.7%	5.0%	34.3%
Asset utilisation	18.6%	22.4%	64.5%	116.7%
Liquidity				
Current ratio	1.7	1.0	3.25	3.0
Risk				
Gearing (W2)	39.2	54.0	0	0
Growth				
Turnover	3.3%		(42.9%)	
Profit	(25%)		(91.7%)	
Capital employed	24.6%		3.3%	

(ii) **Comments on ratios**

Both companies have shown a significant fall in profits. The ratios show that this is due to both a reduction in margins and falling asset utilisation. Capital employed has grown (especially for WSS) and it may be that this extra investment needs more time to generate additional profit.

EA has witnessed a dramatic reduction in sales. Costs seem to be largely fixed as these have only fallen by 17%. Turnover for the regulated monopoly appears to be more stable.

Financial risk (gearing) is high in WSS (although no comparisons with similar companies are available), but the gearing ratio has fallen in the year. High gearing magnifies the effect of volatile turnover on profit. Although it would seem EA has high operating gearing (fixed to total costs), this is somewhat compensated by the fact that it has no financial gearing.

Liquidity for both companies has improved, although no benchmarks against respective industry averages are available.

(iii) **Limitations**

Accuracy of the figures – are the two years under review representative?

Short versus long term – longer-term trends would be useful. Certain events in 20X9 (i.e. expenditure on fixed assets) will reduce short-term performance but fuel longer-term growth (and profit).

The two companies cannot really be compared – one is a regulated monopoly, the other has to compete in a competitive market based on the perception of its products, quality and value for money. As such, comparison may be better carried out using industry benchmarks.

Profitability can only be fully appraised when compared against required returns of the shareholders. This, in turn, reflects the perceived risks they take when investing in each company. This may be lower for a regulated monopoly, and thus ROCEs lower, although the monopoly does have a higher level of gearing.

Workings

(W1) **Profitability ratios (20X9 shown)**

	WSS	EA
ROCE*	14/167 × 100 = 8.4%	1/31 × 100 = 3.2%
Profit margin	14/31 × 100 = 45.2%	1/20 × 100 = 5.0%
Asset utilisation	31/167 × 100 = 18.6%	20/31 × 100 = 64.5%

*Note: profit before interest used as the objective is to measure internal efficiency rather than return to external shareholders.

(W2) **Gearing ratios (20X9 shown)**

	WSS	EA
Debt / Equity	47/120 = 39.2	0

9

Divisional performance appraisal and transfer pricing

Chapter learning objectives

Upon completion of this chapter you will be able to:

- Discuss the appropriateness of, and apply the following as measures of performance:
  - return on investment (ROI)
  - residual income (RI)
  - economic value added (EVA)

- describe, compute and evaluate performance measures relevant in a divisionalised organisation structure including ROI, RI and economic value added (EVA)

- discuss the need for separate measures in respect of managerial and divisional performance

- discuss the circumstances in which a transfer pricing policy may be needed and discuss the necessary criteria for its design

- demonstrate and evaluate the use of alternative bases for transfer pricing

- explain and demonstrate issues that require consideration when setting transfer prices in multinational companies

- evaluate and apply the value-based management approaches to performance management

- evaluate the use and application of strategic models in assessing the business performance of an entity, such as Ansoff, Boston Consulting Group and Porter.

- discuss the problems encountered in planning, controlling and measuring performance levels, e.g. productivity, profitability, quality and service levels, in complex business structures.

1 Assumed knowledge

Chapter 9 builds on the following knowledge from previous papers:

Paper F5

Divisional performance measures

Transfer pricing

Paper P3

BCG matrix

Ansoff's matrix

2 Introduction to divisional performance management

A feature of modern business management is the practice of splitting a business into semi-autonomous units with devolved authority and responsibility. Such units could be described as 'divisions', subsidiaries or strategic business units (SBUs) but the principles are the same.

It is common in Paper P5 to have to apply your knowledge of performance management to more complex business structures such as divisional structures.

This chapter will review some of the methods available for appraising divisional performance.

3 Problems associated with divisional structures

Before looking at the methods for divisional performance appraisal it is worth noting that divisional structures may result in the following **problems**:

- **Co-ordination** – how to co-ordinate different divisions to achieve overall corporate objectives.

- **Goal congruence** – managers will be motivated to improve the performance of their division, possibly at the expense of the larger organisation.

- **Head office costs** – whether/how head office costs should be reapportioned.

- **Transfer prices** – how transfer prices should be set as these effectively move profit from one division to another.

- **Controllability** – divisional managers should only be held accountable for those factors that they can control. The performance of a division's manager must be appraised separately to the performance of the division. It may be difficult to determine exactly what is and what is not controllable.

- **Inter-dependence of divisions** – the performance of one division may depend to some extent on others, making it difficult to measure performance levels.

Illustration 1 – Inter-dependence of divisions

Suppose division A makes components that are subsequently used in division B to make the finished item that is then sold to customers. The following are examples of areas where the performance of B will be affected by problems in A.

- **Productivity** – suppose some staff in division A are ill, slowing down the supply of components to division B. This will slow down division B as well, unless adequate inventories are held.

- **Profitability** – suppose the transfer pricing system includes an element of actual cost. Cost overruns in A would be passed on to B.

- **Quality** – poor quality work in A will ultimately compromise the quality of the finished product.

- **Service levels** – customer queries to B could involve A's component in which case they need to be re-directed. Division A may not be as customer-focused as B, compromising customer goodwill.

Management of a division

The management of a division are normally remunerated on a basis linked to the performance they achieve. Typically, they are given performance targets and only if they achieve those targets do they get a salary bonus.

The central idea is that the manager of a division is in the same position as an independent entrepreneur. If he experiences the risks and rewards of business ownership, then he/she will act in a manner calculated to maximise the value of the division – or that is the theory. The modern variation on this theme is to give management 'share options' – the right to buy shares at a given price. If the share price performs well, (and the stock market is a good judge of business performance), then the manager benefits. The theory is that this promotes goal congruence between managers and shareholders.

Having decentralised, it is essential that senior management monitor and control the performance of the divisions and of those people with direct responsibility for those divisions. An accounting information system (a management control system) must be in place to allow for divisional assessment. The system used must have a close bearing on divisional goals and must recognise that some costs of a division will be controllable by its managers and some will not.

4 Responsibility accounting

Responsibility accounting is based on the principle of **controllability**, i.e. managers should only be made accountable and be assessed on those aspects of performance they can control.

The controllability principle may result in the establishment of different performance measures for the division and its manager. In practice, it can be difficult to establish which items are controllable and which are uncontrollable. For example, an increase in supplier's prices may be seen as something that the divisional manager cannot control. However, it could be argued that the cost is controllable since the divisional manager may be able to change the source or type of supply.

Types of responsibility centres

There are three types of responsibility centre.

When assessing divisional performance it is vital that the measures used match the type of division:

Type of division	Description	Typical measures
Cost centre	• Division incurs costs but has no revenue stream.	• Total cost • Cost variances • Cost per unit and other cost ratios • Non-financial performance indicators (NFPIs), for example related to quality, productivity, efficiency.
Profit Centre	• Division has both costs and revenue • Manager **does not** have the authority to alter the level of investment in the division.	All of the above plus: • sales • profit • sales variances • margins • market share • working capital ratios (depending on the division concerned) • NFPIs related to customer satisfaction.
Investment centre	• Division has both costs and revenue. • Manager **does** have the authority to invest in new assets or dispose of existing ones.	All of the above plus: • return on investment (ROI) • residual income (RI) • economic value added (EVA). These are discussed in more detail below.

5 Return on investment (ROI)

5.1 What is ROI?

ROI is the divisional equivalent of ROCE. It shows the operating profit that is generated for every $1 of assets employed. If ROI is used to appraise the performance of the divisional manager then only the controllable elements of operating profit and capital employed should be included (as discussed in the previous section).

$$ROI = \frac{\text{Controllable profit from operations}}{\text{Controllable capital employed}} \times 100$$

Note: As with ROCE, use PBIT if this is given instead of profit from operations.

Decision rule: If ROI > cost of capital (required return), then accept the project or appraise the division as performing favourably.

5.2 Advantages and disadvantages of ROI

Advantages	Disadvantages
• Widely used and accepted since it is in line with ROCE which is frequently used to assess overall business performance. • As a relative measure it enables comparisons to be made with divisions or companies of different sizes. • It can be broken down into secondary ratios for more detailed analysis, i.e. profit margin and asset turnover.	• May lead to dysfunctional decision making (see below). • Increases with age of asset if net book values (NBVs) are used (see below). • Different accounting policies can confuse comparisons. • Exclusion from capital employed of intangible assets, such as brands and reputation. • The corporate objective of maximising total shareholders' wealth is not achieved by making decisions on the basis of ROI. • It may encourage the manipulation of profit and capital employed figures to improve results and, for example, to obtain a bonus payment.

Two of these disadvantages will be discussed in more detail below.

Dysfunctional decision making

There is a risk that if ROI is used as a performance measure, management may only take decisions which will increase divisional ROI, regardless of wider corporate benefits.

The test your understanding below illustrates the problem of dysfunctional behaviour.

Test your understanding 1

Managers within MV are appraised on the ROI of their division. The company's cost of capital is 15%.

Jon, a divisional manager, has the following results:

	$
Annual profit	30,000
Investment	100,000

Within his division, the purchase of a new piece of equipment has been proposed. This equipment would cost $20,000, would yield an extra $4,000 of profit per annum and would have many other non-financial and environmental benefits to the division and the company as a whole.

Required:

Will Jon invest in the new equipment? Is this the correct decision for the company?

Age of assets

The ROI will increase with the age of the asset. This may encourage divisional managers to hold onto old, and potentially inefficient, assets rather than investing in new ones.

The test your understanding below illustrates this problem.

6.4 Comparison of ROI and RI

Test your understanding 3

Division Z has the following financial performance:

Operating profit	$40,000
Capital employed	$150,000
Cost of capital	10%

Required:

Would the division wish to accept a new possible investment costing $10,000 which would earn an annual operating profit of $2,000 if the evaluation was on the basis of:

(a) ROI

(b) RI?

Is the division's decision in the best interests of the company?

Test your understanding 4

KM is considering a new project and has gathered the following data:

The initial investment is $66 million which will be required at the beginning of the year. The project has a three year life with a nil residual value. Depreciation is calculated on a straight-line basis.

The project is expected to generate revenue of $85m in year 1, $90m in year 2 and $94m in year 3. These values may vary by 6%.

The direct costs will be $50m in year 1, $60m in year 2 and $70m in year 3. These may vary by 8%.

Cost of capital may also vary from 8% to 10% for the life of the project.

Use the written down value of the asset at the start of each year to represent the value of the asset for the year.

Ignore tax.

Required:

Prepare two tables for:

(a) the best outcome and

(b) the worst outcome

showing the annual operating profit, residual income and return on investment for each year of the project and the NPV.

7 Annuity depreciation

Annuity depreciation

- As discussed, the use of ROI and RI does not always result in decisions that are in the best interests of the company.

- Specifically, a project with a positive net present value (NPV) at the company's cost of capital may show poor ROI or RI results in early years, leading to its rejection by the divisional manager.

- Annuity depreciation is one attempt to resolve this problem.

Example:

Division X is currently generating a ROI of 12%. It is considering a new project. This requires an investment of $1.4 million and is expected to yield net cash inflows of $460,000 per annum for the next four years. None of the initial investment will be recoverable at the end of the project.

The company has a cost of capital of 8%. Annual accounting profits are to be assumed to equal annual net cash inflows less depreciation, and tax is to be ignored.

Required:

(a) Calculate and comment on the NPV of the project.

(b) Calculate and comment on the ROI and RI of the project.

(c) Calculate and comment on the ROI and RI of the project using annuity depreciation.

(d) Calculate and comment on the ROI and RI of the project at the project IRR of 12%.

Solution:

(a) NPV calculation

Time	CF ($)	DF 8%	PV ($)
0	(1,400,000)	1	(1,400,000)
1–4	460,000	3.312	1,523,520

NPV = 123,520

Conclusion: the project has a positive NPV and is therefore worthwhile accepting from the company's point of view.

(b) ROI and RI

	Year 1	Year 2	Year 3	Year 4
	$000	$000	$000	$000
NBV at start of year	1,400	1,050	700	350
Net cash inflow	460	460	460	460
Depreciation	(350)	(350)	(350)	(350)
Profit	110	110	110	110
Imputed interest @8%	(112)	(84)	(56)	(28)
RI	(2)	26	54	82
ROI	7.9%	10.5%	15.7%	31.4%

Conclusion: If the manager's performance is measured (and rewarded) on the basis of RI or ROI, he is unlikely to accept the project. The first year's RI is negative, and the ROI does not exceed the company's cost of capital until year 2, or the ROI currently being earned until year 3. Divisional managers will tend to take a short-term view. More immediate returns are more certain, and by year 3 he may have moved jobs.

(c) **ROI and RI using annuity depreciation**

Annuity depreciation is calculated as follows:

Step 1: Calculate the equivalent annual cost (EAC) of the initial investment

EAC = Initial investment ÷ cumulative discount factor at the company's cost of capital

= $1.4m ÷ 3.312

= $422,705

Step 2: Calculate annual depreciation

Annual depreciation = EAC − interest on opening NBV

e.g. for year 1 = 422,705 − (1,400,000 × 8%)

= $310,705

The ROI and RI can now be calculated as follows:

	Year 1	Year 2	Year 3	Year 4
	$000	$000	$000	$000
NBV at start of year	1,400	1,089.3	753.7	391.3
	───	───	───	───
Net cash inflow	460	460	460	460
Depreciation	(310.7)	(335.6)	(362.4)	(391.4)
	───	───	───	───
Profit	149.3	124.4	97.6	68.6
Imputed interest @ 8%	(112)	(87.1)	(60.3)	(31.3)
	───	───	───	───
RI	**37.3**	**37.3**	**37.3**	**37.3**
	───	───	───	───
ROI	**10.7%**	**11.4%**	**12.9%**	**17.5%**

Conclusion: The project now has an equal, positive, RI over its life, which will encourage the manager to invest, a decision compatible with that using NPV.

However, there is still a problem if ROI is used as the performance measure, in that the short-term low rate of return may not encourage investment in what is, in fact, a worthwhile project. A way round this is to use annuity depreciation at a different rate that will ensure a level ROI over the project life. The rate to be used will be the IRR of the project.

(d) ROI and RI using annuity depreciation at the project IRR

12% is now used instead of 8% in computing both the EAC of the investment and the interest on capital, yielding the following results:

	Year 1 $000	Year 2 $000	Year 3 $000	Year 4 $000
NBV at start of year	1,400	1,108	781	414.7
Net cash inflow	460	460	460	460
Depreciation	(292)	(327)	(366.3)	(410.2)
Profit	168	133	93.7	49.8
Imputed interest @12%	(168)	(133)	(93.7)	(49.8)
RI	0	0	0	0
ROI	12%	12%	12%	12%

Conclusion:

The ROI and the RI is now level over the project life, ensuring a consistent decision whether the short-term or long-term view is taken. Using 12% as an appraisal rate for the project yields consistent results under all three methods (NPV, ROI and RI) i.e. the project is at break-even.

This somewhat contrived approach is probably less useful than the one above when RI is used to assess performance.

In addition, the use of annuity depreciation does not produce helpful results when cash flows are uneven.

8 Economic value added

8.1 What is economic value added (EVA)?

- EVA is a measure of performance similar to residual income. However, adjustments are made to financial profits and capital to truly reflect the economic value generated by the company.

- It is a measure of performance that is directly linked to shareholder wealth.

- It is important to note that EVA can be used to appraise organisation-wide performance as well as divisional performance.

8.2 Calculating EVA

	$
Net operating profit after tax (NOPAT)	X
Less: adjusted value of capital employed at beginning of the year × WACC	(X)
EVA	X/(X)

Decision rule: a positive EVA is favourable, since the organisation is providing a return greater than that required by the providers of finance.

8.3 Adjustments required

	Change to profit	Change to capital employed
Depreciation and non-current assets	**Add** back depreciation **Deduct** economic depreciation which reflects the true value of assets during the period	Adjust value to reflect economic depreciation and not accounting depreciation. In addition, adjust value to reflect replacement cost of non-current assets rather than the book value.

Provisions	**Add** increase in provisions in the period, e.g. debt provisions, deferred tax provisions. **Deduct** reduction in provisions in the period. These represent over-prudence in the financial accounts.	**Add** back the value of provisions in the period
Non-cash expenses	**Add** back since they do not represent cash paid and may be as a result of profit manipulation and not real costs.	**Add** to retained profit at the end of the year
Interest paid net of tax, i.e. interest × (1 – tax rate)	Interest payments are taken into account in WACC	
Expenditure on advertising, research and development and employee training	**Add** back, i.e. capitalise the entire expense **Deduct** amortisation for the period (if mentioned)	**Increase** capital employed at the end of the year **Increase** capital employed in respect to similar add backs in previous year's investments
Operating leases	**Add** lease payments **Deduct** depreciation on operating lease assets	Add present value of future lease payments. Operating leases should be treated in the same way as financial leases (i.e. capitalised) to prevent firms from using operating leases to reduce capital employed and hence increase EVA

8.4 Summary NOPAT calculation

	$
Controllable operating profit	X
Add:	
accounting depreciation	X
increase in provisions	X
non-cash expenses	X
advertising, research and development and employee training costs	X
operating lease payments	X
Deduct:	
economic depreciation	(X)
decrease in provisions	(X)
amortisation of advertising, research and development and employee training	(X)
depreciation of operating lease assets	(X)
tax charge plus tax relief on interest (interest × tax rate)	(X)
= NOPAT	**X**

8.5 What is the WACC?

WACC = (proportion of equity × cost of equity) + (proportion of debt × post tax cost of debt)

For example, suppose that a company is 60% financed by equity which has a cost of 10% pa and 40% financed by debt which has an after tax cost of 6%

WACC = (0.60 × 0.10) + (0.40 × 0.06) = 0.084   therefore 8.4%

8.6 Evaluation of EVA

EVA assesses the value created by managers, so is a more appropriate tool for measuring performance than a profit based measure. However, it is not without its drawbacks.

Advantages	Disadvantages
EVA is consistent with NPV. Maximisation of EVA will create real wealth for shareholders.	Requires numerous adjustments to profit and capital employed figures which can be cumbersome.
The adjustments made avoid the distortion of results by the accounting policies in place and should therefore result in goal congruent decisions.	Does not facilitate comparisons between divisions since EVA is an absolute measure (as is RI).

The cost of financing a division is bought home to the division's manager.	There are many assumptions made when calculating the WACC, making its calculation difficult and potentially inaccurate.
Long-term value-adding expenditure can be capitalised, removing any incentive that managers may have to take a short-term view.	Based on historical data where as shareholders are interested in future performance.

Illustration 3 – Adjusting for operating leases

Division A is calculating EVA for the first time. It has operating leases on equipment, for which it pays annual rental charges of $40,000. The current value of the operating leases is estimated at $150,000. The economic life of the leased asset is 5 years.

Calculating NOPAT

- Add back the operating lease charge of $40,000.

- Deduct the annual 'economic' depreciation of $30,000 (assume equal annual depreciation of $150,000 ÷ 5 years).

- NET IMPACT – add back $10,000 (the implied interest charge on the lease).

Calculating the adjusted value of capital employed

- The net book value of the operating leases should be added back, i.e. $150,000.

- The annual economic cost of these assets is $30,000 ($150,000 ÷ 5) and so the capital employed would be depreciated by this amount each year thereafter.

Test your understanding 5

Division B has a reported operating profit of $8.4 million, which includes a charge of $2million for the full cost of developing and launching a new product that is expected to generate profits for 4 years.

The company has an after tax weighted average cost of capital of 10%.

The operating book value of the division's assets is $60 million, and the replacement cost has been estimated at $75 million.

Assume the tax charge is $0.

Required:

Calculate division B's EVA.

Student accountant articles: visit the ACCA website, www.accaglobal.com, to review the two articles on 'economic value added versus profit based measures of performance' from July 2011.

9 Value-based management

This is a slight aside but it is worth covering here since it follows on from our discussion of EVA.

Value-based management (VBM) is an approach to management whereby the company's strategy, objectives and processes are aligned to help the company focus on the **key drivers** of shareholder wealth and hence the maximisation of this value.

Measuring shareholder value

Traditionally, financial measures such as EPS and ROCE were used to quantify shareholder value. However, none of these measures directly correlates with the market value of the company (i.e. shareholder value).

Value-based performance management is an approach which takes the interests of the shareholders as its primary focus.

Companies should set goals in terms of **discounted cash flow value**.

Planning, target setting, performance measurement and incentive schemes need to be linked to value creation at all levels of the organisation.

Key drivers of value should be identified and assigned to the appropriate level of management based on controllability.

Illustration 4 – Value drivers

There are seven key drivers of shareholder value:

- revenue
- operating margin
- cash tax rate
- incremental capital expenditure
- investment in working capital
- cost of capital
- growth period.

Each level of management will be able to link its activities to one or more of these value drivers.

Measures used in VBM

Measures include:

- **EVA** – this is the primary measure used. A positive EVA indicates value creation while a negative one indicates destruction.
- **Market value added** (MVA) – this is the accumulated EVAs generated by an organisation since it was formed.
- **Shareholder value analysis** – this is the application of a discounted cash flow technique to valuing the whole business rather than a single potential investment.

Other value-based measures

As well as EVA, consultants have produced a number of other value based measures, with each claiming its own merits.

(1) Market value added (MVA)

MVA is the value added to the business by management since it was formed, over and above the money invested in the company by shareholders and long term debt holders. A positive MVA means value has been added and a negative MVA means value has been destroyed.

MVA can effectively be seen as the accumulated EVAs generated by an organisation over time. As such it should be highly correlated with EVA values. If year after year a company has a positive EVA then these will add up to give a high MVA.

(2) **Shareholder value analysis.**

SVA is an application of discounted cash flow techniques to valuing the whole business rather than a potential investment.

One problem in the estimation of future values is that theoretically the cash flows go to infinity. A practical way to resolve this is to take free cash flows for a few years into the future (the 'competitive advantage period') and then estimate the residual value of the organisation using either some market multiple or book value. The valuation of the company and hence the individual shares can be directly derived from the SVA.

One criticism of the above is that the estimation of the terminal value is subjective. There is a problem in determining how many years' cash flows can be realistically projected into the future and therefore at which point the terminal value should be calculated. However, all valuation methods depend upon estimating either future dividends, earnings or cash flows and hence they all contain some element of subjectivity.

Implementing VBM

Companies using value-based management have implemented planning and control systems across the organisation to support it.

The implementation will involve **four steps**:

- Step 1 – a strategy is developed to maximise value.
- Step 2 – key value drivers are identified and performance targets (both short and long term) are defined for those value drivers.
- Step 3 – a plan is developed to achieve the targets.
- Step 4 – performance metrics and reward systems are created that are compatible with these targets.

The techniques available for increasing and monitoring value will be/have been covered in other chapters and include:

- the balanced scorecard
- business process re-engineering
- TQM
- JIT
- ABC and ABM
- benchmarking.

VBM evaluation

VBM focuses on value as opposed to profit, thus focusing on the long-term rather than purely the short-term.

However, VBM can become an exercise in valuing everything and changing nothing.

In addition, management information systems may need to be adapted to take account of the need to measure non-financial indicators.

Question practice

Take the time to review and attempt the scenario-based question below. It contains an exam standard EVA calculation and also requires an explanation of VBM.

Test your understanding 6

EcoHomes is an innovative company that was born from the demand of customers for high quality, bespoke homes at affordable prices. The company is based in the country of Geeland and is divided into three geographical areas; North, East and West. The company's mission is 'to make environmentally sound homes available to the general public in a way that ensures accessibility and quality of the product'.

EcoHomes is an off-site timber frame manufacturer, producing the shell of the house in their state of the art factory using sustainably sourced, certified timber. The controlled environment assures customers of the best quality available. EcoHomes prides itself on being a 'one-stop-shop' providing the customer with a full design and build and a fixed price quotation which includes all the planning, demolition, ground works, house build and landscaping.

EcoHomes is starting to lose market share and its key goal of 'being the number one bespoke house builder in Geeland' is starting to slip away. The fall in market share is primarily due to the entry of two new competitors into the market. The first of these, Dream Homes, provides cutting edge house designs and premium quality builds (but at prices to match). The second new competitor, Bespoke Homes 4all, undercuts EcoHomes on price but is not able to provide the same quality, design, build or finish.

EcoHomes has just released a profit warning for the first quarter of the current year, 20X2. This has caused the board to reconsider its position and to take action to address the changed environment. Some cost cutting has already begun, such as the commencement of a voluntary redundancy programme and the introduction of a pay freeze for all employees. However, the board recognises that it will need to take more radical steps to fully address the issues it is facing.

EcoHomes has traditionally used EPS and ROCE to quantify shareholder value. The CEO understands that a number of EcoHomes' rivals are now using a value-based management (VBM) approach to performance management and he thinks that it may be a useful development for EcoHomes given the tough competitive environment. Financial data for EcoHomes for the last two years is provided in appendix 1. The CEO has come to you to advise him on the implications of a switch to VBM.

Appendix: Financial data for EcoHomes

	20X1	20X0
	$m	$m
Operating profit	130	110
Interest	20	18
Profit before tax	110	92
Tax @ 25%	27.5	23
Profit after tax	82.5	69

Further information is as follows:

(1) The allowance for doubtful debts was $6 million at 1 January 20X0, $5 million at 31 December 20X0 and $7 million at 31 December 20X1.

(2) Research and development costs of $10 million were incurred during each of the year's 20X0 and 20X1 on a new project, Project Light which is part completed. These costs were expensed in the income statement.

(3) At 1 January 20X0, the company had completed another research project, Project Glass. Total expenditure on this project was $30 million, none of which had been capitalised in the financial statements. The product developed by Project Glass went on sale on 1 January 20X0. The product has a two year lifecycle and no further sales of this product are expected after 31 December 20X1.

(4) The company incurred non-cash expenses of $0.3 million in both years.

(5) Capital employed was $670 million at 1 January 20X0 and $740 million at 1 January 20X1.

(6) The pre-tax cost of debt was 5% in each year. The estimated cost of equity was 12% in 20X0 and 14% in 20X1. The rate of corporation tax was 25% in both years.

(7) The company's capital structure was 60% equity and 40% debt.

(8) There was no provision for deferred tax.

Required:

Write a report to the CEO of EcoHomes addressing the following:

(a) Perform an assessment of EcoHomes using economic value added (EVA). Briefly comment on the results of your calculations.

(14 marks)

(b) Evaluate the use of value-based management (VBM) approaches to performance management.

(7 marks)

(Total: 21 marks)

10 The use of strategic models in divisional performance appraisal

- The matrices of Ansoff and the Boston Consulting Group (BCG) were met in paper P3 where they were used for strategic portfolio analysis.

- These frameworks can also be used for assessing performance management issues in divisionalised businesses.

10.1 Ansoff's matrix

- Ansoff's matrix is used to analyse the possible strategic directions that a division can follow.

- This in turn will highlight key areas, i.e CSFs, that need to be monitored and controlled.

	Existing products	New products
Existing Markets	**Protect/build** • Consolidation (downsizing, withdrawal, holding market share). • Market penetration (increasing market share in existing markets). • Cost efficiences.	**Product development** • New products for existing markets. • Using existing capabilities or by developing new ones.
New Markets	**Market development** • New markets for existing products. • Options include new geographical areas and new segments of existing markets.	**Diversification** • Related (similar industries). • Unrelated.

• These strategies may result in the development of new divisions, closure of existing divisions or changes within existing divisions.

Ansoff's strategies

Protect/build

Both short-term and long-term performance appraisal of products is required to determine which to divest and which to consolidate. The nature and strength of the firm's competitive advantage is likely to be central.

Market penetration is much easier if the market is growing as larger competitors may not invest sufficiently to meet extra demand. However, the extra investment required may depress reported performance, at least initially.

Market development

Market development involves moving into new markets. Key areas of concern include:

• the attractiveness of the new market

• the risk of not fully understanding customer needs in the new market

• the effectiveness of barriers to entry

• the likely reaction of existing firms

- it may take time to achieve the required critical mass and the associated economies of scale. This is likely to depress performance in earlier years.

- a lack of an established reputation

- a lack of a supply chain infrastructure (e.g. distribution outlets).

Product development

Product development involves new products. Key areas of concern are thus:

- Will customers want the new product? Has enough market research been carried out first?

- Development costs and learning effects may give poor ROI initially.

- Will new products be based on extending existing capabilities or will new capabilities have to be created / acquired first? The strength of such capabilities will have to be monitored carefully.

- Potential quality control problems.

- Production capacity.

Diversification

One would expect diversification to be the riskiest strategy on the matrix, involving the risks of both product development and market development.

10.2 The BCG Matrix

The BCG matrix shows whether the firm has a balanced portfolio in terms of products and market sectors.

Steps include:

(1) Divide the business into divisions (SBUs) or products

(2) Allocate each of these to the matrix.

(3) Assess the prospects of each division or product.

(4) Develop strategies and targets for each division or product.

	Star • Large share of high-growth market. • High reinvestment rate required to hold/build position. • Moderate cash flow.	Problem child • Small share of high-growth market. • Large investment required to grow (so cash user). • **Or** divest.
High **Market growth** **Low**		
	Cash cow • Large share of low-growth market. • Cash generator. • Strategy is minimal investment to keep the product going.	Dog • Small share of low-growth market. • Moderate or negative cash flow. • Divest.
	High **Relative market share** **Low**	

If the relevant information is available, market growth and relative market share should be calculated as follows:

- **Market growth** = the % increase/decrease in annual market revenue

  Note: if market revenue is given for a number of successive years the average % increase/decrease in annual market revenue can be calculated as follows:

  $$1 + g = \sqrt[n]{\text{most recent market revenue} \div \text{earliest market revenue}}$$

  where g = the increase/decrease in annual market revenue as a decimal

  n = the number of periods of growth

  As a guide, 10% is often used as the dividing line between high and low growth.

- **Relative market share** = division's market share ÷ market leader's share

  divisional market share = divisional revenue ÷ market revenue

  A relative market share greater than 1 indicates that the division or product is the market leader. 1 is the dividing line between high and low relative market share.

The BCG matrix

Star	Problem Child

• Is the high investment being spent effectively?
 	
• Is market share being gained, held or eroded?
 	
• Is customer perception (e.g. brand, quality) improving?
 	
• Are customer CSFs changing as the market grows?
 	
• What is the net cash flow?
 	
• Is the star becoming a cash cow?
	(1) **Assuming the strategy is to invest**
	
	   – Is market share being gained?
	
	   – Effectiveness of advertising spend.
	
	(2) **Assuming the strategy is to divest**
	
	   – Monitor contribution to see whether to exit quickly or divest slowly.

Cash Cow	**Dog**
• What is the net cash flow? • Is market share being eroded – could the cash cow be moving towards becoming a dog?	• Monitor contribution to see whether to exit quickly or divest slowly. • Monitor market growth as an increase in the growth rate could justify retaining the product.

Test your understanding 7

Food For Thought (FFT) has been established for over 20 years and has a wide range of food products.

The organisation has four divisions:

(1) Premier

(2) Organic

(3) Baby

(4) Convenience

The Premier division manufactures a range of very high quality food products, which are sold to a leading supermarket, with stores in every major city in the country. Due to the specialist nature of the ingredients these products have a very short life cycle.

The Organic division manufactures a narrow range of food products for a well-established Organic brand label.

The Baby division manufactures specialist foods for infants, which are sold to the largest UK Baby retail store.

The Convenience division manufactures low fat ready-made meals for the local council.

The following revenue data has been gathered:

Year ending 31st March:

		20X3	20X4	20X5	20X6	20X7
Premier	Market size	180	210	260	275	310
	Sales revenue	10	12	18	25	30
Organic	Market size	18.9	19.3	19.6	19.8	20.4
	Sales revenue	13.5	14	14.5	15	16
Baby	Market size	65	69	78	92	96
	Sales revenue	2.5	2.7	2.8	2.9	3
Convenience	Market size	26	27.2	27.6	28	29
	Sales revenue	0.9	0.9	0.92	0.94	0.9

(handwritten above table: 16.7   23 - $m 5.7   12.7)

The management accountant has also collected the following information for 20X7 for comparison purposes.

Market leader		% share
Premier	*14.6 %*	17%
Organic	*1.9*	78%
Baby	*10.2*	25%
Convenience		31%

Required:

Using the BCG matrix assess the competitive position of Food For Thought.

(handwritten working at bottom of page:)

Market growth / Division market share / Relative market share

	Market growth	market share	
Premier	14.7%	10%	10%/17% = 0.53
Organic	1.9%	78%	78%/78% = 1
Baby	10.5%	3%	3%/25 = 0.12
Con	2.7%	3%	3%/31 = 0.10

Where products stand within the BCG matrix

The logical thrust here is that, if you enjoy a high market share, then you will probably have a strong position because of low unit production cost and a high market profile. A product that has a high growth potential offers obvious advantages but it is typically associated with high development costs because of the need to develop the product itself and/or maintain the high market share.

The nature of the four classifications shown above is self-explanatory. An understanding of where given products stand in relation to this matrix can be another essential element in strategic planning. For example, if a product is a cash cow, then it may be very useful, but it should be appreciated that it may be at an advanced stage in its life cycle and the cash it generates should be invested in potential stars.

However, it is not always easy to distinguish between a star and a dog. Many businesses have poured money into the development of products that they believed were potential stars only to find that those products turned into dogs. The Sinclair C5 (a small, battery-powered car) is often quoted as an example of this phenomenon. The promoters of this product in the 1980s proceeded on the basis that there was a market for such a car as a means of urban transport and that the C5 would enjoy a high share of this market. In fact, the only niche it found was as a children's toy and it achieved only a low market share with little growth potential as such. The general point this model makes is that current period cash flow is not an unambiguous statement on the performance of a product or business sector. To appreciate fully the performance of a product, one has to appreciate where the product stands in terms of the above matrix. A poor current cash flow may be acceptable from a product or service considered to be a 'Star'.

Use of BCG analysis as a performance management tool

Benefits	Drawbacks
• Ensures that a balanced portfolio of products or divisions exists, i.e. are there enough cash cows to support our question marks and stars? Are there a minimum number of dogs?	• Too simplistic, e.g. a high market share does not always translate to competitive advantage. A strong brand, for example, may give competitive advantage despite a low market share.
• Can use to manage divisions in different ways, e.g. divisions in a mature market should focus on cost control and cash generation.	• Designed as a tool for product portfolio analysis rather than performance measurement.
• Metrics used by the division can be in line with the analysis, e.g. metrics for high growth prospects may be based on profit and ROI and metrics for lower growth prospects will focus on margin and cash generation.	• Downgrades traditional measures such as profit and so may not be aligned with shareholder's objectives.
• Looks at the portfolio of divisions or products as a whole rather than assessing the performance of each one separately.	• Starting point for performance management only.
• Can be used to assess performance, e.g. if an organisation consists mainly of cash cows we would expect to see static or low growth in revenue.	• Does not consider links between business units, e.g. a dog may be required to complete a product range.

11 Transfer pricing

11.1 Introduction

The **transfer price** is the price at which goods or services are transferred from one division to another within the same organisation.

The transfer price chosen will have a direct impact on the performance of the divisions.

Characteristics of a good transfer price

- **Goal congruence** – the transfer price that is negotiated and agreed upon by the buying and selling divisions should be in the best interests of the company overall.
- **Fairness** – the divisions must perceive the transfer price to be fair since the transfer price set will impact divisional profit and hence performance evaluation.
- **Autonomy** – the system used to set the transfer price should seek to maintain the autonomy of the divisional managers. This autonomy will improve managerial motivation.
- **Bookeeping** – the transfer price chosen should make it straightforward to record the movement of goods or services between divisions.
- **Minimise global tax liability** – multinational companies can use their transfer pricing policies to move profits around the world and thereby minimise their global tax liability.

11.2 The general rules for setting transfer prices

Scenario 1: There is a perfectly competitive market for the product/service transferred

Transfer price = market price

A perfect market means that there is only one price in the market, there are no buying and selling costs and the market is able to absorb the entire output of the primary division and meet all the requirements of the secondary division.

Scenario 2: the selling division has surplus capacity

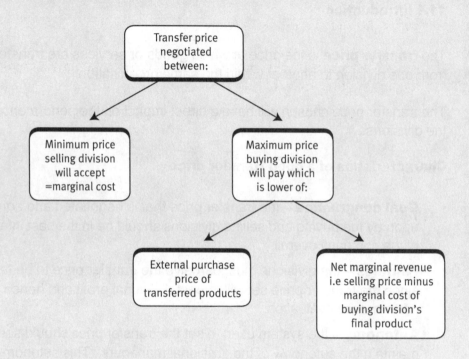

Scenario 3: The selling division does not have any surplus capacity

11.3 Practical methods of transfer pricing

Method 1: Market based approach

- If a perfectly competitive market exists for the product, then the market price is the best transfer price.

- Care must be taken to ensure the division's product is the same as that offered by the market (e.g. quality, delivery terms, etc.).

- The market price should be adjusted for costs not incurred on an internal transfer, e.g. delivery costs.

Method 2: Cost based approach

- Alternatively, if a perfectly competitive market does not exist for the product, the transfer price can be set at **cost + % profit.**

- Standard cost should be used rather than actual cost to avoid inefficiencies being transferred from one department to another and to aid planning and budgeting.

- The cost may be:
  - **the marginal cost** – this will be preferred by the buying division, i.e. they will consider the price to be fair.
  - **the full cost** – this will be preferred by the selling division, i.e. they will consider the price to be fair.
  - **the opportunity cost** – if there is no spare capacity in the selling division, the opportunity cost should be added to the marginal cost/full cost.

- **'Fairness'** is one of the key characteristics of a good transfer price. Two alternative approaches that may be perceived as fair by both the buying and the selling divisions are:
  - **marginal cost plus a lump sum (two part tariff)** – the selling division transfers each unit at marginal cost and a periodic lump sum charge is made to cover fixed costs.
  - **dual pricing** – the selling division records one transfer price (e.g. full cost + % profit) and the buying division records another transfer price (e.g. marginal cost). This will be perceived as fair but will result in the need for period-end adjustments in the accounts.

Illustration 5 – Practical methods of transfer pricing

Manuco

Manuco has been offered supplies of special ingredient Z at a transfer price of $15 per kg by Helpco, which is part of the same group of companies. Helpco processes and sells special ingredient Z to customers external to the group at $15 per kg. Helpco bases its transfer price on total cost-plus 25% profit mark-up. Total cost has been estimated as 75% variable and 25% fixed.

Required:

Discuss the transfer prices at which Helpco should offer to transfer special ingredient Z to Manuco in order that group profit maximising decisions may be taken on financial grounds in each of the following situations.

(a) Helpco has an external market for all its production of special ingredient Z at a selling price of $15 per kg. Internal transfers to Manuco would enable $1.50 per kg of variable packing cost to be avoided.

(b) Conditions are as per (i) but Helpco has production capacity for 3,000kg of special ingredient Z for which no external market is available.

(c) Conditions are as per (ii) but Helpco has an alternative use for some of its spare production capacity. This alternative use is equivalent to 2,000kg of special ingredient Z and would earn a contribution of $6,000.

Solution

(a) Since Helpco has an external market, which is the opportunity foregone, the relevant transfer price would be the external selling price of $15 per kg. This will be adjusted to allow for the $1.50 per kg avoided on internal transfers due to packing costs not required, i.e. the transfer price is $13.50 per kg.

(b) In this situation Helpco has no alternative opportunity for 3,000 kg of its special ingredient Z. It should, therefore, offer to transfer this quantity at marginal cost. This is variable cost less packing costs avoided = $9 – $1.50 = $7.50 per kg (note: total cost = $15 × 80% = $12; variable cost = $12 × 75% = $9). The remaining amount of special ingredient Z should be offered to Manuco at the adjusted selling price of $13.50 per kg (as above).

(c) Helpco has an alternative use for some of its production capacity, which will yield a contribution equivalent to $3 per kg of special ingredient Z ($6,000/2,000 kg). The balance of its spare capacity (1,000 kg) has no opportunity cost and should still be offered at marginal cost. Helpco should offer to transfer: 2,000 kg at $7.50 + $3 = $10.50 per kg; 1,000kg at $7.50per kg (= marginal cost); and the balance of requirements at $13.50 per kg.

Test your understanding 8

X, a manufacturing company, has two divisions: Division A and Division B. Division A produces one type of product, ProdX, which it transfers to Division B and also sells externally. Division B has been approached by another company which has offered to supply 2,500 units of ProdX for $35 each.

The following details for Division A are available:

	$
Sales revenue:	
Sales to division B @ $40 per unit	400,000
External sales @ $45 per unit	270,000
less:	
Variable cost @$22 per unit	352,000
Fixed costs	100,000
	———
Profit	218,000
	———

External sales of Prod X cannot be increased, and division B decides to buy from the other company.

Required:

(a) Calculate the effect on the profit of division A.

(b) Calculate the effect on the profit of company X.

Test your understanding 9

A company operates two divisions, Able and Baker. Able manufactures two products, X and Y. Product X is sold to external customers for $42 per unit. The only outlet for product Y is Baker.

Baker supplies an external market and can obtain its semi-finished supplies (product Y) from either Able or an external source. Baker currently has the opportunity to purchase product Y from an external supplier for $38 per unit. The capacity of division Able is measured in units of output, irrespective of whether product X, Y or a combination of both are being manufactured.

The associated product costs are as follows:

	X	Y
Variable costs per unit	32	35
Fixed overheads per unit	5	5
Total unit costs	37	40

Required:

(a) Using the above information, provide advice on the determination of an appropriate transfer price for the sale of product Y from division Able to division Baker under the following conditions:

   (i) when division Able has spare capacity and limited external demand for product X

   (ii) when division Able is operating at full capacity with unsatisfied external demand for product X.

(b) The design of an information system to support transfer pricing decision making necessitates the inclusion of specific data. Identify the data that needs to be collected and how you would expect it to be used.

11.4 International transfer pricing

Almost two thirds of world trade takes place within multi-national companies. Transfer pricing in multi-national companies has the following complications:

Taxation

The selling and buying divisions will be based in different countries. Different taxation rates in these countries allows the manipulation of profit through the use of transfer pricing.

Illustration 6 – Taxation and transfer pricing

Rosca Coffee is a multinational company. Division A is based in Northland, a country with a tax rate of 50%. This division transfers goods to division B at a cost of $50,000 per annum. Division B is based in Southland, a country with a tax rate of 20%. Based on the current transfer price of $50,000 the profit of the divisions and of the company is as follows:

	Division A ($)	Division B ($)	Company ($)
External sales	100,000	120,000	220,000
Internal transfers to div B	50,000	–	50,000
Fixed and variable costs	(70,000)	(40,000)	(110,000)
Transfer costs from div A	–	(50,000)	(50,000)
Profit before tax	80,000	30,000	110,000
Profit after tax	40,000	24,000	64,000

Rosca Coffee want to take advantage of the different tax rates in Northland and Southland and have decided to reduce the transfer price from $50,000 to $20,000. This will result if the following revised profit figures:

	Division A ($)	Division B ($)	Company ($)
External sales	100,000	120,000	220,000
Internal transfers to div B	20,000	–	20,000
Fixed and variable costs	(70,000)	(40,000)	(110,000)
Transfer costs from div A	–	(20,000)	(20,000)
Profit before tax	50,000	60,000	110,000
Profit after tax	25,000	48,000	73,000

Conclusion: the manipulation of the transfer price has increased the company's profits from $64,000 to $73,000.

Remittance controls

- A country's government may impose restrictions on the transfer of profits from domestic subsidiaries to foreign multinationals.

- This is known as a 'block on the remittances of dividends' i.e. it limits the payment of dividends to the parent company's shareholders.

- It is often done through the imposition of strict exchange controls.

- Artificial attempts at reducing tax liabilities could, however, upset a country's tax authorities. Many tax authorities have the power to alter the transfer price and can treat the transactions as having taken place at a fair arms length price and revise profits accordingly.

Test your understanding 10

Required:

Discuss how a multinational company could avoid the problem of blocked remittances.

Additional example on international issues

A multinational organisation, C, has 2 divisions each in a different country – Divisions A and B. Suppose Division A produces a product X where the domestic income tax rate is 40% and transfers it to Division B, which operates in a country with a 50% rate of income tax. An import duty equal to 25% of the price of product X is also assessed. The full cost per unit is $190, the variable cost $60.

Required:

The tax authorities allow either variable or full cost transfer prices. Determine which should be chosen.

Solution

	$
Effect of transferring at $190 instead of $60:	
Income of A is $130 higher and so A pays $130 × 40% more income tax	(52)
Income of B is $130 lower and so C pays $130 × 50% less income tax	65
Import duty is paid by B on an additional $130, and so C pays $130 × 25% more duty	(32.5)
Net effect (cost) of transferring at $190 instead of $60	(19.5)

Conclusion: C should transfer at variable cost.

Student accountant article: visit the ACCA website, www.accaglobal.com, to review the article on transfer pricing from October 2009.

12 Exam focus

Exam sitting	Area examined	Question number	Number of marks
June 2014	EVA and VBM	1(iii)(iv)	19
June 2013	Transfer pricing	4	25
December 2012	EVA	3(a)	13
June 2012	EVA	1(ii)	3
June 2011	BCG analysis	4	20
June 2011	RI, ROI, EVA, transfer pricing	1(a)(b)	24
December 2010	EVA and VBM	3	20
December 2009	Transfer pricing	3	20
December 2008	Transfer pricing	4(a)	12
June 2008	ROI, RI and EVA	1(a)(i)(ii)	20
December 2007	Divisional performance measures, RI and EVA	2	25
Pilot paper	Transfer pricing	3(a)	10

Note:

*   The current examiner has set the exam papers from the December 2010 sitting onwards.

*   The format of the exam changed in June 2013. Section A now contains 1 × 50 mark question (previously 2 questions worth 60 marks in total) and Section B now contains a choice of 2 from 3 questions worth 25 marks each (previously a choice of 2 from 3 questions worth approximately 20 marks each).

Chapter summary

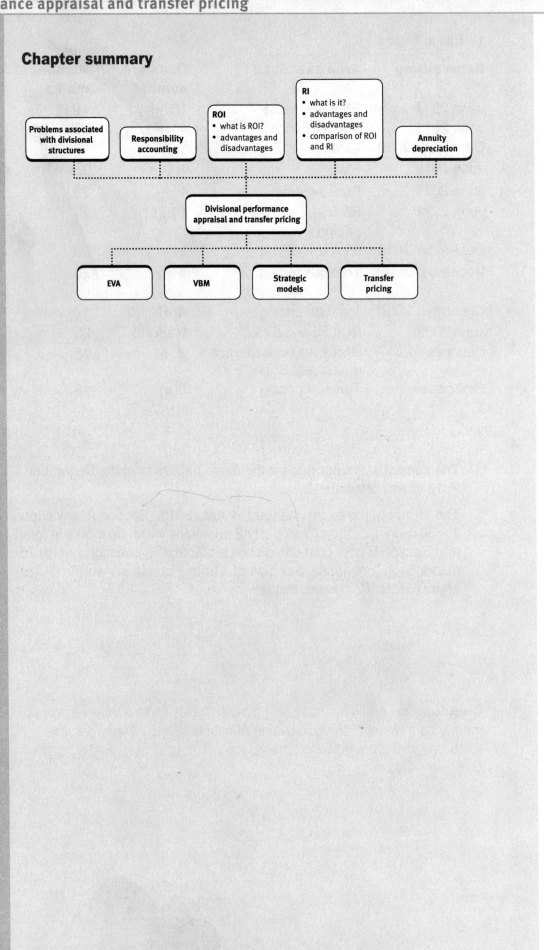

Test your understanding answers

Test your understanding 1

	Before	**After**	**Investment**
Profit ($)	30,000	34,000	4,000
Investment ($)	100,000	120,000	20,000
ROI	30%	28%	20%

- Jon's decision – from a personal point of view, the ROI of Jon's division will go down and his bonus will be reduced or lost as a result. Therefore, Jon will reject the investment.

- However, the new equipment has a ROI of 20%. This is higher than the company's cost of capital (required return) of 15% and therefore Jon should accept the new investment.

Conclusion: dysfunctional behaviour has occurred.

Test your understanding 2

Year	**Opening book value of assets**	Annual book depreciation	Closing value of assets	Pre-dep'n profits	**Post dep'n profits**	**ROI**
	$000	$000	$000	$000	$000	
1	800	80	720	200	120	15%
2	720	80	640	200	120	17%
3	640	80	560	200	120	19%

Conclusion: The ROI increases, despite no increase in annual profits, merely as a result of the book value of assets falling. Therefore, the divisional manager will be rewarded for holding onto old, and potentially inefficient, assets.

Test your understanding 3

(a) **ROI**

Current ROI = ($40k/$150k) × 100	26.7%
ROI with new investment = ($42k/$160k) × 100	26.3%
ROI of the new investment = ($2k/$10k) × 100	20%

Decision: The division would not accept the investment since it would reduce the division's ROI.

However, this is not in the best interests of the company since the ROI (20%) is greater than the company's cost of capital (10%).

(b) **RI**

Current RI = $40k – (10% × $150k)	$25k
RI with new investment = $42k – (10% × $160k)	$26k

Decision: The division would accept the investment since it generates an increase in RI of $1,000.

This decision is in the best interests of the company.

Test your understanding 4

(a) Best outcome

	Year 1	Year 2	Year 3
RI and ROI	$m	$m	$m
NBV @ start of year	(66.0)	(44.0)	(22.0)
Revenue (add 6%)	90.1	95.4	99.6
Less direct cost (minus 8%)	(46.0)	(55.2)	(64.4)
Net cash flow	44.1	40.2	35.2
Less depreciation	(22.0)	(22.0)	(22.0)
Operating profit	**22.1**	**18.2**	**13.2**
Less imputed interest @ 8%	(5.3)	(3.5)	(1.8)
RI	**16.8**	**14.7**	**11.4**
ROI	**33.5%**	**41.4%**	**60.0%**

NPV @ 8% discount factor

Timing	CF	DF	PV
t_0	(66.0)	1.000	(66.0)
t_1	44.1	0.926	40.8
t_2	40.2	0.857	34.5
t_3	35.2	0.794	28.0
NPV			**37.3**

(b) **Worst outcome**

RI and ROI	Year 1	Year 2	Year 3
	$m	$m	$m
NBV @ start of year	(66.0)	(44.0)	(22.0)
Revenue (minus 6%)	79.9	84.6	88.4
Less direct cost (add 8%)	(54.0)	(64.8)	(75.6)
Net cash flow	25.9	19.8	12.8
Less depreciation	(22.0)	(22.0)	(22.0)
Operating profit	**3.9**	**(2.2)**	**(9.2)**
Less imputed interest @ 10%	(6.6)	(4.4)	(2.2)
RI	**(2.7)**	**(6.6)**	**(11.4)**
ROI	**5.9%**	**−5.0%**	**−41.8%**

NPV @ 10% discount factor

Timing	CF	DF	PV
t_0	(66.0)	1.000	(66.0)
t_1	25.9	0.909	23.5
t_2	19.8	0.826	16.4
t_3	12.8	0.751	9.6
NPV			**(16.5)**

Test your understanding 5

NOPAT

	$m
Controllable operating profit	8.4
Add back items that add value: development costs	2
Deduct amortisation of development costs ($2m ÷ 4 years)	(0.5)
	———
NOPAT	9.9
	———

Adjusted value of capital employed

	$m
Opening book value of assets	60
Adjustment to reflect the replacement cost of assets ($75m – $60m)	15
Net book value of development costs ($2m – $0.5m)	1.5
	———
Adjusted value of capital employed	76.5
	———

EVA

	$m
NOPAT	9.9
Less: adjusted value of capital employed × WACC ($76.5m × 10%)	(7.65)
	———
EVA	**2.25**
	———

Test your understanding 6

REPORT

To: CEO

From: A accountant

Date: April 20X2

Subject: EVA calculation and evaluation of VBM

Introduction

This report performs an assessment of EcoHomes using economic value added (EVA) and evaluates the use of value-based management as a tool for managing performance.

(a) **EVA calculation**

(W1) **Calculation of NOPAT**

	20X1	20X0
	$m	$m
Operating profit	130	110
Add research costs expensed (Project Light)	10	10
Less amortisation of prior year expenses (Project Glass)	(15)	(15)
Add increase in allowance for doubtful debts	2	(1)
Add non-cash expenses	0.3	0.3
Less cash taxes (W3)	(32.5)	(27.5)
NOPAT	94.8	76.8

(W2) **Calculation of adjusted capital employed at 1 January**

	20X1	20X0
	$m	$m
Capital at 1 January per statement of financial position	740	670
Add allowance for bad and doubtful debts	5	6
Add capitalisation of research and development (Project Light)	10	30
Add capitalisation of research and development (Project Glass)	15	
Add non-cash expenses incurred during 20X0	0.3	
Adjusted capital employed at 1 January	770.3	706

(W3) **Calculation of net tax**

	20X1	20X0
	$m	$m
Tax charge per income statement	27.5	23
Add tax relief on interest (interest × 25%)	5	4.5
Cash taxes	32.5	27.5

(W4) **Weighted average cost of capital (WACC)**

20X1: (60% × 14%) + ((40% × 5% × (1–25%)) = 9.9%

20X0: (60% × 12%) + ((40% × 5% × (1–25%)) = 8.7%

EVA = NOPAT – (WACC × adjusted capital employed)

20X1: 94.8 – (9.9% × 770.3) = $18.54 million

20X0: 76.8 – (8.7% × 706) = $15.38 million

Conclusion:

EVA is positive in both 20X0 and 20X1 showing that EcoHomes is adding value in both periods. The EVA increased by 20.5% year on year from $15.38 million in 20X0 to $18.54 million in 20X1. This is particularly pleasing given the level of competition within the industry. However, it will be necessary to closely monitor the EVA to ensure that there is no reduction in the figure in 20X2.

(b) **Evaluation of value-based management**

Value-based management (VBM) is an approach to management whereby the company's strategy, objectives and processes are aligned to help the company focus on the key drivers of shareholder wealth and hence the maximisation of value.

Traditionally, EcoHomes used the financial measures of ROCE and EPS to quantify shareholder value. However, neither of these measures directly correlates with the market value of the company (shareholder value).

VBM takes the interests of shareholders as its primary objective. EVA is the primary measure used, (other methods include market value added and shareholder value analysis). A positive EVA indicates value creation (as in 20X0 and 20X1 in EcoHomes) while a negative one indicates destruction. EVA is consistent with net present value (NPV). Maximisation of EVA will create real wealth for shareholders.

Although EVA is calculated using the profit figure, the profit is adjusted in order to bring it closer to a cash flow measure of performance which is less affected by various accounting adjustments such as depreciation. Long-term value added expenditure can be capitalised, removing any incentive that managers may have to take a short-term view.

EVA will also bring the cost of financing home to EcoHomes' managers.

A major disadvantage of VBM measures such as EVA, compared to say EPS or ROCE, is the unfamiliarity and complexity of the calculation. Staff will need to be trained and shareholders educated in order to overcome this.

Another disadvantage of EVA is the large number of assumptions made when calculating the WACC. It should also be remembered that calculations such as EVA are based on historical data where as shareholders are interested in future performance.

Test your understanding 7

	Market growth (% change in annual market revenue)	Division's market share (most recent divisional revenue/market revenue)	Relative market share (division's market share/market leader's share)
Premier	14.6%	10%	0.58
Organic	1.9%	78%	1.00
Baby	10.2%	3%	0.12
Convenience	2.8%	3%	0.10

The management could use the BCG matrix in order to classify its subsidiaries in terms of their rate of market growth and relative market share.

The model has four categories. These are:

Stars

A star product has a relatively high market share in a growth market.

The **Premier** division is experiencing strong growth in a growing market.

It has a 10% market share and therefore it seems reasonable to categorise the Premier division as a star.

Problem child

They have a relatively low market share in a high growth market. The **Baby** division would appear to fall into this category. The market leader enjoys a 25% share whilst the Baby division appear to be struggling to achieve growth in turnover and hence profits.

Cash cow

A cash cow is characterised by a relatively high market share in a low growth market and should generate significant cash flows.

The **Organic** division appears to be a cash cow since it has a very high market share in what can be regarded as a low growth market.

Dog

A dog is characterised by a relatively low market share in a low growth market and might well be loss making. The **Convenience** division would appear to fall into this category since its market share is very low and it has low growth.

Food for thought has a dog and a problem child that both require immediate attention.

Competitors within the sector will resist any attempts to reduce their share of a low growth or declining market. As far as the problem child is concerned, the management need to devise appropriate strategies to convert them into stars.

Test your understanding 8

(a) Division A will lose the contribution from internal transfers to Division B. Contribution foregone = 2,500 × $(40–22) = $45,000 reduction.

(b)

	$ **per unit**
Cost per unit from external supplier	35
Variable cost of internal manufacture saved	22
Incremental cost of external purchase	13
Reduction in profit of X	= $13 × 2,500 units
	= $32,500

Test your understanding 9

(a)

(i) The transfer price should be set between $35 (minimum price Able will sell for) and $38 (maximum price Baker will pay). Able has spare capacity, therefore the marginal costs to the group of Able making a unit is $35. If the price is set above $38, Baker will be encouraged to buy outside the group, decreasing group profit by $3 per unit.

(ii) If Able supplies Baker with a unit of Y, it will cost $35 and they (both Able and the group) will lose $10 contribution from X. Therefore, the minimum price able will sell for is $45. So long as the bought-in external price of Y to Baker is less than $45, Baker should buy from that external source.

(b) The following are required.

– Marginal costs (i.e. unit variable costs) and incremental fixed costs for various capacity levels for both divisions.

– External market prices if appropriate.

– External bought-in prices from suppliers outside the group.

– Opportunity costs from switching products.

– Data on capacity levels and resource requirements.

Test your understanding 10

Blocked remittances might be avoided by means of:

- increasing transfer prices paid by the foreign subsidiary to the parent company (see below)

- lending the equivalent of the dividend to the parent company

- making payments to the parent company in the form of:
    - royalties
    - payments for patents
    - management fees and charges

- charging the subsidiary company additional head office overheads.

Note: The government of the foreign country might try to prevent many of these measures being used.

Performance management in not-for-profit organisations

Chapter learning objectives

Upon completion of this chapter you will be able to:

- highlight and discuss the potential for diversity in objectives depending on organisation type

- discuss the need to achieve objectives with limited funds that may not be controllable

- identify and discuss ways in which performance may be judged in not-for-profit organisations

- discuss the difficulties in measuring outputs when performance is not judged in terms of money or an easily quantifiable objective

- discuss how the combination of politics and the desire to measure public sector performance may result in undesirable service outcomes

- assess 'value for money' service provision as a measure of performance in not-for-profit organisations and the public sector.

Student accountant articles: visit the ACCA website, www.accaglobal.com, to review the two articles on 'not-for-profit organisations' from September and October 2009.

1 Assumed knowledge

Chapter 10 builds on your knowledge of performance measurement in not-for-profit organisations from Paper F5.

2 What is a not-for-profit (NFP) organisation?

NFP organisations display the following characteristics:

*   Most do not have external shareholders and hence the maximisation of shareholder wealth is not the primary objective.

*   They do not distribute dividends.

*   Their objectives normally include some social, cultural, philanthropic, welfare or environmental dimension which would not be readily provided in their absence.

When assessing the performance of NFP organisations it is important to include both financial and non-financial measures.

3 Problems associated with performance measurement in NFP organisations

Problem 1: Non-quantifiable costs and benefits

Introduction

Many of the benefits arising from expenditure by these bodies are non-quantifiable in monetary terms. The same can be true of costs. This is because:

*   **No readily available scale exists.**

    For example, how to measure the impact of a charity providing a help line to people suffering from depression?

*   **How to trade off cost and benefits measured in a different way.**

    For example, suppose funds in a hospital are reallocated to reduce waiting lists (a benefit) but at the expense of the quality of patient care (a cost). Is the time saved enough to compensate for any potential additional suffering?

*   **Time scale problems.**

    Benefits often accrue over a long time period and therefore become difficult to estimate reliably. For example, a school may invest in additional sports facilities that will benefit pupils over many decades.

*   **Externalities.**

    Suppose a council decides to grant planning permission for new houses to be built. The new residents will increase the number of cars on local roads, resulting in greater congestion and pollution, affecting other residents.

Illustration 1 – Non-quantifiable costs and benefits

Non-quantifiable benefits

In 2001, the British government scrapped admission charges to some of the country's most famous museums and galleries. The policy has attracted approximately 50 million extra people to the nation's great artistic and cultural collections. Subjects such as history, art and geography have been enlivened by being able to go to a museum or gallery and see and touch the exhibitions. However, it is difficult to quantify the benefits.

Non-quantifiable costs

A hospital has decided to save money by using a cheaper cleaning firm. However, this decision may create problems in a number of areas:

- It may lead to the spread of infection.

- The general public may lose confidence in the quality of the cleaning.

- Medical staff may become demotivated because they are unable to carry out their work effectively.

However, it is difficult to measure these costs.

Test your understanding 1

In an attempt to improve people's quality of life the UK government has introduced a range of performance measures to measure quality of life, including the following:

- the local bird population

- the stock of 'decent' housing

- traffic volumes.

Required:

A town planning office is considering whether to approve a plan to build new houses on farmland. Assess the plan by reference to the three indicators given.

Solution = cost benefit analysis (CBA)

Some NFP organisations, particularly in the public sector, attempt to resolve the above difficulties by quantifying **in financial terms** all of the costs and benefits associated with a decision.

Illustration 2 – CBA

Suppose a local government department is considering whether to lower the speed limit for heavy goods vehicles (HGVs) travelling on a particular road through a residential area. The affected stakeholders may be identified as follows:

Stakeholder	Cost	Benefit
HGV operators	• Extra journey time • Potential speeding fines	• Fewer accidents
Other road uses	• Extra journey times	• Fewer accidents
Local residents	• Higher noise levels and pollution	• Fewer accidents
Local authority	• Cost of new signs, speed cameras • Cost of enforcement	• Fines collected

These costs and benefits then need to be quantified financially.

Factor	How to measure
Time	• For HGV operators this can be quantified as additional wages, overtime premiums, additional fuel costs, etc. • For other road users we need to quantify how much people value their time. One way this can be done is by comparing the costs of different modes of transport (e.g. coach versus rail versus air) to see the premium travellers will pay to save time. • Another approach is to compare property prices as they get further away from train stations as this will in part reflect longer journey times.
Noise	• Cost of installing double glazing to reduce noise levels. • Difference in house prices between houses next to the busy road and those set further back.

Pollution	• Cost of cleaning off soot and other pollutants.
	• Comparison of house prices near/away from main roads.
Accidents	• Impact on insurance premiums for drivers.
	• For victims of accidents the value of not breaking a leg, say, or not being killed, is estimated in many ways, e.g. the present value of future earnings affected.

Once these have been quantified, it is relatively straightforward to compare overall costs and benefits to see the net impact on society.

Problem 2: Assessing the use of funds

Introduction

Many NFP organisations, particularly public sector organisations, do not generate revenue but simply have a fixed budget for spending within which they have to keep. The funding in public sector organisations tends to come directly from the government.

There are a number of problems associated with this funding:

- The organisation may feel under pressure to hit government targets rather than focusing on what they would normally consider important.

- There is not necessarily a link between providing more service and obtaining more funds. Funding tends to be limited and may not be controllable.

- A failure to achieve objectives sometimes leads to higher levels of funding.

Illustration 3 – Funding

An ineffective or inefficient police force will not be closed down, but is likely to justify and obtain additional funding.

Solution = assess value for money

Value for money (VFM) is often quoted as an objective in NFP organisations, i.e. have they gained the best value from the limited funds available?

VFM can be assessed in a number of ways:

- through benchmarking an activity against similar activities in other organisations

- by using performance indicators/ measures (see TYU 2)

- through conducting VFM studies (possibly in conjunction with other institutions)

- by seeking out and then adopting recognised good practice where this can be adapted to the institution's circumstances

- through internal VFM audit work

- through retaining both documents that show how an activity has been planned to build in VFM, and evidence of the good practices adopted

- by examining the results or outcomes of an activity.

Using performance measures to assess VFM

When assessing VFM using performance measures, it is important to tailor your choice of indicators to the scenario given, focusing on the most relevant measures (for example, measures relating to the organisation's mission or objectives). Once you have calculated the relevant measures you must be prepared to discuss the performance management response to each measure. Statements of which indicator have gone up or gone down will not be adequate in the exam.

Test your understanding 2

Maple Council is concerned about the performance of St George's School, one of the primary schools within its jurisdiction and, in order to substantiate this concern, the Council's Education Department has collected the following information regarding the last two years.

	20X7	20X8
School Roll (no of pupils)	502	584
Number of teaching staff	22	21
Number of support staff	6	6
Number of classes	20	20
Possible teaching days in a year	290	290
Actual teaching days in a year	279	282
Total pupil absences (in pupil teaching days)	2,259	3,066
Total teaching staff absences (in pupil teaching days)	132	189

	$	$
Budgeted expenditure	2,400,000	2,600,000
Actual expenditure	2,200,000	2,900,000

The data has been sent to the council's finance department in which you work for analysis.

Required:

Calculate relevant performance measures for St George's School for each of the last two years.

Based on your calculations analyse the school's performance in terms of value for money and explain the possible management responses to your findings.

Value for money and the 3Es

Value for money is interpreted as providing an economic, efficient and effective service.

Economy – an input measure. Are the resources the cheapest possible for the quality desired?

Effectiveness – an output measure looking at whether objectives are being met.

Efficiency – here we link inputs and outputs. Is the maximum output being achieved from the resources used?

Test your understanding 3

Required:

Explain the meaning of economy, efficiency and effectiveness for a university, incorporating specific examples for each of the 3Es.

Test your understanding 4

A local government housing department (LGHD) has funds which it is proposing to spend on the upgrading of air conditioning systems in its housing inventory.

It is intended that the upgrading should enhance the quality of living for the occupants of the houses.

Preferred contractors will be identified to carry out the work involved in the upgrading of the air conditioning systems, with each contractor being responsible for upgrading of the systems in a proportion of the houses. Contractors will also be required to provide a maintenance and operational advice service during the first two years of operation of the upgraded systems.

Prior to a decision to implement the proposal, LGHD has decided that it should carry out a value for money (VFM) audit.

You have been given the task of preparing a report for LGHD, to help ensure that it can make an informed decision concerning the proposal.

Required:

Prepare a detailed analysis which will form the basis for the preparation of the final report. The analysis should include a clear explanation of the meaning and relevance of each of (a) and (b) below and should incorporate specific references to examples relating to the upgrading proposal.

(a) Value for Money (VFM) audit (including references to the roles of principal and agent).

(6 marks)

(b) Economy, efficiency and effectiveness as part of the VFM audit.

(6 marks)

(Total: 12 marks)

Other methods of evaluating performance

In addition to assessing value for money and the 3Es the following approaches can be used to assess the performance of NFP organisations:

- The '**goal approach**' looks at the ultimate objectives of the organisation, i.e. it looks at output measures.

  For example for a hospital: Have waiting lists been reduced? Have mortality rates gone down? How many patients have been treated?

- The '**systems resources approach**' looks at how well the organisation has obtained the inputs it needs to function.

  For example, did the hospital manage to recruit all the nurses it needed?

- The '**internal processes approach**' looks at how well inputs have been used to achieve outputs – it is a measure of efficiency.

  For example, what was the average cost per patient treated?

Problem 3: Multiple and diverse objectives

Diverse objectives

As mentioned, NFP organisations are unlikely to have an objective of maximisation of shareholder wealth. Instead they are seeking to satisfy the particular needs of their members or sections of society, which they have been set up to benefit.

Illustration 4 – Diverse objectives

Diverse objectives in NFP organisations include:

- A hospital's objective is to treat patients.
- A council's objective is care for the local community.
- A charity's objective may be to provide relief for victims of a disaster.

Multiple objectives

Multiple stakeholders in NFP organisations give rise to multiple objectives. This can be problematic when assessing the performance of these organisations.

Solution

The problem of multiple objectives can be overcome by prioritising objectives or making compromises between objectives.

Illustration 5 – The problem of multiple objectives

A hospital will have a number of different groups of stakeholders, each with their own objectives. For example:

- Employees will seek a high level of job satisfaction. They will also aim to achieve a good work-life balance and this may result in a desire to work more regular daytime hours.

- Patients will want to be seen quickly and will demand a high level of care.

There is potential conflict between the objectives of the two stakeholder groups. For example, if hospital staff only work regular daytime hours then patients may have to wait a long time if they come to the hospital outside of these hours and the standard of patient care will fall dramatically at certain times of the day.

The hospital must prioritise the needs of different stakeholder groups. In this case, the standard of patient care would be prioritised above giving staff the regular daytime working hours that they would prefer. However, in order to maintain staff morale an element of compromise should also be used. For example, staff may have to work shifts but will be given generous holiday allowances or rewards to compensate for this.

Test your understanding 5

Required:

Describe the different groups of stakeholders in an international famine relief charity. Explain how the charity might have conflicting objectives and the impact this conflict may have on the effective operation of the organisation.

Problem 4: The impact of politics on performance measurement

The combination of politics and performance measurement in the public sector may result in undesirable outcomes.

- The public focus on some sectors, such as health and education, make them a prime target for political interference.
- Long-term organisational objectives are sacrificed for short-term political gains.

Illustration 6 – Impact of politics

Politicians may promise 'increased funding' and 'improved performance' as that is what voters want to hear, but it may result in undesirable outcomes.

Increased funding:

- may be available only to the detriment of other public sector organisations
- may be provided to organisations in political hot-spots, not necessarily the places that need more money
- may not be used as efficiently or effectively as it could be
- may only be available in the short-term, as a public relations exercise.

Improved performance:

- may be to the detriment of workers and clients
- may come about as the result of data manipulation, rather than real results
- may be a short-term phenomenon
- may result in more funds being spent on performance measurement when it might better be used on improvements, e.g. hospitals under increasing pressure to compete on price and delivery in some areas may result in a shift of resources from other, less measurable areas, such as towards elective surgery and away from emergency services.

Test your understanding 6 – Long practice question on NFPOs

Public versus private sector

The objective of a health authority (a public sector organisation) is stated in its most recent annual report as:

'To serve the people of the region by providing high-quality health care within expected waiting times'.

The 'mission statement' of a large company in a manufacturing industry is shown in its annual report as:

'In everything the company does, it is committed to creating wealth, always with integrity, for its shareholders, employees, customers and suppliers and the community in which it operates.'

Required:

(a) Discuss the main differences between the public and private sectors that have to be addressed when determining corporate objectives or missions.

(10 marks)

(b) Describe three performance measures which could be used to assess whether or not the health authority is meeting its current objective.

(3 marks)

(c) Explain the difficulties which public sector organisations face in using such measures to influence decision making.

(5 marks)

(Total: 18 marks)

4 Exam focus

Exam sitting	Area examined	Question number	Number of marks
June 2010	VFM and the 3Es	3(i)(ii)	12
June 2009	Assessment of performance in a NFPO	1(a)	20
December 2007	Problems encountered when comparing public and private sector performance and VFM	1(b)(c)	12

Note:

* The current examiner has set the exam papers from the December 2010 sitting onwards.

* The format of the exam changed in June 2013. Section A now contains 1 × 50 mark question (previously 2 questions worth 60 marks in total) and Section B now contains a choice of 2 from 3 questions worth 25 marks each (previously a choice of 2 from 3 questions worth approximately 20 marks each).

Chapter summary

Performance management in not-for-profit organisations

What is a NFP organisation?

Problems associated with performance measurement in NFP organisations
- non-quantifiable costs and benefits
- assessing the use of funds
- multiple and diverse objectives
- impact of politics on performance measurement

Test your understanding answers

Test your understanding 1

	The local bird population	The stock of 'decent' housing	Traffic volumes
Improved quality of life		X	
Reduced quality of life	X		X
Reason	Fewer feeding and nesting areas	New houses should be reasonably habitable!	New homes will result in a higher local population and more traffic

Test your understanding 2

Measure 1	20X7	20X8
Possible pupil teaching days		
(school roll × possible teaching days in the year)	145,580	169,360
Actual pupil teaching days		
(school roll × actual teaching days in the year)	140,058	164,688
Actual to possible teaching days as a %	**96.2%**	**97.2%**

Measure 2	20X7	20X8
Pupils absences as a % of total actual teaching days	2,259	3,066
	140,058	164,688
	1.6%	**1.9%**

Measure 3	20X7	20X8
Staff absences as a % of total actual teaching days	132	189
	140,058	164,688
	0.1%	**0.1%**

Measure 4

Pupil teacher ratio	502:22	584:6
	22.8:1	**27.8:1**

Measure 5

Pupil to non teaching staff ratio	502:6	584:6
	83.7:1	**97.3:1**

Measure 6

Average class size	502	584
(school / number of classes)	20	20
	25.1	**29.2**

Measure 7

	20X7	20X8
Budgeted expenditure per pupil	2,400,000	2,600,000
	502	584
	$4780.88	$4452.05
Actual expenditure per pupil	2,200,000	2,900,000
	502	584
	4382.47	4965.75

Comments

In certain circumstances, the schools performance has been fairly consistent over the two years. Staff and pupil absences as a percentage of total actual pupil teaching days have deteriorated marginally (but the fall may not merit investigation by management), whilst actual to possible total teaching days has shown a slight improvement (managers may investigate the reasons for this improvement and take steps to improve this figure further next year).

The major area of concern is the number of pupils on the school roll is roughly 16% higher than last year. This may have an impact on performance. Management must investigate the reasons for the increase and establish whether the trend is set to continue. Action may be taken if a link to a deterioration in performance is established, e.g. through the recruitment of more teaching staff, building additional classrooms and investing in extra resources such as IT resources and books. However, the increase in student numbers may actually indicate more efficient use of resources and hence value for money. Pupil to teaching staff, pupil to non teaching staff, and average class size has worsened. Whether this is enough to effect the quality of provision is impossible to say without further investigation.

Expenditure per pupil has fallen but this is a function of the increased pupil numbers.

Overall, it is not really possible to arrive at a firm conclusion about the schools performance. This is partly due to a lack of data from the school, and partly because of a lack of data from other schools against which to compare it.

Test your understanding 3

Value for money for a university would comprise three elements:

Economy – this is about balancing the cost with the quality of resources. Therefore, it will review areas such as the cost of books, computers and teaching compared with the quality of these resources. It recognises that the organisation must consider its expenditure but should not simply aim to minimise costs, e.g. low cost but poor quality teaching or books will hinder student performance and will damage the reputation of the university.

Effectiveness – this measures the achievement of the organisation's objectives, for example:

- The % of students achieving a target grade.
- The % of graduates who find full time employment within 6 months of graduating.

Efficiency – this focuses on the efficient use of any resources acquired, for example:

- How often are the library books that are bought by the university taken out by students?

- What is the utilisation of IT resources?

- What % of their working time do academic staff spend lecturing and researching?

Test your understanding 4

(a) Value for money audits may be seen as being of particular relevance in not-for-profit organisations where they are an important performance assessment tool. The VFM audit focuses on the achievement of objectives of the organisation in a way that ensures the most economic, efficient and effective manner. This may be complicated by the inter-relationship of objectives.

In the scenario the principal objective is the provision of the upgrade of the air-conditioning systems, ensuring that the quality of the system is satisfactory to LGHD. A subsidiary objective is to ensure satisfaction of the occupants of the premises with the quality and ease of use of the upgraded system.

An extension of the objectives is to ensure that the upgrade is seen to satisfy cost-benefit criteria, both in terms of the upgrade and the subsequent maintenance and operational advice to be provided by the contractors.

The principals are LCGD as the provider of funds and the house occupiers as recipients of the improved service.

The agents are the contractors who are tasked with the installation and maintenance of the upgrade plus the advice to users (occupants) during the initial two year period.

(b) The focus on the achievement of the objectives of the proposed improvements will benefit from consideration of the relevance of each of Economy, Efficiency and Effectiveness. The three Es are likely to be seen as possibly being in conflict with each other in terms of the achievement of objectives.

Economy will be seen as being achieved by aiming at minimising the average cost per house for the upgrade and subsequent maintenance and advice. This may be aimed at choosing the lowest quote per house for the proposed upgrades. A possible problem with this approach is that the quality of the work done may be compromised resulting in dissatisfaction of occupants.

Efficiency may be seen as the maximisation of the input:output ratio. In this exercise, this may be measured through maximising the number of houses that can have the air-conditioning upgrade with the funds available.

Effectiveness requires the achievement of the objectives (both principal and subsidiary) of the proposal. This may be measured by focusing on factors such as:

- The quality of upgrade obtained

- The level of improvement in air-conditioning achieved

- The extent to which external noise is eliminated

- Residents' feedback indicates that the benefits will outweigh any inconvenience caused by the upgrading work

- LCGD considers that 'value for money' has been achieved.

Test your understanding 5

The stakeholders will include donors, people needing aid, voluntary staff, paid staff, the governments of the countries granting and receiving aid.

There may be conflicting objectives. Donors and people needing aid will want all of the funds to be spent on famine relief. Management staff may require a percentage of the funds to be spent on administration and promotion in order to preserve the long-term future of the charity. Donors may have their own views about how donations should be spent which conflict with management staff.

The charity may wish to distribute aid according to perceived need. Governments in receiving countries may have political reasons for distorting information relating to need. These conflicts may make it difficult to set clear objectives on which all stakeholders agree.

Test your understanding 6 – Long practice question on NFPOs

(a) The main differences between the public and private sector regarding corporate objectives are:

The objectives of a public sector body are usually set out in the Act of Parliament or legal document that brought the body into existence. They are therefore difficult to change, even as environmental conditions change around the body. The directors of a private sector body have more freedom in making up the objectives of the company as they go along, and can change the objectives rapidly in response to changing conditions.

The value of the output of a private sector body can be easily determined in an unbiased way, by looking at the sales revenue achieved. Such numbers can therefore be part of the objectives to be achieved. There is no easy way for determining the economic value of the output of a public sector body; placing a value on the achievements of a country's Navy last year is almost impossible.

The mission statement of the company in the question recognises the role of the company in having responsibilities to different groups of stakeholders: shareholders, customers, the community at large, etc. Some public sector bodies appear to ignore the interests of certain stakeholders; you might for example be able to think of bodies that appear to be run more for the employees of the body itself rather than the public it is supposed to be serving. Private sector bodies that ignore stakeholders go bust and leave the marketplace. Failing public sector bodies often are rewarded with greater slices of public money to finance their inadequacies.

Private sector companies can attract finance in a free marketplace if they wish to expand. Public sector bodies are constrained by short-term cash limits set by the government depending on the state of the public finances. This acts against the construction of long-term strategic plans in the public sector.

The public sector has historically had little understanding of capital as a scarce resource. In the objective quoted in the question for the health authority, there is no mention of giving value for money to the taxpayers who finance the services. Private sector companies have to give value for money to their shareholders; otherwise the shareholders will sell their shares and the share price will fall, making future capital issues more expensive.

(b) In terms of the health authority's current objective, three performance measures that could be used are:

Number of patients who survive serious surgery: this would give a measure of the quality of emergency health care provided, and could be calculated as an absolute figure and a percentage, and compared with the figures for the previous year and nationally.

Length of time (on average) before an ambulance arrives after an emergency call is made: this could be compared with the figure for the previous year and for other similar regions of the country.

Length of waiting list for serious operations, i.e. the average time period between a patient being recommended for an operation by his doctor and the operation actually taking place: this figure could be compared with the figure for the previous year and with national figures.

(c) Decisions have to be made at both a local level (the tactical and operational decisions in running the public sector organisation) and a national level (mainly in terms of the amount of money to be made available to the service).

If insufficient funds have been made available to a health authority, the only way it can maintain standards is to let the waiting list increase. This might reflect badly on the local managers, but the responsibility for the problem really lies with the politicians who have decided to inadequately finance the organisation.

Similar problems exist in other public sector areas. Consider the police, for example. If they arrest more criminals, is this good or bad? Some people would say it is a good thing in that they are detecting more crime; others would say it is a failure of their crime prevention measures. If the statistical percentage of successful prosecutions brought was to be used as a performance measure, this might pressure the police to release on caution all those suspects against whom the police felt they did not have a watertight case. This is surely not in the public interest.

The recommended solution is for public sector organisations to rephrase their statements of objectives to bring more stakeholders into view, and then to construct a range of performance measures, which takes into account the wishes of each of these stakeholders.

KAPLAN PUBLISHING

Non-financial performance indicators and corporate failure

Chapter learning objectives

Upon completion of this chapter you will be able to:

- discuss the interaction of non-financial performance indicators with financial performance indicators

- discuss the implications of the growing emphasis on non-financial performance indicators

- discuss the significance of non-financial performance indicators in relation to employees

- identify and discuss the significance of non-financial performance indicators in relation to product/service quality, e.g. customer satisfaction reports, repeat business ratings, access and availability

- discuss the difficulties in interpreting data on qualitative issues

- discuss the significance of brand awareness and company profile and their potential impact on business performance

- evaluate the 'balanced scorecard' approach as a way in which to improve the range and linkage between performance measures

- evaluate the 'performance pyramid' as a way in which to link strategy, operations and performance

- evaluate the work of Fiitzgerald and Moon that considers performance measurement in business services using building blocks for dimensions, standards and rewards

- discuss and apply the Performance Prism

- assess the potential likelihood of corporate failure, utilising quantitative and qualitative performance measures and models (such as Z-scores and Argenti)

- assess and critique quantitative and qualitative corporate failure prediction models

- identify and discuss performance improvement strategies that may be adopted in order to prevent corporate failure

- discuss how long-term survival necessitates consideration of life-cycle issues

- identify and discuss operational changes to performance management systems required to implement the performance improvement strategies.

1 Assumed knowledge

Chapter 11 builds on your knowledge of financial and non-financial performance measurement from Paper F5.

2 Introduction

In Chapters 8 and 9 we looked at a wide range of financial performance measures. However, in order to fully appraise the performance of an organisation, and to understand if the best techniques are being used to drive its success, it is useful to use a range of financial performance indicators (FPIs) and non-financial performance indicators (NFPIs) to evaluate performance.

The final part of the chapter covers the separate topic of corporate failure. It is important that an organisation can identify situations where there is a risk of corporate failure and take steps to try to prevent that failure from occurring.

3 Drawbacks of sole reliance on financial performance measures

There are a number of problems associated with the sole use of FPIs to monitor performance:

Short-termism

The problem of short-termism was discussed in Chapter 8. Linking rewards to financial performance may tempt managers to make decisions that will improve short-term financial performance but may have a negative impact on long-term profitability. For example, a manager may decide to delay investment in order to boost the short-term profits of their division.

Internal focus

Financial performance measures tend to have an internal focus. In order to compete successfully it is important that external factors (such as customer satisfaction and competitors' actions) are also considered.

Manipulation of results

Most managers will act in good faith and have an honest approach to performance management. However, in order to achieve target financial performance (and hence their reward), some managers may be tempted to manipulate results, e.g. costs recorded in the current year may be wrongly recorded in the next year's accounts in order to improve current year performance.

It is important to point out that NFPIs can also be open to manipulation by managers (in fact they may be even more open to manipulation due to their subjective nature). However, using a comprehensive range of FPIs and NFPIs should assist in achieving a true and fair view of organisational performance and any problems associated with manipulation of results should be minimised.

Do not convey the whole picture

The use of FPIs has limited benefit to the company since they do not convey the full picture regarding the factors that drive long-term success and maximisation of shareholder wealth, e.g. customer satisfaction, ability to innovate, quality. .

Backward looking

Financial performance measures are traditionally backward looking. This is not suitable in today's dynamic business environment.

4 Solution = use financial and non-financial performance indicators

In order to overcome the problems discussed in section 3, a broader range of measures should be used.

The optimum system for performance measurement and control will include:

- Financial performance indicators (FPIs) – it is still important to monitor financial performance, e.g. using ROCE, EBITDA, EVA.

- Non-financial performance indicators (NFPIs) – these measures will reflect the long-term viability and health of the organisation.

The measures used should be tailored to the circumstances in the organisation.

By focusing on the examination and improvement of upstream determinants (e.g. quality, flexibility, resource utilisation and innovation), improvements in downstream results (e.g. competitiveness and financial performance) should occur.

The models used to evaluate financial and non-financial performance will be reviewed in detail in section 7.

FPIs and NFPIs

The following table gives examples of possible FPIs and NFPIs:

Financial performance	<ul><li>cost</li><li>profitability</li><li>liquidity</li><li>budget variance analysis</li><li>market ratios</li><li>level of bad debts</li><li>return on capital employed (ROCE).</li></ul>
Competitiveness	<ul><li>sales growth by product or service</li><li>measures of customer base</li><li>relative market share and position.</li></ul>

Activity	• sales units
	• labour/machine hours
	• number of passengers carried
	• number of material requisitions serviced
	• number of accounts reconciled
	• whichever measurement is used it may be compared against a pre-set target.
Productivity	• efficiency measurements of resources planned against consumed
	• measurements of resources available against those used
	• productivity measurements such as production per person or per hour or per shift.
Quality of service	• quality measures in every unit
	• evaluate suppliers on the basis of quality
	• number of customer complaints received
	• number of new accounts lost or gained
	• rejections as a percentage of production or sales.
Customer satisfaction	• speed of response to customer needs
	• informal listening by calling a certain number of customers each week
	• number of customer visits to the factory or workplace
	• number of factory and non-factory manager visits to customers.
Quality of working life	• days' absence
	• labour turnover
	• overtime
	• measures of job satisfaction.
Innovation	• proportion of new products and services to old ones
	• new product or service sales levels.

5 NFPIs and business performance

5.1 Introduction

There are a number of areas that are particularly important for ensuring the success of a business and where the use of NFPIs plays a key role. These include:

- the management of human resources
- product and service quality
- brand awareness and company profile.

Each of these will be reviewed in turn.

5.2 The management of human resources

- Traditionally the main performance measure for staff was cost (a FPI).
- However, many businesses (particularly service organisations) have started to view staff as a major asset and recognise that it is important to attract, motivate and retain highly qualified and experienced staff. As a result, NFPIs are now also used to monitor and control staff.
- Measurement of factors such as skill levels, training, absenteeism and employee turnover will assist in checking that the organisation is utilising its employees effectively in the pursuit of organisational objectives.

Test your understanding 1

Required:

Discuss, with reasons, two non-financial performance indicators that can be used to monitor and control employees.

5.3 Product and service quality

Problems with product or service quality can have a long-term impact on the business and they can lead to customer dissatisfaction and loss of future sales.

NFPIs are particularly useful when assessing product and service quality. Measures may focus on:

- the **quality of incoming supplies**, e.g. a sample of incoming supplies may be inspected to determine the level of quality

- the **quality of work completed** – again, a sample of output may be checked to verify the levels of quality

- **customer satisfaction** – one definition of quality is 'the ability of a product or service to meet customers' needs'. Customer satisfaction, loyalty and repeat business go hand in hand and it is important to measure customer satisfaction, e.g. using customer surveys.

Product and service quality

- A product (or service) and its components should be critically and objectively compared both with competition and with customer expectation and needs, for example:
    - Is it good value?
    - Can it really deliver superior performance?
    - How does it compare with competitor offerings?
    - How will it compare with competitor offerings in the future given competitive innovations?

- Product and service quality are usually based on several critical dimensions that should be identified and measured over time. Performance on all these dimensions needs to be combined to give a complete picture. For example:
    - an automobile firm can have measures of defects, ability to perform to specifications, durability and ability to repair
    - a bank might be concerned with waiting time, accuracy of transactions, and making the customer experience friendly and positive
    - a computer manufacturer can examine relative performance specifications, and product reliability as reflected by repair data.

- The relative importance of different factors will vary from company to company and between customers, but achieving high quality means ensuring all the factors of the product or service package meet customer requirements.

- Measures should be tracked over time and compared with those of competitors. It is the relative comparisons and changes that are most important.

- One of the most important assets of many firms is the loyalty of the customer base. Measures of sales and market share are useful but are crude indicators of how customers really feel about a firm.

- Often the most sensitive and insightful information comes from those who have decided to leave a brand or firm. Thus, 'exit interviews' for dissatisfied customers who have 'left' a brand can be very productive.

- Another key area is access and availability of products and services, as failure in these areas can cause a loss of customers.

- Other possible sources of non-financial information related to product and service quality and customer satisfaction are:

    - repeat business ratings, which is useful as a complement to measurements of absolute sales.

    - general customer satisfaction surveys

    - monitoring of complaints both in terms of numbers and type of complaint.

Illustration 1 – Quality of service at BAA

BAA (the former state owned British Airports Authority) uses regular customer surveys for measuring customer perceptions of a wide variety of service quality attributes, including, for example, the cleanliness of its facilities, the helpfulness of its staff and the ease of finding one's way around the airport. Public correspondence is also analysed in detail, and comment cards are available in the terminals so that passengers can comment voluntarily on service levels received. Duty terminal managers also sample the services and goods offered by outlets in the terminals, assessing them from a customer perspective.

They check the cleanliness and condition of service facilities and complete detailed checklists which are submitted daily to senior terminal managers. The company has also a wealth of internal monitoring systems that record equipment faults and failures, and report equipment and staff availability. These systems are supported by the terminal managers who circulate the terminals on a full-time basis, helping customers as necessary, reporting any equipment faults observed and making routine assessments of the level of service provided by BAA and its concessionaires.

 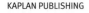

BAA plc

Quality characteristic	Measures	Mechanisms
Access	Walking distance/ease of finding way around	Surveys/operational data
Aesthetics	Staff appearance/airport appearance/quality of catering	Surveys/inspection
Availability	Equipment availability	Internal fault monitors
Cleanliness	Environment and equipment	Surveys/inspection
Comfort	Crowdedness	Surveys/inspection
Communication	Information clarity/clarity of labelling and pricing	Surveys/inspection
Competence	Staff efficiency	Management inspection
Courtesy	Courtesy of staff	Surveys/inspection
Friendliness	Staff attitude	Surveys/inspection
Reliability	Equipment faults	Surveys/inspection
Responsiveness	Staff responsiveness	Surveys/inspection
Security	Efficiency of security checks/ number of urgent safety reports	Surveys/internal data

5.4 Brand awareness and company profile

Brand awareness is an indicator of the strength of a product's/ service's place in the customers' minds.

Developing and maintaining a brand and/or a company profile can be expensive. However, it can also enhance performance due to customer loyalty which results in repurchasing and continued use of the products. The value of a brand/company profile is based on the extent to which it has:

- high loyalty

- name awareness

- perceived quality

- other attributes such as patents or trademarks.

Measuring customer loyalty

FPIs may focus on areas such as:

- marketing spend against sales
- market share
- elasticity of demand to price and
- profit margins compared to other companies who make similar products but whose brand strength is much stronger/ weaker.

NFPIs may focus on areas such as:

- customer awareness and
- consumer opinions.

Brand awareness and company profile

- If potential customers do not know about a company, they will not purchase from it. Therefore, one of the main goals of any business should be to build brand awareness.

- Assessment of brand awareness means identifying the product or company's associations in the minds of customers, and its perceived quality. This is related to but can be very different from actual quality – but ultimately it is the consumer who decides what a brand is really worth.

- Associations can be monitored in an effective way by talking to groups of customers informally on a regular basis. The identification of changes in important associations is likely to emerge from such efforts. More structured tools are also available.

- A brand or firm can be scaled on its key dimensions using a representative sample of customers. Key dimensions can then be tracked over time.

- For companies with a high company profile it is particularly important that brand awareness is positive.

- Measures of brand awareness can either look at the direct link between the brand and overall results, e.g. by considering the price premiums which the company obtains, or monitor the more intangible aspects such as awareness and consumer opinion.

Test your understanding 2

Required:

How are the measures of product and service quality related to brand awareness and company profile?

6 Difficulties in using and interpreting qualitative data

Most NFPIs are in qualitative terms. These qualitative factors can often:

- be difficult to measure. For example, two separate customers may be provided with an identical product or service but may have different perceptions as to how well it satisfied their needs.

- be difficult to express in quantitative terms. This problem can be addressed, for example, by using a scoring system on a customer survey for the level of customer satisfaction.

In Chapter 6 we discussed the difficulties in recording and processing data of a qualitative nature and looked at how a business can deal with qualitative data.

Qualitative data

Difficulties in using and interpreting qualitative information

Particularly at higher levels of management, non-financial information is often not in numerical terms, but qualitative, or soft, rather than quantitative. Qualitative information often represents opinions of individuals and user groups. However there are issues related to its use:

- Decisions often appear to have been made on the basis of quantitative information; however qualitative considerations often influence the final choice, even if this is not explicit.

- Conventional information systems are usually designed to carry quantitative information and are sometimes less able to convey qualitative issues. However the impact of a decreased output requirement on staff morale is something that may be critical but it is not something that an information system would automatically report.

- In both decision making and control, managers should be aware that an information system may provide a limited or distorted picture of what is actually happening. In many situations, sensitivity has to be used in interpreting the output of an information system.

- Information in the form of opinions is difficult to measure and interpret. It also requires more analysis.

- Qualitative information may be incomplete.

- Qualitative aspects are often interdependent and it can be difficult to separate the impact of different factors.

- Evaluating qualitative information is subjective, as it is not in terms of numbers – there are no objective formulae as there are with financial measures.

- The cost of collecting and improving qualitative information may be very high.

- Difficulties in measurement and interpretation mean that qualitative factors are often ignored.

Working with qualitative information

Despite the challenges it presents, there may be ways of improving the use of qualitative information.

- Where it is important to make use of qualitative information, it is essential to ensure that users are aware of any assumptions made in analysis and of the difficulties involved in measuring and counting it.

- It is sometimes possible to quantify issues which are initially qualitative, by looking at its impact, e.g. when looking at service quality, considering the cost of obtaining the same quality of service elsewhere.

- Even if it is not possible to quantify issues precisely, attempting to do so is likely to improve decision making as the issues are likely to have been thought through more thoroughly.

Test your understanding 3

Required:

Your company is considering replacing its current products with a new range which will use different production techniques. What qualitative issues will you need to consider?

7 Models for evaluating financial and non-financial performance

7.1 Introduction

There are four key models that an organisation can use to evaluate its financial and non-financial performance.

- Kaplan and Norton's balanced scorecard
- Fitzgerald and Moon's building block model
- The performance pyramid
- The Performance Prism

These are highly examinable. Each one will be reviewed in turn but remember that questions may ask you to compare and contrast the methods rather than just discussing each one is isolation.

7.2 Benefits of models for evaluating financial and non-financial performance

The benefits of these models are as follows:

- financial and non-financial performance measures are included
- they are linked in to corporate strategy
- include external as well as internal measures
- include all important factors regardless of how easy they are to measure
- show clearly the tradeoffs between different dimensions of performance
- show how measures will motivate managers and employees.

7.3 Kaplan and Norton's balanced scorecard

What is the balanced scorecard?

The balanced scorecard provides a framework which can be utilised to develop a multi-dimensional set of performance measures for strategic control of the business.

The balanced scorecard includes:

- financial measures (these reveal the results of actions already taken)
- non-financial measures (these are drivers of future financial performance)
- external as well as internal information.

The balanced scorecard allows managers to look at the business from four important perspectives:

Within each of these perspectives a business should seek to:

* identify a series of goals (i.e. CSFs) and
* to establish appropriate measures (KPIs).

These should be in line with the overall strategic objectives and vision of the organisation.

Illustration 2 – Examples of goals and measures

A balanced scorecard for an electronics company could include the following goals and measures:

	Goals (CSFs)	Measures (KPIs)
Customer perspective	Low cost	Benchmark cost vs competitor's cost
	High quality	% defects
	Responsive service	% on-time deliveries
Internal perspective	Operational excellence	Production cycle time, rectification time, % of production completed on time and within budget
	Employee satisfaction	Staff turnover
Innovation and learning	Innovation	% of income from new products
	Internal learning	Number of employee suggestions and % implemented, % of time spent on staff development
Financial perspective	Growth and development	Quarterly sales growth
	Survival	Cash flow
	Profitability	ROCE

It would be beneficial to rank the goals and measures in order of importance.

Test your understanding 4

Required:

Suggest some performance measures for a building company involved in house building and commercial property and operating in a number of different countries.

Evaluation of the balanced scorecard as a performance measurement tool

The balanced scorecard provides a balanced view of organisational performance in that:

- it includes a mixture of financial and non-financial measures
- it covers internal and external matters
- it links the fulfilment of long-term and short-term objectives to the achievement of overall strategy and vision.

However, the balanced scorecard is not without its problems.

Test your understanding 5

Required:

Discuss the disadvantages of the balanced scorecard.

Implementing the balanced scorecard

There are four essential activities which have to be executed rigorously if the implementation of the balanced scorecard is to succeed:

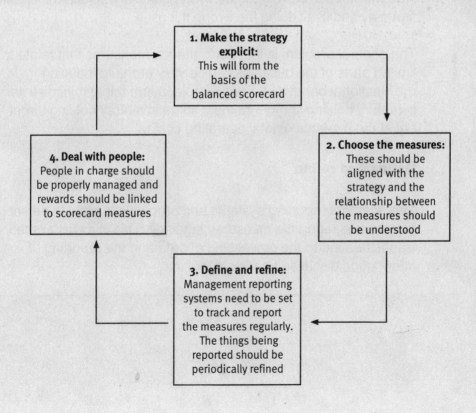

1. Make the strategy explicit:
This will form the basis of the balanced scorecard

2. Choose the measures:
These should be aligned with the strategy and the relationship between the measures should be understood

3. Define and refine:
Management reporting systems need to be set to track and report the measures regularly. The things being reported should be periodically refined

4. Deal with people:
People in charge should be properly managed and rewards should be linked to scorecard measures

Steps involved in implementing the scorecard

(1) Make the strategy explicit

The starting point in producing a balanced scorecard is identifying the strategic requirements for success in the firm. Typically, those strategic requirements will relate to products, markets, growth and resources (human, intellectual and capital).

For example, businesses like Dell may want to be low-cost producers achieving competitive advantage from selling undifferentiated products at lower prices than those of competitors, or a business may have a product development strategy to become a leader in technology and command a premium like Apple. Their strategy may also be to develop and maintain market share, like Microsoft, or their strategy may be to occupy the number-one or number-two position in their lines of business.

(2) Choose the measures

Performance measures have to be selected that clearly relate to the achievement of the strategies identified in the earlier process. As has been seen throughout the discussion of performance measures in this text, the selection of appropriate indicators and measures is critical. The selected measures form the goals that management communicates to staff as being important. Those goals are what staff will strive to achieve. If the wrong goals are selected then the firm may find itself doing the wrong things.

The general problem is that performance measures that relate to limited parts of the business can be very prone to inducing dysfunctional behaviour. For example, a firm might minimise its inventory holding in order to meet some inventory holding target – but at the expense of total operating costs.

(3) Define and refine

Management reporting systems and procedures need to be set up to track and report the measures regularly. This involves all the issues relating to the processing of data and the reporting of information discussed earlier in this text.

The precise requirements of reporting associated with the use of the balanced scorecard will make demands on both the management accounting and IT systems in an organisation. Fully satisfying those demands has a cost and sometimes compromises may have to be made in order to contain that cost.

All sorts of practical problems may be encountered in reporting on an indicator. For example, when reporting on revenue:

- How is revenue calculated and when is it recorded?
- Should it include the non-core business activity?
- Should revenue be reported under product, region or customer headings?
- How should interdivisional transactions be reported?

Operating the management accounting system associated with the balanced scorecard requires that the things being reported should be defined and periodically refined.

(4) **Deal with people**

The balanced scorecard is an exercise in modifying human behaviour. It is its interaction with people that determines whether or not it will work.

Balanced scorecards can easily become a confusing mass of measures, some of which even contradict each other. There may be too many measures and action to achieve some of them may contribute to failure to achieve others. The measures may not always be prioritised.

To be effective, the measures contained in the scorecard should be limited in number, reasonably consistent and ranked in some order of priority. Further, performance measures should be aligned with the management structure. Career progression and remuneration should be appropriately linked to scorecard measure linked performance. Organisations which adopt a balanced scorecard but continue to reward managers on the basis of a narrow range of traditional financial measures are likely to be disappointed by the results.

Practical example of scorecard implementation

One example reported in management literature of how the balanced scorecard might be applied is the US case of Analog Devices (a semi-conductor manufacturer) in the preparation of its five-year strategic plan for 1998–2002.

Analog Devices had as its main corporate objective: 'Achieving our goals for growth, profits, market share and quality creates the environment and economic means to satisfy the needs of our employees, stockholders, customers and others associated with the firm. Our success depends on people who understand the interdependence and congruence of their personal goals with those of the company and who are thus motivated to contribute towards the achievement of those goals.'

Three basic strategic objectives identified by the company were market leadership, sales growth and profitability.

The company adopted targets as follows:

Customer perspective

- Percentage of orders delivered on time: a target was set for the five-year period to increase the percentage of on-time deliveries from 85% to at least 99.8%.

- Outgoing defect levels: the target was to reduce the number of defects in product items delivered to customers, from 500 per month to fewer than 10 per month.

- Order lead time: a target was set to reduce the time between receiving a customer order to delivery from 10 weeks to less than three weeks.

Internal perspective

- Manufacturing cycle time: to reduce this from 15 weeks to 4 to 5 weeks over the five-year planning period.

- Defective items in production: to reduce defects in production from 5,000 per month to fewer than 10 per month.

Learning and innovation perspective

- Having products rated 'number one' by at least 50% of customers, based on their attitudes to whether the company was making the right products, performance, price, reliability, quality, delivery, lead time, customer support, responsiveness, willingness to co-operate and willingness to form partnerships.

- The number of new products introduced to the market.

- Sales revenue from new products.

- The new product sales ratio: this was the percentage of total sales achieved by products introduced to the market within the previous six quarters.

- Average annual revenues for new products in their third year.

- Reducing the average time to bring new product ideas to market.

Financial targets were set for revenue, revenue growth, profit and return on assets, but the idea was that the financial targets would flow from achieving the other targets stated above.

Analog Devices sought to adopt financial and non-financial performance measures within a single system, in which the various targets were consistent with each other and were in no way incompatible.

Strategy mapping

Strategy mapping was developed by Kaplan and Norton as an extension to the balanced scorecard and to make the implementation of the scorecard more successful.

The steps involved are:

- At the head of the strategy map is the overriding objective of the organisation which describes how it creates value. This is then connected to the organisation's other objectives, categorised in terms of the four perspectives of the balanced scorecard, showing the cause-and-effect relationships between them.

- The strategy map helps organisations to clarify, describe and communicate the strategy and objectives, both within the organisation and to external stakeholders by presenting the key relationships between the overall objective and the supporting strategy and objectives in one diagram.

Issues when implementing the strategy map:

- Organisations have often found it difficult to translate the corporate vision into behaviour and actions which achieve the key corporate objectives.

- In practice, many employees do not understand the organisation's strategy, and systems such as performance management and budgeting are not linked to the strategy.

Question practice

The following question is of the same standard and style as the real exam. It examines the balanced scorecard, amongst other areas, and effectively demonstrates the linkages between different performance management techniques. Take the time to attempt the question in full and learn from the answer, considering both content and style.

Test your understanding 6

Jump is a listed business operating a chain of quality health clubs in a European country. The company has a strong reputation for the quality of its service but there are a number of other health clubs operating in the country and the market is fiercely competitive.

The country in which Jump is located is currently in recession. Consumer spending is falling throughout the economy and there is no immediate likelihood of a resumption of growth. Appendix 1 shows the financial data for Jump for the past two years.

Jump's Chief Executive Officer (CEO) has recently conducted a strategic review of the business in the context of the current economic recession. He has identified the following strategy as critical for Jump's success:

(1) Focus on key customers

(2) Ensure Jump's offerings meet the needs of these customers.

(3) Reduce or eliminate costs which do not address the needs of these customers.

(4) Build for the future using a programme of sustainable development.

Jump recognises that it operates in a highly competitive environment and periodically monitors its share of the market and compares its prices with those of its competitors. The CEO has identified the need to operate a more systematic method of performance improvement. To this end, he believes that competitor benchmarking is necessary and has information that at least one of Jump's main competitors benchmark already. Appendix 2 contains data analysing Jump and its two main competitors; Fitness Matters and Active First.

Appendix 1: Financial data for Jump

	20X0	20X1
	€m	€m
Operating profit	51.9	42.7
Interest	4.2	6.1
Profit before tax	47.7	36.6
Profit for the year	37.2	26.3
EVA	20.6	7.2

	20X0	20X1
Average number of shares in issue	140 million	140 million
Stock market information:		
Country's market index	1,020.7	704.3
Health club sector index	1,711.3	1,320.3
Jump's average share price	€1.22	€1.03

Appendix 2: Comparative data

	Fitness Matters		Active First		Jump	
	20X0	20X1	20X0	20X1	20X0	20X1
Revenue €m	246	239	521	508	483	522
Profit for the year €m	19.3	17.4	40.4	25.9	37.2	26.3
No. of health clubs	18	20	26	35	20	21
Market share	12.4%	12.2%	16.9%	15.6%	16.0%	16.0%
Revenue per health club €m	13.7	12.0	20.0	14.5	24.2	24.9

Required:

(a) Describe the different perspectives of the balanced scorecard showing how the new strategy as outlined by the CEO links to these perspectives. Suggest appropriate performance measures for Jump for each of the detailed points within the strategy.

(8 marks)

(b) Assess the financial performance of the company using share price, EPS and EVA. Critically evaluate the use of these performance metrics and how they may affect management behaviour.

(11 marks)

(c) Prepare a report for the board on a benchmarking exercise using the information given in appendix 2.

  (i) Evaluate the benefits and difficulties of benchmarking in this situation.

  (ii) Evaluate the performance of Jump using the data given in the question. Conclude as to the performance of the company.

(13 marks)

Professional marks for appropriateness of format, style and structure of the report.

(3 marks)

(Total: 35 marks)

Student accountant articles: visit the ACCA website, www.accaglobal.com, to review the article on 'performance measures to support competitive advantage'.

7.4 Fitzgerald and Moon's building block model

Fitzgerald and Moon have developed an approach to improving the performance measurement system in **service organisations**. It suggests that the performance measurement system should be based on the three building blocks of dimensions, standards and rewards.

Dimension
Competitiveness
Financial performance
Quality of service
Flexibility
Resource utilisation
Innovation

Standards	Rewards
Ownership	Clarity
Achievability	Motivation
Fairness	Controllability

Dimensions

The dimensions are the goals, i.e. the CSFs for the business and suitable metrics must be developed to measure each performance dimension.

Dimensions fall into two categories: downstream results (competitiveness and financial performance) and upstream determinants (quality of service, flexibility, resource utilisation and innovation).

Dimension	Type of measure
Competitiveness	Relative market share
Financial performance	Turnover growth
Quality of service	Product reliability
Flexibility	Delivery time
Resource utilisation	Productivity
Innovation	New product numbers

Dimensions of performance

The table above identifies the dimensions of performance. The first two of these relate to downstream results, the other four to upstream determinants. For example, a new product innovation will not impact on profit, cash flow and market share achieved in the past – but a high level of innovation provides an indicator of how profit, cash flow and market share will move in the future. If innovation is the driver or determinant of future performance, it is a key success factor.

Standards

The standards are the targets (KPIs) set for the metrics chosen from the dimensions measured. The standards set should have the following characteristics:

- **Ownership**: Managers who participate in the setting of standards are more likely to accept and be motivated by the standards than managers on whom standards are imposed.

- **Achievability**: An achievable, but challenging, standard is a better motivator than an unachievable one.

- **Fairness**: When setting standards across an organisation, care should be undertaken to ensure that all managers have equally challenging standards.

Rewards

Rewards are the motivators for the employees to work towards the standards set. Remember:

- what gets measured gets done

- what gets measured and fed back gets done well

- what gets rewarded gets repeated.

To ensure that employees are **motivated** to meet standards, the standards need to be **clear** (e.g. the target is to 'achieve four product innovations per year' rather than to simply 'innovate') and linked to **controllable** factors. The actual means of motivation may involve performance related pay, a bonus or a promotion.

Fitzgerald and moon example			
Fitzgerald and Moon applied to a Washing Machine Manufacturer:			

Dimension = CSF	Flexibility – On time delivery	Quality of service	Financial performance
Standard = KPI	Delivery speed	Reliability	Profitability
Reward	Points for each on time delivery – leading to a bonus	% commission for repair engineers from fee or warranty paid	Management profit related bonuses

Test your understanding 7

FL provides training on financial subjects to staff of small and medium-sized businesses. Training is at one of two levels – for clerical staff, instructing them on how to use simple financial accounting computer packages, and for management, on management accounting and financial management issues.

Training consists of tutorial assistance, in the form of workshops or lectures, and the provision of related material – software, texts and printed notes.

Tuition days may be of standard format and content, or designed to meet the client's particular specifications. All courses are run on client premises and, in the case of clerical training courses, are limited to 8 participants per course.

FL has recently introduced a 'helpline' service, which allows course participants to phone in with any problems or queries arising after course attendance. This is offered free of charge.

FL employs administrative and management staff. Course lecturers are hired as required, although a small core of technical staff is employed on a part-time basis by FL to prepare customer-specific course material and to man the helpline.

Material for standard courses is bought in from a group company, who also print up the customer-specific course material.

Required:

Suggest a measure for each of the six dimensions of the building block model.

Question practice

The question below is an extract from a past exam question. It is a great question to attempt to ensure that you fully understand the building block model and that you can apply your knowledge in the context of the scenario.

Test your understanding 8

The Sentinel Company (TSC) offers a range of door-to-door express delivery services. The company operates using a network of depots and distribution centres throughout the country of Nickland. The following information is available:

(1) Each depot is solely responsible for all customers within a specified area. It collects goods from customers within its own area for delivery both within the specific area covered by the depot and elsewhere in Nickland.

(2) Collections made by a depot for delivery outside its own area are forwarded to the depots from which the deliveries will be made to the customers.

(3) Each depot must therefore integrate its deliveries to customers to include:

    (i) goods that it has collected within its own area; and

    (ii) goods that are transferred to it from depots within other areas for delivery to customers in its area.

(4) Each depot earns revenue based on the invoiced value of all consignments collected from customers in its area, regardless of the location of the ultimate distribution depot.

(5) Depot costs comprise all of its own operating costs plus an allocated share of all company costs including centralised administration services and distribution centre costs.

(6) Bonuses for the management team and all employees at each depot are payable quarterly. The bonus is based on the achievement of a series of target values by each depot.

(7) Internal benchmarking is used at TSC in order to provide sets of absolute standards that all depots are expected to attain.

(8) The Appendix shows the target values and the actual values achieved for each of a sample group of four depots situated in Donatellotown (D), Leonardotown (L), Michaelangelotown (M), and Raphaeltown (R). The target values focus on three areas:

    (i) depot revenue and profitability

    (ii) customer care and service delivery; and

    (iii) credit control and administrative efficiency.

The bonus is based on a points system, which is also used as a guide to the operational effectiveness at each depot. One point is allocated where the target value for each item in the Appendix is either achieved or exceeded, and a zero score where the target is not achieved.

Appendix: Target and actual value statistics for Donatellotown (D), Leonardotown (L), Michaelangelotown (M), and Raphaeltown (R) for the Quarter ended 31 October 2008

Revenue and Profit Statistics:

	Revenue (1)		Profit (2)	
	Target	**Actual**	**Target**	**Actual**
	$m	$m	$m	$m
Company overall	200	240	30	32
Selected depots:				
D	16	15	2.4	2.3
L	14	18	2.1	2.4
M	12	14	1.8	2.2
R	18	22	2.7	2.8

Note: For the purpose of calculation of each depot's points it is essential that actual profit as a percentage of actual revenue must exceed the target profit (%).

Customer Care & Service Delivery Statistics:

	Target	Actual			
Selected Depots:		**D**	**L**	**M**	**R**
	%	%	%	%	%
Measure (% of total):					
(3) Late collection of consignments	2.0	1.9	2.1	1.8	2.4
(4) Misdirected consignments	4.0	4.2	3.9	3.3	5.1
(5) Delayed response to complaints	1.0	0.7	0.9	0.8	1.2
(6) Delays due to vehicle breakdown	1.0	1.1	1.4	0.3	2.0
Measure (% of revenue):					
(7) Lost items	1.0	0.6	0.9	0.8	1.9
(8) Damaged items	2.0	1.5	2.4	1.5	1.8
Credit Control & Administration Efficiency Statistics:					
(9) Average debtor weeks	5.5	5.8	4.9	5.1	6.2
(10) Debtors in excess of 60 days (% of total)	5%	?	?	?	?
(11) Invoice queries (% of total)	5%	1.1%	1.4%	0.8%	2.7%
(12) Credit notes as a % of revenue	0.5%	?	?	?	?

Other information:

	D	L	M	R
Aged Debtor analysis (extract):	$000	$000	$000	$000
Less than 30 days	1,300	1,500	1,180	2,000
31–60 days	321	133	153	552
Value of credit notes raised during the period ($000)	45	36	28	132

Note: TSC operates all year round.

Required:

Prepare a report for the directors of TSC which:

(a) contains a summary table which shows the points gained (or forfeited) by each depot. The points table should facilitate the ranking of each depot against the others for each of the 12 measures provided in the Appendix

(9 marks)

(b) evaluates the relative performance of the four depots as indicated by the analysis in the summary table prepared in (a)

(5 marks)

(c) assesses TSC in terms of financial performance, competitiveness, service quality, resource utilisation, flexibility and innovation and discusses the interrelationships between these terms, incorporating examples from within TSC; and

(10 marks)

(d) critiques the performance measurement system at TSC.

(5 marks)

Note: this requirement includes 4 professional marks.

(Total: 33 marks)

Evaluation of the building block model

The building block model has a number of advantages:

- All key determinants of success (financial and non-financial) in performance will be measured.

- It is specifically tailored to the service industry.

- The reward system will operate in a way to optimally motivate the individual staff members.

- Targets are set in such a way to engage and motivate staff, i.e. through ownership, achievability and fairness.

However, it is not without its drawbacks:

- It is not suitable for non-service companies.

- It can be difficult to see how the building blocks link to the strategic objectives.

7.5 Performance pyramid

- The performance pyramid, developed by Lynch and Cross, includes a hierarchy of financial and non-financial performance measures.

- The aim is to produce a set of performance measures which are comprehensive in examining the results and the determinants of those results for the organisation.

- It is based on the belief that each level of the organisation has different concerns but they must support each other in order to achieve the overall objective of the organisation.

- The pyramid shape is to emphasise that the measures from the operational up to the strategic levels should support the corporate vision.

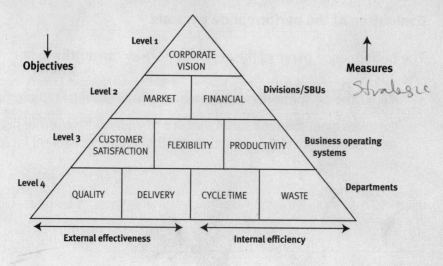

Level 1: At the top of the organisation is the corporate vision through which the organisation describes how it will achieve long-term success and competitive advantage.

Level 2: This focuses on the achievement of an organisation's CSFs in terms of market-related measures and financial measures. The marketing and financial success of a proposal is the initial focus for the achievement of corporate vision.

Level 3: The marketing and financial strategies set at level 2 must be linked to the achievement of customer satisfaction, increased flexibility and high productivity at the next level. These are the guiding forces that drive the strategic objectives of the organisation.

Level 4: The status of the level 3 driving forces can be monitored using the lower level departmental indicators of quality, delivery, cycle time and waste.

The left hand side of the pyramid contains measures which have an external focus and which are predominantly non-financial. Those on the right are focused on the internal efficiency of the organisation and are predominantly financial.

> **Test your understanding 9**
>
> **Required:**
>
> Suggest two measures (KPIs) for each of the three categories at the business operating systems level, i.e. customer satisfaction, flexibility and productivity.

Student accountant article: visit the ACCA website, www.accaglobal.com, to review the article on 'the pyramids and pitfalls of performance measurement' from September 2005.

Evaluation of the performance pyramid

The performance pyramid has a number of key **strengths** in that:

- it links the performance measures at different levels of the organisation.

- it makes clear the measures that are of interest to external parties (such as customer satisfaction) and those that focus on internal factors (such as waste).

However, there are a number of **drawbacks**:

- Implementation of the performance pyramid will use vital management time and resource.

- Some measures may conflict, for example there will be a trade off between quality and cost.

7.6 The Performance Prism

The Performance Prism is a performance management framework. Most frameworks focus on the needs of the owners of the organisation. Other stakeholders such as customers, employees and suppliers tend to be forgotten about.

The Performance Prism aims to manage the performance of an organisation from five interrelated 'facets':

(1) **Stakeholder satisfaction**

The first facet of the Prism focuses on who are the stakeholders and what do they want.

It is important to not only identify the stakeholders and their needs but to also establish the relative degree of power and interest of each of the stakeholder groups.

The organisation needs to identify the most important stakeholders and what they want from the organisation. They must then identify performance measures to ascertain how well the organisation is meeting these needs.

(2) **Stakeholder contribution**

The organisation will need to become more demanding of what it expects of its own stakeholders. It will need to identify exactly what it is that the organisation wants from those stakeholders, and then come up with ways to measure whether or not the stakeholders are providing it. The relationship between the company and its stakeholders should be seen as a two way relationship based on establishing the needs of each party and taking steps to fulfil those needs.

A good example is customers. The organisation will want profit from its customers and may therefore start to perform customer profitability analysis. Regarding the other major stakeholders, the following are examples of what the organisation may want from them:

– Shareholders – capital for growth and the willingness to take on more risk.

– Employees – flexibility and multiple skills.

(3) **Strategies**

In the Performance Prism, strategy is the route the organisation takes to reach the goal and not the goal itself. The goals are defined in the first two facets of the Prism, i.e. what strategies should the organisation be adopting to ensure that the wants and needs of its stakeholders are satisfied, while ensuring that its own requirements are satisfied too?

(4) **Processes**

After identifying the strategies, the organisation will need to identify if they have the right business processes to support the strategies. Business process re-engineering (BPR) may be used at this stage to identify any redundant processes. Value chain analysis may also be employed to identify what are the key processes. For example, when reviewing the organisation's processes it may be found that the current employee training and development scheme is not adequately meeting the needs of its employees and the organisation itself. Therefore, an entirely new training and development process may be designed and implemented.

Measures will then be developed to see how well these processes are working. Management will have to identify which are the most important processes, and focus attention on these, rather than simply measuring the functioning of all processes.

(5) **Capabilities**

Capabilities are the people, practices, technologies and infrastructure required to enable a process to work. It is important that the right capabilities exist within the organisation in order to support the processes identified, e.g. do we have the right people designing and implementing the new training programme?

In the capabilities facet of the Performance Prism, the organisation will need to identify which capabilities are required, and identify performance measures to see how well these capabilities are being performed. For example, at the end of each training course, employees may give written feedback on the tutors running the course and may grade the tutor as say good or excellent.

Benchmarking is likely to be used extensively in measuring the organisation's capabilities. In this respect, benchmarking is used to determine if the organisation has the right skills, not just currently but to take the organisation forward into the future. The McKinsey 7s model may also be used. The model identifies the hard elements as the strategy, organisation structure and systems alongside the soft elements of shared values, style, staff and skills. Performance measures in these areas may reflect, for example, any new research and development.

The framework

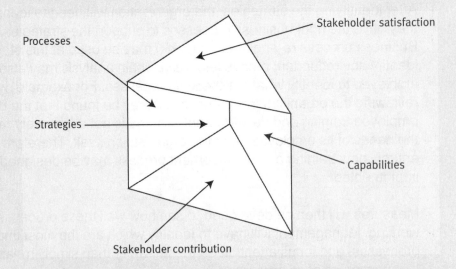

Processes

Stakeholder satisfaction

Strategies

Capabilities

Stakeholder contribution

Illustration 3 – The Performance Prism at DHL

In 2000, the board of DHL (UK) decided to replace monthly performance meetings (which focused too much on operational data) with quarterly meetings which took a more strategic approach. The Performance Prism was used as a framework at these meetings.

What do DHL's regular customers want and need?	• Delivery speed • Confidence in DHL • Relationship • Information accessibility
What strategies has/will DHL adopt(ed) to ensure that these wants and needs are satisfied?	• Local contact • Proactive availability of information • Promote superiority of core service
What processes has/will DHL put in place to ensure that these strategies are delivered?	• Customer service strategy • Proactive traces • Local sales & courier network • Customer access tools

What capabilities does DHL require to ensure that these processes can be operated?	• Teamwork • Technology • Robust network • Skills
What does DHL want from its stakeholders to allow the above to happen?	• Confidence in data • Empowerment • People-based culture

Test your understanding 10

Phoenix Fund Management (PFM) has been responsible for the investment of pension and life insurance funds for the past twenty years. It claims to be a 'fund manager with a difference' by seeking to gain active involvement in under-performing or poorly managed businesses. PFM requires that companies it has invested in be run in the long-term interests of the shareholders. PFM assesses such companies in terms of communication, financial, strategic and ethical performance against certain principles it has developed. (For instance, one financial principle is that 'companies should have performance evaluation and incentive systems to provide managers with an incentive to deliver long term shareholder value').

PFM's belief is that there is a lack of 'real' accountability between boards of directors and shareholders and that too often shareholders concentrate on short-term financial gains. PFM argues that if other investors believe that a company is poorly run they merely sell their shares and invest elsewhere. Thus boards of directors are not held properly to account over poor performance. Where it believes companies it invests in are under-performing, PFM enters into dialogue with the board and seeks changes in practice. PFM is increasingly being recognised as a major driver of change in corporate life.

Required:

Explain how the Performance Prism can assist companies in developing performance management indicators which take account of the needs of stakeholders such as PFM.

Evaluation of the Performance Prism

The main advantage of the Performance Prism is that it focuses on the wants and needs of a range of stakeholders.

However, there is little detail as to the performance measures that should be used for each perspective.

Student accountant article

Visit the ACCA website, www.accaglobal.com, to review the article on the 'Performance Prism' from February 2012.

8 Corporate failure

8.1 Introduction

So far we have focused on how effective performance management and measurement can help an organisation in achieving its goals. However, not all businesses will achieve their goals successfully. If left unchecked, these businesses are at risk of corporate failure. It is imperative that steps are taken to identify the potential symptoms of failure and address any issues before corporate collapse occurs.

Corporate failure occurs when a company cannot achieve a satisfactory return on capital over the longer-term. If unchecked, the situation is likely to lead to an inability of the company to pay its obligations as they become due. The company may still have an excess of assets over liabilities, but if it is unable to convert those assets into cash it will be insolvent.

Test your understanding 11

Required:

Identify some of the reasons for corporate failure.

8.2 Why to companies fail?

There are many businesses why companies fail. Two key reasons include:

- failing to adapt to changes in the environment
- strategic drift, i.e. a rigid approach to strategic planning. Strategy is developed in accordance with unchanged assumptions (which may have proved successful in the past) and may drift away from environmental fit.

Why do companies fail?

Reasons include:

(1) **Failing to adapt to changes in the environment**

Reasons for failing to adapt include:

– complacency

– risk-averse decision making

– economies of production and administration

– limited opportunities for innovation and diversification

– limited mental models.

Complacency is a charge frequently levelled at managers, and there are, no doubt, occasions when senior managers convince themselves that everything is fine, when it is not. However, the charge is frequently made with the benefit of hindsight, rather than observation of the efforts made by those managers at the time. There are several entirely sensible reasons why managers are reluctant to make large strategic changes.

First, it is not possible to quantify the risks of making a major change. Several studies have shown that predicting changes in the environment and devising appropriate counter-measures is among the most difficult things a manager is required to do. Only in hindsight are the dynamics clear. It is worth remembering that case studies are written backwards, where a known outcome is traced back to its origins.

Faced with such difficulties, managers are reluctant to make large-scale changes that might risk increasing the problems, and might be very difficult to implement adequately. Rather, they select options of relatively limited impact – a process referred to as logical incrementalism.

Secondly, changes to production can reduce the opportunities for economies of scale, and raise the firm's cost base. There is always a temptation to try to retain share, by reducing price, rather than make fundamental changes to a product of its method of production and risk escalating costs.

Thirdly, it may be that management is entirely aware that the strategic situation is worsening, but be unable to see opportunities to innovate or diversify out of trouble. It must be accepted that there are situations where there are no feasible solutions, and there might be better uses of the shareholders' funds than attempts to turn the business round.

Finally, a large part of the problem is caused by the mental models of those who have control of the strategy within an organisation. A mental model is the way that individuals think about problems and issues. We look (below) at Johnson's notion of strategic drift, where the firm's mental models stop the company from changing quickly enough to keep up with environmental change.

(2) **Strategic drift**

Strategic drift is a term devised by **Johnson** (1988) to describe as a warning to those who champion the idea of strategy emerging as a series of logical, incremental steps. Johnson argues that this limits the rate of change to the speed at which management might feel comfortable, which has many advantages (particularly in implementation), but might be inappropriate in periods when the environment moves very quickly.

As outlined above, the organisation takes a series of logical, incremental steps that enables it to change ahead of the market, developing a competitive advantage. However, the rate of change in the market place speeds up, and the firm's incrementalist approach is not enough to maintain its advantage, and it is left behind. At this point, the firm must abandon the approach, and adopt radical, discontinuous change in order to stay with the market leaders.

Johnson's main argument is that the reasons for failing to increase the tempo of change are largely cultural, rather than technical. He argues that the corporate paradigm, as revealed by its cultural web and described in an earlier chapter, is the biggest constraint on strategic thinking and action. It is important to see that management cannot change a corporate paradigm, partly because they are themselves caught up in it, and partly because some elements of it are not amenable to management techniques. Logical incrementalism is successful because it does not challenge the underlying paradigm, allowing change to take place relatively smoothly. More revolutionary change must damage the paradigm before it can begin.

KAPLAN PUBLISHING

8.3 Symptoms of failure

The following information can be used when assessing the likelihood of corporate failure:

Quantitative information	Qualitative information
• Analysis of the company accounts to identify problems relating to key ratios such as liquidity, gearing and profitability.	• Information in the chairman's report and the director's report (including warnings, evasions and changes in the composition of the board since last year).

• Other information in the published accounts such as:
 	
  – very large increases in intangible fixed assets
 	
  – a worsening cash position shown by the cash flow statement
 	
  – very large contingent liabilities
 	
  – important post balance sheet events.
	• Information in the press (about the industry and the company or its competitors).
	
	• Information about environmental or external matters such as changes in the market for the company's products or services.

Test your understanding 12

Required:

You have been asked to investigate a chain of convenience stores and assess the likelihood of corporate failure. What would you include in your analysis?

Additional example

Insureme was the market leader in home and motor vehicle insurance with a 28% market share. The company has lost its market share over the last two years and this may lead to the demise of the company.

Required:

Discuss five performance indicators, other than decreasing market share, which might indicate Insureme might fail as a corporate entity.

Solution:

Poor cash flow

Poor cash flow might render an organisation unable to pay its debts as and when they fall due for payment. This might mean, for example, that providers of finance might be able to invoke the terms of a loan covenant and commence legal action against an organisation which might eventually lead to its winding-up.

Lack of new production/service introduction

Innovation can often be seen to be the difference between 'life and death' as new products and services provide continuity of income streams in an ever-changing business environment. A lack of new product/service introduction may arise from a shortage of funds available for re-investment. This can lead to organisations attempting to compete with their competitors with an out of date range of products and services, the consequences of which will invariably turn out to be disastrous.

General economic conditions

Falling demand and increasing interest rates can precipitate the demise of organisations. Highly geared organisations will suffer as demand falls and the weight of the interest burden increases. Organisations can find themselves in a vicious circle as increasing amounts of interest payable are paid from diminishing gross margins leading to falling profits/increasing losses and negative cash flows. This leads to the need for further loan finance and even higher interest burden, further diminution in margins and so on.

Lack of financial controls

The absence of sound financial controls has proven costly to many organisations. In extreme circumstances it can lead to outright fraud (e.g. Enron and WorldCom).

Internal rivalry

The extent of internal rivalry that exists within an organisation can prove to be of critical significance to an organisation as managerial effort is effectively channeled into increasing the amount of internal conflict that exists to the detriment of the organisation as a whole. Unfortunately the adverse consequences of internal rivalry remain latent until it is too late to redress them.

Loss of key personnel

In certain types of organisation the loss of key personnel can 'spell the beginning of the end' for an organisation. This is particularly the case when individuals possess knowledge which can be exploited by direct competitors, e.g. sales contacts, product specifications, product recipes, etc.

8.4 Corporate failure prediction models

Two types of model

Quantitative models
Indentify financial ratios with values which differ markedly between surviving and failing companies

Qualitative models
Assign scores to particular qualitative risk factors

Quantitative models

Model	Explanation
Beaver's univariate model (1966)	A simple, but flawed, model that assesses the financial status of a company by reviewing one ratio at a time.
The Z score (1968)	A more sophisticated model that combines key ratios into a single discriminate score. This is a **key model** and will be discussed in more detail below.
Taffler and Tishaw's model (1977)	Developed their own version of the Z score model based on a combination of four ratios.
The ZETA model (1977)	This model addressed some of the problems associated with the Z score model.
Performance analysis score	Ranks all company Z scores in percentile terms, measuring relative performance from 0 to 100. Any downward trend over time should be investigated.
H score model	Similar to the previous model in that it is a ranked percentile score of between 0 and 100. The threshold is 25, below which companies are described as being in the 'Warning Area'. This score means that only 25% of companies have characteristics even more indicative of failed companies and therefore corporate failure is a real concern.

Calculating a Z score

The Z score model uses publicly available financial information about an organisation in order to predict whether it is likely to fail within a two year period.

The Z score is generated by calculating five ratios, which are then multiplied by a pre-determined weighting factor and added together to produce the Z score. The formula is:

$$Z \text{ score} = 1.2X1 + 1.4X2 + 3.3X3 + 0.6X4 + 1.0X5$$

Where:

X1 = working capital/total assets

X2 = retained earnings/total assets

X3 = earnings before interest and tax/total assets

X4 = market value of equity/total liabilities

X5 = sales/total assets

The score indicates the likelihood of failure:

- **Less than 1.81** – companies with a Z score of below 1.81 are in danger and possibly heading towards bankruptcy

- **Between 1.81 and 2.99** – companies with scores between 1.81 and 2.99 need further investigation to assess the likelihood of failure

- **3 or above** – companies with a score of 3 or above are financially sound and are expected to survive.

Test your understanding 13

Required:

Using the data below calculate the Z score for each of the four companies and comment on your findings.

	Company B	Company C	Company D	Company E
X1 = Working Capital / Total Assets	0.717	0.06	1.3	0.25
X2 = Retained earnings/ Total Assets	0.847	0.03	0.8	0.21
X3 = EBIT / Total Assets	3.107	0.09	1.1	0.5
X4 = Market value of Equity / Total Liabilities	0.42	0.541	–	–
X5 = Sales / Total Assets	0.998	–	0.5	0.16

(handwritten annotations: 12×0.717; 1.4×0.847; 3.3×3.107; 0.6×0.42; 1.0×0.998)

Evaluation of quantitative models

The **advantages** of quantitative methods are:

- calculations are simple
- an objective measure of failure is provided.

However, **limitations** include:

- the prediction of failure for firms with a score below 1.8 (or indeed success for firms with a score of 3 or above) is highly probable but not guaranteed.
- the model is based on a statistical analysis of historic patterns of trading by a group of companies and may not be relevant unless the company under examination falls within the same economic circumstances and industry sector as those used to set the coefficients in the model
- further analysis is needed to fully understand the situation, e.g. cash flow projections, detailed cost information, environmental review.
- scores are only good predictors in the short-term.
- Figures are open to manipulation through creative accounting which can be a feature of companies in trouble.
- The Z score model only gives guidance below the danger level of 1.81. Further investigation is needed for those organisations with scores between 1.81 and 2.99.

Qualitative models – Argenti's A score

Qualitative models are based on the realisation that financial measures are limited in describing the circumstances of a company.

The most notable qualitative model is Argenti's A score model. This model relies on subjective scores to certain questions given by the investigator.

Argenti suggested that the failure process follows a predictable sequence:

(1) **Defects** – include management weaknesses (such as an autocratic chief executive or the failure to separate the role of the chairman and chief executive) and accounting deficiencies (such as no budgetary control or lack of cash flow planning). Each defect is given a score. A mark of 10 or more out of a possible 45 is considered unsatisfactory.

(2) **Mistakes** – will occur over time as a result of the defects above. Mistakes are scored under three headings; high gearing, overtrading or failure of a big project. A score of more than 15 out of a possible 45 is considered unsatisfactory.

(3) **Symptoms of failure** – mistakes will eventually lead to visible symptoms of failure, e.g. deteriorating ratios, creative accounting or non-financial signs such as delayed investment or frozen salaries.

If the overall score is more than 25, the company has many of the signs preceding failure and is therefore a cause for concern.

Failing companies often score highly, around 60.

Evaluation of qualitative models

The key **advantages** of these models are:

- the ability to use non-financial as well as financial measures
- the ability to use the judgement of the investigator.

However, these strengths can also be seen as **weaknesses** since the models:

- are based on the subjective judgement of the expert
- require a large amount of financial and non-financial information.

8.5 Performance improvement strategies

The key to preventing corporate failure is to spot the warning signs early, and take corrective action quickly.

- The actions needed will depend on the particular situation. Once the signs of impending failure are seen, it is important to investigate and identify the causes.
- These may be related to a range of different functions within the business, such as financial management, marketing or production.
- It may sometimes be necessary to seek external advice to help to identify the problem.

- It is important that the managers of the business accept that there is a problem and that mistakes have been made and to move on to a solution, rather than apportioning blame.

- Actions may involve major strategic change, such as getting out of a loss-making business, or making changes to the way operations are managed, such as changes to production management.

- The action needed may include putting in controls to prevent further loss.

- The best strategy to prevent failure is to have effective management systems in place to begin with.

The **performance management system** will need to reflect the performance improvement strategies:

- a link should be established between the new strategic goals and CSFs

- performance targets should be set at all levels and these should relate to the achievement of strategic objectives

- continuous review of actual performance against targets will be required

- additional training and development needs must be met.

Test your understanding 14

You have been asked to recommend actions which need to be taken to prevent failure of an electronics manufacturer which is in financial difficulties. On investigation, you ascertain that the company has been making losses for the last two years. Although the product is well thought of in the market, sales are decreasing slightly. Returns and customer complaints are high. The manufacturing time for the products is 30 days and raw materials inventories are generally held for two weeks. There are also high levels of finished goods inventories. Receivables days are 100.

Required:

What actions do you suggest should be taken?

8.6 Long-term survival and the product life cycle

Classic life cycle

The 'classic' life cycle for a product has four phases, with different CSFs.

- An **introduction phase**, when the product or service is first developed and introduced to the market. Sales demand is low whilst potential customers learn about the item. There is a learning process for both customers and the producer, and the producer might have to vary the features of the product or service, in order to meet customer requirements more successfully.

- A **growth phase**, when the product or service becomes established and there is a large growth in sales demand. The number of competitors in the market also increases, but customers are willing to pay reasonably high prices. The product becomes profitable. Variety in the product or service increases, and customers are much more conscious of quality issues.

- A **maturity phase**, which might be the longest stage in the product life cycle. Demand stabilises, and producers compete on price.

- A **decline phase**, during which sales demand falls. Prices are reduced to sustain demand and to slow the decline in sales volume. Eventually the product becomes unprofitable, and producers stop making it.

Long-term survival necessitates consideration of life-cycle issues:

Issue 1: There will be different CSFs at different stages of the life cycle. In order to ensure that performance is managed effectively KPIs will need to vary over different stages of the life cycle.

Issue 2: The stages of the life cycle have different intrinsic levels of risk:

- The introduction period is clearly a time of high business risk as it is quite possible that the product will fail.

- The risk is still quite high during the growth phase because the ultimate size of the industry is still unknown and the level of market share that can be gained and retained is also uncertain.

- During the maturity phase the risk decreases and the final phase should be regarded as low risk because the organisation knows that the product is in decline and its strategy should be tailored accordingly.

Understanding and responding to these risks is vital for the future success of the organisation.

If there is an analysis of the developing risk profile it should be compared with the financial risk profiles of various strategic options, making it much easier to select appropriate combinations and to highlight unacceptably high or low total risk combinations. Thus for an organisation to decide to finance itself with debt during the development stage would represent a high total risk combination.

Student accountant articles: visit the ACCA website, www.accaglobal.com, to review the article on 'business failure' from July 2008.

9 Exam focus

Exam sitting	Area examined	Question number	Number of marks
December 2013	Performance pyramid	2(a)	15
June 2013	Balanced scorecard and building block model	1(iii)(iv)(v)	33
December 2012	Corporate failure	4	20
June 2012	Performance prism	2(b)	14
December 2011	Performance pyramid	2(b)(c)	18
June 2011	Building block model	3	20
June 2011	Balanced scorecard	2(a)(b)(d)	21
December 2010	Corporate failure	5	20
June 2010	NFPIs and the balanced scorecard	1(i)	13
June 2010	Performance pyramid	5(b)	12
December 2009	Assessment of financial and non-financial performance	1(ii)	10
June 2009	Balanced scorecard	1	35
June 2009	Drawbacks of sole reliance on financial performance measures	2(c)	6
December 2008	Evaluation of performance including building block model	1(a)	29
December 2007	Indicators of corporate failure	5(b)	10
Pilot paper	Assessment of financial performance and performance pyramid	2	25

Note:

- The current examiner has set the exam papers from the December 2010 sitting onwards.

- The format of the exam changed in June 2013. Section A now contains 1 × 50 mark question (previously 2 questions worth 60 marks in total) and Section B now contains a choice of 2 from 3 questions worth 25 marks each (previously a choice of 2 from 3 questions worth approximately 20 marks each).

Chapter summary

Test your understanding answers

Test your understanding 1

The following NFPIs could be used:

- Absenteeism
- Productivity
- Turnover rate (analyse further to identify reasons for leaving)

These give an indication of the morale of employees.

Test your understanding 2

The experience of existing customers and their perception of the quality of the products or services will help to determine whether the company profile is positive or negative. This is particularly important for a high profile company, about which everyone will have an opinion whether or not they have any experience as a customer. This will be based on the opinions of customers with whom they have contact, and on press reports which discuss the quality of the company's offering.

Test your understanding 3

- The impact on and the views of employees. Any decision which affects working practices will have a morale effect on employees. Some decisions, such as to close a department, will have a greater effect than others, for example an increase in production, but both will affect employees.

- The impact on and opinion of customers who will be affected by any decision which changes the finished product or its availability. For example, the deletion of a product will force customers to choose an alternative item.

- Suppliers will be affected by changes to production which require different raw materials or delivery schedules. For example, an increase in production may cause the supplier to increase production of the raw material.

- The response of competitors. Any decision to changes in product specification or pricing will affect competitors who will then choose whether or not to respond.

- The impact on demand for scarce resources. A change in production as a result of the decision may alter the demand for individual resources and the result of the decision may alter availability.

- Any social and environmental effects.

Test your understanding 4

Financial perspective

- ROCE and RI – overall and by SBU.
- Margins – overall and by product/customer/country.
- Different costs as a percentage of sales – e.g. labour costs/sales, sub-contractor costs/sales.
- Sales growth.
- Cash flow targets.
- Market share.

Customer perspective

- Percentage of scheduled targets met – especially whether contracts are finished on time.
- Percentage of repeated business.
- Number of complaints received.
- Targets for new customers won.
- Percentage of apartments sold off-plan.

Internal business perspective

- Percentage of tenders won.
- Percentage of utilisation of fixed assets – vehicles, plant and machinery.
- Percentage of contracts with cost overruns.
- Cost overrun as percentage of budgeted cost.
- Targets for employee productivity.
- For staffing, environmental and health and safety measures.

Innovation and learning perspective

- Number of patents established for new methods/technologies.
- Percentage of new materials used compared with total materials.
- Percentage of total revenue coming from new buildings using new structural innovations in their design.

Test your understanding 5

The disadvantages are as follows:

- It is **difficult to record and process data of a non-financial**, i.e. qualitative, **nature**.

- **Information overload** due to the large number of measures that may be chosen. However, Kaplan and Norton recommended that only a handful of measures are used.

- Potential **conflict between measures**, e.g. profitability may increase in the short-term through a reduction in product development.

- The **measures chosen may not align with the strategy and/or vision** of the organisation.

- **Poor communication to employees/managers** – organisations which adopt the balanced scorecard but continue to reward managers on the basis of a narrow range of traditional financial measures are likely to be disappointed with the results.

- **Lack of commitment by senior management** will lead to an inevitable failure of the scorecard.

- The **cost** involved in establishing suitable measures and in measuring the performance of all four perspectives.

- It focuses on the **strategic level**. However, a similar approach can be implemented at the tactical or operational level.

Test your understanding 6

(a) The balanced scorecard allows managers to look at the business from four important perspectives:

Customer – how do our customers see us and how do we present ourselves to them?

Internal business process – what processes must we excel at in order to meet the needs of our customers and shareholders?

Innovation and learning – can we continue to improve and create value?

Financial – how do we look to our shareholders and how do we optimally serve their interests?

KAPLAN PUBLISHING

The new strategy focuses on four key areas which will address the balanced scorecard perspectives in different ways:

Focus on key customers – this will directly address the customer perspective but will also have implications for the other three perspectives.

In terms of appropriate performance measures, Jump should begin by segmenting the market, e.g. by age, gender, income or the family lifecycle. Jump should then analyse each segment in terms of profitability and changing market share and should then target the most profitable segment(s) of the market.

Ensure Jump's offerings meet the needs of these customers – this will directly address the customer perspective but may also result in a change in internal business processes and an increase in innovation and learning. This, in turn, should have a knock on impact on the financial perspective.

In terms of appropriate performance measures, from a customer perspective, Jump should monitor levels of customer satisfaction (e.g. via surveys) and repeat business. Internal business processes could be benchmarked against competitors or could be monitored internally, again through the review of customer satisfaction. Innovation and learning could be monitored by looking at the number of new products and staff training time, e.g. are target customers satisfied with a range of new aerobics classes offered and the competence of the staff leading these classes? The financial perspective could be monitored using, say, ROCE, EPS or profit margin.

Cost cutting – this focuses mainly on the internal business process perspective and seeks to focus the business on value added activities.

Appropriate performance measures may include efficiency savings generating by removing or reducing unnecessary processes or products.

Build for the future using sustainable development – the future focus ties into the innovation and learning perspective but may also have a knock on impact on the other three perspectives.

In terms of appropriate performance measures, Jump may monitor its energy efficiency.

(b) **Assessment of financial performance**

The year on year performance has declined. EPS (W1) has fallen by 29% which would normally result in a fall in shareholder satisfaction. However, when reviewing the share price it would seem that Jump's shareholders would be encouraged by the company's future prospects. Although Jump's share price has fallen by 16% year on year, the market as a whole has fallen by 31% and more importantly the health sector has fallen by 23%.

Furthermore, even though Jump's EVA has fallen by 65% year on year it has remained positive so the company continues to create value for its shareholders.

(W1) **EPS**

	20X0	20X1
EPS = PAT ÷ average number of shares in issue	€37.2m ÷ 140m = €0.266	€26.3m ÷ 140m = €0.188

Evaluation of performance metrics

	Advantages	Disadvantages
EPS	• Widely used measure. • Important to shareholders since relates to dividend growth.	• Based on accounting profit which is subject to manipulation. • Comparison is only between two years which can be misleading.
Share price	Widely used by shareholders to monitor investments.	• Volatile • Subject to fluctuations outside of manager's control. • Managers may be encouraged to make decisions which boost short term share price.
EVA	• Widely used and measured. • Adjustments are made to profit.	Numerous adjustments to profit must be made.

Conclusion as to impact of metrics on management

Both EPS and share price may encourage managers to make decisions which improve short term financial performance but may impact on long term profitability. EVA aims to partially tackle this issue through the adjustment of accounting figures but the large number of adjustments can make this measure unwieldy.

(c) **To**: Board of Jump

From: A Accountant

Date: Today

Subject: Benchmarking performance

This report describes the benefits and problems associated with benchmarking the company's performance. Then, the performance of Jump and its two main competitors is calculated and evaluated.

Benchmarking is the use of a yardstick to compare performance. The yardstick, or benchmark, is based upon the best in class. Competitor benchmarking uses a direct competitor with the same or similar processes as the benchmark.

(i) Advantages of benchmarking

Improved performance

Benchmarking could be a key tool in enabling Jump to improve its performance and increase profitability in this highly competitive market. There should be improvements across all areas, e.g. quality, customer service.

Achievability

The improvements will be seen as achievable since the new methods have actually been used in another organisation. This should encourage managers and employees to buy-in to the change process.

Improved understanding of environmental pressures

The benchmarking process should enable Jump to get back in touch with the needs of its customers and to better understand its competitors. The industry is highly competitive and so this greater awareness will be essential for future success.

Eliminates complacency

Benchmarking can help Jump to overcome complacency and to drive organisational change.

Continuous improvement

Benchmarking can be carried out at regular intervals and can therefore drive continuous improvement in the business.

Disadvantages of benchmarking

Identifying best practice

In may prove difficult to identify the organisations that are best in class.

Cost

The actual benchmarking exercise will be costly for Jump. It is essential that the benefits of the exercise are greater than the associated costs.

Impact on motivation

If comparisons are unfavourable the information could have a negative impact on employee motivation and this would result in further inefficiencies.

Deciding which activities are to be benchmarked

This is a difficult process. Jump may not realise that there are better ways of doing things until they have seen their competitors carrying out certain processes.

Managers become too target driven

Benchmarking can result in managers becoming obsessed with hitting targets. This could sometimes be counterproductive.

Collection of data

The actual collection of data can be time consuming and costly. Data may not be readily accessible for all areas of performance measurement and competitors may be unwilling to share details.

(ii) Comparing Jump to its competitors, it is clear that Jump has done well to increase its total revenue (8% increase) but this comes at the cost of a significant fall in profit compared with Fitness matters (Fitness Matter's fall in profit was 10% compared with a 29% fall for Jump). Jump should look into its pricing policy since it may have been buying sales by offering heavy discounts and these may not be sustainable in the long term.

Active Matters drop in profit is greatest of all but this may be explained by problems in the range and quality of its services. Active matters opened nine new health clubs in the period but there has been an overall fall in revenue of 2%. Jump could analyse Active Matter's offerings to its customers in order to avoid making the same mistakes.

In terms of market share, Jump has maintained its position against slight falls in its competitors.

In revenue per health club, Jump has outperformed its competitors. However, this may be due to Jump having a larger average health club. The average club area for the three companies should be investigated.

Conclusion

In conclusion, Jump seems to be performing well with increased revenues and the maintenance of market share during the decline. The company must guard against the danger of eroding margins too far.

Test your understanding 7

Possible measures include:

Financial performance

- Fee levels.
- Material sales.
- Costs.
- Net profit.
- Outside lecturer costs.

Competitiveness

- Market share.
- Sales growth.
- Success rate on proposals.

Quality of service

- Repeat business levels.
- Number of customer complaints.
- Help-line use may be related to tuition quality.

Flexibility

- Availability and use of freelance staff.
- Breadth of skills and experience of lecturers.

Resource utilisation

- Use of freelance lecturers.
- Levels of non-chargeable staff time.

Innovation

- Number of new in-company courses.
- Time to develop new courses.
- New course formats.

Note: only one measure was required for each dimension.

KAPLAN PUBLISHING

Test your understanding 8

Report:

To: The Directors of TSC

From: Management Accountant

Subject: The performance of our depots

Date: 5 December 2008

(a) **Summary analysis of points gained (1) or forfeited (0) for quarter ended 31 October 2008**

Revenue and Profit Statistics:	D	L	M	R
Revenue	0	1	1	1
Profit (see note below)	1	0	1	0
Customer Care and Service Delivery Statistics:				
Late collection of consignments	1	0	1	0
Misdirected consignments	0	1	1	0
Delayed response to complaints	1	1	1	0
Delays due to vehicle breakdown	0	0	1	0
Lost items	1	1	1	0
Damaged items	1	0	1	1
Credit Control & Administration Efficiency Statistics:				
Average debtor weeks	0	1	1	0
Debtors in excess of 60 days	1	1	1	1
Invoice queries (% of total)	1	1	1	1
Credit notes as a % of revenue	1	1	1	0
Total points gained	**8**	**8**	**12**	**14**

Workings:

(i) Profit point calculation:

Actual results, e.g. Donatellotown = 2.3/15 = 15.3% (1 point) and
Leonardotown = 2.4/18 = 13.3% (0 point)

(ii) Debtors in excess of 60 days (% of total)

	D	L	M	R
Revenue ($000)	15,000	18,000	14,000	22,000
Debtor weeks	5.8	4.9	5.1	6.2
Therefore debtors	1,673	1,696	1,373	2,623
Less than 30 days	(1,300)	(1,500)	(1,180)	(2,000)
31–60 days	(321)	(133)	(153)	(552)
More than 60 days	52	63	40	71
Debtors in excess of 60 days (% of total)	3.1	3.7	2.9	2.7

(iii) Value of credit notes raised as a % of revenue

e.g. Donatellotown = $45,000/$15,000,000 = 0.3%

(b) The summary analysis in (a)(i) shows that using overall points
gained, Michaelangelotown has achieved the best performance with
12 points. Donatellotown and Leonardotown have achieved a
reasonable level of performance with eight points each.
Raphaeltown has under performed, however, gaining only four out of
the available 12 points.

Michaelangelotown is the only depot to have achieved both an
increase in revenue over budget and an increased profit:revenue
percentage.

In the customer care and service delivery statistics,
Michaelangelotown has achieved all six of the target standards,
Donatellotown four; Leonardotown three. The Raphaeltown statistic
of achieving only one out of six targets indicates the need for
investigation.

With regard to the credit control and administrative efficiency
statistics, Leonardotown and Michaelangelotown achieved all four
standards and Donatellotown achieved three of the four standards.
Once again, Raphaeltown is the 'poor performer' achieving only two
of the four standards.

(c) The terms listed may be seen as representative of the dimensions of performance. The dimensions may be analysed into results and determinants.

The results may be measured by focusing on financial performance and competitiveness. **Financial performance** may be measured in terms of revenue and profit as shown in the data in the appendix of the question in respect of TSC. The points system in part (a) of the answer shows which depots have achieved or exceeded the target set. In addition, liquidity is another aspect of the measurement of financial performance. The points total in part (a) showed that Leonardotown and Michaelangelotown depots appear to have the best current record in aspects of credit control.

Competitiveness may be measured in terms of sales growth but also in terms of market share, number of new customers, etc. In the TSC statistics available we only have data for the current quarter. This shows that three of the four depots listed have achieved increased revenue compared to target.

The **determinants** are the factors which may be seen to contribute to the achievement of the results. Quality, resource utilisation, flexibility and innovation are cited by Fitzgerald and Moon as examples of factors that should contribute to the achievement of the results in terms of financial performance and competitiveness. In TSC a main **quality** issue appears to be customer care and service delivery. The statistics in the points table in part (a) of the answer show that the Raphaeltown depot appears to have a major problem in this area. It has only achieved one point out of the six available in this particular segment of the statistics.

Resource utilisation for TSC may be measured by the level of effective use of drivers and vehicles. To some extent, this is highlighted by the statistics relating to customer care and service delivery. For example, late collection of consignments from customers may be caused by a shortage of vehicles and/or drivers. Such shortages could be due to staff turnover, sickness, etc or problems with vehicle maintenance.

Flexibility may be an issue. There may, for example, be a problem with vehicle availability. Possibly an increased focus on sources for short-term sub-contracting of vehicles/collections/deliveries might help overcome delay problems.

The 'target v actual points system' may be seen as an example of **innovation** by the company. This gives a detailed set of measures that should provide an incentive for improvement at all depots. The points system may illustrate the extent of achievement/non-achievement of company strategies for success. For example TSC may have a customer care commitment policy which identifies factors that should be achieved on a continuing basis. For example, timely collection of consignments, misdirected consignments re-delivered at no extra charge, prompt responses to customer claims and compensation for customers.

(d)   The performance measurement system used by TSC appears simplistic. However, it may be considered to be measuring the right things since the specific measures used cover a range of dimensions designed to focus the organisation on factors thought to be central to corporate success, and not confined to traditional financial measures.

Internal benchmarking is used at TSC in order to provide sets of absolute standards that all depots are expected to attain. This should help to ensure that there is a continual focus upon the adoption of 'best practice' at all depots. Benchmarks on delivery performance place an emphasis upon quality of service whereas benchmarks on profitability are focused solely upon profitability!

Incentive schemes are used throughout the business, linking the achievement of company targets with financial rewards. It might well be the case that the profit incentive would act as a powerful motivator to each depot management team. However, what is required for the prosperity of TSC is a focus of management on the determinants of success as opposed to the results of success.

(Alternative relevant discussion would be acceptable)

Test your understanding 9

Possible measures (KPIs)

Customer satisfaction

- Repeat purchases.
- Numbers of complaints.
- Value of refunds.
- Sales growth by market segment.

Flexibility

- Product/service introduction time.
- Product/service mix flexibility.
- Internal setup times – the time taken to switch production from one product to another.
- Delivery response time – the time taken to meet customer delivery requests.

Productivity

- Revenue per employee.
- Sales and administration costs as a percentage of sales revenue.
- Units of output per unit of resource.
- Capital asset utilisation.

Note: only two measures were required for each category.

Test your understanding 10

The Performance Prism is an approach to performance measurement which is designed to take account of the interests of all stakeholders, such as suppliers, employees, legislators, and local communities. In doing this it takes a broader approach to stakeholder interests than many other performance management models which pay limited attention to stakeholders other than customers and shareholders. The Performance Prism is based on the principle that the performance of an organisation depends on how effectively it meets the needs and requirements of all its stakeholders takes stakeholder requirements as the start point for the development of performance measures rather than the strategy of the organisation. It also recognises the need to work with stakeholders to ensure that their needs are met. The framework can be used to identify measures at all levels within the organisation.

The Performance Prism has five facets which are different perspectives on performance which prompt specific questions. The answers to these questions form the starting point for defining performance measures.

These facets are as follows:

Stakeholder satisfaction – Who are our key stakeholders and what do they want and need? PFM is a key stakeholder of the investee companies, and invested in, with a clear requirement for long term shareholder value. It also has other wants and needs relating to communication, financial, strategic and ethical performance.

Stakeholder contribution – What contributions do we want and need from our stakeholders? PFM appears to be a company which wants to make a significant contribution to the companies it invests in and presumably has experience which investee businesses can benefit from.

Strategies – What strategies do we need to put in place to satisfy the wants and needs of our key stakeholders, while satisfying our own requirements too? For example, strategies to deliver long term shareholder value are likely to meet the requirements of an investee company as well as PFM's.

Processes – What processes do we need to put in place to enable us to execute our strategies? Depending on the strategy chosen, companies will identify changes which need to be made to the company and its operations to meet the strategic objectives. These should be reflected in the performance indicators for the company.

Capabilities – What capabilities do we need to put in place to allow us to operate, maintain and enhance our processes? An example of this has already been identified by PFM in the performance evaluation and incentive scheme for managers.

Test your understanding 11

Reasons include:

- Poor leadership leading to poor business planning, financial planning, marketing and management.

- Failure to focus on a specific market because of poor research.

- Failure to control cash by carrying too much stock, paying suppliers too promptly, and allowing customers too long to pay.

- Failure to control costs ruthlessly.

- Failure to adapt your product to meet customer needs.

- Failure to carry out decent market research.

- Failure to build a team that is compatible and has the skills to finance, produce, sell and market.

- Failure to pay taxes.

- Failure of businesses' need to grow, merely attempting stability or having less ambitious objectives.

- Failure to gain new markets.

- Under-capitalisation.

- Cash flow problems.

- Tougher market conditions.

- Poor management.

- Companies diversifying into new, unknown areas without a clue about the costs.

- Company directors spending too much money on frivolous purposes thus using all available capital.

Test your understanding 12

Examples of issues to include:

- an analysis of key ratios, such as liquidity, gearing, cash flow and activity ratios, including trends

- changes in the cash flow of the business

- any history of significant losses

- liability position

- ability to pay creditors on time

- human resources, for example level of dependence on key staff, labour difficulties

- skills and abilities of senior management and an assessment of the strengths and weaknesses of the company

- developments in the market, such as the likelihood of new supermarkets being built near stores

- any regulatory changes which are likely to affect the company

- an analysis of the company report to identify any significant changes over the year.

Test your understanding 13

	Company B	Company C	Company D	Company E
1.2X1	0.86	0.07	1.56	0.3
1.4X2	1.19	0.04	1.12	0.29
3.3X3	10.25	0.3	3.63	1.65
0.6X4	0.25	0 .32	0	0
1.0X5	1	0	0.5	0.16
Z score	**13.55**	**0.74**	**6.81**	**2.4**

Companies with a Z score of below 1.81 are in danger and possibly heading towards bankruptcy, i.e. company C.

A score between 1.81 and 2.99 means that they need further investigation, i.e. company E.

A score of 3 or above companies are financially sound, i.e. companies B and D.

Test your understanding 14

The evidence suggests that the company has problems in financial management, production, purchasing and marketing.

Actions required:

- Improve credit control to reduce the debtor days.

- Address the production process to:
  - reduce manufacturing time and stock levels to reduce the requirement for working capital and save costs. This should also improve the ability to respond to customer demands and reduce the need to hold stocks of finished goods

  - improve final product quality to reduce returns and improve customer satisfaction.

- Improve marketing activity to address customer satisfaction issues and increase sales.

The role of quality in performance management

Chapter learning objectives

Upon completion of this chapter you will be able to:

- discuss and evaluate the application of Japanese business practices and management accounting techniques, including:
  - Kaizen costing
  - Target costing
  - Just-in-time, and
  - Total Quality Management
- discriminate between quality, quality assurance, quality control and quality management
- assess the relationship of quality management to the performance management strategy of an organisation
- advise on the structure and benefits of quality management systems and quality certification
- justify the need and assess the characteristics of quality in management information systems
- discuss and apply Six Sigma as a quality improvement method using tools such as DMAIC for implementation.

1 Assumed knowledge

Chapter 12 builds on your knowledge of quality from Paper F5.

2 Introduction

In today's competitive global business environment, quality is one of the key ways in which a business can differentiate its product or service, improve performance and gain competitive advantage. Quality can form a key part of a strategy.

Quality can be defined in a number of ways:

- Is the product/service free from errors and does it adhere to design specifications?

- Is the product/service fit for use?

- Does the product/service meet customers' needs?

Test your understanding 1
Required:
Explain the reasons why quality may be important to an organisation?

Some other important definitions include:

Quality management involves planning and controlling activities to ensure the product or service is fit for purpose, meets design specifications and meets the needs of customers. Quality management should lead to improvements in performance.

Quality control involves a number of routine steps which measure and control the quality of the product/service as it is developed.

Quality assurance involves a review of the quality control procedures, usually by an independent third party, such as ISO (see section 3). It aims to verify that the desired level of quality has been met.

3 Quality certification

The International Organisation for Standardisation (**ISO**) is one of the major bodies responsible for producing quality standards that can be applied to a variety of organisations.

The ISO 9000 quality standards have been adopted by many organisations. An ISO 9000 registered company must:

- submit its quality procedures for external inspection
- keep adequate records
- check outputs for differences
- facilitate continuous improvement.

A certified company will be subject to continuous audit.

Test your understanding 2

Required:

Explain the advantages and disadvantages to a fast growing UK based mobile phone company of becoming ISO certified.

4 Quality-related costs

- Monitoring the costs of quality is central to the operation of any quality improvement programme.

- KPIs should be developed based on the costs of quality and these can be used as a basis for staff rewards.

- The organisation's costing system should be capable of identifying and collecting these costs. This will lead to a greater management focus on quality since 'what gets measured gets done'.

Test your understanding 3

Required:

Provide an example for each of the four sub-categories of quality cost.

Test your understanding 4

The following information has been supplied for Company X.

	$000
Revenue	320,000
Costs:	
Design engineering P	5,000
Warranty E	8,950
Estimated lost contribution from public knowledge of poor quality	9,561
Training P	560
Process engineering P	3,450
Rework I	7,545
Customer support per repaired unit E	645
Product testing A	65
Transportation costs per repaired unit E	546
Inspection A	13,800

Required:

Prepare a cost analysis that shows the prevention, appraisal, internal failure and external failure costs for Company X. Your statement should show each cost heading as a % of turnover and clearly show the total cost of quality (including any opportunity costs).

5 Quality management systems

5.1 What is a quality management system?

A **quality management system** (QMS) is a set of co-ordinated activities to direct and control an organisation in order to continually improve its performance.

The total cost of conformance is the cost of operating a QMS. The more rigorous the QMS, the lower the costs of non-conformance will be.

5.2 Implementing a QMS

Delivering products which meet the desired level of quality will only occur if all the factors that have an impact on quality are managed effectively.

A QMS should pervade the whole organisation recognising the quality impact of all areas of the organisation. There are a number of ways of implementing a QMS. For example, ISO 9001:2005 recommends that the design should be based on 8 principles:

Test your understanding 5

Required:

Explain how the 8 principles of ISO 9001:2005 should result in quality improvements.

5.3 Impact of a QMS on performance management

The adoption of a QMS should complement an organisation's strategy and help it in achieving its quality objectives. An effective QMS should:

- minimise the overall costs of quality

- improve customer satisfaction due to higher levels of quality

- improve staff morale and productivity due to the involvement and pride taken in the work done.

6 Quality practices

QUALITY PRACTICES

KAIZEN COSTING | TOTAL QUALITY MANAGEMENT | JUST-IN-TIME | SIX SIGMA | TARGET COSTING

6.1 Kaizen Costing

What is Kaizen?

Kaizen is a Japanese term for the philosophy of continuous improvement in performance via small, incremental steps.

Characteristics:

- Kaizen involves setting standards and then continually improving these standards to achieve long-term sustainable improvements.

- The focus is on eliminating waste, improving processes and systems and improving productivity.

- Involves all areas of the business.

- Employees often work in teams and are empowered to make changes.

- Allows the organisation to respond quickly to changes in the competitive environment.

Illustration 1 – Kaizen

Many Japanese companies have introduced a Kaizen approach:

- In companies such as Toyota and Canon, a total of 60–70 suggestions per employee are written down and shared every year.

- It is not unusual for over 90% of those suggestions to be implemented.

- In 1999, in one US plant, 7,000 Toyota employees submitted over 75,000 suggestions, of which 99% were implemented.

Continuous improvement explained

Continuous improvement is the continual examination and improvement of existing processes and is very different from approaches such as business process re-engineering (BPR), which seeks to make radical one-off changes to improve an organisation's operations and processes. The concepts underlying continuous improvement are:

- The organisation should always seek perfection. Since perfection is never achieved, there must always be scope for improving on the current methods.

- The search for perfection should be ingrained into the culture and mindset of all employees. Improvements should be sought all the time.

- Individual improvements identified by the work force will be small rather than far-reaching.

What is Kaizen costing?

Kaizen costing focuses on producing small, incremental cost reductions throughout the production process through the product's life.

KAPLAN PUBLISHING

The steps in Kaizen costing are as follows:

| During the design phase, a target cost is set for each production function. |

| The target costs are totalled to give a total target cost for the product. This becomes the baseline for the first year of production. |

| As the production process improves, cost reductions reduce the baseline cost. |

| Cost reduction targets are set on a regular (e.g. monthly) basis and variance analysis is carried out at the end of each period to compare the target cost reduction with the actual cost. |

One of the main ways to reduce costs is through the elimination of the seven main types of waste:

- **Over-production** – produce more than customers have ordered.

- **Inventory** – holding or purchasing unnecessary inventory.

- **Waiting** – production delays/idle time when value is not added to the product.

- **Defective units** – production of a part that is scrapped or requires rework.

- **Motion** – actions of people/equipment that do not add value.

- **Transportation** – poor planning or factory layout results in unnecessary transportation of materials/work-in-progress.

- **Over-processing** – unnecessary steps that do not add value.

Test your understanding 6

Although the Kaizen costing approach was developed in the manufacturing industry it could also be applied in the service sector.

Required:

Identify some possible sources of waste in a restaurant business and categorise them according to the seven main types of waste described above.

Impact of Kaizen on traditional management accounting techniques

There is a marked distinction between a traditional standard costing system and a modern Kaizen costing approach.

- A traditional standard costing system would not be suitable in a Kaizen environment. Workers who are used to a command and control structure will have to change their behaviour and speak out about possible improvements.

- Standard costs will have much less value as they are fixed over a relevant period where as Kaizen costing can respond more easily in a dynamic environment.

- Standard costing is used to control costs where as Kaizen costing has the advantage of focusing on cost reductions.

- In a standard costing system, employees are often seen as the source of problems where as in a Kaizen system, employees often work in teams and are empowered to make changes.

6.2 Total Quality Management

What is total quality management?

Total Quality Management (TQM) is a philosophy of quality management that originated in Japan in the 1950s.

Fundamental features of TQM:

- **Prevention of errors before they occur**: The aim of TQM is to get things right first time. This contrasts with the traditional approach that less than 100% quality is acceptable. TQM will result in an increase in prevention costs, e.g. quality design of systems and products, but internal and external failure costs will fall to a greater extent.

- **Continual improvement**: Quality management is not a one-off process, but is the continuous examination and improvement of processes.

- **Real participation by all**: The 'total' in TQM means that everyone in the value chain is involved in the process, including:

  - Employees – they are expected to seek out, identify and correct quality problems. Teamwork will be vital.

  - Suppliers – quality and reliability of suppliers will play a vital role.

  - Customers – the goal is to identify and meet the needs of customers.

- **Management commitment**: Managers must be committed and encourage everyone else to be quality conscious.

Illustration 2 – TQM success/failure

A TQM success story

Corning Inc is the world leader in speciality glass and ceramics. This is partly due to the implementation of a TQM approach. In 1983 the CEO announced a $1.6 billion investment in TQM. After several years of intensive training and a decade of applying the TQM approach, all of Corning's employees had bought into the quality concept. They knew the lingo – continuous improvement, empowerment, customer focus, management by prevention and they witnessed the impact of the firm's techniques as profits soared.

An example of TQM failure

British Telecom launched a total quality program in the late 1980s. This resulted in the company getting bogged down by quality processes and bureaucracy. The company failed to focus on its customers and later decided to dismantle its TQM programme. This was at great cost to the company and they have failed to make a full recovery.

Performance measures in a TQM environment

Examples of performance measures in a TQM environment include:

- monetary measure – cost of rectification

- non-monetary measures – percentage of wastage

- variance analysis – care must be taken with regard to traditional performance reports such as favourable price variances, these can arise because of using poorer quality resources
- targets or benchmarks must be set against which the performance of suppliers can be measured
- outputs too must be measured for quality against pre-determined targets.

6.3 Just-in-time

What is just-in-time?

Just-in-time (JIT) is a demand-pull system of ordering from suppliers which aims to reduce inventory levels to zero.

JIT applies to both production within an organisation and to purchasing from external suppliers.

JIT purchasing is a method of purchasing that involves ordering materials only when customers place an order. When the goods are received they go straight into production.

JIT production is a production system that is driven by demand for the finished products (a 'pull' system), whereby each component on a production line is produced only when needed for the next stage.

JIT is often used in conjunction with other continuous improvement methods.

Illustration 3 – Toyota

Toyota pioneered the JIT manufacturing system, in which suppliers send parts daily – or several times a day – and are notified electronically when the production line is running out.

More than 400 trucks a day come in and out of Toyota's Georgetown plant in the USA, with a separate logistics company organising shipment from Toyota's 300 suppliers – most located in neighbouring state within half a day's drive of the plant.

Toyota aims to build long-term relationships with suppliers, many of whom it has a stake in, and says it now produces 80% of its parts within North America.

Requirements for successful operation of a JIT system

Requirements include:

- **High quality and reliability** – disruptions cause hold ups in the entire system and must be avoided. The emphasis is on getting the work right first time:
    - Highly skilled and well trained staff should be used.
    - Machinery must be fully maintained.
    - Long-term links should be established with suppliers in order to ensure a reliable and high quality service and to minimise any stoppages in production.

- **Elimination of non-value added activities** – for example, value is not added whilst storing the products and therefore inventory levels should be minimised.

- **Speed of throughput** – the speed of production should match the rate at which customers demand the product. Production runs should be shorter with smaller stocks of finished goods.

- **Flexibility** – a flexible production system and workforce is needed in order to be able to respond immediately to customers' orders.

- **Lower costs** – another objective of JIT is to reduce costs by:
    - Raising quality and eliminating waste.
    - Achieving faster throughput.
    - Minimising inventory levels.

Test your understanding 7

Required:

Explain the advantages and disadvantages to an organisation of operating a JIT system.

JIT and supplier relationships

A company is a long way towards JIT if its suppliers will guarantee the quality of the material they deliver and will give it shorter lead-times, deliver smaller quantities more often, guarantee a low reject rate and perform quality-assurance inspection at source. Frequent deliveries of small quantities of material to the company can ensure that each delivery is just enough to meet its immediate production schedule. This will keep its inventory as low as possible. Materials handling time will be saved because as there is no need to move the stock into a store, the goods can be delivered directly to a workstation on the shop floor. Inspection time and costs can be eliminated and the labour required for reworking defective material or returning goods to the supplier can be saved.

The successful JIT manufacturer deliberately sets out to cultivate good relationships with a small number of suppliers and these suppliers will often be situated close to the manufacturing plant. It is usual for a large manufacturer that does not use the JIT approach to have multiple suppliers. When a new part is to be produced, various suppliers will bid for the contract and the business will be given to the two or three most attractive bids.

A JIT manufacturer is looking for a single supplier that can provide high quality and reliable deliveries, rather than the lowest price. This supplier will often be located in close proximity to the manufacturing plant.

There is much to be gained by both the company and its suppliers from this mutual dependence. The supplier is guaranteed a demand for the products as the sole supplier and is able to plan to meet the customer's production schedules. If an organisation has confidence that suppliers will deliver material of 100% quality, on time, so that there will be no rejects, returns and hence no consequent production delays, usage of materials can be matched with delivery of materials and stocks can be kept at near zero levels.

Jaguar, when it analysed the causes of customer complaints, compiled a list of 150 areas of faults. Some 60% of them turned out to be faulty components from suppliers. One month the company returned 22,000 components to different suppliers. Suppliers were brought on to the multi-disciplinary task forces the company established to tackle each of the common faults. The task force had the simple objective of finding the fault, establishing and testing a cure, and implementing it as fast as possible. Jaguar directors chaired the task forces of the 12 most serious faults, but in one case the task force was chaired by the supplier's representative.

JIT and service operations

Although it originated with manufacturing systems, the JIT philosophy can also be applied to some service operations.

- Whereas JIT in manufacturing seeks to eliminate inventories, JIT in service operations will seek to eliminate internal or external queues of customers.

- Other concepts of JIT, such as eliminating wasteful motion and seeking ways of achieving continuous improvement are also applicable to services as much as to manufacturing activities.

The impact on management accounting

The introduction of a JIT system will have a number of effects on the costing system and performance management.

- Allowances for waste, scrap and rework are moved to the ideal standard, rather than an achievable standard.

- Costs are only allowed to accumulate when the product is finished.

- The inevitable reduction in inventory levels will reduce the time taken to count inventory and the clerical cost.

- Minimal inventory makes it easier for a firm to switch to backflush accounting (a simplified method of cost bookkeeping).

- Traditional performance measures such as inventory turnover and individual incentives are replaced by more appropriate performance measures, such as:
  - total head count productivity
  - inventory days
  - ideas generated and implemented
  - customer complaints
  - bottlenecks in production
  - amount and effectiveness of staff training.

6.4 Six Sigma

- Six Sigma is a quality management programme that was pioneered by Motorola in the 1980s.

- The aim of the approach is to achieve a reduction in the number of faults that go beyond an accepted tolerance level. It tends to be used for individual processes.

- The sigma stands for the standard deviation. For reasons that need not be explained here, it can be demonstrated that, if the error rate lies beyond the sixth sigma of probability there will be fewer than 3.4 defects in every one million units produced.

- This is the tolerance level set. It is almost perfection since customers will have room to complain fewer than four times in a million.

e.g

Illustration 4 – The Six Sigma approach

A hospital is using the Six Sigma process to improve patient waiting times. An investigation of the views of patients has revealed that:

- patients do not want to be called before their appointment time as they do not want to feel that they have to be at the hospital early to avoid missing an appointment

- the maximum length of time they are prepared to wait after the appointment time is 30 minutes.

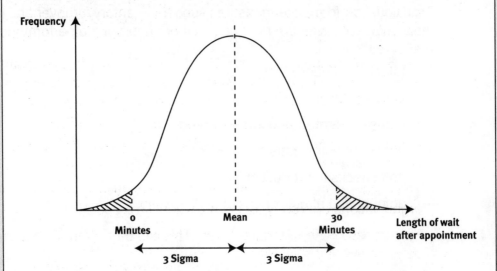

The aim of the Six Sigma programme will be to ensure that no more than 3.4 waits in every million occurrences exceed 30 minutes or are less than 0 minutes.

Key requirements and criticisms

There are a number of **key requirements** for the implementation of Six Sigma.

- Six Sigma should be focused on the customer and based on the level of performance acceptable to the customer.

- Six Sigma targets for a process should be related to the main drivers of performance.

- To maximise savings Six Sigma needs to be part of a wider performance management programme which is linked to the strategy of the organisation. It should not be just about doing things better but about doing things differently.

- Senior managers within the organisation have a key role in driving the process.

- Training and education about the process throughout the organisation are essential for success.

- Six Sigma sets a tight target, but accepts some failure – the target is not zero defects.

Literature on Six Sigma contains some **criticisms** of the process and identifies a number of limitations as follows.

- Six Sigma has been criticised for its focus on current processes and reliance on data. It is suggested that this could become too rigid and limit process innovation.

- Six Sigma is based on the use of models which are by their nature simplifications of real life. Judgement needs to be used in applying the models in the context of business objectives.

- The approach can be very time consuming and expensive. Organisations need to be prepared to put time and effort into its implementation.

- The culture of the organisation must be supportive – not all organisations are ready for such a scientific process.

- The process is heavily data-driven. This can be a strength, but can become over-bureaucratic.

- Six Sigma can give all parts of the organisation a common language for process improvement, but it is important to ensure that this does not become jargon but is expressed in terms specific to the organisation and its business.

- There is an underlying assumption in Six Sigma that the existing business processes meet customers' expectations. It does not ask whether it is the right process.

The five steps of the Six Sigma process (DMAIC)

Step 1: Define customer requirements/problem
- customer requirements can be divided into those that are the minimum that is acceptable, those that improve the customer's experience and those that go beyond the customer's expectations.
- quality problem defined in specific, quantifiable terms.
- a mission statement is prepared explaining what will be done about the problem. This should also be in specific, quantifiable terms
- a project team is set up from across the organisation and is given the resources to address the problem.

Step 2: Measure existing performance
- the project team does some preliminary work to measure how the current process is working and identifies what is causing the quality problem
- measures should focus on areas where customers will value improvement
- the performance measurement system must be reliable (redesign may be required).

Step 3: Analysis the existing process
- the project team investigates their preliminary concerns and test different theories to get to the root cause of the problem
- techniques such as Pareto analysis will improve the focus of action on the issues that give rise to the majority of quality problems (i.e. 20% of the causes will give rise to 80% of the problems).

Step 4: Improve the process
- Potential solutions are developed for process re-design. The most appropriate solution will be one that achieves the mission statement within the cost and resource constraints of the organisation.

Step 5: Control the process
New controls are designed to compare actual performance with targeted performance to make sure the improvements to the process are being sustained

How does Six Sigma improve the quality of performance?

Six Sigma improves quality in a number of ways:

- An increased focus on the customer.

- The identification of business process improvements as key to success

- Management decision making is driven by data and facts, for example the number of customer complaints as a key performance measure.

- The proactive involvement of management and effective leadership to co-ordinate the different Six Sigma projects.

- It involves collaboration across functional and divisional boundaries focusing the whole organisation on quality issues.

- The increased profile of quality issues and the increased knowledge of quality management that comes from the use of different layers of trained experts.

Test your understanding 8

Required:

How can management accountants contribute to the Six Sigma process?

6.5 Target costing

The target cost is an estimate of a product's cost which is derived by subtracting a desired profit margin from a competitive market price.

Steps in target costing:

(1) Estimate a selling price for the product - consider how much customers will pay and how much competitors charge for similar products.

(2) Deduct the required profit.

(3) Produce a target cost figure.

(4) Reduce cost gap, i.e the difference between the current cost and the target cost.

Techniques to reduce the cost gap

Many of the techniques used to reduce the cost gap have a **'quality'** focus. These include:

- JIT

- TQM

- Kaizen

- ABC

- Value analysis: a systematic examination of the product which asks questions such as:

  - can another dependable supplier be found for less cost?

  - does it need all of its features?

Key features of target costing

- **Target costing forces a focus on the customer:** Product decisions and cost analysis have to take account of customer requirements such as quality, features and price. This is not always the case with other cost management methods.

- **Successful target costing considers all costs** related to production and distribution of the products and involves the whole supply chain. This may even include joint working between suppliers and manufacturers to share information and enable cost reductions, particularly for products for which raw materials contribute a high proportion of the manufactured cost.

- **Target costing considers the entire life-cycle** of the product, so that total costs to the manufacturer are minimised.

- **Target costing begins very early in the development** phase of new products, so that changes are made before production begins. Decisions made at this stage generally determine a high proportion of the costs of any product.

- **Target costing is a multi-disciplinary approach** which involves staff from all functions in the analysis and decision making.

- **Target costing is an iterative process** in which teams are making judgements and trade-offs between product features, price, sales volumes, costs and investment requirements.

- **Target costing provides cost targets** for individual inputs and processes which can be used for performance monitoring.

Additional question on quality

Question

Edward Electronics assembles and sells many types of radio. It is considering extending its product range to include digital radios. These radios produce a better sound quality than traditional radios and have a large number of potential additional features not possible with the previous technologies (station scanning, more choice, one touch tuning, station identification text and song identification text etc).

A radio is produced by assembly workers assembling a variety of components. Production overheads are currently absorbed into product costs on an assembly labour hour basis.

Edward Electronics is considering a target costing approach for its new digital radio product.

Required:

(a) Briefly describe the target costing process that Edward Electronics should undertake.

(3 marks)

(b) Explain the benefits to Edward Electronics of adopting a target costing approach at such an early stage in the product development process.

(4 marks)

A selling price of $44 has been set in order to compete with a similar radio on the market that has comparable features to Edward Electronics' intended product. The board have agreed that the acceptable margin (after allowing for all production costs) should be 20%.

Cost information for the new radio is as follows:

Component 1 (Circuit board) – these are bought in and cost $4.10 each. They are bought in batches of 4,000 and additional delivery costs are $2,400 per batch.

Component 2 (Wiring) – in an ideal situation 25 cm of wiring is needed for each completed radio. However, there is some waste involved in the process as wire is occasionally cut to the wrong length or is damaged in the assembly process. Edward Electronics estimates that 2% of the purchased wire is lost in the assembly process. Wire costs $0.50 per metre to buy.

Other material – other materials cost $8.10 per radio.

Assembly labour – these are skilled people who are difficult to recruit and retain. Edward Electronics has more staff of this type than needed but is prepared to carry this extra cost in return for the security it gives the business. It takes 30 minutes to assemble a radio and the assembly workers are paid $12.60 per hour. It is estimated that 10% of hours paid to the assembly workers is for idle time.

Production Overheads – recent historic cost analysis has revealed the following production overhead data:

	Total production overhead ($)	Total assembly labour hours
Month 1	620,000	19,000
Month 2	700,000	23,000

Fixed production overheads are absorbed on an assembly hour basis based on normal annual activity levels. In a typical year 240,000 assembly hours will be worked by Edward Electronics.

Required:

(c) Calculate the expected cost per unit for the radio and identify any cost gap that might exist.

(13 marks)

(Total: 20 marks)

Answer

(a) The target costing process should be undertaken as follows:

Step 1: Establish the selling price by considering how much customers will be willing to pay and how much competitors charge for similar products.

Step 2: Deduct the required profit from the selling price.

Step 3: Calculate the target cost, i.e. selling price minus profit.

Step 4: Find ways to reduce the cost gap, e.g. cheaper materials, cheaper labour, increased productivity, reduced waste.

(b) The benefits are as follows:

- Target costing has an external focus, i.e. it considers how much customers will pay/competitors will charge.

- Cost control can occur earlier in the design process and the required steps can be taken to reduce the cost gap.

- The performance of the business should be enhanced due to better management of costs.

- The focus will be on getting things right first time which should reduce the development time.

(c) (W1) **Production overhead** (using high low method)

	Production overhead ($)	Labour hours
High	700,000	23,000
Low	620,000	19,000
Difference	80,000	4,000

- Variable overhead = $80,000 ÷ 4,000 = $20 per hour

- Total cost $700,000 = fixed cost + variable cost ($20/hour × 23,000). This gives a monthly fixed cost of $240,000. (Note: the total cost at the low level of production could also be used to find the fixed cost).

- Annual fixed cost = $240,000 × 12 = $2,880,000

- Overhead absorption rate (OAR) = $2,880,000 ÷ 240,000hours = $12 per hour

Cost card and cost gap calculation

	$ per radio
Component 1	4.10
Component 1 delivery = $2,400 ÷ 4,000	0.60
Component 2 wiring = $0.50 × 0.25metres × 100/98	0.128
Other material	8.10
Assembly labour = $12.60 × 0.5hours × 100/90	7.00
Variable production overhead = $20/hour (W1) × 0.5hours	10.00
Fixed production overhead = $12/hour (W1) × 0.5hours	6.00
Total cost	**35.928**
Desired cost	35.20
Cost gap	**0.728**

Additional question on quality

Required:

Explain how management accounting/management techniques such as total quality management, just in time, value analysis, activity based costing and the balanced scorecard could contribute towards the analysis of the relationship between costs and quality.

Answer:

Total Quality Management (TQM)

TQM is an approach that seeks to ensure that all aspects of providing goods and services are delivered at the highest possible standard, and that standards keep improving. The underlying principle is that the cost of preventing deficient quality is less than the costs of correcting poor quality. This denies the idea that improved quality can only be secured with greater expenditure, but adopts the approach that improved quality will reduce costs.

Quality related costs are concerned with both achieving quality and failure to achieve quality.

Quality costs can categorised as:

- **Prevention costs** – communicating the concept, training, establishing systems to deliver quality services

- **Appraisal costs** – e.g. inspection and testing

- **Internal failure costs** – wasted materials used in rejects, down time resulting from internal service quality failures, resources devoted to dealing with complaints

- **External failure costs** – loss of goodwill and future business, compensation paid to customers and rectification costs

The TQM view is that by getting it right first time and every time, the prevention and appraisal costs will be outweighed by the savings in failure costs, hence lower costs and improved quality are congruent goals. TQM requires everyone in the organisation to have identified customers, whether external or internal, so that a continuous service quality chain is maintained all the way through the organisation to the final customer.

Just In Time (JIT)

JIT is a manufacturing and supply chain process that is intended to reduce inventory levels and improve customer service by ensuring that customers receive their orders at the right time and in the right quantity. The system should facilitate a smooth workflow throughout the business and reduce waste. Goods are produced to meet customer needs directly, not for inventory.

Cost reductions should arise from:

- Lower raw material and finished goods inventory levels, therefore reduced holding costs

- Reduced material handling

- Often a reduction in the number of suppliers and lower administration and communication costs

- Guaranteed quality of supplies reduces inspection and rectification costs

Quality improvements should arise from:

- Fewer or even single sourcing of supplies strengthens the buyer–supplier relationship and is likely to improve the quality.

- The absence of customer stockholding compels the supplier (if they want continued business) to guarantee the quality of the material that they deliver.

- The necessity to work regularly and closer with hauliers strengthens the relationship with them. The deliveries become high priority and more reliable.

- Customers are not faced with the traditional problems of having to wait until their suppliers inventories are replenished. The system is designed to respond to customers' needs rapidly.

- Direct focus on meeting an identified customer's need, production is merely to add to an anonymous pile of inventory.

Value Analysis

Value analysis is concerned with concentrating on activities that add value to the product/service as perceived by the customer. It examines business activities and questions why they are being undertaken and what contribution do they make to customer satisfaction. Value added activities include designing products, producing output and developing customer relationships. Non-value added activities include returning goods, inventory holding, and checking on the quality of supplies received. Wherever possible eliminate the non-value added activities.

Value analysis commences with a focus on customers. What do they want? What do they regard as significant in the buying decision: function, appearance, longevity or disposal value? This is concerned with identifying what customers regard as quality and then providing it: do not expend effort on what they regard as unimportant. It is about clarifying what the constituents of quality are on the Costs and Quality diagram. Having decided this there is a need to develop alternative designs, estimate costs and evaluate alternatives.

Activity Based Costing (ABC)

ABC is concerned with attributing/assigning costs to cost units on the basis of the service received from indirect activities e.g. public relations, recruitment, quality assurance general meetings. The organisation needs to identify cost drivers – the specific activities that cause costs to arise e.g. number of orders taken, telephone calls made, number of breakdowns or the number of visitors to an attraction.

ABC intends to avoid the arbitrary allocation of overheads to products/services by identifying a causal link between costs, activities and outputs. Because of higher degrees of automation, the increasing significance of overheads in the cost make up of output intensifies the need to improve the apportionment of them. Accountants can contribute towards providing better cost information to the value analysis referred to above. Product managers need to know what they are getting for their money – what is the real cost of quality? What are the cost driving activities that do not impact on quality? What activities that generate minimal costs have a significantly favourable impact on quality?

The Balanced Scorecard (Kaplan and Norton)

The Balanced Scorecard provides a framework for a business to achieve its strategic objectives include both financial and non-financial objectives. The approach claims that performance has four dimensions: financial, customer, internal business, and innovation and learning. The customer perspective asks: How does the business appear to the customers? The internal business perspective asks :What do we need to do to satisfy shareholders and customers, including the monitoring of unit costs? The innovation and learning perspective looks at how products and processes should be changed and improved.

The scorecard is concerned with monitoring and measuring the critical variables that comprise the customer and internal perspective. The choice of variables for inclusion in the scorecard is significant because the scorecard report is a design for action. Inappropriate indicators will trigger damaging responses. For example, the organisation needs to monitor what factors customers regard as contributing to improved quality, not what the business thinks it should provide. Therefore the scorecards would be suitable for inclusion as quantifiable indicators on the axis on the Costs and Quality diagram. The Balanced Scorecard attempts to improve the range and relationship between alternative performance measures, in the case under discussion, costs and quality.

7 Quality in management information systems

7.1 Features of a quality system

Four features of a quality system

Functionality
- system performs task it was designed for

Reliability
- system is not susceptible to downtime and outputs are accurate and complete

Usability
- the system is user friendly

Build quality
- eg ease of maintenance and upgrade

Test your understanding 9

Required:

Explain the consequences of failing to include these four features in a management information system.

7.2 Designing a quality system

Designing a quality system

In order to ensure that the system fulfils the quality criteria of functionality, reliability, usability and build quality a structured approach to development should be used. One such approach is the systems development life cycle (SDLC):

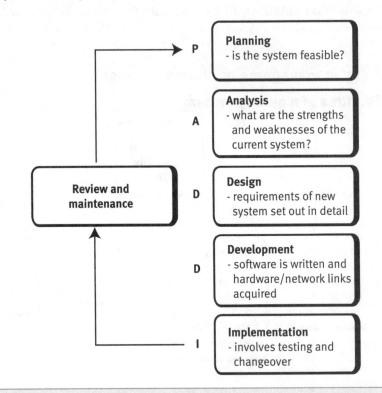

8 Exam focus

Exam sitting	Area examined	Question number	Number of marks
June 2012	Six Sigma	3	17
December 2011	Quality costs, Kaizen and JIT	5	20
June 2010	Cost targets and quality costs	5(a)	8
June 2009	Six Sigma	5	20
December 2008	Software quality and service quality	2(c)(d)	7
December 2008	Quality costs	4(b)	8
June 2008	Quality costs and elimination of quality problems	5	20
Pilot paper	Service quality	1(e)	6

Note:

- The current examiner has set the exam papers from the December 2010 sitting onwards.

- The format of the exam changed in June 2013. Section A now contains 1 × 50 mark question (previously 2 questions worth 60 marks in total) and Section B now contains a choice of 2 from 3 questions worth 25 marks each (previously a choice of 2 from 3 questions worth approximately 20 marks each).

Chapter summary

Definitions
- quality management
- quality control
- quality assurance

Quality certification
- ISO

Quality-related costs
- prevention
- appraisal
- internal failure
- external failure

The role quality in performance management

Quality management systems
- what is a QMS?
- implementing a QMS
- impact on performance management

Quality practices
- Kaizen costing
- TQM
- JIT
- Six sigma
- Target costing

Quality in MIS
- features of a quality system
- designing a quality system

Test your understanding answers

Test your understanding 1

Higher quality can help to increase revenue and reduce costs:

- Higher quality improves the perceived image of a product or service. As a result, more customers will be willing to purchase the product/service and may also be willing to pay a higher price.

- A higher volume of sales may result in lower unit costs due to economies of scale.

- Higher quality in manufacturing should result in lower waste and defective rates, which will reduce production costs.

- The need for inspection and testing should be reduced, also reducing costs.

- The level of customer complaints should fall and warranty claims should be lower. This will reduce costs.

- Better quality in production should lead to shorter processing times. This will reduce costs.

Test your understanding 2

Advantages

- Recognised standard – the company's reputation for quality will be enhanced since ISO is a recognised international standard of quality.

- Marketing – ISO certification will act as an excellent marketing tool. It will help to differentiate the company, on the grounds of quality, in the customers' eyes.

- Improved profitability – fulfilment of the ISO criteria should help the company to improve quality. This, in turn, should reduce costs and improve quality.

- International competitiveness – ISO certification is becoming increasingly useful in international markets and may help the company to compete on a world stage.

Disadvantages

- Cost – fees are upward of $1,500 depending on the size of the company.

- Time – documentation can be time consuming to produce.

- Bureaucracy – the scheme encourages bureaucracy with lots of form filling and filing rather than positive actions.

- Rigid policies – these might discourage initiative and innovation and may therefore hinder the quality process.

- Not all embracing – ISO certification will form a small part of a quality practice such as TQM.

Test your understanding 3

Prevention costs

- Cost of designing products and services with built in quality.

- Cost of training employees in the best way to do their job.

- Cost of equipment testing to ensure it conforms with quality standards required.

Appraisal costs

- Inspection and testing, for example of a purchased material or service.

Internal failure costs

- Cost of scrapped material due to poor quality.

- Cost of re-working parts.

- Reinspection costs.

- Lower selling prices for sub-quality products.

External failure costs

- Cost of recalling and correcting products.

- Cost of lost goodwill.

Test your understanding 4

	$000	% of revenue
Prevention costs:		
Design engineering	5,000	1.56
Process engineering	3,450	1.08
Training	560	0.18
Total	**9,010**	**2.82**
Appraisal costs:		
Inspection	13,800	4.31
Product testing	65	0.02
Total	**13,865**	**4.33**
Internal failure costs	7,545	2.36
Total	**7,545**	**2.36**
External failure costs:		
Warranty	8,950	2.80
Customer support	645	0.20
Transportation	546	0.17
Total	**10,141**	**3.17**
Sub-total	**40,561**	**12.68**
Opportunity costs	9,561	2.99
Total quality costs	**50,112**	**15.66**

Test your understanding 5

The 8 principles of ISO 9001:2005 should result in quality improvements as follows:

- **Customer focus** – quality may be defined as 'the product/service meeting the customer's needs' and therefore a customer focus should improve quality.

- **Leadership** – leaders should communicate the importance of quality and drive a culture of quality.

- **Involvement of people** – everyone in the organisation should have a quality focus.

- **Process approach** – related activities and resources should be managed in an integrated quality process.

- **Systems approach to management** – groups of related processes should be managed in an integrated quality system.

- **Continual improvement** – quality management is not a one off process, but is the continuous examination and improvement of processes.

- **Factual approach to decision making** – quality procedures should be documented and applied consistently.

- **Mutually beneficial supplier relationships** – long-term links should be established with suppliers in order to ensure a reliable and high quality service.

Test your understanding 6

Suggestions could include:

- Pre-preparing plated servings of perishable desserts which are not ordered and need to be thrown away – over-production.

- Poor kitchen layout which could lead to unnecessary movement of staff and result in waste from motion and from transportation of material or lead to accidents and spillages and waste in processes and methods.

- Poorly trained cooking staff who produce sub-standard meals which cannot be served – product defects.

- Producing too many pre-prepared components such as sauces to be incorporated in dishes which are then not needed – waste from inventory.

- Poor scheduling in the kitchen leading to serving staff waiting for meals to be ready – waste from waiting time.

Test your understanding 7

Advantages of JIT

- Lower stock holding costs means a reduction in storage space which saves rent and insurance costs.

- As stock is only obtained when needed, less working capital is tied up in stock.

- There is less likelihood of stock perishing, becoming obsolete or out of date.

- Avoids the build up of unsold finished products that occurs with sudden changes in demand.

- Less time is spent checking and re-working the products as the emphasis is on getting the work right first time.

- Increased flexibility in meeting the customer's individual needs.

The result is that costs should fall and quality should increase. This should improve the company's competitive advantage.

Disadvantages of JIT

- There is little room for mistakes as little stock is kept for re-working a faulty product.

- Production is very reliant on suppliers and if stock is not delivered on time or is not of a high enough quality, the whole production schedule can be delayed.

- There is no spare finished product available to meet unexpected orders, because all products are made to meet actual orders.

- It may be difficult for managers to empower employees to embrace the concept and culture.

- It won't be suitable for all companies. For example, supermarkets must have a supply of inventory.

- It can be difficult to apply to the service industry. However, in the service industry a JIT approach may focus on eliminating queues, which are wasteful of customers' time.

Test your understanding 8

- The provision of data at all stages in the process.

- Providing expertise in the identification of appropriate output, input and process measures (financial and non-financial) and ways to collect the data.

- Analysis of data.

- Evaluation of possible solutions.

- Identification of performance measures for the control process and monitoring after changes have been implemented.

- Taking part in multi-disciplinary Six Sigma teams.

Test your understanding 9

- **Poor functionality and reliability** may result in:
  - user dissatisfaction, e.g. because the system does not perform the desired task
  - additional costs, e.g. to correct inaccurate reports.

- **Poor usability** may result in:
  - staff dissatisfaction
  - excessive staff training
  - excessive time spent by staff trying to operate the system.

- **Poor build quality** will result in difficulties maintaining and upgrading the system which will impact long-term profit.

KAPLAN PUBLISHING

Current developments in performance management

Chapter learning objectives

Upon completion of this chapter you will be able to:

- discuss, evaluate and apply environmental management accounting using for example lifecycle costing, input/output analysis and activity-based costing

- discuss the use of benchmarking in public sector performance (league tables) in public sector performance and its effects on operational and strategic management and behaviour

- discuss the issues surrounding the use of targets in public sector organisations

- discuss contemporary issues in performance management

- discuss how changing organisation's structure, culture and strategy will influence the adoption of new performance measurement methods and techniques.

1 Assumed knowledge

Chapter 13 builds on your knowledge of environmental management accounting from Paper F5.

2 Introduction

The area of performance management is constantly evolving. The techniques and systems used today are very different from those of 50 years ago and there are current issues and pressures which are likely to lead to further developments:

- changes in technology may have a significant impact on measuring performance

- a recognition that there is a broader picture than just financial performance

- issues relating to governance.

Contemporary issues in performance management

Changes in technology

Improvements in technology have a significant impact on performance management.

- It is possible to measure more and more different indicators of performance – the challenge now is to ensure that the aspects being measured and managed are the right ones.

KAPLAN PUBLISHING

- Improved technology also means that it is possible to produce information much more quickly and in real time.

- Information is now made directly available to managers on their desks at the touch of a button. The production of performance reports is no longer the responsibility of a small number of specialists – rather their role is to design the overall system to ensure that it provides the information required by managers.

- The availability of more data does not automatically mean that there is more useful information – it is still important to ensure that the data is interpreted to ensure that it is useful.

- Performance management is about more than the information produced – however much information is provided, what is important is how it is used and how the organisation acts in response to it.

Broadening performance management

There is a growing recognition that the performance of organisations depends on more than purely financial performance.

- There has been significant growth in the use of non-financial measures of performance.

- Techniques have been developed to enable measurement of performance in a number of different dimensions, and this trend looks set to continue. Examples are the balanced scorecard and the performance prism.

- Historically the focus of performance management has been on outputs of the organisation's activities. Organisations are now beginning to focus on outcomes, or achievements, and then using output measures to achieve those outcomes.

- There is a recognition that everyone in the organisation needs to be involved in performance management.

- There is also a need to extend involvement outside the organisation to the entire supply chain, as organisations recognise that others have an influence on their performance.

Governance

Over recent years, the issue of corporate governance has become a major area for concern in many countries. Organisations are now under increased pressure to demonstrate that they are effectively managed. This has led to:

- pressure to demonstrate improvements in performance

- more demands for accountability from external agencies

- legislation and regulation relating to performance reporting

- companies looking for ways to measure and report on improvements in governance.

3 The influence of structure, culture and strategy

The way in which new techniques and methods are adopted will vary between organisations and will be influenced by organisational structure, culture and strategy.

Factor	Explanation
Organisational **structure**	• Highly centralised and/ or functional structures will tend to inhibit the manager's discretion to try out new techniques. • A task centred and/ or decentralised structure will have the opposite effect.
Organisational **culture**	• A restrictive, bureaucratic culture will be less open to the adoption of new techniques. • An innovative or creative culture will be a lot more willing to embrace new techniques.
Organisational **strategy**	• The techniques adopted by an organisation will be influenced by the strategy it is pursuing. • For example, an organisation that focuses on quality may adopt a TQM approach whereas an organisation that focuses on cost reduction may adopt an activity-based approach.

KAPLAN PUBLISHING

4 Environmental management accounting

4.1 Introduction

Organisations are becoming increasingly aware of the environmental implications of their actions.

Test your understanding 1

Required:

Discuss the potential benefits to a company of reducing the negative environmental impact of its operations, products or services.

Illustration 1 – Environmental management at BP

BP plc's previous Annual Review describes a number of activities aimed at reducing the environmental impact of the company's operations:

- improving the integrity of its equipment and pipelines to reduce the spillage of oil

- reducing the emissions of greenhouse gases, which is measured and reported within the Annual Review

- introducing environmental requirements for new projects

- supporting the use of market mechanisms to bring about emission reductions across the industry

- launching a new business providing energy from alternative sources

- investing in research into biofuels

- developing and marketing fuel which produces lower emissions compared with standard fuels.

4.2 Drawbacks of traditional management accounting

Management accounts provide us with an analysis of the performance of the business. However, traditional accounting systems are unable to deal adequately with environmental costs. As a result, managers are unaware of these costs and have no information with which to manage or reduce them.

Environmental cost category	Description	Problem
Conventional costs	Costs such as raw material and energy costs	Will not be prioritised by management since often hidden within overheads
Contingent costs	Costs such as future compliance costs or remediation costs when a site is decommissioned	Often incurred towards the end of a project so are ignored by managers who focus on short-term performance
Relationship costs	Image costs such as the cost of producing environmental information for public reporting	Ignored by managers who are unaware of their existence
Reputational costs	Costs associated with failing to address environmental issues, e.g. lost sales	Ignored by managers who are unaware of the risk of incurring them

Illustration 2 – Reputational costs

In April 2010 a blast at the Deepwater Horizon rig in the Gulf of Mexico killed eleven people and caused one of the worst oil spills in history. The US presidential commission concluded that the oil spill was an avoidable disaster caused by a series of failures and blunders made by BP, its partners and the government departments assigned to regulate them. It also warned that such a disaster was likely to recur because of complacency in the industry.

For BP, the company at the heart of the disaster, the effects have had a deep and widespread impact. The company has become synonymous with everything that is dangerous about oil exploration causing massive reputational damage.

4.3 Using environmental management accounting to address these problems

To ensure that environmental costs are fully considered and to improve the environmental performance of an organisation, a new technique called environmental management accounting (EMA) has been introduced. EMA:

- identifies and estimates the costs of environment-related activities and seeks to control these costs

- identifies and separately monitors the usage and cost of resources such as water, electricity and fuel and enables these costs to be reduced

- ensures environmental considerations form a part of capital investment decisions

- assesses the likelihood and impact of environmental risks

- includes environment-related indicators as part of routine performance monitoring

- benchmarks activities against environmental best practice.

In summary, the focus of EMA is not all on financial costs but it also considers the environmental cost or benefit of any decisions made.

4.4 EMA techniques

Four key techniques exist. The techniques can assist an organisation in improving its performance. They are not mutually exclusive.

Activity-based costing (ABC)

ABC distinguishes between:

- environment-related costs which can be attributed directly to a cost centre, e.g. a waste filtration plant, and

- environment-driven costs which are generally hidden in overheads.

The environment-driven costs are removed from general overheads and traced to products or services. This means that cost drivers are determined for these costs and products are charged for the use of these environmental costs based on the amount of cost drivers that they contribute to the activity. This should give a good attribution of environmental costs to individual products and should result in better control of costs.

Advantages and disadvantages of ABC

Advantages	Disadvantages
• Better/fairer product costs	• Time consuming
• Improved pricing – so that the products which have the biggest environmental impact reflect this by having higher selling prices	• Expensive to implement
	• Determining accurate costs and appropriate cost drivers is difficult
• Better environmental control	• External costs, i.e. not experienced by the company (e.g. carbon footprint) may still be ignored/unmeasured
• Facilitates the quantification of cost savings from 'environmentally-friendly' measures	• A company that integrates external costs voluntarily may be at a competitive disadvantage to rivals who do not do this
• Should integrate environmental costing into the strategic management process	• Some internal environmental costs are intangible (e.g. impact on employee health) and these are still ignored

Input/output analysis

This technique compares the physical quantities input into a process and compares this with the output quantities. The physical quantities can be translated into monetary terms.

Illustration 3 – Input/output analysis

		Physical units (kgs)	Revenue/ (cost) ($)
Input		100	(700,000)
Output	Product	60	900,000
	Scrap for recycling	20	45,000
	Disposed of as waste	20	(300,000)
	Total		**(55,000)**

A reduction in waste could help to eliminate the loss.

KAPLAN PUBLISHING

Flow cost accounting

This is associated with input/output analysis since it looks at the physical quantities of material involved in different processes. The aim is to reduce the quantities of material and hence the cost.

Lifecycle costing

Lifecycle costing considers the costs and revenues of a product over its whole life rather than one accounting period. Therefore, the full environmental cost of producing a product will be taken into account. In order to reduce lifecycle costs an organisation may adopt a TQM approach.

It is arguable that TQM and environmental management are inextricably linked insofar as good environmental management is increasingly recognised as an essential component of TQM. Such organisations pursue objectives that may include zero complaints, zero spills, zero pollution, zero waste and zero accidents. Information systems need to be able to support such environmental objectives via the provision of feedback – on the success or otherwise – of the organisational efforts in achieving such objectives.

Note: The benefit of each of the techniques must be weighed against the cost of providing the additional information.

Illustration 4 – Cost reduction at McCain Foods

One example of energy saving is McCain Foods, which buys an eighth of the UK's potatoes to make chips. It has cut its Peterborough plant's CO_2 footprint by two-thirds, says corporate affairs director Bill Bartlett. It invested £10m (approximately $15m) in three 3MW turbines to meet 60 per cent of its annual electricity demand. McCain spent another £4.5m (approximately $6.75m) on a lagoon to catch the methane from fermenting waste water and particulates, which generates another 10 per cent of the site's electricity usage. It also wants to refine its used cooking oil, either for its own vehicles fleet or for selling on.

McCain want to become more competitive and more efficient.

Question practice

The question below is taken from the December 2010 exam. It is an excellent question on EMA. Make sure that you take the time to attempt the question and review/ learn from the answer.

Test your understanding 2

FGH Telecom (FGH) is one of the largest providers of mobile and fixed line telecommunications in Ostland. The company has recently been reviewing its corporate objectives in the light of its changed business environment. The major new addition to the strategic objectives is under the heading: 'Building a more environmentally friendly business for the future'. It has been recognised that the company needs to make a contribution to ensuring sustainable development in Ostland and reducing its environmental footprint. Consequently, it adopted a goal that, by 2017, it would have reduced its environmental impact by 60% (compared to year 2001).

The reasons for the board's concern are that the telecommunications sector is competitive and the economic environment is increasingly harsh with the markets for debt and equities being particularly poor. On environmental issues, the government and public are calling for change from the business community. It appears that increased regulation and legislation will appear to encourage business towards better performance. The board have recognised that there are threats and opportunities from these trends. It wants to ensure that it is monitoring these factors and so it has asked for an analysis of the business environment with suggestions for performance measurement.

Additionally, the company has a large number of employees working across its network. Therefore, there are large demands for business travel. FGH runs a large fleet of commercial vehicles in order to service its network along with a company car scheme for its managers. The manager in charge of the company's travel budget is reviewing data on carbon dioxide emissions to assess FGH's recent performance.

Recent initiatives within the company to reduce emissions have included:

(a) the introduction in 2010 of a homeworking scheme for employees in order to reduce the amount of commuting to and from their offices and

(b) a drive to increase the use of teleconferencing facilities by employees.

Data on FGH Telecom:

Carbon Dioxide emissions

Measured in millions of kgs	2001 Base year	2009	2010
Commercial Fleet Diesel	105.4	77.7	70.1
Commercial Fleet Petrol	11.6	0.4	0.0
Company Car Diesel	15.1	14.5	12.0
Company Car Petrol	10.3	3.8	2.2
Other Road Travel (Diesel)	0.5	1.6	1.1
Other Road Travel (Petrol)	3.1	0.5	0.3
Rail Travel	9.2	9.6	3.4
Air Travel (short haul)	5.0	4.4	3.1
Air Travel (long haul)	5.1	7.1	5.4
Hire Cars (Diesel)	0.6	1.8	2.9
Hire Cars (Petrol)	6.7	6.1	6.1
Total	172.6	127.5	106.6

Required:

(a) Perform an analysis of FGH's business environment to identify factors which will affect its environmental strategy. For each of these factors, suggest performance indicators which will allow FGH to monitor its progress.

(8 marks)

(b) Evaluate the data given on carbon dioxide emissions using suitable indicators. Identify trends from within the data and comment on whether the company's behaviour is consistent with meeting its targets.

(9 marks)

(c) Suggest further data that the company could collect in order to improve its analysis and explain how this data could be used to measure the effectiveness of the reduction initiatives mentioned.

(3 marks)
(Total: 20 marks)

Student accountant article: visit the ACCA website, www.accaglobal.com, to review the article on 'environmental management accounting' from July 2010.

5 The use of league tables (benchmarking) in the public sector

5.1 Introduction

A **league table** is a chart or list which compares one organisation with another by ranking them in order of ability or achievement.

League tables have become a popular performance management tool in the public sector in recent years, for example in hospitals and schools.

> ### Illustration 5 – The use of league tables in schools
>
> In January 2010 the secondary schools league tables showed that London is the highest performing region in England at GCSE level (exams sat by students at the age of 16) with 54% of pupils achieving the benchmark at GCSE of five A* to C grades including English and mathematics. This is a striking turnaround in just over a decade. In 1997 only 29.9% of London pupils reached this level.

5.2 Advantages of league tables

- Implementation stimulates competition and the adoption of best practice. As a result, the quality of the service should improve.

- Monitors and ensures accountability of the providers.

- Performance is transparent.

- League tables should be readily available and can be used by consumers to make choices.

5.3 Disadvantages of league tables

> ### Test your understanding 3
>
> **Required:**
>
> Discuss the disadvantages of using league tables in the public sector.

KAPLAN PUBLISHING

Test your understanding 4

A government has decided to improve school performance by the use of league tables with schools assessed on the following:

- percentage pass rates in examinations
- absenteeism.

It has been proposed that funding be linked to these measures.

Required:

Suggest some potentially negative outcomes of this system.

5.4 Benchmarking

Benchmarking will be used to rank the organisations in the league table.

This is a key technique but is not without its problems:

- Dysfunctional behaviour – managers focus on achieving targets to the detriment of overall performance.
- Poor results may lead to users switching to alternative providers resulting in a downward spiral in the quality of the service provided.
- Benchmarking is often a measuring exercise, not a learning exercise.
- Benchmarking will not lead to improvements if pressure is not exerted by stakeholders.

Student accountant article: visit the ACCA website, www.accaglobal.com, to review the article on 'benchmarking and the use of targets in the public sector' from September 2012.

6 The use of targets in public sector organisations

6.1 Introduction

'A **performance target** represents the level of performance that the organisation aims to achieve for a particular activity. Such targets should be consistent with the SMART criteria' (Government and Audit Commission).

The results from the benchmarking process (discussed above) can be used to set attainment targets for public sector organisations such as schools, hospitals and the police force.

6.2 Advantages and disadvantages of targets

Targets should act as an invaluable tool for improvement:

- improving the efficiency and effectiveness of public expenditure
- reducing overall expenditure
- increasing accountability and transparency
- increasing responsiveness to stakeholder needs.

However, there are a number of **issues** associated with the use of targets:

- **Central control** – most targets are set centrally by government. It may be more appropriate for targets to be drawn up locally by professionals who are aware of the challenges faced in different parts of the country.

- **Difficulty level** – targets that are too difficult tend to debilitate rather than motivate and those that are too easy lead to complacency.

- **All or nothing** – not meeting the target can be seen as a sign of failure. However, if an aspirational target is set it may not be met but may still result in improvements and act as a motivator.

- **Too many targets** – there is a tendency to set too many targets to try to measure every aspect of service delivery. However, a manager responsible for service delivery will be unable to concentrate on more than a handful of targets at any one time.

- **Targets not always appropriate** – it is not always appropriate to set targets, e.g. if the activity is not within the control of the person responsible for meeting the target or it is difficult to quantify the outputs of the organisation.

- **Cost** – the cost of setting the target may outweigh the benefit.

- **Lack of ownership of targets** – each target should have a named person who is accountable for the performance and achievement of the objective.

- **Gaming** – there may be a tendency for people to 'play the system' rather than using the targets as a tool for improvement, i.e. people want to look good rather than be good.

- **Conflict** – conflict between targets may occur, e.g. a reduction in the number of children on the Child Protection Register may coincide with an increase in child abuse cases.

KAPLAN PUBLISHING

7 Exam focus

Exam sitting	Area examined	Question number	Number of marks
December 2013	League tables	4	25
June 2012	Public sector benchmarking	4	17
June 2011	EMA	5	20
December 2010	Environmental performance	4	20
December 2008	League tables	1(b)	6

Note:

- The current examiner has set the exam papers from the December 2010 sitting onwards.

- The format of the exam changed in June 2013. Section A now contains 1 × 50 mark question (previously 2 questions worth 60 marks in total) and Section B now contains a choice of 2 from 3 questions worth 25 marks each (previously a choice of 2 from 3 questions worth approximately 20 marks each).

Chapter summary

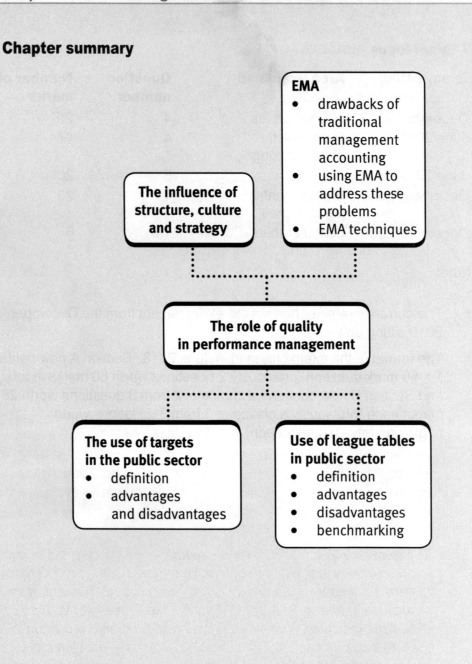

EMA
- drawbacks of traditional management accounting
- using EMA to address these problems
- EMA techniques

The influence of structure, culture and strategy

The role of quality in performance management

The use of targets in the public sector
- definition
- advantages and disadvantages

Use of league tables in public sector
- definition
- advantages
- disadvantages
- benchmarking

Test your understanding answers

Test your understanding 1

The benefits are as follows:

- An environmental approach ensures the organisation meets with legal and regulatory standards.

- Increased sales as a result of meeting with customers' needs.

- Helps to maintain a positive public image.

- Manages risk, e.g. of an environmental disaster.

- Can reduce costs, e.g. through improved use of fuel and water.

Test your understanding 2

(a) Government regulations relevant to FGH's environmental strategy include requirements to recycle materials, limits on pollution and waste levels along with new taxes such as carbon levies to add additional costs. Performance indicators would be additional costs resulting from failure to recycle waste, fines paid for breaches and the level of environmental tax burdens.

The general economic climate is relevant to the strategy including factors such as interest, inflation and exchange rates. For FGH, the general economic environment is not good and cost savings from reductions in energy use would help to offset falling profits. Also, the difficulties indicated in raising capital could be monitored through the firm's cost of capital. This would be especially relevant if the environmental initiatives lead to significant capital expenditure for FGH.

Trends and fashions among the general public appear to be relevant for FGH as the public will be end-users of its services and environmental action could improve the brand image of FGH. Suitable performance indicator would be based around a score in a customer attitude survey.

Technological changes in the capabilities available to FGH and its competitors will affect its environmental strategy. New environmentally efficient technologies such as hybrid cars and solar recharging cells would be relevant to the cost and product sides of FGH. Performance indicators would involve measuring the impact of the use of new technology on existing emission data.

(b) The company has a target of cutting emissions by 60% of their 2001 values by the year 2017. Overall, it has cut emissions by 38% in the first nine years of the 16-year programme. There was a reduction of 16% in the last year of measurement. If this rate of improvement is maintained then the company will reduce its emissions by 82% (62% × (84% ^ 7)) by 2017. However, it should be noted that it is unlikely that there will be a constant rate of reduction as it normally becomes more difficult to improve as the easy actions are taken in the early years of the programme.

The initial data are rather complex and so to summarise, three categories for the three types of transport were considered (Road, Rail and Air). The largest cut has been in rail related emissions (63%) while the contribution from road transport has only fallen by 38%. The road emissions are the dominant category overall and they are still falling within the programmed timetable to reach the target. However, it is clear that air travel is not falling at the same pace but this may be driven by factors such as increasing globalisation of the telecommunication industry which necessitates travel by managers abroad to visit multinational clients and suppliers.

One unusual feature noted is that the mix of transport methods appears to be changing. Rail travel appears to be declining. This is surprising as rail is widely believed to be the lowest emitting method from these forms of travel. However, caution must be exercised on this conclusion which may be due to a change in the emissions technology relating to each category of travel rather than the distance travelled using each method.

The major change that is apparent from the basic data is the move from petrol to diesel-powered motor vehicles which in the commercial fleet appears nearly complete. It will be more difficult to move company and private cars to diesel-power as there will be an element of choice on the part of the car user in the type of car driven.

Working

Measured in millions of kgs	2001	2009	2010	Change on base year
	Base year			
Commercial Fleet Diesel	105.4	77.7	70.1	−33%
Commercial Fleet Petrol	11.6	0.4	0.0	−100%
Company Car Diesel	15.1	14.5	12.0	−21%
Company Car Petrol	10.3	3.8	2.2	−79%
Other Road Travel (Diesel)	0.5	1.6	1.1	120%
Other Road Travel (Petrol)	3.1	0.5	0.3	−90%
Rail Travel	9.2	9.6	3.4	−63%
Air Travel (short haul)	5.0	4.4	3.1	−38%
Air Travel (long haul)	5.1	7.1	5.4	6%
Hire Cars (Diesel)	0.6	1.8	2.9	383%
Hire Cars (Petrol)	6.7	6.1	6.1	−9%
Total	172.6	127.5	106.6	
Index	100%	74%	62%	
YoY change		−16%		

Simplifying categories

Road travel	153.3	106.4	94.7	−38%
Air travel	10.1	11.5	8.5	−16%
Rail travel	9.2	9.6	3.4	−63%
Total	172.6	127.5	106.6	−38%

Mix of travel method in each year

Road travel	89%	83%	89%	
Air travel	6%	9%	8%	
Rail travel	5%	8%	3%	

(c) The analysis could be improved by collecting data on the total distances travelled so that employee behaviour can be tracked. This would allow measurement of the effect of switching away from physical meetings and using teleconferencing facilities. This may be particularly effective in cutting air travel which has been noted as a problem area.

It would also allow assessment of the homeworking scheme which should reduce total distance travelled. Although, the full environmental benefit will not be apparent as much of the travel would have been a regular commute to work which an employee will not be able to claim and so is unlikely to record.

Finally, the collection of distance travelled data will allow a measure of the effect of changing modes of transport by calculating an average emission per km travelled.

Test your understanding 3

- Encourages providers to focus on performance measures rather than the quality of the service.

- Costly and time consuming.

- May encourage creative reporting.

- The value of any performance indicator depends on the quality of any data in the calculation. The data management systems in the public sector do not always provide quality data.

- Many of the outcomes valued by society are not measurable but many of the performance indicators have been selected on the basis of what is practical rather than what is meaningful.

- Differences between public sector organisations may make comparisons meaningless, e.g. a school in a deprived area will be at a natural disadvantage. This may result in employees being held responsible for things over which they have no control.

- A poor ranking may have a negative impact on public trust and employee morale.

- A poor ranking may lead to a worsening of future performance, e.g. gifted children are no longer sent to a poorly performing school and this results in an even lower ranking in future years.

Test your understanding 4

- Children with special needs/disabilities will find it harder to gain school places as they may be perceived as having less chance of passing examinations reducing school performance and funding. (The irony here is that schools which are willing to accept children with disabilities often need more funding, not less.)

- Truants are likely to be expelled at the school's first realistic opportunity. This may result in the school performing better but only transfers the 'problem' somewhere else.

- Schools may focus on examination performance to the detriment of other educational goals, e.g. art, sports.

- Schools facing difficulties will receive less funding to help overcome those problems.

- There will be increased competitiveness and decreased collaboration between schools.

Index

Index

KAPLAN PUBLISHING

Index

Index